Common Along California's Coast

Harbor Seal
(Phoca vitulina)

habitat range

While the sea lion is more commonly associated with the California coast, there are also many different types of seals there, including the harbor seal. Harbor seals are five-to-six feet long and can swim as soon as they are born.

Buuuuuuuuuull!

These seals can't walk, but they wriggle over the rocks on their bellies.

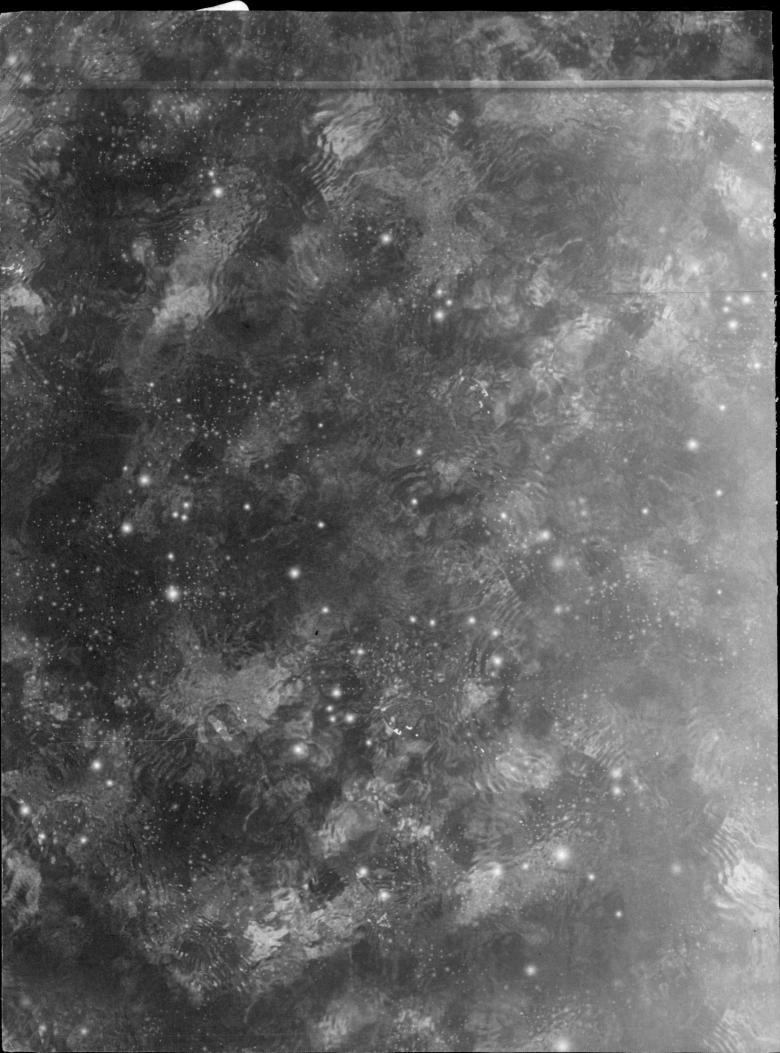

HOUGHTON MIFFLIN

California
Science

 HOUGHTON MIFFLIN   BOSTON

Program Authors

William Badders
Director of the Cleveland Mathematics and
Science Partnership
Cleveland Municipal School District, Cleveland, Ohio

Douglas Carnine, Ph.D.
Professor of Education
University of Oregon, Eugene, Oregon

James Feliciani
Supervisor of Instructional Media and Technology
Land O' Lakes, Florida

Bobby Jeanpierre, Ph.D.
Assistant Professor, Science Education
University of Central Florida, Orlando, Florida

Carolyn Sumners, Ph.D.
Director of Astronomy and Physical Sciences
Houston Museum of Natural Science, Houston, Texas

Catherine Valentino
Author-in-Residence
Houghton Mifflin, West Kingston, Rhode Island

Primary Grade Consultant

Kathleen B. Horstmeyer
Past President SEPA
Carefree, Arizona

Content Consultants
See Teacher's Edition for a complete list

California Teacher Reviewers

Robert Aikman
Cunningham Elementary
Turlock, California

Christine Anderson
Rock Creek Elementary
Rocklin, California

Dan M. Anthony
Berry Elementary
San Diego, California

Patricia Babb
Cypress Elementary
Tulare, California

Ann Balfour
Lang Ranch Elementary
Thousand Oaks, California

Colleen Briner-Schmidt
Conejo Elementary
Thousand Oaks, California

Mary Brouse
Panama Buena Vista Union
School District
Bakersfield, California

Monica Carabay
Four Creeks Elementary
Visalia, California

ISBN-13: 978-0-618-68619-3
ISBN-10: 0-618-68619-3

1 2 3 4 5 6 7 8 9-VH-15 14 13 12 11 10 09 08 07 06

California Teacher Reviewers (cont'd.)

Sheri Chu
Vineyard Elementary
Ontario, California

Teena Collins
Frank D. Parent Elementary
Inglewood, California

Gary Comstock
Cole Elementary
Clovis, California

Jenny Dickinson
Bijou Community School
South Lake Tahoe, California

Cheryl Dultz
Kingswood Elementary
Citrus Heights, California

Tom East
Mountain View Elementary
Fresno, California

Sharon Ferguson
Fort Washington Elementary
Fresno, California

Robbin Ferrell
Hawthorne Elementary
Ontario, California

Mike Freedman
Alta-Dutch Flat Elementary
Alta, California

Linda Gadis-Honaker
Banyan Elementary
Alta Loma, California

Lisa Gomez
Marshall James Elementary
Modesto, California

Lisa Green
Jordan Elementary
Orange, California

Tina Hubbard
Brentwood Elementary
Victorville, California

Carey Iannuzzo
Fitzgerald Elementary
Rialto, California

Teresa Lorentz
Banta Elementary
Tracy, California

Christine Luellig
Henderson Elementary
Barstow, California

Peggy MacArthur
Montevideo Elementary
San Ramon, California

Jeffrey McPherson
Parkview Elementary
Garden Grove, California

Susan Moore
Lang Ranch Elementary
Thousand Oaks, California

William Neddersen
Tustin Unified School District
Tustin, California

Josette Perrie
Plaza Vista School
Irvine, California

Lisa Pulliam
Alcott Elementary
Pomona, California

Jennifer Ramirez
Skyline North Elementary
Barstow, California

Lynda Rogers
Santa Cruz County Office of
Education
Capitola, California

Nancy Scali
Arroyo Elementary
Ontario, California

Janet Sugimoto
Sunset Lane School
Fullerton, California

Laura Valencia
Kingsley Elementary
Montclair, California

Sally Van Wagner
Antelope Creek Elementary
Rocklin, California

Jenny Wade
Stockton Unified School District
Stockton, California

Judy Williams
Price Elementary
Anaheim, California

Karen Yamamoto
Westmore Oaks Elementary
West Sacramento, California

Contents

UNIT A
Systems in Living Things

Big Idea Plants and animals have structures for respiration, digestion, waste disposal, and transport of materials.

Activities

California poppies

Contents

UNIT B
Water on Earth

Big Idea Water on Earth moves between the oceans and land through the processes of evaporation and condensation.

Activities

California

Contents

UNIT C
Weather and the Solar System

Big Ideas Energy from the Sun heats Earth unevenly, causing air movements that result in changing weather patterns. The solar system consists of planets and other bodies that orbit the Sun in predictable paths.

California

Activities

Lightning over the California Desert

Contents

UNIT D
Elements and their Combinations

Big Idea Elements and their combinations account for all the varied types of matter in the world.

Activities

Using Your Textbook

The Nature of Science
People all over the world do science. You can do science, too. You probably already do.

The Nature of Science

In the front of your book, you will be introduced to scientists and to ways of investigating science.

Every unit in your book has two or more chapters.

EARTH **B** SCIENCE

Water on Earth

Chapter 4
Water Resources 106

Independent Books
• Water Resources
• Niagara Falls, The Power of Water
• Where Does Drinking Water Come From?

Chapter 5
The Water Cycle 142

Independent Books
• The Water Cycle
• The End of the Ice Age
• A Drop of Water

Big Idea!
Standard Set 3.
Earth Sciences

Water on Earth moves between the oceans and land through the processes of evaporation and condensation.

Clouds over the Sierra Nevadas

105

Independent Books are books you can read on your own.

Big Idea! tells you the part of your **California Science Standards** that connects the Main Ideas of each lesson.

Lesson Preview gives information and asks questions about each lesson.

Writing Journal tells you to write or draw answers to the questions.

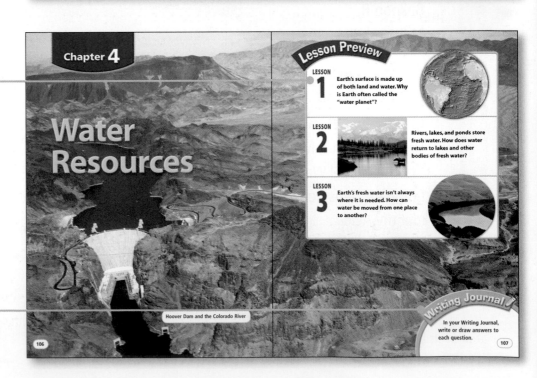

Chapter 4

Water Resources

Hoover Dam and the Colorado River

106

Lesson Preview

LESSON 1
Earth's surface is made up of both land and water. Why is Earth often called the "water planet"?

LESSON 2
Rivers, lakes, and ponds store fresh water. How does water return to lakes and other bodies of fresh water?

LESSON 3
Earth's fresh water isn't always where it is needed. How can water be moved from one place to another?

Writing Journal
In your Writing Journal, write or draw answers to each question.

107

Vocabulary Preview

introduces important science terms, with pictures, and vocabulary skills.

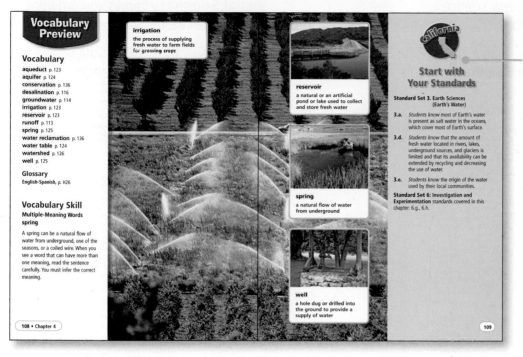

California Science Standards are identified for each chapter.

Every lesson in your book has two parts.
Lesson Part 1: Directed Inquiry

Building Background gives you science facts and information.

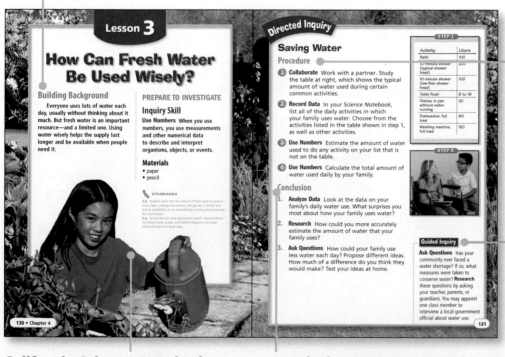

Procedure lists the steps you will follow to conduct your Investigation.

Guided Inquiry lets you take your investigation further.

California Science Standards appear in blue throughout each lesson.

Conclusion guides you in thinking about your investigation.

Lesson Part 2: Learn by Reading

Vocabulary lists the new science words that you will learn.

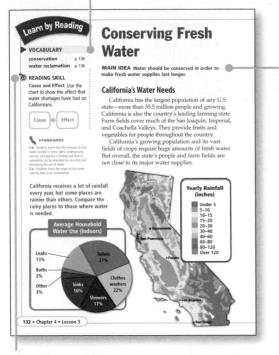

Main Idea tells you what is important.

Reading Skill helps you understand and organize information as you read.

Lesson Wrap-Up

Visual Summary shows you different ways to summarize what you've read.

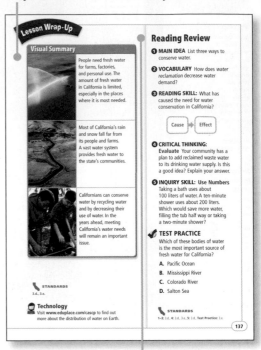

Reading Review lets you check your understanding after you read.

Focus On

Focus On lets you learn more about a key concept in a chapter.

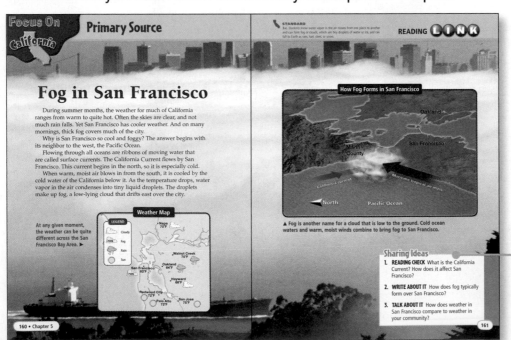

Focus On types include: History of Science, Technology, Primary Source, Literature, and Reader's Theater.

Sharing Ideas has you check your understanding and write and talk about what you have learned.

Extreme Science

Compares and contrasts interesting science information.

Writing Journal provides writing guidance for the Extreme Science lesson.

Links and Careers/People in Science

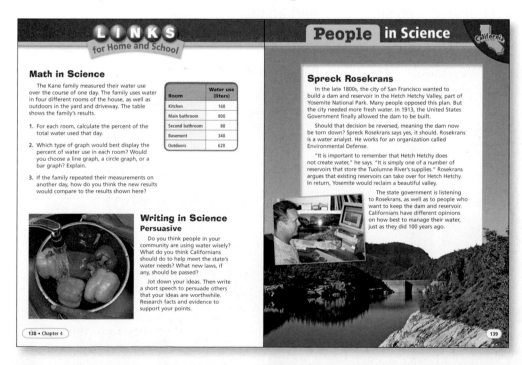

Links connects science to other subject areas.

Careers/People in Science tells you about the work of real scientists.

Chapter and Unit Review and Test Practice

Helps you to know you are on track with learning California science standards.

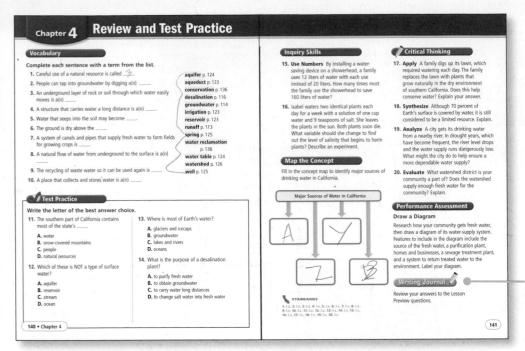

Chapter 4 — Review and Test Practice

Vocabulary

Complete each sentence with a term from the list.

1. Careful use of a natural resource is called ___
2. People can tap into groundwater by digging a(n) ___
3. An underground layer of rock or soil through which water easily moves is a(n) ___
4. A structure that carries water a long distance is a(n) ___
5. Water that seeps into the soil may become ___
6. The ground is dry above the ___
7. A system of canals and pipes that supply fresh water to farm fields for growing crops is ___
8. A natural flow of water from underground to the surface is a(n) ___
9. The recycling of waste water so it can be used again is ___
10. A place that collects and stores water is a(n) ___

aquifer p. 124
aqueduct p. 123
conservation p. 136
desalination p. 116
groundwater p. 114
irrigation p. 123
reservoir p. 123
runoff p. 113
spring p. 125
water reclamation p. 136
water table p. 124
watershed p. 126
well p. 125

Test Practice

Write the letter of the best answer choice.

11. The southern part of California contains most of the state's ___
   A. water
   B. snow-covered mountains
   C. people
   D. natural resources

12. Which of these is NOT a type of surface water?
   A. aquifer
   B. reservoir
   C. stream
   D. ocean

13. Where is most of Earth's water?
   A. glaciers and icecaps
   B. groundwater
   C. lakes and rivers
   D. oceans

14. What is the purpose of a desalination plant?
   A. to purify fresh water
   B. to obtain groundwater
   C. to carry water long distances
   D. to change salt water into fresh water

140 • Chapter 4

Inquiry Skills

15. **Use Numbers** By installing a water-saving device on a showerhead, a family uses 12 liters of water with each use instead of 20 liters. How many times must the family use the showerhead to save 160 liters of water?

16. Isabel waters two identical plants each day for a week with a solution of one cup water and 9 teaspoons of salt. She leaves the plants in the sun. Both plants soon die. What variable should she change to find out the level of salinity that begins to harm plants? Describe an experiment.

Map the Concept

Fill in the concept map to identify major sources of drinking water in California.

Major Sources of Water in California

Critical Thinking

17. **Apply** A family digs up its lawn, which required watering each day. The family replaces the lawn with plants that grow naturally in the dry environment of southern California. Does this help conserve water? Explain your answer.

18. **Synthesize** Although 70 percent of Earth's surface is covered by water, it is still considered to be a limited resource. Explain.

19. **Analyze** A city gets its drinking water from a nearby river. In drought years, which have become frequent, the river level drops and the water supply runs dangerously low. What might the city do to help ensure a more dependable water supply?

20. **Evaluate** What watershed district is your community a part of? Does the watershed supply enough fresh water for the community? Explain.

Performance Assessment

Draw a Diagram

Research how your community gets fresh water, then draw a diagram of its water-supply system. Features to include in the diagram include the source of the fresh water, a purification plant, homes and businesses, a sewage treatment plant, and a system to return treated water to the environment. Label your diagram.

Writing Journal
Review your answers to the Lesson Preview questions.

STANDARDS
1: 3.d., 2: 3.d., 3: 3.d., 4: 3.e., 5: 3.e., 6: 3.a., 7: 3.e., 8: 3.d., 9: 3.a., 10: 3.a., 11: 3.e., 12: 3.d., 13: 3.a., 14: 3.e., 15: 3.e., 16: 3.a., 17: 3.e., 18: 3.a., 19: 3.a., 20: 3.e.

141

Writing Journal instructs you to review the questions you answered at the start of the chapter.

Unit Wrap-Up

Learn more about science using the **Discover More** question. Also find a link to a simulation on the EduPlace web site.

UNIT B Wrap-Up

You Can...

Discover More

Stalactites are rock formations that form on the ceilings of limestone caves. Droplets of groundwater trickle through tiny cracks in the cave roof. The water dissolves some of the limestone rock. When a water droplet evaporates, it leaves behind a tiny deposit of limestone sediment. Drop by drop, the water adds more limestone sediment to the deposit. Over thousands of years, the deposit grows downward to form a huge stalactite. One stalactite is thought to have taken 4,000 years to grow to a length of 2 m (7 ft).

Stalactites form when drops of water containing minerals drip from the ceiling of a limestone cave.

Stalagmites form when water drops fall to the floor of the cave and evaporate.

Sometimes, stalactites and stalagmites meet. When this happens they form a single column.

Stalactite • Stalagmite • Column

See a cave system grow. Go to www.eduplace.com/cascp/ to witness a cave's growth over thousands of years.

176 • Unit B

References

The back of your book includes sections you will refer to again and again.

Index • Glossary • Health and Fitness Handbook

in circulatory system, 74 in respiratory system

aquifer (AK wuh fur) an underground layer of rock or soil through which water easily moves (124)

Science and Math Toolbox

Science and Math Toolbox

Using a Microscope H2
Making a Bar Graph H3
Using a Calculator H4
Using Variables H5
Using a Tape Measure or Ruler H6
Measuring Volume H7
Using a Thermometer H8
Using a Balance H9
Using an Equation or Formula H10
Making a Chart to Organize Data H11
Reading a Circle Graph H12
Making a Line Graph H13
Measuring Elapsed Time H14
Measurements H16

Start with Your Standards

Your California Science Standards

Your California
Science Standards

Welcome to the adventure of science!

Many famous scientists and inventors have lived and worked in California. Someday, you could be one, too!

Your science standards tell you what you should know by the end of Grade 5. They also tell what you should be able to do when you investigate and experiment. When you use your science book, you will find the standards printed next to each section of the lesson and chapter.

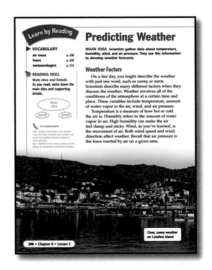

Houghton Mifflin Science will lead you to mastering your standards. Along the way, you will ask questions, do hands-on investigations, think critically, and read what scientists have discovered about how the world works. You will also get to know real people who do science every day.

How Families Can Help

- Get to know the California Science Content Standards on the pages that follow. If you want to learn more about science education, you can find the Science Framework for California Public Schools online at **www.cde.ca.gov/ci/**

- Relate the science of the standards to activities at home such as cooking, gardening, and playing sports.

- Get to know your child's science textbook, encouraging him or her to use the table of contents, index, and glossary. Point out the importance of titles and headings as a means to finding the information needed.

- Help your child choose library books to read about science, nature, inventors, and scientists. You can use the Recommended Literature for Math & Science online database at **www.cde.ca.gov/ci/sc/ll/**

- Find opportunities for your child to use numbers and mathematics skills and to measure and to estimate measurements, such as when planning a trip.

- Encourage your child to do experiments and enter science fairs.

Mount Shasta

Science Content Standards

These Science Content Standards are learning goals that you will achieve by the end of fifth grade. Below each standard is the unit or chapter in this book where that standard is taught. In that unit and chapter, there are many opportunities to master the standard—by doing investigations, reading, writing, speaking, and drawing concept maps.

Set 1

Physical Sciences

Elements and their combinations account for all the varied types of matter in the world. As a basis for understanding this concept:

Unit D: Elements and Their Combinations

1.a. *Students know* that during chemical reactions the atoms in the reactants rearrange to form products with different properties.
Chapter 9: Chemical Compounds
Chapter 10: Characteristics of Matter

1.b. *Students know* all matter is made of atoms, which may combine to form molecules.
Chapter 8: Atoms and Elements

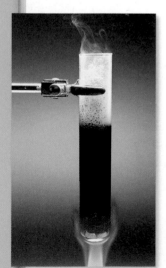

1.c. *Students know* metals have properties in common, such as high electrical and thermal conductivity. Some metals, such as aluminum (Al), iron (Fe), nickel (Ni), copper (Cu), silver (Ag), and gold (Au), are pure elements; other, such as steel and brass, are composed of a combination of elemental metals.
Chapter 8: Atoms and Elements
Chapter 10: Characteristics of Matter

1.d. *Students know* that each element is made of one kind of atom and that the elements are organized in the periodic table by their chemical properties.
Chapter 8: Atoms and Elements

1.e. *Students know* scientists have developed instruments that can create discrete images of atoms and molecules that show that the atoms and molecules often occur in well-ordered arrays.
Chapter 8: Atoms and Elements

1.f. *Students know* differences in chemical and physical properties of substances are used to separate mixtures and identify compounds.
Chapter 9: Chemical Compounds
Chapter 10: Characteristics of Matter

1.g. *Students know* properties of solid, liquid, and gaseous substances, such as sugar ($C_8H_{12}O_6$), water (H_2O), helium (He), oxygen (O_2), nitrogen (N_2), and carbon dioxide (CO_2).
Chapter 8: Atoms and Elements
Chapter 10: Characteristics of Matter

1.h. *Students know* living organisms and most materials are composed of just a few elements.
Chapter 8: Atoms and Elements

1.i. *Students know* the common properties of salts, such as sodium chloride (NaCl).
Chapter 9: Chemical Compounds

Set 2

Life Sciences

Plants and animals have structures for respiration, digestion, waste disposal, and transport of materials. As a basis for understanding this concept:
Unit A: Systems in Living Things

2.a. *Students know* many multicellular organisms have specialized structures to support the transport of materials.
Chapter 1: Cells
Chapter 2: Plant Systems

2.b. *Students know* how blood circulates through the heart chambers, lungs, and body and how carbon dioxide (CO_2) and oxygen (O_2) are exchanged in the lungs and tissues.
Chapter 3: Human Body Systems

2.c. *Students know* the sequential steps of digestion and the roles to teeth and the mouth, esophagus, stomach, small intestine, large intestine, and colon in the function of the digestive system.
Chapter 3: Human Body Systems

2.d. *Students know* the role of the kidney in removing cellular waste from blood and converting it into urine, which is stored in the bladder.
Chapter 3: Human Body Systems

2.e. *Students know* how sugar, water, and minerals are transported in a vascular plant.
Chapter 2: Plant Systems

2.f. *Students know* plants use carbon dioxide (CO_2) and energy from sunlight to build molecules of sugar and release oxygen.
Chapter 2: Plant Systems

2.g. *Students know* plant and animals cells break down sugar to obtain energy, a process resulting in carbon dioxide (CO_2) and water (respiration).
Chapter 1: Cells

Earth Sciences (Earth's Water)

Water on Earth moves between the oceans and land through the processes of evaporation and condensation. As a basis for understanding this concept:
Unit B: Water on Earth

3.a. *Students know* most of Earth's water is present as salt water in the oceans, which cover most of Earth's surface.
Chapter 4: Water Resources
Chapter 5: The Water Cycle

3.b. *Students know* when liquid water evaporates, it turns into water vapor in the air and can reappear as a liquid when cooled or as a solid if cooled below the freezing point of water.
Chapter 5: The Water Cycle

3.c. *Students know* water vapor in the air moves from one place to another and can form fog or clouds, which are tiny droplets of water or ice, and can fall to Earth as rain, hail, sleet, or snow.
Chapter 5: The Water Cycle

3.d. *Students know* that the amount of fresh water located in rivers, lakes, underground sources, and glaciers is limited and that its availability can be extended by recycling and decreasing the use of water.
Chapter 4: Water Resources

3.e. *Students know* the origin of the water used by their local communities.

▲ **Bridal Veil Falls**

Set 4 — Earth Sciences (Weather)

Energy from the Sun heats Earth unevenly, causing air movements that result in changing weather patterns. As a basis for understanding this concept:
Unit B: Water on Earth
Unit C: Weather and the Solar System

4.a. *Students know* uneven heating of Earth causes air movements (convection currents).
Chapter 5: The Water Cycle
Chapter 6: Weather

4.b. *Students know* the influence that the ocean has on the weather and the role that the water cycle plays in weather patterns.
Chapter 5: The Water Cycle

4.c. *Students know* the causes and effects of different types of severe weather.
Chapter 6: Weather

4.d. *Students know* how to use weather maps and data to predict local weather and know that weather forecasts depend on many variables.
Chapter 6: Weather

4.e. *Students know* that the Earth's atmosphere exerts a pressure that decreases with distance about Earth's surface and that at any point it exerts this pressure equally in all directions.
Chapter 6: Weather

Set 5 — Earth Sciences (The Solar System)

The solar system consists of planets and other bodies that orbit the Sun in predictable paths. As a basis for understanding this concept:
Unit C: Weather and the Solar System

5.a. *Students know* the Sun, an average star, is the central and largest body in the solar system and is composed primarily of hydrogen and helium.

5.b. *Students know* the solar system includes the planet Earth, the Moon, the Moon, the Sun, eight other planets and their satellites, and smaller objects, such as asteroids and comets.
Chapter 7: The Solar System

5.c. *Students know* the path of a planet around the Sun is due to the gravitational attraction between the Sun and the planet.
Chapter 7: The Solar System

Set 6

Investigation and Experimentation

Scientific progress is made by asking meaningful questions and conducting careful investigations. As a basis for understanding this concept and addressing the content in the other three strands, students should develop their own questions and perform investigations. Students will:

Directed Inquiry and Guided Inquiry investigations in every lesson

6.a. Classify objects (e.g., rocks, plants, leaves) in accordance with appropriate criteria.
Directed Inquiry and Guided Inquiry investigations

6.b. Develop a testable question.
Directed Inquiry and Guided Inquiry investigations

6.c. Plan and conduct a simple investigation based on a student-developed question and write instructions others can follow to carry out the procedure.
Directed Inquiry and Guided Inquiry investigations

6.d. Identify the dependent and controlled variables in an investigation.
Directed Inquiry and Guided Inquiry investigations

6.e. Identify a single independent variable in a scientific investigation and explain how this variable can be used to collect information to answer a question about the results of the experiment.
Directed Inquiry and Guided Inquiry investigations

6.f. Select appropriate tools (e.g., thermometers, metersticks, balances, and graduated cylinders) and make quantitative observations.
Directed Inquiry and Guided Inquiry investigations

6.g. Record data by using appropriate graphic representations (including charts, graphs, and labeled diagrams) and make inferences based on those data.
Directed Inquiry and Guided Inquiry investigations

6.h. Draw conclusions form scientific evidence and indicate whether further information is needed to support a specific conclusion.
Directed Inquiry and Guided Inquiry investigations

6.i. Write a report of an investigation that includes conducting tests, collecting data or examining evidence, and drawing conclusions.
Directed Inquiry and Guided Inquiry investigations

The Nature of Science

Science is an adventure.
People all over the world do
science. You can do science, too.
You probably already do.

Big Idea

Scientific progress is made by asking meaningful questions and conducting careful investigations.

Start with Your Standards

STANDARD SET 6. Investigation and Experimentation

6. Scientific progress is made by asking meaningful questions and conducting careful investigations. As a basis for understanding this concept and addressing the content in the other three strands, students should develop their own questions and perform investigations.

6.a. Classify objects (e.g., rocks, plants, leaves) in accordance with appropriate criteria.

6.b. Develop a testable question.

6.c. Plan and conduct a simple investigation based on a student-developed question and write instructions others can follow to carry out the procedure.

6.d. Identify the dependent and controlled variables in an investigation.

6.e. Identify a single independent variable in a scientific investigation and explain how this variable can be used to collect information to answer a question about the results of the experiment.

6.f. Select appropriate tools (e.g., thermometers, metersticks, balances, and graduated cylinders) and make quantitative observations.

6.g. Record data by using appropriate graphic representations (including charts, graphs, and labeled diagrams) and make inferences based on those data.

6.h. Draw conclusions from scientific evidence and indicate whether further information is needed to support a specific conclusion.

6.i. Write a report of an investigation that includes conducting tests, collecting data or examining evidence, and drawing conclusions.

The Nature of Science

You Can...

Do What Scientists Do

Meet Dr. Dale Brown Emeagwali. She works as a teacher and researcher at Morgan State University in Baltimore, Maryland. Dr. Emeagwali is a microbiologist, which is a biologist who specializes in studying single-celled organisms, or microorganisms. The goal of her investigations is to gain a better understanding of the processes that take place inside cells. Depending on the question she is investigating, Dr. Emeagwali may observe these living things in nature or conduct an experiment in the laboratory.

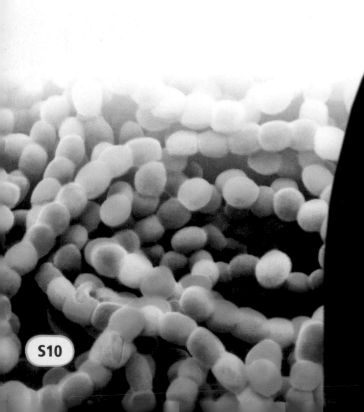

Scientists ask questions. Then they answer the questions by investigating and experimenting. Dr. Emeagwali has asked many questions about how microorganisms carry out their life processes, as well as how they affect human health.

In one investigation, she demonstrated that a certain chemical exists in a type of bacteria called *Streptomyces parvulus.* Such discoveries add to the basic knowledge of microbiology. Dr. Emeagwali is pleased, though, when her work has practical applications in medicine. In another experiment, she demonstrated that certain molecules could be used to stop the formation of tumors in people with cancer.

Dr. Emeagwali understands that for each investigation she carries out she must repeat the procedure many times and get the same results before she can conclude that her results are true.

Science investigations involve communicating with other scientists.

In addition to laboratory research, Dr. Emeagwali spends time writing papers about her work in order to communicate with other scientists. She wants other scientists to be able to repeat her investigations in order to check that her results are valid. Dr. Emeagwali also spends time reading about the work of other scientists to keep informed about the progress others have made in microbiology.

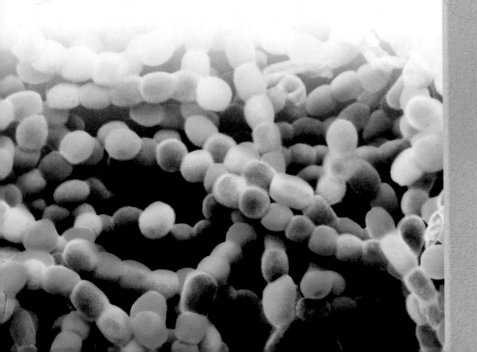

You Can...

Think Like a Scientist

The ways scientists ask and answer questions about the world around them is called **scientific inquiry.** Scientific inquiry requires certain attitudes, or approaches to thinking about a problem. To think like a scientist you have to be:

- curious and ask a lot of questions.

- willing to answer them by planning careful experiments.

- able to keep an open mind. That means you consider the ideas of others.

- willing to use measurement, estimation, and other mathematics skills.

- open to changing what you think when your investigation results surprise you.

- willing to question what other people tell you.

What kind of rock is this? How did this rock form? Where did the different materials that make up the rock come from?

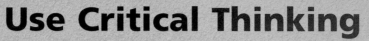

Use Critical Thinking

When you think critically, you make decisions about what others tell you or what you read. Is what you heard on TV or read in a magazine a fact or an opinion? A *fact* can be checked to make sure it is true. An *opinion* is what someone thinks about the facts.

Did you ever hear a scientific claim that was hard to believe? When you think, "What evidence is there to support that claim?" you are thinking critically. You'll also think critically when you evaluate investigation results. Observations can be interpreted in many ways. You'll judge whether a conclusion is supported by the data collected.

The book states that a sedimentary rock forms when rock fragments and other sediments are pressed and cemented together.

It looks like fragments of different kinds of rock came together to make this rock. This must be a type of sedimentary rock.

Science Inquiry

Applying scientific inquiry helps you understand the world around you. Suppose you have decided to investigate which color is easiest to see clearly in the dimmest light.

Observe In the evening, as daylight fades, you observe the different colored objects around you. As the light becomes dimmer and dimmer, you notice which color remains clear to your eyes.

Ask a Question When you think about what you saw, heard, or read, you may have questions.

Hypothesis Think about facts you already know. Do you have an idea about the answer? Write it down. That is your *hypothesis*.

Experiment Plan a test that will tell if the hypothesis is true or not. Choose the tools and materials you will need. List the steps you will follow. Make sure you keep all the conditions the same except the one you are testing. That condition is called the *independent variable*.

Conclusion Think about your results. What do they tell you? Did your results support your hypothesis or show it to be false? Or, do you need more information?

Describe your experiment to others. Communicate the tests you conducted, the results and conclusion.

STANDARDS
6.b. Develop a testable question.
6.e. Identify a single independent variable in a scientific investigation and explain how this variable can be used to collect information to answer a

question about the results of the experiment.
6.f. Select appropriate tools (e.g., thermometers, metersticks, balances, and graduated cylinders) and make quantitative observations.

My Color Experiment

Observe As the light dims, dark colors such as dark blue seem to disappear from sight first.

Ask a question I wonder which color can be seen most clearly in the dimmest light?

Hypothesis Yellow is the color that can be seen most clearly in the dimmest light.

Experiment I'm going to use objects of different colors in a room with a light controlled by a dimmer switch. The brightness of the light will be the *independent variable*. First, I will observe the colors in bright light. Then I will slowly dim the light to observe which color I can see the most clearly in the dimmest light.

Conclusion The results support my hypothesis. Yellow is the color that can be seen most clearly in the dimmest light.

Inquiry Process

The methods of science may vary from one area of science to another. Here is a process that some scientists follow to answer questions and make new discoveries.

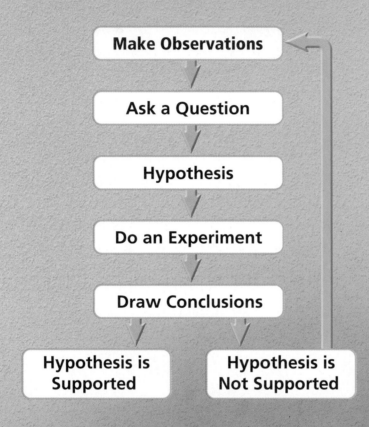

Make Observations

Ask a Question

Hypothesis

Do an Experiment

Draw Conclusions

Hypothesis is Supported

Hypothesis is Not Supported

Science Inquiry Skills

You'll use many of these skills of inquiry when you investigate and experiment.

- Ask Questions
- Observe
- Compare
- Classify
- Predict
- Measure

- Hypothesize
- Use Variables
- Experiment
- Use Models
- Communicate
- Use Numbers

- Record Data
- Analyze Data
- Infer
- Collaborate
- Research

STANDARDS
6.b. Develop a testable question.
6.c. Plan and conduct a simple investigation based on a student-developed question and write instructions others can follow to carry out the procedure.

6.e. Identify a single independent variable in a scientific investigation and explain how this variable can be used to collect information to answer a question about the results of the experiment.

Try It Yourself!

Experiment With Energy Beads

When you hold Energy Beads in your fist for a while and then go outdoors and open your hand, the beads change from off-white to many different colors.

1 What questions do you have about the Energy Beads?

2 How would you find out the answers?

3 How could you use Energy Beads to test a hypothesis?

4 Write your plan for an experiment with a single independent variable using Energy Beads. Predict what will happen.

Be an Inventor

Cassandra "Cassie" Wagner became an inventor when she was 11 years old. At that time, she was in middle school. During the summer, she wanted to make a toy for her pet cat. Cats are attracted to catnip, a plant with a strong odor. Cassie considered including catnip as part of her toy.

When Cassie researched about catnip on the Internet, she discovered that some people thought an oil in the plant will repel insects. She could find no proof of that hypothesis, and so she decided to test it herself. In her first experiment, Cassie put a small amount of the oil from catnip onto a cotton ball. She then observed whether mosquitoes were repelled by the ball. They were.

With the help of a professor at a nearby university, Cassie ran further experiments in a laboratory. She proved that the spray she made with the catnip oil repelled insects just as well as bug sprays sold in stores.

Cassie called her bug repellent Bugnip, and she planned to have it produced and sold to consumers. In the future, her efforts may lead to other inventions and better ways of repelling bothersome bugs.

"It was over the summer, and I didn't have much going on. I was just fooling around."

What Is Technology?

The tools people make and use, the things they build with tools, and the methods used to accomplish a practical purpose are all **technology**. A toy train set is an example of technology. So is a light rail system that provides transportation in a major city.

Scientists use technology, too. For example, a telescope makes it possible for scientists to see objects far into space that cannot be seen with just the eyes. Scientists also use measurement technology to make their observations more exact.

Many technologies make the world a better place to live. Sometimes, though, a technology that solves one problem can cause other problems. For example, burning coal in power plants provides power for generators that produce electricity for homes, schools, and industries. However, the burning of coal also can cause acid rain, which can be very harmful to living things.

A Better Idea

"I wish I had a better way to _____." How would you fill in the blank? Everyone wishes he or she could do a job more easily or have more fun. Inventors try to make those wishes come true. Inventing or improving an invention requires time and patience.

A company in Canada had a better idea in 1895. It invented the first power tool. Today, many other tools are powered by electricity—including this cordless power screwdriver. Today, inventors are still improving power tool technology, including using lasers and microwaves to drill into steel, stone, and glass. Maybe, someday, you will have a better idea for a new power tool.

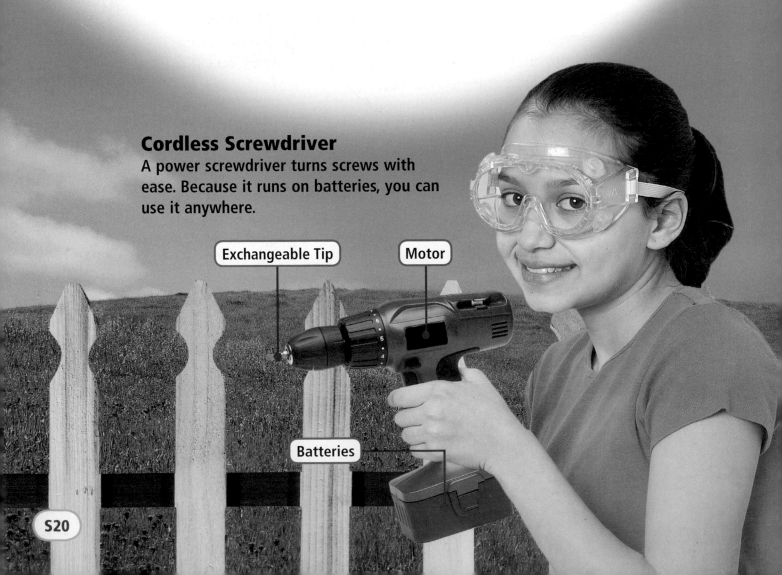

Cordless Screwdriver
A power screwdriver turns screws with ease. Because it runs on batteries, you can use it anywhere.

Exchangeable Tip

Motor

Batteries

How to Be an Inventor

1. **Identify a problem.** It may be a problem at school, at home, or in your community.

2. **List ways to solve the problem.** Sometimes the solution is a new tool. Other times it may be a new way of doing an old job or activity.

3. **Choose the best solution.** Decide which idea you predict will work best. Think about which one you can carry out.

4. **Make a sample.** A sample, called a *prototype*, is the first try. Your idea may need many materials or none at all. Choose measuring tools that will help your design work better.

5. **Try out your invention.** Use your prototype, or ask some else to try it. Keep a record of how it works and what problems you find. The more times you try it, the more information you will have.

6. **Improve your invention.** Use what you learned to make your design work better. Draw or write about the changes you made and why you made them.

7. **Share your invention.** Show your invention to others. Explain how it works. Tell how it makes an activity easier or more fun. If it did not work as well as you wanted, tell why.

Make Decisions

Trouble for Manatees

Manatees are large, slow-moving marine mammals. An average manatee is about 3 meters long and has a mass of about 500 kilograms. Manatees are gentle planteaters.

In summer, manatees can be seen along the ocean coasts of Alabama, Georgia, Florida, and South Carolina. In winter, they migrate to the warm waters of bays and rivers along the Gulf Coast of Florida. Living near the coast protects the manatees from diseases they might catch in colder waters. However, there are dangers in living so close to land. The great majority of manatee deaths are caused by collisions with boats. Almost all manatees have scars on their backs from being hit by fast-moving boats.

Deciding What to Do

What can be done to protect manatees from harm?

Here's how to make your decision about the manatees. You can use the same steps to help solve problems in your home, in your school, and in your community.

1 LEARN Learn about the problem. Take the time needed to get the facts. You could talk to an expert, read a science book, or explore a website.

2 LIST Make a list of actions you could take. Add actions other people could take.

3 DECIDE Think about each action on your list. Identify the risks and benefits. Decide which choice is the best one for you, your school, or your community.

4 SHARE Communicate your decision to others.

Boat Slow Speed Zone!

Science Safety

☑ Know the safety rules of your school and classroom and follow them.

☑ Read and follow the safety tips in each Investigate activity.

☑ When you plan your own investigations, write down how to keep safe.

☑ Know how to clean up and put away science materials. Keep your work area clean, and tell your teacher about spills right away.

☑ Know how to safely plug in electrical devices.

☑ Wear safety goggles when your teacher tells you.

☑ Unless your teacher tells you to, never put any science materials in or near your ears, eyes, or mouth.

☑ Wear gloves when handling live animals.

☑ Wash your hands when your investigation is done.

Caring for Living Things

☑ Learn how to care for the plants and animals in your classroom so that they stay healthy and safe. Learn how to hold animals carefully.

LIFE **A** SCIENCE

UNIT

Systems in Living Things

California Connection

Visit www.eduplace.com/cascp
to learn more about Earth's
living things.

California Field Trip

Monterey Bay Aquarium

The Monterey Bay Aquarium has over 550 different species of aquatic plants and animals on display.

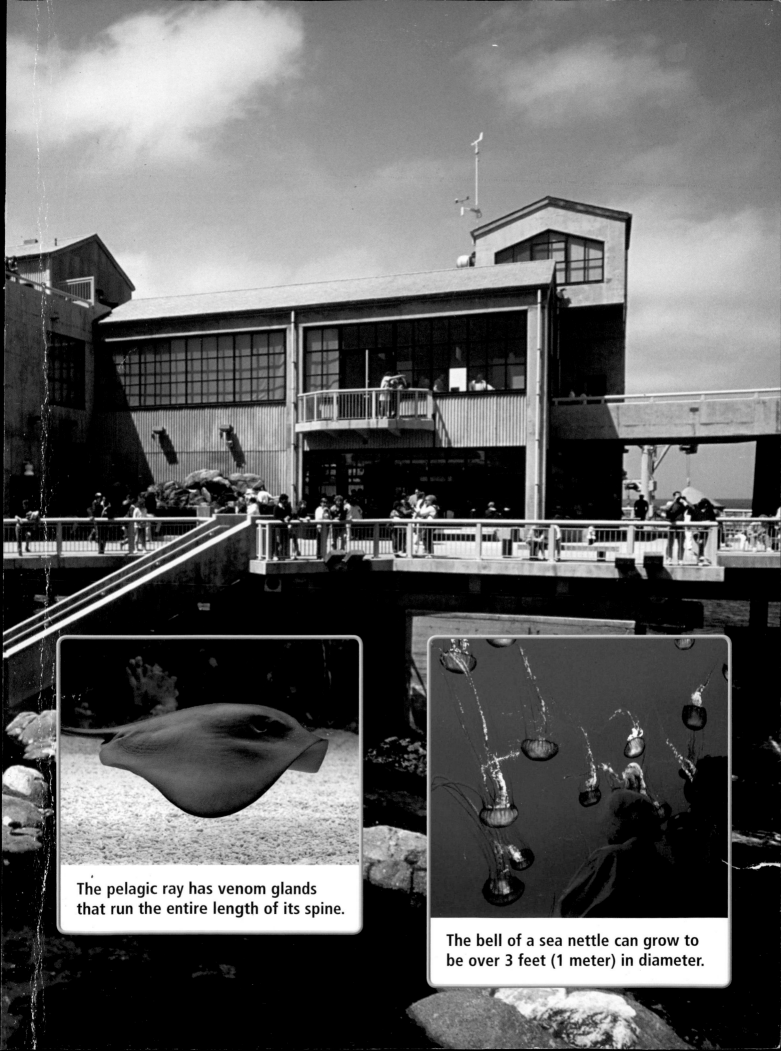

The pelagic ray has venom glands that run the entire length of its spine.

The bell of a sea nettle can grow to be over 3 feet (1 meter) in diameter.

LIFE — UNIT A — SCIENCE

Systems in Living Things

Plants and animals have structures for respiration, digestion, waste disposal, and transport of materials.

The American White Pelican lives in California and elsewhere.

1

Cells

Nerve cells (false-color image)

LESSON 1

A typical cell is so small that you need a microscope to see it. What are cells, and what do they do?

LESSON 2

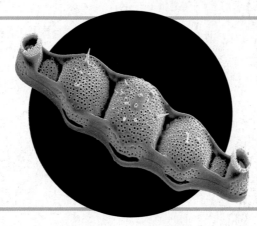

Cells need energy to carry out life functions and to keep organisms alive. How do cells get and use energy?

LESSON 3

When you perform any activity, such as swinging a baseball bat, different body systems are working together. How are cells organized to keep your body healthy and active?

Writing Journal

In your Writing Journal, draw or write answers to each question.

Vocabulary Preview

Vocabulary

Glossary

English-Spanish, p. H24

Vocabulary Skill

Word Roots
organelle

The prefix *organ-* means "tool, instrument, sense organ." The suffix *-elle* changes the meaning of the word to the diminutive. Say each word part. Then say them together.

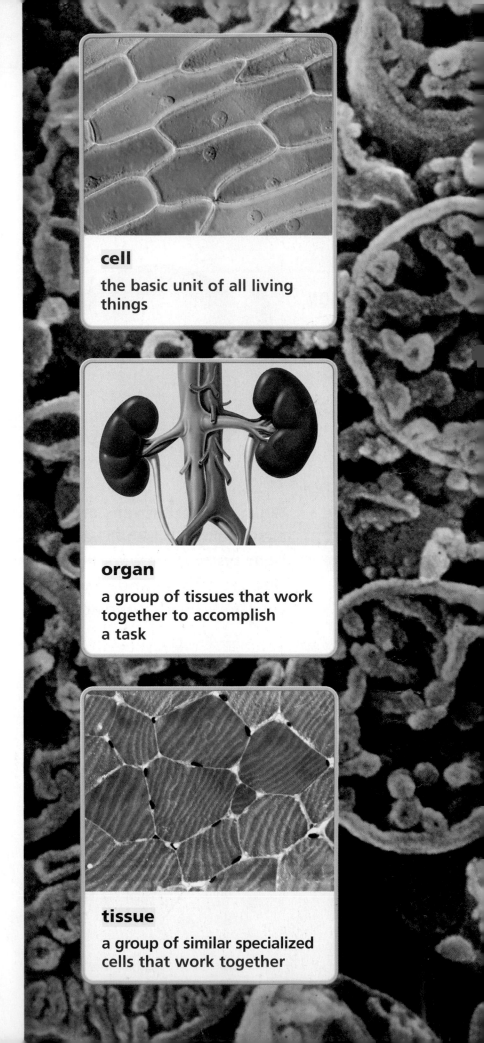

cell
the basic unit of all living things

organ
a group of tissues that work together to accomplish a task

tissue
a group of similar specialized cells that work together

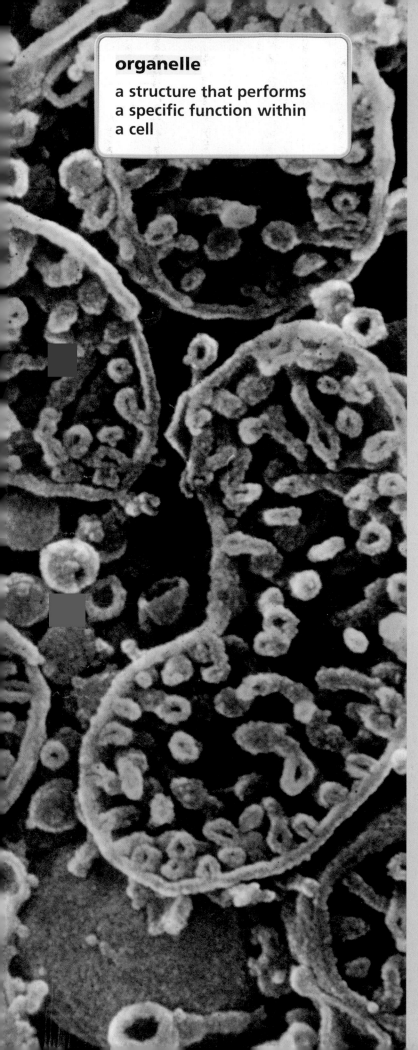

> **organelle**
>
> a structure that performs a specific function within a cell

Start with Your Standards

Standard Set 2. Life Sciences

2.a. *Students know* many multicellular organisms have specialized structures to support the transport of materials.

2.g. *Students know* plant and animal cells break down sugar to obtain energy, a process resulting in carbon dioxide (CO_2) and water (respiration).

Standard Set 6: Investigation and Experimentation standards covered in this chapter: 6.d., 6.g., 6.h.

What Are the Parts of a Cell?

Building Background

All living things, from water plants to hippos, are made of cells. When you compare cells and their parts, you can better understand how organisms like this hippopotamus live and interact with their environments.

STANDARDS

2.a. *Students know* many multicellular organisms have specialized structures to support the transport of materials.
6.g. Record data by using appropriate graphic representations (including charts, graphs, and labeled diagrams) and make inferences based on those data.

PREPARE TO INVESTIGATE

Inquiry Skill

Record Data You can record and display the data you collect in the form of charts, graphs, and labeled diagrams.

Materials

- microscope
- prepared slides of various plant and animal tissues

Science and Math Toolbox

For step 1, review **Using a Microscope** on page H2.

Get Closer!

Procedure

1. **Collaborate** Work in a small group. Take turns looking through a microscope at each slide. Note the titles of the slides, which tell the sources of the samples.

2. **Record Data** Draw a picture of the cells in each sample. Next to the picture write the name of the sample, and whether it comes from a plant or an animal.

3. **Compare** Compare drawings with those of other members of your group. Discuss how all the plant cells are similar. Discuss how all the animal cells are similar.

4. **Infer** After you discuss the cells with your group, draw a diagram of a typical plant cell and a diagram of a typical animal cell.

Conclusion

1. **Communicate** Discuss how your diagrams of typical cells show the differences between plant and animal cells.

2. **Infer** Compare the outer boundaries of an animal cell and a plant cell. Which appears to be more flexible? Which appears to be stronger?

3. **Hypothesize** Do you think the cells of all plants and animals share the characteristics you identified? How could you test your hypothesis?

Guided Inquiry

Experiment Cells vary a great deal in size. Your cells are almost 100 times bigger than a bacteria cell. Build or draw a model to **compare** the difference in size between a human and a bacteria cell.

VOCABULARY

cell	p. 8
cytoplasm	p. 10
nucleus	p. 10
organelle	p. 10

READING SKILL

Compare and Contrast
Use a Venn diagram to list similarities and differences between animal cells and plant cells.

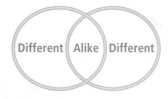

Different · Alike · Different

STANDARD

2.a. *Students know* many multicellular organisms have specialized structures to support the transport of materials.

Cells

MAIN IDEA Cells are the basic building blocks of living things. Cells contain special structures to transport cell materials.

The Cell Theory

The basic unit that makes up living things is the **cell.** All living things, from the tiniest insect to the largest whale, are made of cells.

When you look at most living things, you cannot see individual cells. That is because most cells are much too small to be seen with the unaided eye. Cells were not discovered until the microscope was invented in the 1600s. As scientists began using newer, more powerful microscopes, they learned more and more about cells and their structure.

By the late 1800s, scientists had organized their conclusions about cells into a single theory. The cell theory states:

- All living things are made of one or more cells.
- The cell is the basic unit of a living organism.
- Cells come from other cells.

Today, scientists continue to use new equipment and techniques to study cells. They are learning more about the way cells work.

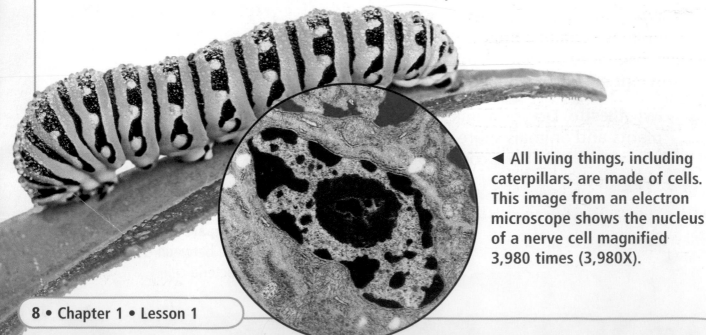

◄ All living things, including caterpillars, are made of cells. This image from an electron microscope shows the nucleus of a nerve cell magnified 3,980 times (3,980X).

Comparing Plant and Animal Cells

Need	Plant cells	Animal cells
Energy source	Sunlight, for making own food	Other living things, eaten for food
Support and protection	Thick cell walls and fluid-filled cell parts	Cell membrane and other parts
Growth and reproduction	DNA and proteins	DNA and proteins

Algae

Animal

▲ Cells of animals, such as these fish, are quite different from cells of plants and algae.

What Cells Do

All living things have the same basic needs. They need to make or take in food, which is their source of energy. They need a way to support and protect their bodies, and to get rid of wastes. They also need to grow and reproduce.

Some organisms consist of just a single cell. That means that one cell carries out all of the functions of life listed above. Bacteria, yeasts, and many kinds of algae all live as single cells.

Other organisms are multicellular, meaning they contain a huge number of cells. Even a small animal, such as a worm or a snail, contains billions of cells. These cells work together to provide all the needs of the organism.

Typically, the cells of multicellular organisms cannot survive apart from one another. Each cell can perform only some of the activities needed to stay alive.

Cells in different kinds of living things may perform life functions very differently. For example, cells in plants and algae make their own food from raw materials and sunlight. Animal cells cannot do this. Animals must eat other living things for food.

Other life functions are very similar in all living things. Cells make copies of themselves by using the same type of molecule, which is called DNA. Most cells also use the same kinds of parts, as you will discover on the next few pages.

COMPARE AND CONTRAST How do the functions of cells compare in a single-celled and a multicellular organism?

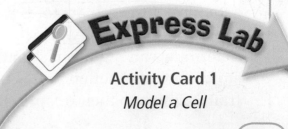

Express Lab

Activity Card 1
Model a Cell

9

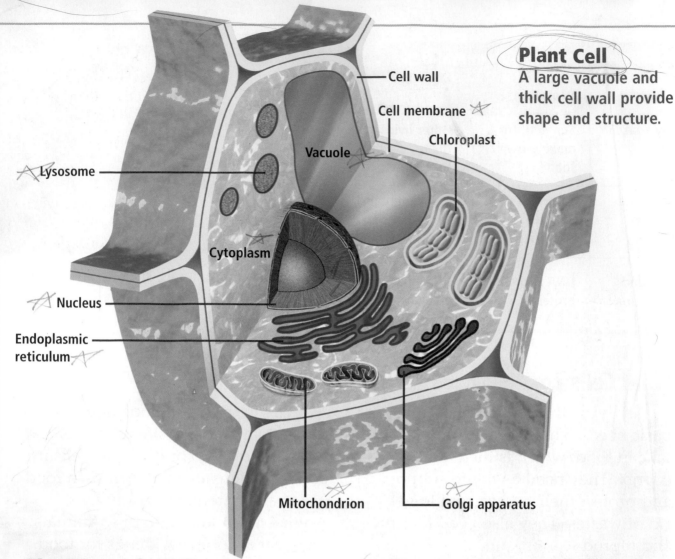

Cell wall

Cell membrane

Chloroplast

Vacuole

Lysosome

Cytoplasm

Nucleus

Endoplasmic reticulum

Mitochondrion

Golgi apparatus

Plant Cell
A large vacuole and thick cell wall provide shape and structure.

The Parts of a Cell

All plant and animal cells contain even smaller structures called **organelles.** These structures perform specific functions in the cell.

Animal cells and plant cells have many of the same organelles, but some are quite different. As you read through this section, refer to the organelle or other cell part in the illustrations.

Nucleus The **nucleus** directs the activities of the cell. It stores a molecule called DNA, which determines an organism's traits. DNA stores the information that is passed from parents to their offspring.

Cell Membrane The cell membrane is a thin, flexible covering that surrounds all types of cells. It allows food, water, and gases to enter the cell and wastes to leave.

Cell Wall In plant cells, the cell wall is a rigid outer layer that surrounds the cell membrane. The cell wall protects the cell and helps the plant stay upright. Pores in the cell wall allow materials to pass in and out.

Cytoplasm Between the nucleus and the cell membrane is the **cytoplasm.** All of the remaining organelles are located within the cytoplasm. They are suspended there in a thick fluid.

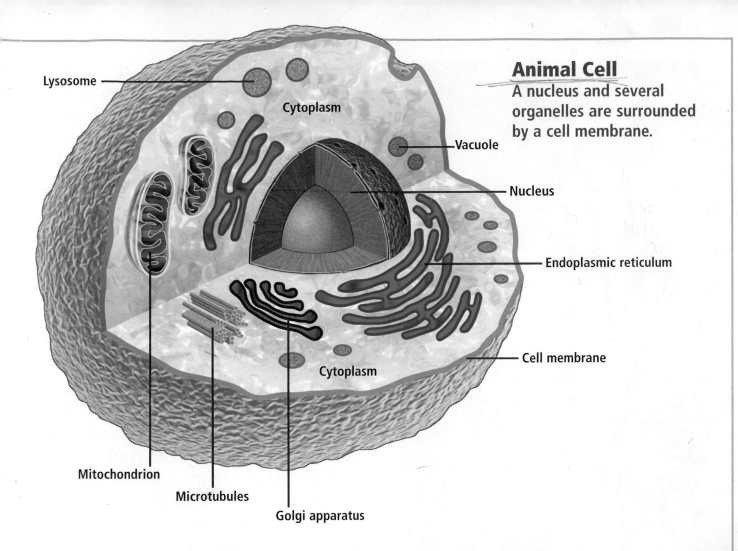

Animal Cell
A nucleus and several organelles are surrounded by a cell membrane.

Lysosome

Cytoplasm

Vacuole

Nucleus

Endoplasmic reticulum

Cell membrane

Cytoplasm

Mitochondrion

Microtubules

Golgi apparatus

Ribosomes Tiny ribosomes are scattered throughout the cell. Unlike most other organelles, ribosomes are not surrounded by membranes. Ribosomes help assemble compounds called proteins. Proteins make up the structural components of cells, and they allow the cell to perform nearly all chemical reactions.

Lysosomes Lysosomes are small, ball-shaped organelles that help the cell break down nutrients and old cell parts. Lysosomes are common in animal cells, but rare in plants.

Vacuoles Vacuoles are membrane-bound sacs that are filled with fluid. They store water, food, waste, and other substances the cell processes.

Animal cells may have several vacuoles. Plant cells, however, often have one large, central vacuole. When the vacuole in a plant cell is full, the cell is rigid. If the vacuoles in many cells lose water, the plant will wilt.

Golgi Apparatus The Golgi apparatus receives proteins, then processes them for "shipment" outside the cell. This organelle is a system of membranes. It modifies and refines proteins, sometimes adding compounds that will protect them from being broken apart.

COMPARE AND CONTRAST Describe differences between plant cells and animal cells.

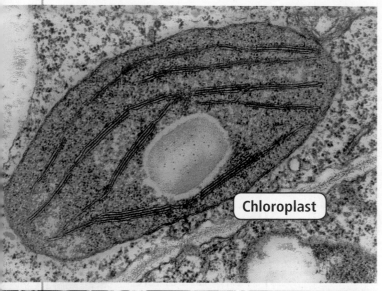

Chloroplast

Chloroplasts Found only in plants and some protists, chloroplasts contain pigments that absorb sunlight. They use the energy to make food—a unique process among the organelles! The pigment chlorophyll gives plants their green color.

Mitochondria Large, peanut-shaped organelles, called mitochondria, are known as the "power plants" of the cell. Inside them, sugars break apart as they react with oxygen. This process releases carbon dioxide, water, and a lot of energy.

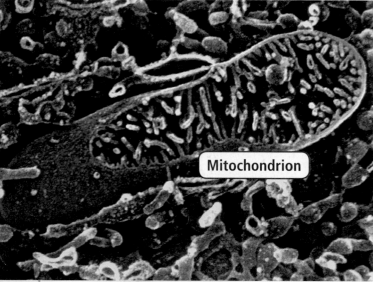

Mitochondrion

In both plant and animal cells, the number of mitochondria depends on the amount of energy the cell needs. For example, a muscle cell requires a great deal of energy, and so it has a large number of mitochondria (singular: mitochondrion).

Endoplasmic Reticulum The endoplasmic reticulum (ER) is a system of membranes and tubes. The membranes twist and turn through the cell, providing passages through which materials can pass.

A cell usually contains two kinds of ER, called rough and smooth. Rough ER is dotted with ribosomes. This type of ER is common in cells that secrete lots of proteins. Smooth ER is not covered by ribosomes. Its activities include breaking down toxic substances and controlling the levels of certain chemicals.

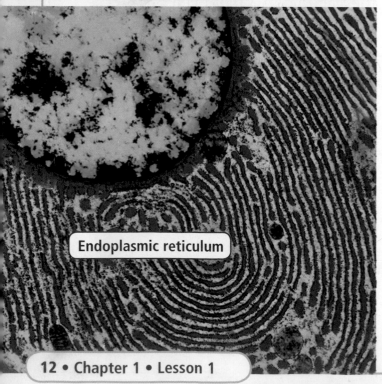

Endoplasmic reticulum

COMPARE AND CONTRAST How is smooth ER different from rough ER?

Lesson Wrap-Up

Visual Summary

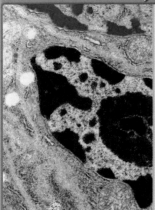

All living things are made of cells. Cells are the basic units of all living things, and all cells come from other cells.

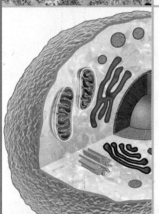

Cells—from single-celled algae to complex organisms with trillions of cells—carry out the basic functions of life.

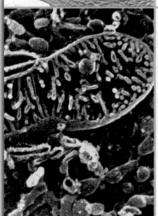

Cells contain smaller structures called organelles. Each performs a specific function.

 STANDARD

2.a.

 **Technology**
Visit **www.eduplace.com/cascp** to find out more about the parts of a cell.

Reading Review

❶ MAIN IDEA What do all cells have in common?

❷ VOCABULARY Write a sentence using the terms *cell* and *nucleus*. Explain the role of the nucleus in the cell.

❸ READING SKILL Compare single-celled organisms with those having many cells. How are they alike and different?

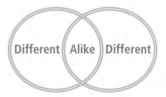

Different Alike Different

❹ CRITICAL THINKING:
Evaluate How would you determine whether a cell came from an animal or a plant? Discuss cell parts in your answer.

❺ INQUIRY SKILL: Record Data
Draw a picture of a typical plant cell and an animal cell. Label the organelles and other cell parts.

 TEST PRACTICE
Which is part of a plant cell but not an animal cell?

A. mitochondria

B. cell membrane

C. chloroplast

D. nucleus

 STANDARD

1–5: 2.a., **Test Practice:** 2.a.

History of the Microscope

Today's microscopes are much more complex and powerful than those used hundreds of years ago. As you read about the different microscopes, compare them to the ones you use in your classroom.

Egyptians polished rock crystals in the shape of convex lenses.

Eyeglasses were invented in Italy.

Anton van Leeuwenhoek used a microscope to observe free-living protists, which he called "animalcules."

~2600 B.C.   ~1285   1665   1673

Robert Hooke used a microscope of magnification 30× to observe cells in cork.

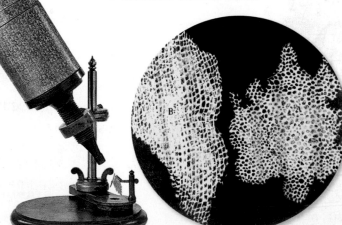

◄ Drawing of cork cells made by Robert Hooke

STANDARD
1.e. *Students know* scientists have developed instruments that can create discrete images of atoms and molecules that show that the atoms and molecules often occur in well-ordered arrays.

READING

Modern Microscopes

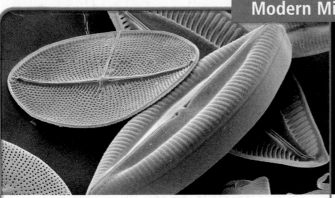

SEM (3-D)
This scanning electron micrograph shows two kinds of diatoms, magnified 1,750×.

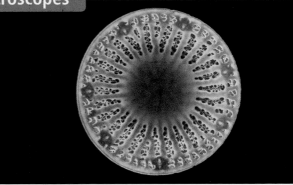

TEM (cross section)
This transmission electron micrograph shows a diatom that lives in fresh water.

Carl Zeiss produced the first commercial microscope that formed images from ultraviolet (UV) light.

A scanning tunneling microscope produced this image of silicon atoms.

1904   **1931**   **1982**

The first electron microscope was built.

Sharing Ideas

1. **READING CHECK** Compare the microscopes of the past to those you use today.

2. **TALK ABOUT IT** Why do you think many scientists name the microscope as the most important tool for studying living things?

15

How Do Cells Make and Use Energy?

Building Background

Every organism on Earth needs energy to carry out life processes. This energy comes from a class of compounds called sugars. Plants make their own sugars, while animals get them by eating food.

STANDARDS

2.g. *Students know* plant and animal cells break down sugar to obtain energy, a process resulting in carbon dioxide (CO_2) and water (respiration).
6.d. Identify the dependent and controlled variables in an investigation.

PREPARE TO INVESTIGATE

Inquiry Skill

Use Variables The controlled variables are the conditions unchanged in an experiment.

Materials

- measuring cup
- warm water
- cup or bowl
- teaspoon
- sugar
- packet of yeast
- 2 sealable plastic bags
- cafeteria tray
- paper towels
- lamp

Science and Math Toolbox

For step 3, review **Using Variables** on page H5.

Watch Yeast Feast!

Procedure

STEP 1

Time	Yeast + Water + Sugar	Yeast + Water
1 hour		
2 hours		
4 hours		
8 hours		
24 hours		

1. **Collaborate** Work in a small group. In your *Science Notebook,* make a chart like the one shown.

2. **Experiment** Pour 100 mL of warm water (not hot) into a cup or bowl. Stir in 15 g of sugar and 5 g yeast. Pour the mixture into a sealable plastic bag. Squeeze out as much air as you can. Seal the bag completely.

3. **Use Variables** Repeat step 2 using a second bag, but this time do not include sugar.

STEP 3

4. Place both sealed bags on a tray lined with a paper towel. Set the tray on a shelf or tabletop under a lit lamp.

5. **Record Data** Check the bags throughout the next 24 hours. Record what you observe. Use either words or pictures to describe what you see.

STEP 4

Conclusion

1. **Compare** Describe how the content of the two bags changed over time. Note important differences in the bags.

2. **Hypothesize** What do you think might have caused the effects you observed? Propose a hypothesis. Describe how you could test this hypothesis.

3. **Use Variables** In this experiment, what were the independent and dependent variables? Which variables did you control?

4. **Communicate** Write a report describing your investigation.

Guided Inquiry

Experiment Do yeasts grow better in warm or cold temperatures? Do they need light to grow? **Ask questions** about yeast growth. Plan and carry out an experiment to test one of these questions.

VOCABULARY

cellular respiration   p. 19
diffusion   p. 21
osmosis   p. 21

READING SKILL

Problem/Solution Use the chart to tell how organisms solve the problem of getting energy.

Problem	Solution

STANDARDS

2.g. *Students know* plant and animal cells break down sugar to obtain energy, a process resulting in carbon dioxide (CO_2) and water (respiration).
2.a. *Students know* many multicellular organisms have specialized structures to support the transport of materials.

Using Energy

MAIN IDEA To get energy, plant and animal cells break down sugar, releasing water and carbon dioxide.

Glucose

All organisms need energy to stay alive. This energy comes from food that they make for themselves or that they take in from the outside.

As you know, foods can look and taste very different from one another. Yet after food is broken down, the energy it provides comes from just a few different kinds of molecules. The most important of these molecules is glucose.

Glucose is an example of a sugar. It is a building block for all sorts of other sugars, including the kind used to sweeten foods. Plants are able to make their own glucose, which they store in very large molecules. Starches, which are found in potatoes and grains, are huge chains of glucose molecules strung together. So is cellulose, which makes up wood and other tough plant parts.

Unlike plants, animals cannot make their own glucose. This is why all animals need plants for food. Many animals eat plants; other animals eat plant-eaters.

◄ Like other animals, a koala uses a system of organs—the digestive system—to break down the food it eats. The system supplies glucose and other energy-rich compounds to the blood.

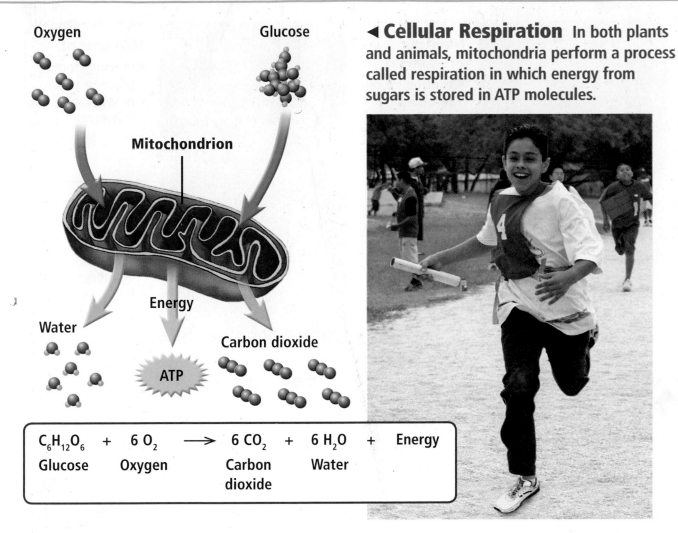

Oxygen

Glucose

Mitochondrion

Energy

Water

ATP

Carbon dioxide

$$C_6H_{12}O_6 + 6\,O_2 \longrightarrow 6\,CO_2 + 6\,H_2O + \text{Energy}$$

Glucose   Oxygen   Carbon   Water
                                            dioxide

◄ **Cellular Respiration** In both plants and animals, mitochondria perform a process called respiration in which energy from sugars is stored in ATP molecules.

Cellular Respiration

How do cells use glucose for energy? In plants and animals, cells break down glucose in a process called **cellular respiration**. The process involves a series of chemical reactions. It begins in the cytoplasm of the cell, then continues in mitochondria. You learned about these cell parts in Lesson 1.

Cellular respiration serves to change glucose and oxygen into carbon dioxide gas and water. It also releases a lot of energy, which the cell traps in a molecule called ATP. This special molecule is like a battery for the cell. The cell breaks apart ATP whenever it needs energy.

Plants and animals are able to store glucose very well. Many animals will change glucose into fat tissue, especially when they eat more than their energy needs demand.

Yet animals are not able to store gases, such as oxygen and carbon dioxide. This is why you and other animals need to breathe all the time! With every breath, you take in the oxygen gas that you need for cellular respiration. You also breathe out carbon dioxide, the waste product of the process.

PROBLEM AND SOLUTION How do cells get the energy they need to stay alive?

Making Proteins
• controlling cell reactions
• providing structure and support

Movement
• moving from place to place, or within the organism

Cell Division
• growing new body parts
• repairing or replacing damaged parts

Transport
• pumping materials across cell membranes

Why Cells Need Energy

Cells need energy to stay alive. Here are four important examples of life functions of a cell:

Making Proteins All cells make and use an important class of large molecules called proteins. Proteins allow cells to control the chemical reactions inside them.

Other proteins provide structure and support for organisms. Your skin, nails, and hair are made from proteins, as are a bird's feathers.

Movement Muscle cells are able to shrink and expand, and the body moves in response. Such movement takes a lot of energy, so muscle cells typically have many mitochondria.

In single-celled organisms, sometimes the cell itself moves from place to place. Some use tiny oar-like structures. Others use a structure that acts like a propellor.

Cell Division New cells form when old cells divide in two. You grew from a single cell inside your mother into the trillion-celled organism you are today. Each cell division needed a lot of energy.

Transport of Materials Recall that a cell membrane surrounds every cell. The membrane keeps some materials outside or inside the cell, but lets others pass through. Often—but not always—the transport of materials across the cell membrane requires energy.

Express Lab

Activity Card 2
Make an Energy Reaction

Moving Materials

As you have read, cells need all sorts of materials to stay alive. In most organisms, these materials include water, glucose, oxygen, and minerals such as sodium and potassium. Cells also produce wastes that must be removed. One waste is carbon dioxide gas.

How do these materials move in and out of the cell? In some cases, they do so without the cell using any energy. This kind of movement is called passive transport.

The simplest kind of passive transport is **diffusion,** a process that spreads substances through a gas or liquid. You can smell dinner across the room because food molecules diffuse through the air. Diffusion also spreads materials into and out of cells. Materials diffuse from areas of high concentration to areas of low concentration.

A special form of diffusion is called **osmosis** (ahz MOH sihs). Osmosis takes place across a membrane that lets water pass, but keeps out many things that are dissolved in the water. Osmosis works to keep water inside cells.

In other cases, a cell needs to move materials opposite to the way diffusion would move them. This kind of movement is called active transport, and it requires the cell to use energy. In active transport, materials are moved from regions of low to high concentration.

Nerve cells, for example, must use energy to pump sodium out of the cell and potassium into the cell. Nerves are able to work because they move sodium and potassium in this way.

PROBLEM AND SOLUTION **What are two ways that cells transport materials?**

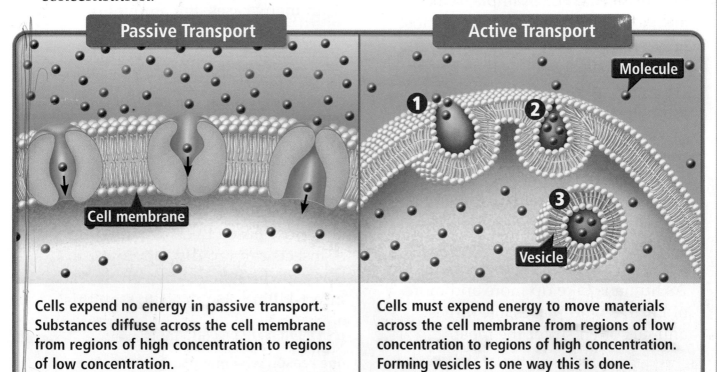

Passive Transport	Active Transport

Cell membrane

Molecule

Vesicle

Cells expend no energy in passive transport. Substances diffuse across the cell membrane from regions of high concentration to regions of low concentration.

Cells must expend energy to move materials across the cell membrane from regions of low concentration to regions of high concentration. Forming vesicles is one way this is done.

Cheetah   **Snake**   **Grasshopper**

▲ All three of these animals need energy, which they gain from their food. Which do you think needs the most food? Why?

Organisms and Energy

Individually, a cell does not need much energy. But remember that Earth is home to a huge number of organisms, each made of between one cell and trillions of cells!

Not all organisms have the same energy needs. For example, which animal do you think needs the most energy: a grasshopper, a snake, or a cheetah? The answer is the cheetah. As a general rule, warm-blooded animals with bigger bodies and greater speeds need far more energy than smaller, slower animals.

The need for energy is an important reason why many large animals are now endangered. The greater an animal's need for food, the larger an area it must travel to find it. As humans take up more and more of Earth's wild places, the largest animals often suffer the most.

A plant also needs energy, but not nearly as much as an animal of equal size. One reason is that plants do not move from place to place. A plant needs energy for growth and for transporting materials. Sunlight provides enough energy for such tasks, but not for rapid movement.

In many cases, the amount of energy available determines how organisms grow and reproduce. For example, if you cut open a peach or a pear and let it sit, colonies of bacteria and fungi from the air will grow rapidly upon it. The fruit supplies energy for these organisms.

On a larger scale, a farm crop can be a huge energy source for insects and other pests. Even a small number of insects can rapidly reproduce to cover a whole field. Farmers spread insect-killing chemicals to stop this.

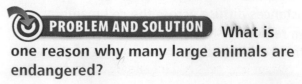 **PROBLEM AND SOLUTION** What is one reason why many large animals are endangered?

Lesson Wrap-Up

Visual Summary

All living things need energy to survive. The main source of this energy is glucose, a type of sugar.

In the process of cellular respiration, cells break down glucose and capture its energy. They use oxygen to do this and release water and carbon dioxide.

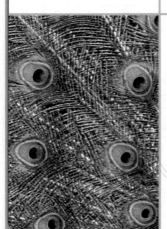

Cells need energy to carry out life functions that include movement, cell division, making proteins, and transporting materials.

STANDARDS

2.a., 2.g.

Technology

Visit **www.eduplace.com/cascp** to find out more about how cells and organisms use energy.

Reading Review

❶ MAIN IDEA How do cells use energy?

❷ VOCABULARY What is the process of cellular respiration, and what does it provide cells?

❸ READING SKILL What problem does a digestive system help an animal solve? How does it solve this problem?

Problem	Solution

❹ CRITICAL THINKING: Compare and Contrast Explain how the energy needs of a maple tree might differ from those of a squirrel.

❺ INQUIRY SKILL: Use Variables Does temperature affect the speed that food dye diffuses through water? Write a procedure to find out.

 TEST PRACTICE

During a process of _____, cells use energy to move materials across cell membranes.

A. diffusion

B. active transport

C. osmosis

D. passive transport

STANDARDS

1–2: 2.g., 3–4: 2.a., 5: 2.g., 6.d., **Test Practice:** 2.a.

23

How Are Cells Organized?

Building Background

How are you able to digest food, or move from place to place? How are you able to catch a baseball, or dance in time to music, or solve a math problem? In humans and other multicellular organisms, cell organization makes all the processes of life happen.

 STANDARDS

2.a. *Students know* many multicellular organisms have specialized structures to support the transport of materials.
6.h. Draw conclusions from scientific evidence and indicate whether further information is needed to support a specific conclusion.

PREPARE TO INVESTIGATE

Inquiry Skill

Ask Questions Scientists ask questions about organisms, objects, and events. Science inquiry helps test the answers.

Materials

- microscope
- prepared slides of various animal tissues

Science and Math Toolbox

For step 2, review **Using a Microscope** on page H2.

Exploring Tissues

Procedure

1 **Collaborate** Work in a small group. In your *Science Notebook,* draw a chart like the one shown. Use the chart to record your observations of different types of tissues.

2 **Observe** Take turns looking through the microscope at each type of tissue.

3 **Record Data** Record your observations by drawing one cell in the tissue. Then draw several cells, showing how they are arranged.

4 **Communicate** With the group, discuss the function of each type of tissue you studied. What part of the body did the tissue come from? What was the shape of the cells in the tissue?

Conclusion

1. **Analyze Data** How do all the cells in a single kind of tissue compare?

2. **Infer** What can you infer about the functions of all the cells in one kind of tissue? How would you define tissue?

3. **Infer** Humans and other animals have a wide variety of tissues in their bodies. What advantage does this variety provide?

STEP 1

Slide Number	Type of Tissue	Observations

STEP 2

Guided Inquiry

Ask Questions You have seen several examples of animal tissues. Make a list of questions you have about what you saw. Share your list with your class. Choose one question and **research** the answer at the library or on the Internet.

Cell Organization

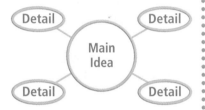
MAIN IDEA Cells join together to perform basic life functions in multicellular organisms.

From Cells to Organisms

Unlike a single-celled organism, a multicellular organism is made up of more than one cell. In these organisms the cells work together to perform life processes. The cells are specialized, which means that they perform only certain functions. By working together, these cells meet the needs of the organism as a whole.

Cells come in many shapes and sizes. The shape of a cell often relates to its function. Nerve cells, for example, are long and have many branches. This shape allows them to deliver electrical impulses over long distances. Skin cells are generally flat and arranged close together. In this way, they form a protective layer around the body. Muscle cells are larger than other cells. Their many fibers can contract and relax to cause movement.

In most multicellular organisms, cells are organized as the chart shows. ▼

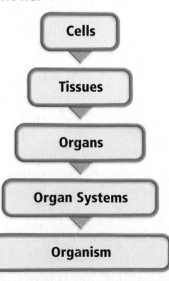

Cells → Tissues → Organs → Organ Systems → Organism

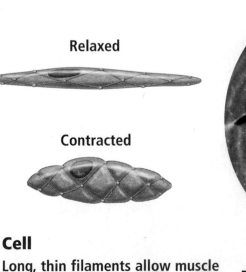

Relaxed

Contracted

Cell
Long, thin filaments allow muscle cells to relax and contract.

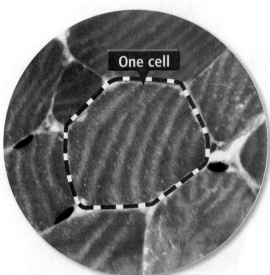

One cell

Tissue
Muscle cells are bundled to create a strong, contracting tissue.

Cells in multicellular organisms are organized at different levels. First, they are organized into tissues. A **tissue** is a large group of similar specialized cells. Muscle tissue, for example, consists of long bundles of muscle cells. Each bundle of muscle tissue is held together by its own covering. Like their component cells, muscle tissues contract and relax.

Similarly, nerve cells form nerve tissue, bone cells form bone tissue, and skin cells form the tissues of the skin. A tissue gets its characteristics from the particular type of specialized cell that forms it.

Together, tissues of different types make up organs. An **organ** is a group of related tissues that perform a specific function. The heart, brain, stomach, and liver are examples of organs.

Even if two organs are made from the same kind of tissue, they can be very different in appearance and function. For example, bones in the middle ear look and function much differently from the bones in arms and legs.

Plants have organs, too. Roots, stems, leaves, and fruits are organs of a plant. Each plant organ consists of related tissues made up of specialized cells that perform a certain function.

MAIN IDEA AND DETAILS Why do complex organisms have more than one kind of tissue?

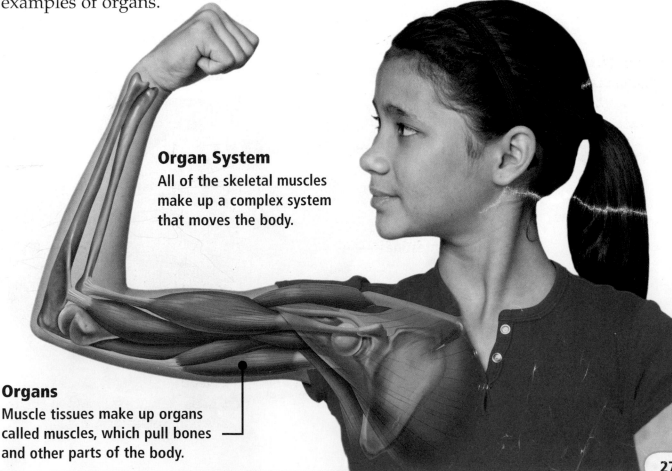

Organism
The muscular system works with other systems to help the girl live and grow.

Organ System
All of the skeletal muscles make up a complex system that moves the body.

Organs
Muscle tissues make up organs called muscles, which pull bones and other parts of the body.

Working Together

To meet the needs of the whole organism, organs are organized into organ systems. An **organ system** is a group of related organs that work together to perform a specific function. Most multicellular organisms have several organ systems. Organ systems combine to form the entire organism.

The diagram below shows parts of organ systems for a frog. The digestive system breaks down food into nutrients that cells can absorb. The respiratory system brings oxygen to the body and removes carbon dioxide. The circulatory system brings oxygen and nutrients to body cells, and it removes wastes. Other systems provide motion, senses, and protection.

Plants, too, have organ systems. A plant's leaves form one system. Tubes that carry water nutrients through a plant form another system.

In Chapter 3, you will read about different organ systems in humans. They work together to keep you alive and healthy.

MAIN IDEA AND DETAILS Why do organisms need organ systems?

Like other animals, a frog uses many organs to keep itself alive and healthy. Organs are organized into organ systems.

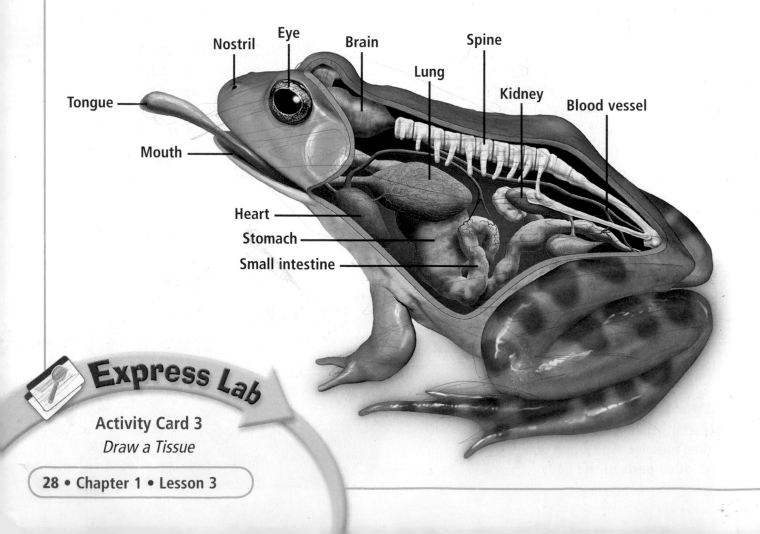

Tongue

Nostril

Eye

Brain

Spine

Lung

Kidney

Blood vessel

Mouth

Heart

Stomach

Small intestine

Express Lab

Activity Card 3
Draw a Tissue

Visual Summary

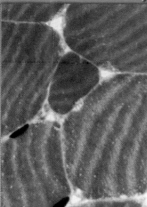

Specialized cells of the same type are grouped together to form tissues. Tissues are grouped together to form organs.

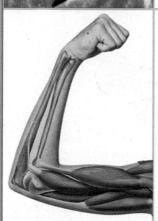

Examples of organs include the heart, kidneys, muscles, and bones. Each organ performs a specific function, such as pumping blood or filtering wastes.

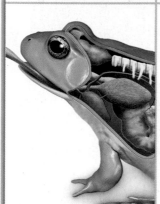

An organ system is a group of related organs that work together to perform a specific function. Organ systems combine to form the entire organism.

STANDARD
2.a.

Technology
Visit **www.eduplace.com/cascp** to find out more about how cells and organisms use energy.

Reading Review

❶ MAIN IDEA Explain how cells join and work together in multicellular organisms.

❷ VOCABULARY Write a sentence or short paragraph that explains how *tissues* are a part of *organs*.

❸ READING SKILL Give two examples of how organs work together in an organ system.

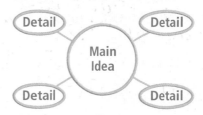

❹ CRITICAL THINKING: Predict Could a cell from a multicellular organism survive apart from the organism? Explain your prediction.

❺ INQUIRY SKILL: Ask Questions A patient complains that he is coughing and feels out of breath. What questions do you think the doctor should ask? Should the questions cover only the respiratory system? Explain.

TEST PRACTICE
An example of an organ system is
_____.

A. a frog's head

B. the heart of a snake

C. a bird's leg muscles

D. your digestive system

STANDARD
1–5: 2.a., **Test Practice:** 2.a.

29

Blue Blood

You don't need a time machine to see a prehistoric creature. Just go to the beach and look for a horseshoe crab. Most prehistoric animals changed over time or became extinct. But horseshoe crabs and their ancestors have existed basically unchanged for well over 250 million years!

Their survival record isn't all that's extreme about them. For one thing, horseshoe crabs aren't really crabs. They belong to the same class of animals as spiders and scorpions. Another curious thing is their blood. It's blue! Human blood is red because of the iron in it. The blood of horseshoe crabs is blue because it contains a copper compound that turns blue when exposed to air.

The medical profession uses an extract from the horseshoe crab's blue, copper-based blood called lysate to test the purity of medicines.

Invasion!

Every spring, millions of horseshoe crabs come ashore to mate and lay billions of eggs. Most of the eggs are eaten by birds and other predators, but enough survive to ensure continuation of the species.

Writing Journal

Horseshoe crabs grow by molting, or shedding their shells. If a horseshoe crab grows 25 percent with each molt, calculate how big a 10 cm crab will be after 5 molts.

31

LINKS
for Home and School

Math in Science

The science teachers of Sheldon Elementary School want to purchase hand lenses and microscopes for a new laboratory. They researched data on the Internet, and the results are shown in the table.

Product	Maximum Magnification	Cost
Hand lens, small	5x	$1.30
Hand lens, large	10x	$8.90
Light microscope, student model	100x	$18.20
Light microscope, lab model	400x	$256.00
Light microscope, advanced model	2,000x	$620.00
Scanning electron microscope	40,000x	$162,600

1. How many small hand lenses could they purchase for the cost of the least expensive microscope?

2. The teachers have budgeted $3,000 to spend on hand lenses and microscopes. Propose one way to spend this money. Describe why you think your plan makes sense.

3. How many times more powerful is the scanning electron microscope than the light microscope, advanced model? How many times more costly is it?

Writing in Science
Narrative

What if the narrator of a story could be the size of a cell, or even smaller? Tell a story about someone or something that travels among cells and can move throughout the body. Use details to show the events of your story. What is your plot? What happens to the main character?

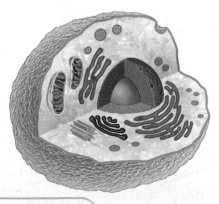

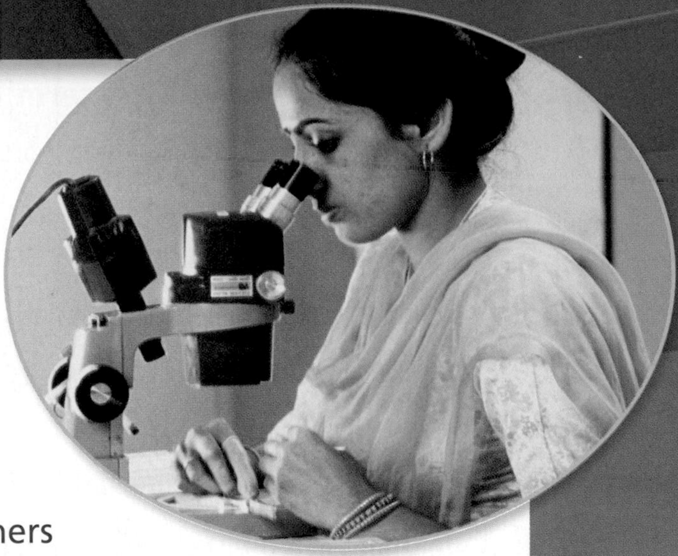

Microbiologist

Microbiologists study bacteria, protists, and other microoorganisms—living things too tiny to see with the unaided eye. They also study viruses, which are not alive.

Microbiologists work closely with doctors, food scientists, and researchers at drug companies. Microorganisms affect people in all sorts of ways, some that scientists are just beginning to understand.

What It Takes!

• An advanced degree in biology or microbiology

• Good analytical and math skills

Chef

Chefs prepare all kinds of dishes. They work at restaurants, schools, office buildings, and other places that serve food. Because food comes from living things, chefs need to know the nutritional value of different plants, animals, and fungi. They make different foods look appealing and taste delicious!

What It Takes!

• A certificate from a cooking school or training on the job

• Keen senses of taste and smell

• An artistic flair for preparing food

Vocabulary

Complete each sentence with a term from the list.

1. Energy is released when mitochondria break down glucose in a process known as ____.

2. The simplest kind of passive transport is called ____.

3. The basic unit that makes up living things is the ____.

4. A small structure within the cell that performs specific functions for the cell is a(n) ____.

5. The activities of the cell are directed by the ____.

6. One form of passive transport that takes place across a membrane that lets water pass, but keeps out many things that are dissolved in the water is called ____.

7. A group of related organs that work together to perform a specific function is a(n) ____.

8. A group of related tissues that perform a specific function is a(n) ____.

9. A large group of similar specialized cells that work together is a(n) ____.

10. Between the nucleus and cell membrane is a substance called ____.

cell p. 8
cellular respiration p. 19
cytoplasm p. 10
diffusion p. 21
nucleus p. 10
organ p. 27
organelle p. 10
organ system p. 28
osmosis p. 21
tissue p. 27

✓ Test Practice

Write the letter of the best answer choice.

11. According to the cell theory, cells are the ____.

   A. same in plants and animals
   B. largest parts of the body
   C. basic units of life
   D. smallest particles on Earth

12. The skin and the heart are two kinds of ____.

   A. cells   B. organs
   C. tissues   D. organ systems

13. Proteins are assembled at organelles called ____.

   A. ribosomes
   B. vacuoles
   C. chloroplasts
   D. mitochondria

14. A substance called glucose provides energy for ____.

   A. animals only   B. plants only
   C. large animals only D. all living things

Inquiry Skills

15. Record Data List some rules you should follow to make sure your charts, graphs, and diagrams are as accurate as possible.

16. From measuring the size of a plant cell, could you learn the size of the plant it came from? Explain why or why not.

Map the Concept

The chart shows two categories. Place each term within a category.

organelle
tissue
nucleus
organ
mitochondria
organ system
Golgi apparatus

Cell	Organism

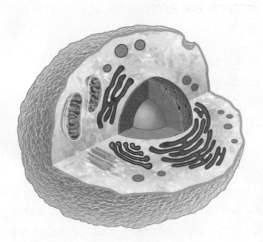

Critical Thinking

17. Apply Plants use sunlight to make glucose, from which they get their energy. What would happen to a plant that did not get enough sunlight?

18. Synthesize What are four things that plant and animal cells use energy to do?

19. Analyze You have discovered a new species of bat. It is a small, very fast hunter of insects. How would you compare its energy needs to an animal of about the same size that moves much more slowly?

20. Evaluate A teacher compares your body to a community of people working together. Do you agree or disagree? Explain your answer. What might happen if some cells were no longer able to work together?

Performance Assessment

Diagram Levels of Organization

Draw a diagram that shows the relationship among cells, tissues, organs, and organ systems in an organism.

Writing Journal

Review your answers to the Lesson Preview questions.

STANDARDS

1: 2.g., **2–13:** 2.a., **14:** 2.g., **15:** 6.g., **16:** 6.h., **17–19:** 2.g., **20:** 2.a., **Map the Concept:** 2.a., **Performance Assessment:** 2.a.

Chapter 2

Plant Systems

Venus flytrap

LESSON 1

Tiny structures inside plant cells use energy from the Sun to make food. Just how do they do this?

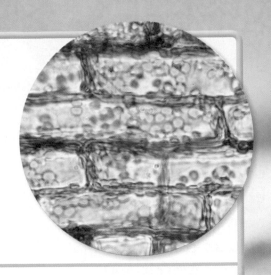

LESSON 2

Water enters this plant through roots in the soil. How does a plant move water up its stem?

Writing Journal

In your Writing Journal, draw or write answers to each question.

Vocabulary Preview

Vocabulary

Glossary

Vocabulary Skill

Word Roots
photosynthesis

The prefix *photo-* means "light." The word part *synthesis* means "putting parts together." Say the prefix and the word part. Then say them together.

vascular plant
a plant that has structures for transporting food, water, and other materials between plant parts

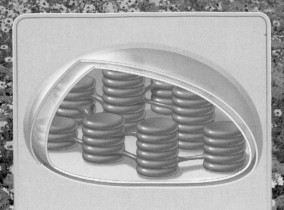

chloroplast

an organelle in which photosynthesis takes place

stomata

small openings in the bottom of a leaf through which gases move

transpiration

the evaporation of water through the stomata of a plant's leaves

Start with Your Standards

Standard Set 2. Life Sciences

2.a. *Students know* many multicellular organisms have specialized structures to support the transport of materials.

2.e. *Students know* how sugar, water, and minerals are transported in a vascular plant.

2.f. *Students know* plants use carbon dioxide (CO_2) and energy from sunlight to build molecules of sugar and release oxygen.

Standard Set 6: Investigation and Experimentation standards covered in this chapter: 6.a., 6.e.

How Do Plants Produce Food?

Building Background

Plants use a process called photosynthesis to make food and give off oxygen. Without plants performing photosynthesis, life as you know it could not exist. All animals, including humans, need the products that plants make.

 STANDARDS

2.f. *Students know* plants use carbon dioxide (CO_2) and energy from sunlight to build molecules of sugar and release oxygen.
6.e. Identify a single independent variable in a scientific investigation and explain how this variable can be used to collect information to answer a question about the results of the experiment.

PREPARE TO INVESTIGATE

Inquiry Skill

Hypothesize When you hypothesize, you use observations or prior knowledge to suggest a possible answer to a question.

Materials

- geranium plant with at least 4 leaves
- squares of cotton cloth (10 cm x 10 cm)

Science and Math Toolbox

Review **Using Variables** on page H5.

Keeping Green

Procedure

Time	Uncovered Leaves	Covered Leaves
2 days		
4 days		
6 days		

1. **Hypothesize** Work in a small group. In your *Science Notebook*, draw a chart like the one shown. Using what you already know about plants, form a hypothesis about the way leaves would change without sunlight.

2. **Experiment** Place your plant in a sunny window or other sheltered spot. Use the cloth squares to cover at least three leaves. Keep at least one leaf uncovered to serve as a control. Aside from the cloth covers, keep all conditions the same for the leaves.

3. **Predict** How do you think the different leaves will change over time? Record your prediction.

4. **Record Data** Check the plant every day and give it water if the soil is dry. Every two days, remove the cover from one or more leaves. Record your observations, then cover the leaves again.

5. **Analyze Data** Discuss the differences that you observed and recorded. Compare the effects of blocking sunlight for two days, four days, and six days.

Conclusion

1. **Use Variables** What was the independent variable in this investigation? What was the dependent variable? Which variables did you control?

2. **Analyze Data** Review the hypothesis and your results. Did you find evidence to support the hypothesis? Explain why or why not.

Guided Inquiry

Experiment Plan and conduct an experiment on plants that tests another independent variable, such as water or soil quality. Describe how you **use variables** in your experiment.

ree-Project

Producing Food

Learn by Reading

▶ VOCABULARY

chlorophyll	p. 43
chloroplast	p. 43
grana	p. 43
photosynthesis	p. 42
stomata	p. 44

◎ READING SKILL

Sequence Use a chart to show the sequence of steps in photosynthesis.

> Step 1
> ↓
> Step 2
> ↓
> Step 3

STANDARDS

2.f. *Students know* plants use carbon dioxide (CO_2) and energy from sunlight to build molecules of sugar and release oxygen.
2.a. *Students know* many multicellular organisms have specialized structures to support the transport of materials.

MAIN IDEA Plants use energy from the Sun to make food. They combine carbon dioxide and water to make sugar, and release oxygen in the process.

Photosynthesis

You are constantly using energy to conduct all of your life processes. You need energy to breathe, eat, move, think, and even sleep. The original source of your energy is the Sun.

As you learned in Chapter 1, plants transform the energy of sunlight into chemical energy. This energy is stored in food. Plants, along with algae and some bacteria, accomplish this through a process called photosynthesis. During **photosynthesis,** plants combine water and carbon dioxide into compounds called sugars. They release oxygen in the process.

Sugars are a plant's food. The plant stores sugars in its tissues and breaks them down when it needs energy. When an animal eats the plant, it can use the stored sugars. And when a larger animal eats the plant-eater, it too obtains energy originally stored in plants. In this way, animals depend on plants for energy.

Plant cells contain organelles called chloroplasts. Inside them, light energy is changed to chemical energy. ▼

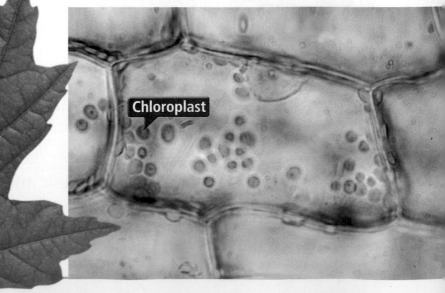

Chloroplast

A plant leaf uses photosynthesis to make food.

In Chapter 1 you learned that photosynthesis takes place in organelles called **chloroplasts.** The number of chloroplasts in a cell depends on the organism. Some tiny algae cells have only one chloroplast, while the cells in the leaves of a tree may each contain more than fifty.

Most chloroplasts have the same basic structure. Each is surrounded by two membranes. Another system of membranes winds through the interior of the chloroplast. These membranes look like flat sacs. They are arranged in stacks called **grana.**

Inside the membranes are a variety of pigments. A pigment is a substance that absorbs light. The most important pigment in a chloroplast is **chlorophyll.** Chlorophyll absorbs most colors of light, but not green.

How does photosynthesis work? When light strikes chlorophyll, the energy is used to split apart water molecules into hydrogen and oxygen. Later, during a series of chemical reactions, hydrogen joins with carbon from carbon dioxide to form sugars. Oxygen gas is released into the atmosphere.

Photosynthesis is a unique process, and it's hard to imagine life on Earth without it. The next time you see a tree or other plant, remember that almost all of its matter came from only water and carbon dioxide.

SEQUENCE What must happen in order for the process of photosynthesis to begin?

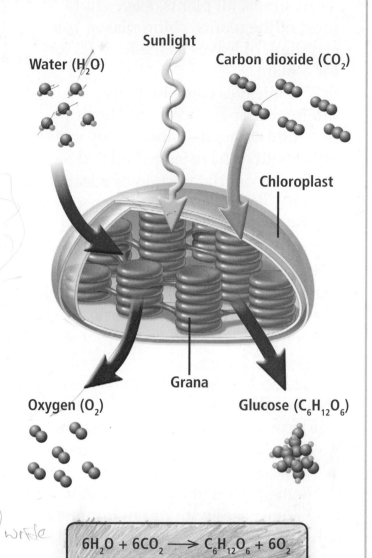

Photosynthesis

Sunlight

Water (H_2O)

Carbon dioxide (CO_2)

Chloroplast

Grana

Oxygen (O_2)

Glucose ($C_6H_{12}O_6$)

$$6H_2O + 6CO_2 \longrightarrow C_6H_{12}O_6 + 6O_2$$

Inside a chloroplast, stacks of membranes called grana contain chlorophyll, which absorbs sunlight.

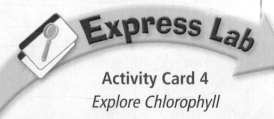

Express Lab

Activity Card 4
Explore Chlorophyll

Plant Leaves

In almost all plants, leaves hold most of the plants' chloroplasts. You can think of leaves as the food factory for a plant.

Plant leaves come in many different shapes and sizes. They can be round or heart-shaped. They can be smooth or have jagged edges.

The broad, flat portion of a leaf is called the blade. Scientists group leaves by the structure of the blade. A simple leaf has a single blade. Oak trees and apple trees have simple leaves. A compound leaf has a blade that is divided into parts. Rose bushes and palm trees have compound leaves.

Leaves are made of different tissues. The outer layer is called the epidermis. The cells in this tissue have a waterproof coating that prevents water loss.

Remember that a plant needs to exchange gases with its environment. Small openings in the epidermis allow oxygen and carbon dioxide to enter or exit the leaf. They also allow water vapor to exit.

These openings are called **stomata** and are scattered about the underside of the leaf. One opening is called a stoma, a Greek word that means "mouth." You can see from the picture that stomata look like small mouths.

Specialized structures that act like gates control the opening and closing of the stomata. When they open, carbon dioxide enters the leaf while oxygen and water vapor exit.

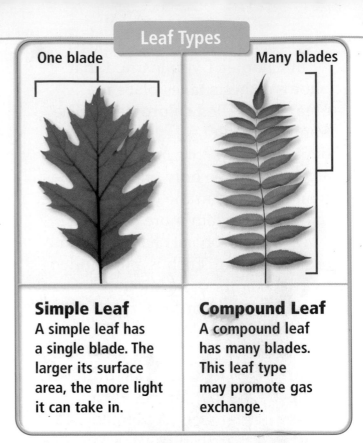

Leaf Types

One blade | Many blades

Simple Leaf
A simple leaf has a single blade. The larger its surface area, the more light it can take in.

Compound Leaf
A compound leaf has many blades. This leaf type may promote gas exchange.

Stomata often open during daylight when photosynthesis occurs. At night, stomata usually close to keep water in. Stomata can also open and close in response to changes in the environment. During dry spells or hot days, a plant's stomata might stay closed to conserve water.

Most of the cells that perform photosynthesis lie just below the epidermis. These cells are arranged with many air spaces between them so that carbon dioxide, oxygen, and water vapor can flow freely.

Running through leaves are long, thin structures called veins. Veins carry materials in and out of the leaf, serving to connect the leaf's cells to the rest of the plant. You will read more about these structures later in this chapter.

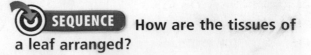 **SEQUENCE** How are the tissues of a leaf arranged?

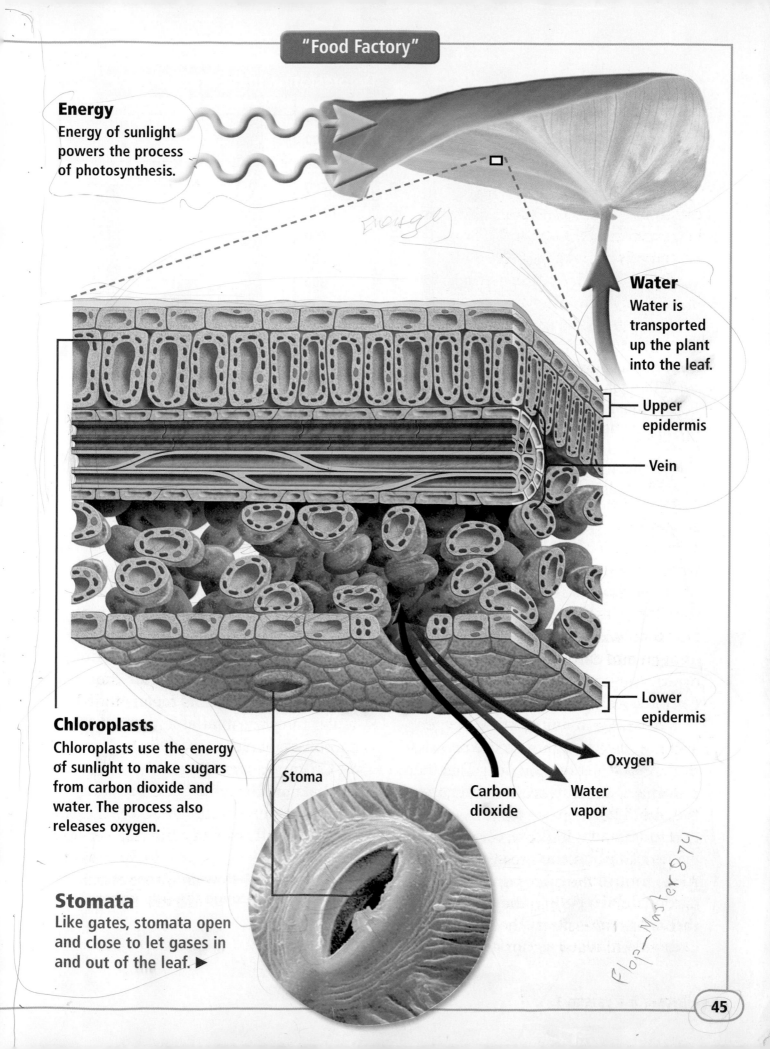

"Food Factory"

Energy
Energy of sunlight powers the process of photosynthesis.

Water
Water is transported up the plant into the leaf.

Upper epidermis

Vein

Lower epidermis

Oxygen

Carbon dioxide

Water vapor

Chloroplasts
Chloroplasts use the energy of sunlight to make sugars from carbon dioxide and water. The process also releases oxygen.

Stoma

Stomata
Like gates, stomata open and close to let gases in and out of the leaf. ▶

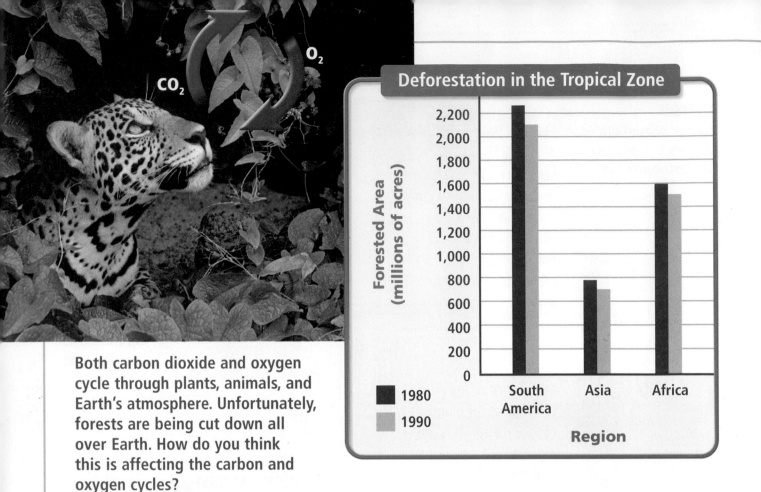

Deforestation in the Tropical Zone

Forested Area (millions of acres)

2,200
2,000
1,800
1,600
1,400
1,200
1,000
800
600
400
200
0

South America   Asia   Africa

Region

■ 1980
▨ 1990

Both carbon dioxide and oxygen cycle through plants, animals, and Earth's atmosphere. Unfortunately, forests are being cut down all over Earth. How do you think this is affecting the carbon and oxygen cycles?

Carbon and Oxygen Cycles

Why doesn't the air run out of oxygen, or fill up with carbon dioxide? The reason is that oxygen and carbon dioxide cycle through the atmosphere and the environment.

As you have read, plants take in carbon dioxide and give off oxygen. Both plants and animals use oxygen to break down sugars. In the process, they release carbon dioxide. Together, plants and animals recycle the gases they both need.

Human activities can upset the cycles of carbon and oxygen. Fossil fuels, for example, contain stored carbon. When people burn these fuels, including coal, oil, and natural gas, the carbon is released as carbon dioxide.

Today, people are burning fossil fuels at a very fast rate. The result is a rapid return of carbon to the atmosphere. In addition, people are cutting down forests, including huge areas of rain forests in South America and other places. This means that fewer trees are available to remove carbon and release oxygen.

Cutting down forests can upset the balance that this cycle provides. Unfortunately, deforestation continues all over Earth.

SEQUENCE How do carbon and oxygen cycle through the atmosphere?

Lesson Wrap-Up

Visual Summary

A plant's leaves use carbon dioxide, water, and energy from sunlight to build molecules of sugar and release oxygen. Veins carry materials to and from leaves.

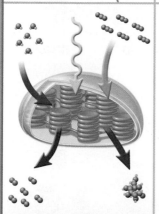

Photosynthesis takes place in the chloroplasts of plant cells. Chlorophyll is the pigment in chloroplasts that absorbs light.

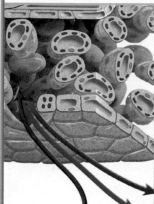

Stomata are openings in the bottom of leaves that let carbon dioxide enter the leaf. Oxygen and water vapor move out of the leaf through the stomata.

 **STANDARDS**

2.f., 2.a.

 Technology

Visit **www.eduplace.com/cascp** to find out more about plant leaves and photosynthesis.

Reading Review

❶ **MAIN IDEA** How do plants make sugar and release oxygen?

❷ **VOCABULARY** What is *chlorophyll* and where is it located? How is it important to plants?

❸ **READING SKILL** Show the steps of photosynthesis.

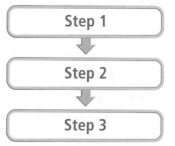

```
┌──────────────┐
│    Step 1    │
└──────────────┘
       │
       ▼
┌──────────────┐
│    Step 2    │
└──────────────┘
       │
       ▼
┌──────────────┐
│    Step 3    │
└──────────────┘
```

❹ **CRITICAL THINKING: Analyze** Describe two reasons that animals need plants.

❺ **INQUIRY SKILL: Hypothesize** What would happen to a plant if the undersides of its leaves were covered with petroleum jelly? Form a hypothesis. Then design an experiment to test your hypothesis.

 TEST PRACTICE

Plants change gases in the air by ____.

A. removing both oxygen and carbon dioxide

B. removing oxygen only

C. adding oxygen and removing carbon dioxide

D. adding a wide variety of gases

 STANDARDS

1–4: 2.f., **5:** 2.a., 6.e., **Test Practice:** 2.f.

THE WORLD OF PLANTS

How do people use plants? The setting is the Chung family living room. Ben reaches for the remote control to find something worth watching. However, just as he's about to change channels . . .

Characters

TV Announcer

Ben Chung:
A fifth-grade boy

Julia Chung:
Ben's sister

Dr. Luisa Galvez:
A research chemist

Emily:
A girl at a California farm

Dr. George Washington Carver:
Scientist

Dad:
Ben and Julia's father

STANDARD

2.f. *Students know* plants use carbon dioxide (CO_2) and energy from sunlight to build molecules of sugar and release oxygen.

READING LINK

Announcer: Stay tuned for our next program, "The World of Plants."

Ben (*yawning*): Do you mind if I find something else to watch?

Julia: Go ahead. This show sounds really boring.

Announcer: You're quite wrong, Ben and Julia Chung of 333 Portland Road!

Ben: Julia! Did you hear that? He's talking to us! (*Ben and Julia lean toward the TV.*)

Announcer: That's right. Plants aren't boring at all. In fact, some are quite surprising.

Julia: Surprising? I doubt it. I already know all about plants and how important they are. Plants use photosynthesis to make the food we eat and to add oxygen to the air.

Ben: And trees give us wood and paper products. So you see, we already know everything. Can we please change the channel now?

Announcer: Hold on! Plants use photosynthesis to make other useful products.

Scene switches quickly to a grove of rubber trees. Birds, monkeys, and other animals chatter in the background.

Julia: Where are we?

Announcer: We're at a rubber tree plantation in Brazil. You can find farms like this in tropical regions all over the world.

Ben (*pressing on a tree*): These trees don't seem bouncier than other trees.

Dr. Galvez (*entering*): That's because rubber comes from the sap of a rubber tree, not from the wood.

Ben: Who are you?

Dr. Galvez: I'm a research chemist. I study ways to change raw rubber into sturdy, useful products.

Julia: Like what? Car tires?

Dr. Galvez: Yes. And many other things, too—escalators, rain gear, windshield wipers, and even pencil erasers.

Ben (*looking around*): I'm glad you're putting these rubber trees to good use.

Rubber
The rubber in most tires begins as sap in rubber trees.

Dr. Galvez: Oh, yes. Today, people use more rubber than ever before. To meet the demand, scientists are mixing natural rubber with rubber made in laboratories.

Announcer: Thanks, Dr. Galvez. Time to meet another interesting plant.

Scene switches to a desert.

Julia: Now what?

Announcer: Welcome to southeast California. Meet the jojoba plant.

Ben: It looks like an ordinary shrub to me.

Announcer: Maybe so, but take a look at these seeds. They're filled with a very unusual oil.

Julia: What's so unusual about it?

Emily *(entering):* Allow me to answer. I'm Emily, and this is my farm. Oil from jojoba seeds is used in shampoo and makeup. Researchers are studying how to use it as a fuel, too.

Ben: Like gasoline or diesel fuel?

Emily: Yes. Think how useful that might be! Instead of digging up fossil fuels, we might raise plants like the jojoba.

Julia: I bet the seeds grow year after year, too. We'd never run out of them!

Announcer: Aha! Maybe now you believe me when I say plants can be surprising! Did you know that citronella oil comes from dried grasses? People use it to repel insects, especially mosquitoes.

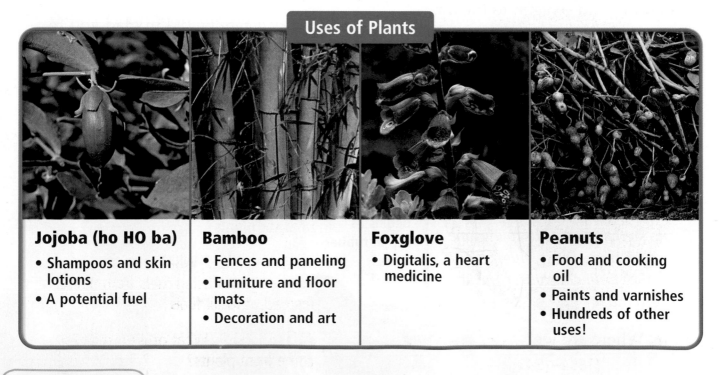

Uses of Plants

Jojoba (ho HO ba)
- Shampoos and skin lotions
- A potential fuel

Bamboo
- Fences and paneling
- Furniture and floor mats
- Decoration and art

Foxglove
- Digitalis, a heart medicine

Peanuts
- Food and cooking oil
- Paints and varnishes
- Hundreds of other uses!

Emily: Don't forget sap from the chicle tree. It's used to make chewing gum!

Dr. Galvez: How about soapwort? It's used to make soap that cleans delicate fabrics.

Soapwort plant

Dr. Carver *(entering)*: Hello, everyone. I'm Dr. George Washington Carver. I'd like to remind you about another important plant: peanuts. Why, I invented more uses for peanuts than anyone ever imagined! Today, peanuts are used to make ink, grease, shaving cream, paint, construction materials—

Ben: OK, OK! I'm convinced! Plants aren't boring!

Julia: They're downright amazing!

**Dr. George Washington Carver
(1864–1943)**

▲ Soap from the soapwort plant is used to clean valuable tapestries.

Dad *(shaking Ben and Julia gently)*: Hey, wake up, kids!

Ben and Julia: What? What happened?

Dad: You slept through a TV show about plants. I came in part way. I thought plants were dull, but I was wrong! Why, did you know . . .

Sharing Ideas

1. **READING CHECK** What are three unusual uses for plants?

2. **WRITE ABOUT IT** What are the advantages of using fuels from plants instead of fossil fuels?

3. **TALK ABOUT IT** What other products come from plants?

How Do Plants Move Materials?

Building Background

Plant leaves need water and minerals that are found in soil. Without them, photosynthesis could not occur. Almost all plants have a way to move materials upward, against the downward pull of gravity.

 STANDARDS

2.e. *Students know* how sugar, water, and minerals are transported in a vascular plant.
6.a. Classify objects (e.g., rocks, plants, leaves) in accordance with appropriate criteria.

PREPARE TO INVESTIGATE

Inquiry Skill

Predict When you predict, you state what you think will happen, based on past observations and experiences.

Materials

- large plastic cup or glass jar
- water
- red food coloring
- eyedropper
- plastic spoon
- stalk of celery with leaves
- microscope
- microscope slide and coverslip

Science and Math Toolbox

For step 5, review **Using a Microscope** on page H2.

Moving Water in Celery

Procedure

1 **Collaborate** Work with a partner. Add water to the cup until it is about three-fourths full.

2 **Measure** Add 4 to 5 drops of food coloring to the water, then stir. Add additional drops if necessary to color the water brightly.

3 **Collaborate** Your teacher will give you a stalk of celery that has just had about 3 cm cut from its bottom. Immediately place the cut end of the celery in the cup of colored water.

4 **Predict** What do you think will happen to the celery? Record your prediction in your *Science Notebook.*

5 **Observe** After one hour, observe the celery. Have your teacher cut off about 3 cm from the bottom of your celery and then cut off a thin cross-section. Prepare a slide and observe the cross-section with a microscope. Draw your observations.

Conclusion

1. **Infer** What did you observe in the cross-section of the celery? Infer the cause.

2. **Predict** What do you think would happen to the celery if you left it in the colored water overnight?

3. **Hypothesize** What if the bottom of a celery stalk was split lengthwise, and only one half was placed in colored water? Form a hypothesis. Test it with your teacher's help.

STEP 2

STEP 3

STEP 5

Guided Inquiry

Ask Questions Collect leaf samples from trees, grasses, and other plants. **Classify** the leaves according to the patterns of their veins. What questions do you have about these patterns?

Moving Materials

MAIN IDEA Plants have specialized tissues and use natural forces to transport water, minerals, and nutrients.

Limits to Growth

Most plants you can name, including all that grow more than a few centimeters tall, are examples of vascular plants. A **vascular plant** has specialized tissues that transport materials throughout it. Veins, which you read about in Lesson 1, carry materials in and out of leaves and through roots and stems. Veins are examples of vascular tissues.

Have you ever observed moss on the side of a tree? Mosses are examples of **nonvascular plants,** which lack structures that transport sugar, water, and other materials between plant parts. They also lack true leaves, stems, and roots. The nonvascular plants also include liverworts and hornworts.

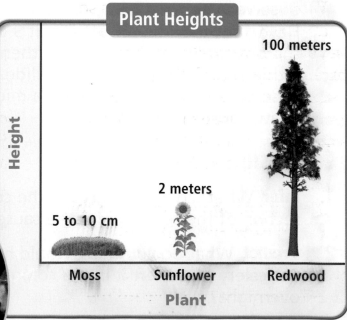

Plant Heights

100 meters

2 meters

5 to 10 cm

Moss — Sunflower — Redwood

Plant

Height

Liverwort

Moss

◀ **Mosses and Liverworts**
Nonvascular plants lack complex organs. Some of their leaf-like tissues are only one cell thick.

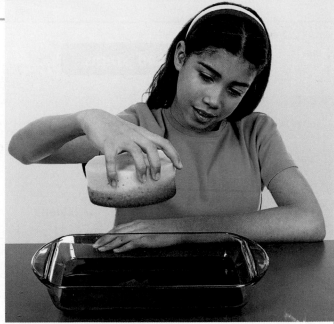

Like this sponge, a cell will slowly take up water from the outside.
The slow speed serves to limit cell size and the size of the organism.

Nonvascular plants are almost always small. Notice the size of the moss in the graph. Compare it with the size of a sunflower and a redwood. Both sunflowers and redwoods are vascular plants.

Why are nonvascular plants so small? One reason is that they lack ways to deliver water to distant parts. So, most of their cells must be close to a source of water, such as the ground or the side of a tree. Gases, water, and minerals move only by diffusion between the environment and the cells.

The photos show a model of this problem. After sitting in pink water for 1 minute, only part of the sponge got wet. If the sponge were a group of cells, then the cells toward the top would dry out quickly and not survive.

Although they are small, nonvascular plants fill important roles in their environments. Because they absorb water, they help hold soil in place and keep it from drying out. They also help form soil, as they slowly break down rocks that they grow on. In addition, these plants provide food and habitats for insects and other small animals.

Unlike many other plants, mosses can grow well without much light. So, many are found on the floor of a wet, dark forest. Sometimes moss grows into a dense mat that covers the forest floor like a carpet.

COMPARE AND CONTRAST What is the main difference between the tissues of vascular and nonvascular plants?

Express Lab

Activity Card 5
Show How a Nonvascular Plant Works

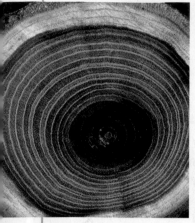

Trunks

Growth rings mark each year's new xylem, or wood tissue. The darker parts show where growth slowed at the end of each season.

Phloem   Xylem

Stems

Stems grow wider by adding new layers of xylem and phloem. New layers grow on either side of the vascular cambium.

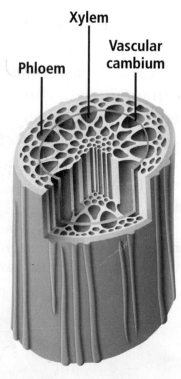

Xylem

Phloem   Vascular cambium

Vascular Plants

The organs of vascular plants include roots, stems, and leaves. Roots anchor a plant in the ground. They also absorb water and minerals from the soil. Some roots store food for the plant as well.

The stem supports the plant and holds its leaves up in the air so they can receive sunlight. The stem also provides a way for water, minerals, and sugars to move between the roots and the leaves.

Roots, stems, and leaves contain two important kinds of vascular tissues: xylem and phloem. **Xylem** conducts water and minerals from the roots to the stem and to the leaves. It carries water only in one direction. **Phloem** conducts sugar that is made in the leaves downward to the rest of the plant. The food is either used or stored. Phloem also can conduct sugar upward, from where it is stored to where it is needed.

A typical plant stem has bundles of vascular tissues containing both xylem and phloem. Some soft-stemmed plants have vascular bundles scattered throughout the stem. Other soft-stemmed plants, as well as plants with woody stems, have a ring of vascular bundles. In this ring, a strip of tissue called the vascular cambium lies between the xylem and phloem. Here, xylem and phloem cells are produced and the stem grows wider.

COMPARE AND CONTRAST What do the two types of vascular tissue conduct?

Transpiration Evaporation from the leaves creates a pull that draws water up through the stem.

The Upward Flow of Water

Plants do not have water pumps like those on a fire truck. So how does water move up a plant's stem, from the roots to the distant leaves? Water moves up plants because of three factors: root pressure, cohesion, and transpiration.

Water enters roots because roots are dryer than the surrounding soil. The outer walls of roots have specialized cells that keep the water from leaking back out. Eventually, pressure builds and pushes water upward.

Yet root pressure alone is not strong enough to push water through an entire plant. Water travels the remainder of the trip because it is pulled upward.

Water molecules cling to each other as a result of a force called cohesion. They cling to molecules of other substances, too, and this force is called adhesion. This forces water to climb up tubes of xylem tissue.

An additional pull is needed to move water to the tops of taller plants. That pull is provided by transpiration. During **transpiration,** liquid water evaporates through plant leaves. As water moves from the plant to the air, water is pulled upward through the plant to take its place. About 99 percent of the water that enters the roots is transpired by the leaves!

COMPARE AND CONTRAST Compare the different forces that move water up a plant.

Gravity Sugar from photosynthesis is pulled down to nourish the plant.

Cohesion Water and minerals cling to each other and to the xylem walls. This forms a column under tension that rises up the stem.

Root Pressure Root pressure pushes water and minerals up.

Root Hairs

How Wide? How Tall?

Vascular plants can be very small or they can be very large. The largest vascular plants are trees. They have woody stems that can grow wider and taller each year until they reach their mature height.

A tree's growth each year is limited by environmental conditions. A tree grows best when it gets all of the nutrients, water, and sunlight it needs. It grows less tall if conditions are too wet or too dry, too hot or too cold, or too windy.

Even under ideal growing conditions, each kind of tree has a different maximum size it can reach. Probably the most important factor that limits the height of a tree is its vascular system. New stems and leaves will grow only with enough water and minerals, which come from the roots.

Some of the tallest trees in the world are California's redwoods. Scientists have observed that the leaves at the top of redwoods are much smaller and shaped differently than leaves farther down. This difference is due to the reduced supply of water and minerals at the upper levels. Scientists propose that the maximum height of a redwood tree is 130 meters (430 feet).

Trees grow in all sorts of places. You can find trees along windy ocean coasts, snowy mountainsides, and the banks of rushing rivers. Such trees show how hardy plants can be.

COMPARE AND CONTRAST Why are the leaves near the bottom of a redwood tree different from the leaves at the top?

◀ Strong winds helped shape this lone tree along the California coast.

Visual Summary

Mosses and other nonvascular plants lack structures to transport food, water, and minerals. These materials move by diffusion from cell to cell.

Vascular plants use specialized tissues called xylem and phloem to transport food, water, and minerals. All large plants are vascular plants.

Root pressure, cohesion, and transpiration move water upward through the xylem in vascular plants. Gravity moves sugar down through the phloem. Phloem also transports sugar and water upward.

STANDARDS

2.a., 2.e.

 Technology
Visit www.eduplace.com/cascp to find out more about vascular and nonvascular plants.

Reading Review

❶ **MAIN IDEA** What specialized tissues transport water, minerals, and sugar in vascular plants?

❷ **VOCABULARY** How does *transpiration* allow a plant to grow tall?

❸ **READING SKILL** How does a vascular plant compare with a nonvascular plant? Explain why one grows much taller than the other.

Compare	Contrast

❹ **CRITICAL THINKING: Apply** A scientist observes mosses growing on a hard rock, but not any vascular plants. Why might vascular plants not be able to grow on the rock?

❺ **INQUIRY SKILL: Predict** Do you think redwood trees would grow as tall or taller if they were planted in wetter, warmer places, such as a tropical rain forest? Explain.

 TEST PRACTICE
In a nonvascular plant, water moves by _____ from cell to cell.

A. gravity

B. diffusion

C. root pressure

D. transpiration

 STANDARDS

1: 2.a., **2:** 2.e., **3–5:** 2.a., **Test Practice:** 2.a.

EXTREME Science

GOING UP

It's extremely tall. It's extremely old. And at the top—it's extremely hard to get a drink! The enormous coast redwood trees are only found along a single strip of the northern California coast. The record-holder stands a majestic 112 meters high. That's taller than a football field is long! So how do these ancient plants raise water to branches hundreds of feet in the air?

It's a feat of extreme capillary action. Hundred of microscopically small vessels lead up the trunk. Each one utilizes the tendency of water molecules to link up, so that a long, super-thin chain can be created. In a process called transpiration, the molecules at the top evaporate off the stomata, hauling the whole chain up a tiny bit each time they do so.

The tallest coast redwood is taller than the Statue of Liberty!

Coast redwoods are huge as well as tall. The largest is about 8 m (26 feet) thick at its base and weighs more than 2,400 tons. That's thicker than a giraffe is tall and heavier than 20 blue whales!

Writing Journal

If you climbed the 112 meter coast redwood at the rate of 1.8 meters per minute, how long would it take to reach the top? Write it out in your journal.

Math in Science

An adult human takes in about 53 liters of oxygen (O_2) every hour from the atmosphere. On a certain tree, each leaf produces 4.8 mL of oxygen every hour.

How many trees will provide enough oxygen for one adult human? Follow the following steps to find out.

1. Convert 53 liters into an equal value of milliliters.

2. Assume that the tree has 500 leaves. How much oxygen in milliliters does this tree produce in one hour?

3. How many of these trees will provide oxygen for one human?

Writing in Science
Narrative

Write a story about a day in the life of a plant, perhaps from the plant's point of view. Choose a plant of any size, from moss to a tall tree. Describe what the plant does, the parts and structures it uses, and challenges it might face to stay alive.

People in Science

Nilsa Bosque-Perez

If you are a farmer or a gardener, you probably dislike aphids. Aphids are small insects that suck out fluids from plants. They also can spread plant viruses. To kill aphids and other pests, farmers typically spray crops with dangerous chemicals.

Nilsa Bosque-Perez is trying to find a better way to stop aphids. She is researching a way to make wheat plants more resistant to aphids and the viruses they spread.

Dr. Bosque-Perez is an entomologist, a scientist who studies insects. Her career began at the University of California. As she would tell you, not all insects are pests. Many insects fill important and useful roles in Earth's communities of living things.

Aphids feed in colonies. They can ruin wheat and other crops. ▶

Vocabulary

Complete each sentence with a term from the list.

1. The green pigment that absorbs sunlight is called *chlorophyll*

2. The process by which green plants use energy from sunlight to make food is *photosynthesis*

3. Openings that let air and water move in and out of leaves are called *stomata*

4. Specialized tissues that transport sugar, water, and minerals are found in a(n) *vascular plant*

5. Water is transported from a plant's roots to its leaves in a tissue called *xylem*

6. Sugar made in a plant's leaves is transported to other parts of a plant in a tissue called *phloem*

7. The process during which water evaporates through a plant's leaves is called *transpiration*

8. Photosynthesis takes place in an organelle called a(n) *chloroplast*

9. No specialized structures for transporting water are found in a(n) *nonvascular plant*

10. Stacks of membranes inside a chloroplast are *grana*

chlorophyll p. 43
chloroplast p. 43
grana p. 43
nonvascular plant p. 54
phloem p. 56
photosynthesis p. 42
stomata p. 44
transpiration p. 57
vascular plant p. 54
xylem p. 56

Test Practice

Write the letter of the best answer choice.

11. People rely on photosynthesis in plants for food and _____.
   A. oxygen
   B. minerals
   C. chlorophyll
   D. carbon dioxide

12. Vascular tissues are important for the _____.
   A. diffusion of water
   B. absorption of energy
   C. transport of materials
   D. opening of stomata

13. To make food, plants use energy from sunlight to combine water and _____.
   A. sugar
   B. oxygen
   C. minerals
   D. carbon dioxide

14. A plant cell in a nonvascular plant gets water from _____.
   A. gravity
   B. diffusion
   C. cohesion
   D. root pressure

Inquiry Skills

15. **Predict** What would happen if you put the stem of a white flower in water colored red? Explain your prediction.

16. How much leaf area does a plant need to survive? Design an experiment to answer this question. Identify the independent variable and the controlled variables in your experiment.

Map the Concept

Fill in the concept map by listing the following terms in one column or both columns. Terms may apply to one or both kinds of plants.

chlorophyll
phloem
photosynthesis
stomata
xylem

Nonvascular Plant	Vascular Plant

Critical Thinking

17. **Application** Why do moss plants grow best in damp areas, such as the floor of a forest? Would moss grow well in dry, sandy soil? Explain.

18. **Synthesis** Could a tree keep growing taller and taller? Explain why or why not.

19. **Evaluation** What would you say to someone who said that people don't need plants? Include at least three reasons in your answer.

20. **Analysis** What is the relationship between stomata and transpiration? When might it be an advantage to a plant to have its stomata closed? Explain.

Performance Assessment

Moving Materials

Draw a diagram of a plant with arrows that show the transport of water and minerals and the transport of sugar. Write captions for your diagram that explain xylem, phloem, root pressure, cohesion, and transpiration.

Writing Journal

Review your answers to the Lesson Preview questions.

STANDARDS

1–2: 2.f., **3–4:** 2.a., **5–7:** 2.e., **8–10:** 2.a., **11:** 2.f., **12:** 2.a., **13:** 2.f., **14:** 2.e., **15:** 2.e., **16:** 6.c., 6.d., 6.e., **17:** 2.a., **18:** 2.e., **19:** 2.f., **20:** 2.a.

Chapter 3

Human Body Systems

A gymnast must be in peak physical condition.

LESSON

1

Your heart and lungs work together to move gases between the air and your body. What are these gases? Why are they important?

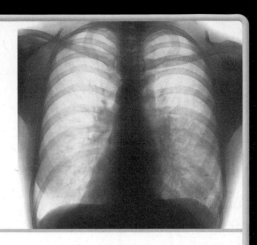

LESSON

2

The food you eat provides energy and helps keep you healthy. How does your body break down food?

LESSON

3

Inside your kidneys, wastes filter out of blood to form urine. Where do these wastes come from?

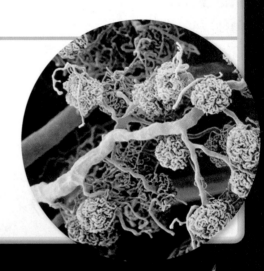

Writing Journal

In your Writing Journal, write or draw answers to each question.

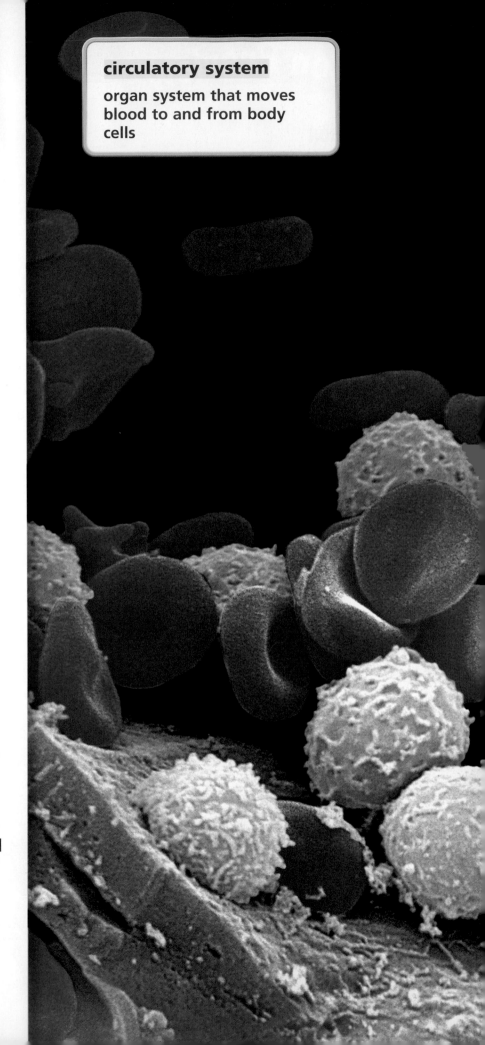

Vocabulary Preview

Vocabulary

artery p. 74
bladder p. 93
capillary p. 74
circulatory system p. 74
digestive system p. 82
esophagus p. 85
excretory system p. 92
heart p. 74
kidney p. 93
large intestine p. 86
respiratory system p. 72
small intestine p. 86
stomach p. 85
vein p. 74

Glossary

English-Spanish, page H26

Vocabulary Skill

Word Origins
Respiratory System

The word *respiratory* comes from the Latin word *respirare,* which means "to breathe out." Other words that come from the same Latin root include *inspiration, transpiration,* and *respiration.*

circulatory system
organ system that moves blood to and from body cells

esophagus

a muscular tube that pushes food toward the stomach

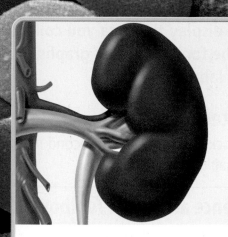

kidney

a bean-shaped organ that filters wastes from the blood

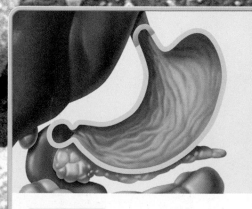

stomach

a muscular organ that mixes and stores food and passes it to the small intestine

Start with Your Standards

Lesson 1

What Are the Respiratory and Circulatory Systems?

Building Background

To breathe underwater, these divers are carrying oxygen in tanks. Humans and all other animals need oxygen to live. The respiratory and circulatory systems deliver oxygen to body cells. They also remove carbon dioxide, a waste gas.

 STANDARDS

2.b. *Students know* how blood circulates through the heart chambers, lungs, and body and how carbon dioxide (CO_2) and oxygen (O_2) are exchanged in the lungs and tissues.
6.c. Plan and conduct a simple investigation based on a student-developed question and write instructions others can follow to carry out the procedure.

PREPARE TO INVESTIGATE

Inquiry Skill

Record Data You can record and display the data you collect in the form of charts, graphs, and labeled diagrams.

Materials

- clock or watch with a second hand
- chair

Science and Math Toolbox

For steps 2 and 4, review **Measuring Elapsed Time** on page H14.

How You Rate

Procedure

1. **Collaborate** Work in a group. Have one group member be the timekeeper. Copy the chart into your *Science Notebook.*

2. **Measure** Have a group member take your pulse while you sit at rest. The group member will count beats for 15 seconds. You count the number of breaths you take during the same time.

3. **Record Data** Record your pulse and breathing rate. Repeat steps 2 and 3 for each group member.

4. **Measure** Jump in place for 1 minute. Immediately have a group member take your pulse for 15 seconds. During the same time count your breaths. Record your new pulse and breathing rate. Repeat this step for each group member.

5. **Use Numbers** Find your pulse and breathing rate for one minute. Use this formula:

Number in 15 seconds	x 4 =	Number in 1 minute

    Record the data in your chart.

Conclusion

1. **Analyze Data** How did your pulse and breathing rates change with exercise?

2. **Infer** Why do breathing and pulse rates increase with exercise?

3. **Infer** Athletes often have much lower pulse rates and breathing rates after exercise compared with most people. Why do you think this is true?

STEP 1

	Pulse		Breathing	
	Beats in 15 s	Beats in 1 min	Beats in 15 s	Beats in 1 min
At Rest				
After Exercise				

STEP 2

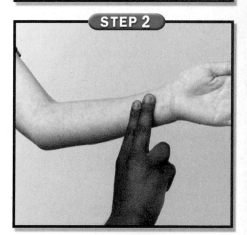

STEP 4

Guided Inquiry

Ask Questions What other factors do you think affect pulse rate? Plan an **experiment** to test your ideas. Conduct the experiment with your teacher's permission.

71

VOCABULARY

artery	p. 74
capillary	p. 74
circulatory system	p. 74
heart	p. 74
respiratory system	p. 72
vein	p. 74

READING SKILL

Compare and Contrast
Use the Venn diagram to compare and contrast what happens when you inhale and exhale.

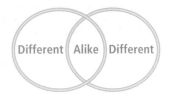

Different Alike Different

STANDARDS

2.b. *Students know* how blood circulates through the heart chambers, lungs, and body and how carbon dioxide (CO_2) and oxygen (O_2) are exchanged in the lungs and tissues.
2.a. *Students know* many multicellular organisms have specialized structures to support the transport of materials.

Respiratory and Circulatory Systems

MAIN IDEA The respiratory system brings oxygen into the body and removes wastes. The circulatory system carries oxygen to the cells and carries away wastes.

The Respiratory System

You could not live for very long without breathing in and breathing out. You breathe so your body can exchange gases with the air. With every breath, your body takes in oxygen and releases carbon dioxide.

Humans and many other animals rely on a system of organs that work together—the **respiratory system**—to meet their need for gas exchange. The respiratory system includes the lungs and the airways that lead to the mouth and nose.

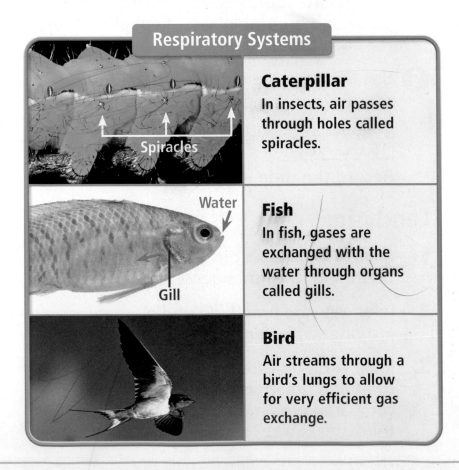

Respiratory Systems

Caterpillar
In insects, air passes through holes called spiracles.

Spiracles

Fish
In fish, gases are exchanged with the water through organs called gills.

Water

Gill

Bird
Air streams through a bird's lungs to allow for very efficient gas exchange.

When you inhale, you take oxygen-filled air into your nose or mouth. The air moves into a sturdy tube called the trachea, which leads down your chest toward the lungs.

The trachea divides into two main tubes called bronchi (singular: bronchus). Inside the lungs, each bronchus divides into smaller and smaller tubes. The smallest tubes lead to grapelike sacs called alveoli (singular: alveolus). Alveoli are tiny air sacs.

The lungs contain millions of alveoli. Each of these tiny structures borders a capillary, which is a thin tube that contains blood. Oxygen diffuses from the alveoli into the blood. At the same time, carbon dioxide diffuses from the blood to the alveoli. Carbon dioxide is a waste product from cells. When you exhale, your body releases carbon dioxide into the air.

Why does air move in and out of the lungs so easily? The reason is because the chest changes size. When you inhale, muscles attached to the ribs tighten and pull upward. The diaphragm, which is located at the bottom of the chest, contracts and pulls downward. These actions expand the chest, making more space. Air flows into the body as a result.

The opposite process occurs when you exhale. When the chest muscles and diaphragm relax, the space in the chest decreases. This forces air out of the body.

All animals need oxygen, and most animals have some sort of respiratory system. Insects take in air through tiny holes called spiracles. Fish take in oxygen through organs called gills. Birds in flight need a great deal of oxygen, so they have extremely efficient respiratory systems. Instead of being pumped in and out, gases move through a bird's lungs in one direction only.

COMPARE AND CONTRAST Compare how a fish and a human breathe.

Nasal passages

Bronchial tube

Trachea

Lungs

Alveoli

Diaphragm

Express Lab

Activity Card 6
Find Your Pulse in Three Locations

The Circulatory System

The **circulatory system** works to bring oxygen and nutrients to all the cells of your body. It also takes carbon dioxide and wastes away from the cells. The gases, nutrients, and wastes all travel in a moveable tissue called blood.

You can think of the circulatory system as a set of highways that connect every cell of your body. The highways are called blood vessels. Like highways for cars, a few blood vessels are quite wide, while most are narrow.

At the center of the circulatory system is a muscular organ called the **heart.** The heart pumps blood through the network of blood vessels. Your heart needs to be strong because it works all the time, even while you are sleeping!

Use the diagram to trace the path of blood through the body. First, blood picks up oxygen in the lungs. From there it travels to the heart, then through arteries to all other parts of the body. An **artery** is a blood vessel that carries blood away from the heart.

Arteries branch into thinner and thinner blood vessels. Eventually they branch into tiny, very thin vessels called **capillaries.** Gases, sugars, minerals, and wastes pass between capillaries and body cells.

Capillaries lead into veins. A **vein** is a blood vessel that carries blood back to the heart. The blood in veins has little oxygen but a lot of carbon dioxide. Veins combine to bring blood back to the heart, which pumps the blood to the lungs again.

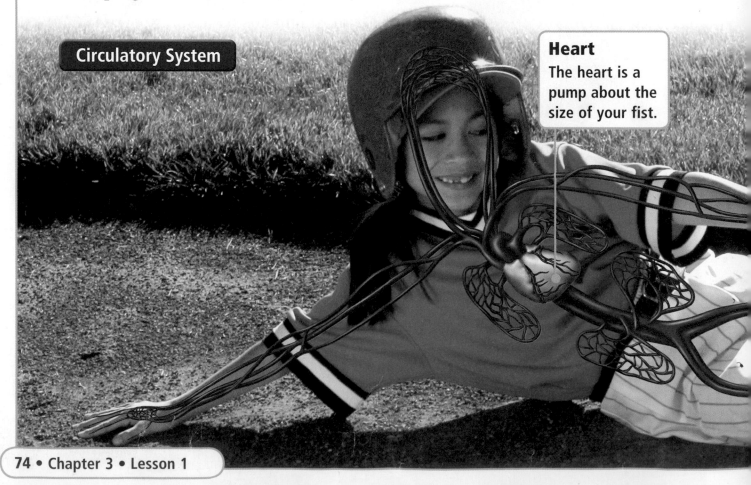

Circulatory System

Heart
The heart is a pump about the size of your fist.

Blood may look like a simple red liquid. In fact, it is much more complex. Blood contains a wide variety of blood cells and other parts.

Red blood cells are disc shaped. These cells use a substance called hemoglobin to carry oxygen and carbon dioxide. Hemoglobin contains iron, which is why iron is important in your diet. Hemoglobin also gives blood its red color.

The other cells in blood are called white blood cells. These are larger cells that help the body fight disease. Blood also contains platelets, which are small pieces of cells. When activated, platelets help the blood clump together into a clot. This helps to heal cuts and other injuries.

Blood cells and platelets are carried in the liquid part of blood, which is called plasma. The plasma also carries sugars and water to the cells, and it carries wastes to the kidneys.

COMPARE AND CONTRAST What does blood bring to cells? What does it carry away?

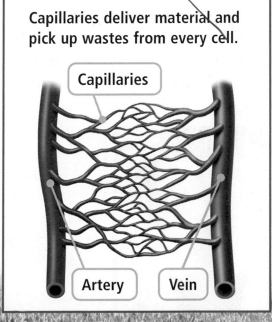

Capillaries deliver material and pick up wastes from every cell.

Capillaries

Artery   Vein

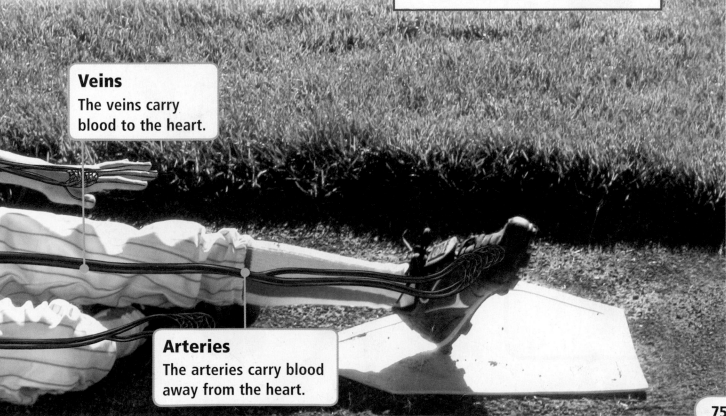

Veins
The veins carry blood to the heart.

Arteries
The arteries carry blood away from the heart.

The Heart

The human heart is divided into four chambers, or separate sections. The two upper chambers are the atria (singular: atrium). The atria receive blood from the veins. The two lower chambers are the ventricles. The ventricles pump blood to the body.

You can feel your ventricles at work by holding your fingers against your wrist or neck. The throbbing you feel is the blood rushing through your arteries. The rhythm of throbbing is your pulse.

Like humans, most animals have some type of heart and circulatory system. A frog's heart has three chambers instead of four. Fish hearts have only two chambers. An earthworm has five hearts, each with only one chamber.

COMPARE AND CONTRAST Describe and compare the different chambers of the human heart.

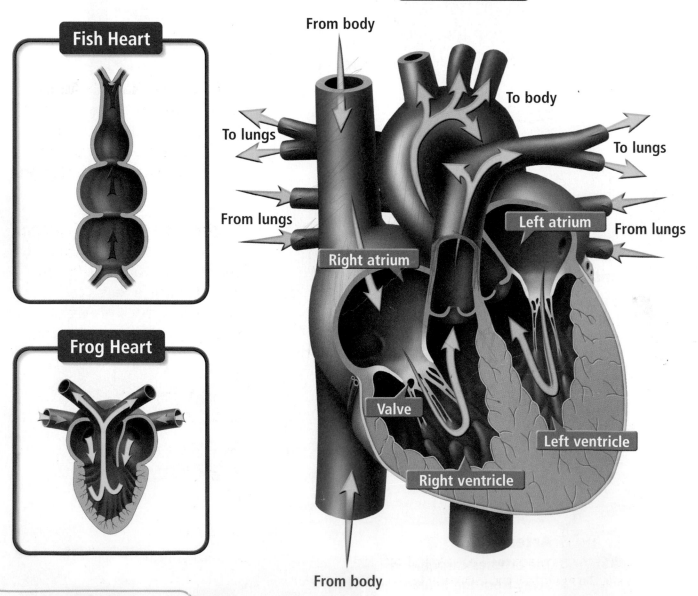

Fish Heart

Frog Heart

Human Heart

From body

To body

To lungs

To lungs

From lungs

From lungs

Left atrium

Right atrium

Valve

Left ventricle

Right ventricle

From body

Visual Summary

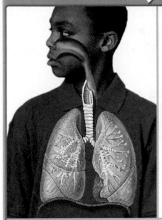

The respiratory system brings oxygen to the blood, and it removes carbon dioxide from the blood.

The circulatory system brings oxygen, sugars, and minerals to all the cells. It also takes carbon dioxide and wastes away from the cells.

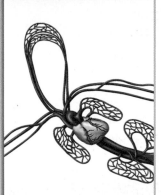

The heart is the central organ of the circulatory system. It is a muscular pump that pushes the blood through the network of blood vessels.

 **STANDARDS**

2.b., 2.a.

 Technology
Visit **www.eduplace.com/cascp** to find out more about the respiratory and circulatory systems.

Reading Review

❶ **MAIN IDEA** Why are the respiratory and circulatory systems necessary for life?

❷ **VOCABULARY** Use the terms *veins* and *arteries* to describe how blood flows.

❸ **READING SKILL:** How are the circulatory and respiratory systems alike? How are they different?

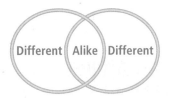

Different | Alike | Different

❹ **CRITICAL THINKING: Apply** Cardiac arrest is the formal name for a heart attack. During this event, the heart stops working or works very poorly. Why is such an event dangerous?

❺ **INQUIRY SKILL: Use Numbers** You inhale and exhale about 500 mL of air with each breath. If you breathe 20 times each minute, how much air passes through your lungs in 1 minute?

 TEST PRACTICE
Gases, sugars, and wastes diffuse across blood vessels called _____.

A. arteries

B. capillaries

C. veins

D. alveoli

 STANDARDS

1: 2.b., **2–3:** 2.a., 2.b., **4–5:** 2.b., **Test Practice:** 2.a., 2.b.

TECHNOLOGY FOR THE HEART

The heart is the hardest working muscle in the body—and the most important. Keeping hearts healthy and curing heart diseases are the goals of a cardiologist. A cardiologist is a medical doctor who is an expert on the heart and the circulatory system.

Like other doctors, cardiologists rely on the latest technology. Special tools help them find and cure diseases that would have been deadly a hundred years ago.

No tool, however, is as important as the doctor's eyes, ears, and brain. A cardiologist always will interview the patient, listen to the heartbeat, feel the pulse, and apply knowledge gained from years of study and practice.

If you would like to be a cardiologist, California has many excellent medical schools. Be prepared, however, for many years of study and hard work.

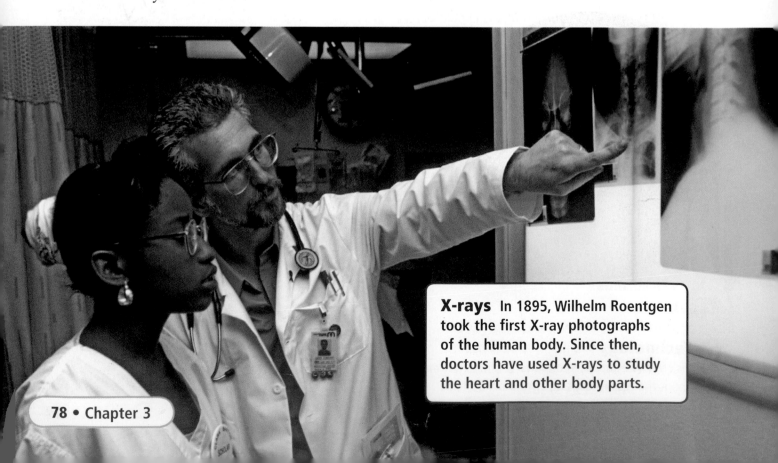

X-rays In 1895, Wilhelm Roentgen took the first X-ray photographs of the human body. Since then, doctors have used X-rays to study the heart and other body parts.

STANDARD
2.b. *Students know* how blood circulates through the heart chambers, lungs, and body and how carbon dioxide (CO_2) and oxygen (O_2) are exchanged in the lungs and tissues.

READING LINK

EKG

Did you know that an electric current controls how the heart beats? Doctors can measure and model this current with an electrocardiogram (EKG). An EKG machine uses wires connected to the patient's skin.

In the EKG shown here, each peak of the wavy line represents one heartbeat. The distance between the peaks shows the heart rate.

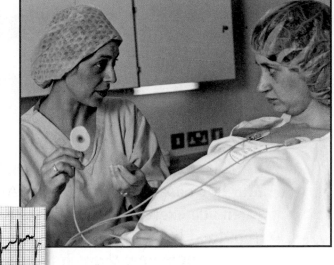

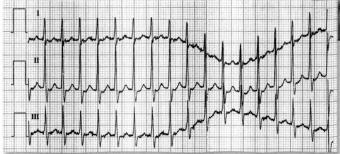

Angioplasty

Blood flow may stop when an artery becomes too narrow. To widen the artery, doctors slide in a balloon along a thin wire. Then they inflate the balloon!

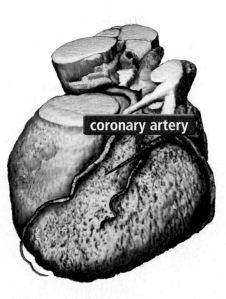

coronary artery

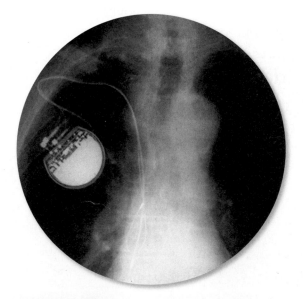

Pacemaker

If a patient's heart weakens, a surgeon may put in a device called a pacemaker. A pacemaker provides electric current to keep the heartbeat steady.

Sharing Ideas

1. **READING CHECK** How does a cardiologist study and treat heart disease?

2. **WRITE ABOUT IT** How has modern technology changed cardiology—the study of the heart?

3. **TALK ABOUT IT** Would you like a career in medicine? Why or why not?

What Is the Digestive System?

Building Background

What happens to the food you eat? Your body uses most of it for energy. When you exercise, you use the energy from food you ate earlier.

As food moves through the digestive system, it breaks down into smaller and smaller pieces. Eventually the pieces are small enough to enter the bloodstream and move into cells.

PREPARE TO INVESTIGATE

Inquiry Skill

Compare When you compare two things, you observe how they are alike and how they are different.

Materials

- 2 plastic spoons
- 2 clear plastic cups
- 2 plastic dishes
- breadcrumbs
- 3 droppers
- water
- iodine solution
- saliva solution
- clock or watch
- goggles
- disposable gloves

Science and Math Toolbox

For step 1, review **Making a Chart to Organize Data** on page H11.

STANDARDS

2.c. *Students know* the sequential steps of digestion and the roles of teeth and the mouth, esophagus, stomach, small intestine, large intestine, and colon in the function of the digestive system.
6.d. Identify the dependent and controlled variables in an investigation.

Saliva Science

Procedure

Safety: Wear goggles and gloves. Iodine solution is poisonous and stains.

1 **Collaborate** Work with a partner. In your *Science Notebook,* make a chart like the one shown. Put a quarter spoonful of breadcrumbs in a clear plastic cup. Add 20 drops of water. Stir for 2 minutes.

2 **Experiment** Transfer a small amount of the mixture to a dish labeled *No Saliva.* Add 1 drop of iodine solution. Stir thoroughly, then put the cup in a warm, sunny place for 8 minutes. Record any changes and the time they took.

3 **Use Variables** Put a quarter spoonful of breadcrumbs in another cup. Add 20 drops of water. Then add 5 mL of saliva solution. Stir thoroughly, then put the cup in a warm, sunny place for 8 minutes.

4 **Compare** Add another 5 mL of saliva solution. Stir thoroughly, and return the cup to the sunny place for 8 minutes. Then transfer a small amount of the mixture to a dish labeled *Saliva.* Test with 1 drop of iodine solution. Record your observations.

Conclusion

1. **Use Variables** What is the independent variable in this experiment? What variables were controlled?

2. **Compare** How did the results of the iodine test in steps 2 and 4 compare?

3. **Infer** What can you infer about what saliva does in the mouth?

STEP 1

Dish	Change	Time
No Saliva		
Saliva		

STEP 2

No Saliva

STEP 4

Saliva

Guided Inquiry

Experiment What foods contain starch? Write out a plan to **analyze data** from a variety of foods. Get permission to carry out your plan. Use a chart to share your results.

Digestive System

VOCABULARY

digestive system	p. 82
esophagus	p. 85
large intestine	p. 86
small intestine	p. 86
stomach	p. 85

READING SKILL

Main Idea and Details
Use the diagram to show three ways the body uses nutrients.

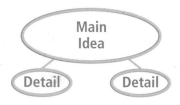

Main Idea

Detail   Detail

STANDARD

2.c. *Students know* the sequential steps of digestion and the roles of teeth and the mouth, esophagus, stomach, small intestine, large intestine, and colon in the function of the digestive system.

MAIN IDEA To function properly, living things need the nutrients found in food. The digestive system breaks down food to release these nutrients.

Energy from Nutrients

From the day you were born, your body has been taking in food. Food provides nutrients, which are materials that the body can use. As the chart on the next page shows, your body uses different kinds of nutrients for different purposes.

How does your body release the nutrients from food? This happens in a process called digestion, which takes place in the digestive system. The **digestive system** is a group of organs that breaks down food into small pieces the body can use.

As you will discover, the organs of the digestive system work like an assembly line at a factory. Each organ accepts food pieces, processes them or changes them, then passes them to the next organ in line. The finished products are small particles of food that enter the blood. There also are waste products that leave the body.

Like humans, most other animals have a digestive system. Cows, horses, and other grazing animals have unusually long and complex digestive systems. This allows them to digest the tough plant matter found in grass and leaves.

Animals that eat meat typically have shorter, simpler digestive systems. Meat breaks down in fewer steps than plant matter does.

◀ **A long digestive system with many chambers helps a horse digest grasses.**

Nutrients			
Carbohydrates	**Proteins**	**Vitamins and Minerals**	**Fats**
Carbohydrates are the main source of energy for the body.	Proteins are used to replace, repair, and grow new cells and tissue.	Vitamins and minerals help in various ways, including helping nerves work.	Fats provide energy and keep skin healthy. They also help the body use vitamins and cushion body organs.
Sources • whole-grain bread • pasta • rice and other grains • potatoes	**Sources** • fish • beef • chicken • beans	**Sources** • fruits • vegetables • fortified milk	**Sources** • butter • oil • salad dressing • ice cream

A few animals don't have digestive systems. Sponges, for example, filter food particles from the water. They use a layer of cells to digest this food, without the aid of organs or an organ system.

To stay healthy, you should eat a balanced diet made from a variety of different foods. Doing so will provide the nutrients your body needs. In addition, drinking lots of water helps to keep you healthy and to keep your digestive system working properly.

You also should avoid eating too many fats and sweets.

It's important to eat right every day, too. Your body can store certain nutrients, especially those used for energy. Many vitamins and minerals, however, cannot be stored. Your body needs a steady supply of these nutrients to stay healthy.

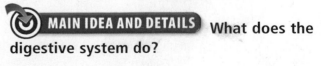 **MAIN IDEA AND DETAILS** What does the digestive system do?

Stages of Digestion

It's lunchtime, and you just bit into a sandwich. What happens next? To find out, follow the path of the sandwich through the digestive system. It's a long path—the average length of an adult's digestive system is about 9 meters (30 feet)!

Digestion begins in the mouth. When you chew, your teeth grind food into smaller pieces. This allows the food to begin moving through the digestive system. Your tongue pushes the food around in your mouth and mixes it with saliva.

Saliva is the watery liquid in the mouth. It moistens the food and begins to break it down. Saliva is produced by salivary glands that are located at the back and bottom of your mouth. Saliva contains chemicals called enzymes. There are hundreds of different enzymes in your body.

The enzymes in saliva break down the starch in foods like bread and potatoes. When the enzymes have done their job, the starch is changed into sugar. Chew a salty cracker for a long time, and you will notice it change from a salty to a sweet taste.

Starches and sugars are carbohydrates, one of the main types of nutrients your body needs. You get most of your energy from carbohydrates.

Digestion Begins

When you finish chewing, food passes down a tube called the esophagus. ▶

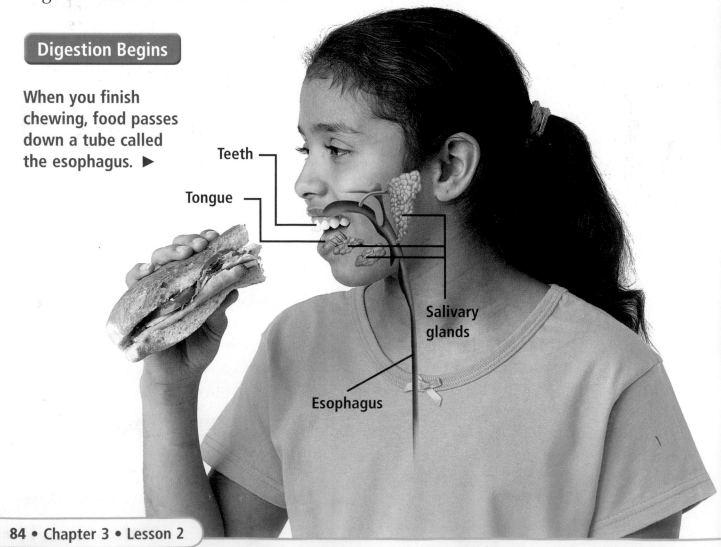

Teeth

Tongue

Salivary glands

Esophagus

Digestive System

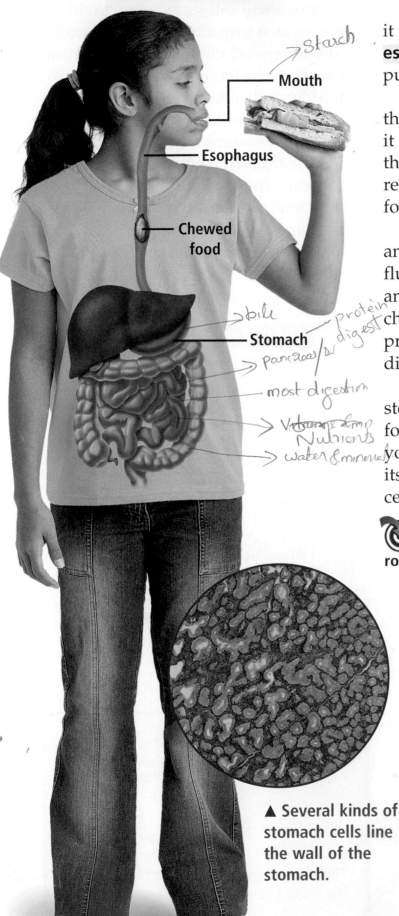

Mouth → Starch

Esophagus

Chewed food

Stomach

→ bile

protein digest

→ pancreas/liver

— most digestion

→ Vitamins & amp Nutrients

→ water & minerals

▲ Several kinds of stomach cells line the wall of the stomach.

When you swallow chewed food it moves into the esophagus. The **esophagus** is a muscular tube that pushes food toward the stomach.

The **stomach** is a muscular organ that mixes and stores food and turns it into a soupy mix. When food enters the stomach, cells lining the stomach release fluids that break down the food further.

The stomach squeezes the food and mixes it with these digestive fluids. The fluids contain enzymes and an acid. This acid is a strong chemical that breaks down food. The proteins in your sandwich are partly digested in your stomach.

After your lunch has been in your stomach for one to three hours, the food, now a soupy liquid, leaves your stomach. Your sandwich is on its way to becoming nutrients your cells can use.

MAIN IDEA AND DETAILS What is one role of the stomach?

Express Lab

Activity Card 7
Show Chewing Effects

Completing Digestion

When food leaves the stomach, it enters the small intestine. The **small intestine** is the long, coiled organ where most digestion takes place. Food remains in the small intestine from one to six hours.

Chemicals from the liver and the pancreas enter the first part of the small intestine, where they break down food even further. These chemicals help to digest fats and carbohydrates. The digestion of proteins is also completed here.

The small intestine is lined with millions of tiny, fingerlike folds called villi (singular: villus). Nutrients from the digested food pass from villi into the blood, then to every cell in the body.

Undigested food and other substances pass to the large intestine. In the **large intestine,** water and minerals from food are absorbed into the blood. Most of the large intestine is a tube called the colon.

Food stays in the large intestine from 12 to 36 hours. Any remaining food passes as solid waste.

 **MAIN IDEA AND DETAILS** Where does most digestion take place?

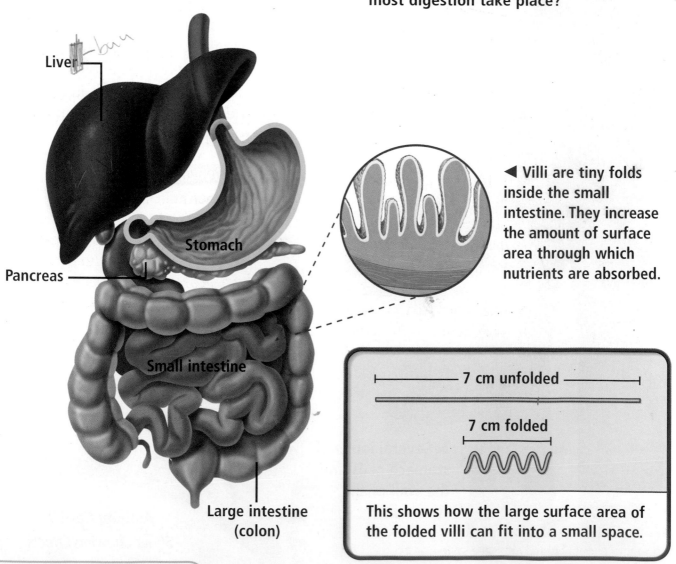

◄ Villi are tiny folds inside the small intestine. They increase the amount of surface area through which nutrients are absorbed.

|───── 7 cm unfolded ─────|

7 cm folded

This shows how the large surface area of the folded villi can fit into a small space.

Liver

Stomach

Pancreas

Small intestine

Large intestine (colon)

Visual Summary

The digestive system breaks down food into nutrients that the body's cells can use. Starches break down into sugars in the mouth.

The stomach mixes and stores food. It further breaks down food into a soupy mix.

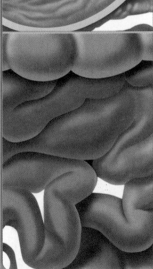

The small intestine finishes the digestion of food and allows the absorption of nutrients into the blood. Water and minerals are absorbed from the large intestine. Undigested food is eliminated as solid waste.

STANDARD

2.c.

 Technology
Visit **www.eduplace.com/cascp** to find out more about how the digestive system works.

Reading Review

① MAIN IDEA How does the digestive system help you use the nutrients in food?

② VOCABULARY How is the *large intestine* different from the *small intestine*?

③ READING SKILL How does food change as it moves through the digestive system?

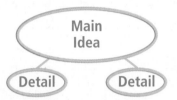

④ CRITICAL THINKING: Analyze
Make a flow chart to show the path of food through the digestive system. Where does the flow chart branch?

⑤ INQUIRY SKILL: Compare
How does the digestive system compare in plant-eating animals and meat-eating animals? What would be the best way to provide evidence for your answer?

 TEST PRACTICE
In which digestive organ are villi found?

A. pancreas

B. small intestine

C. stomach

D. liver

 STANDARD

1–5: 2.c., **Test Practice:** 2.c.

87

STANDARDS 2.c. *Students know* the sequential steps of digestion and the roles of teeth and the mouth, esophagus, stomach, small intestine, large intestine, and colon in the function of the digestive system.

Leaping Teeth!

Digestion begins with the teeth. And nothing in the sea is more famous for its snapping, shredding bite than the great white shark.

The great white swallows down huge chunks of its prey—usually seals or sea lions—without chewing. It has a large, U-shaped stomach that takes over from there, dissolving the food until it is ready to be passed to the spiral-shaped intestines.

Great whites strike fast, eat a lot, and then take a break. Their digestion is so slow that this great fish may not need to eat another big meal for a month or two. Sometimes great whites swallow things they can't digest at all. Scientists have found a straw hat, a lobster trap, and even a cuckoo clock in great white stomachs!

The prehistoric shark Megalodon was even bigger than the great white. The shark that owned this tooth may have been 15 meters long—nearly 50 feet!

This shark seems to be trying to leap at the camera. In fact, it is flying into the air after striking at a seal from below. This time the seal was lucky!

Writing Journal

A great white has about 3000 teeth. If it loses 8% of its teeth every year, calculate in your journal how many replacement teeth it grows in a decade.

What Is the Excretory System?

Building Background

More than half the weight of your body comes from a very simple substance—water. All cells are mostly water, and they use water for all life functions.

One important life function is to flush away wastes. This means you lose water every day. It's important to replace that water to stay healthy.

 STANDARDS

2.d. *Students know* the role of the kidney in removing cellular waste from blood and converting it into urine, which is stored in the bladder.
6.f. Select appropriate tools (e.g. thermometers, meter sticks, balances, graduated cylinders) and make quantitative observations.

PREPARE TO INVESTIGATE

Inquiry Skill

Analyze Data When you analyze data, you look for patterns or other evidence that you can use to make an inference.

Materials

- 6 medium (8 oz) paper cups
- paper towel
- marker
- pencil
- colored sugar
- plastic spoon
- water
- graduated cylinder or measuring cup

Science and Math Toolbox

For step 4, review **Measurement** on page H16.

Pass the Sugar

Procedure

Safety: Wear goggles during this activity. Be careful using scissors.

1. **Collaborate** Work with a partner. Trace the bottom of a paper cup on a paper towel. Repeat twice to make three circles. Cut out the circles.

2. **Experiment** Use a marker to label 3 paper cups IN-1, IN-2, and IN-3. Then use a pencil to punch three small holes in the bottom of each cup near the center.

3. **Experiment** Cover the holes in the IN cups with the paper-towel circles. Add 4 heaping spoonfuls of colored sugar to each IN cup. Label three additional cups OUT-1, OUT-2, and OUT-3.

4. **Measure** While your partner holds cup IN-1 over cup OUT-1, add 10 mL of water to the IN cup. Allow all of the water to drain.

5. Repeat Step 4 with the second pair of cups, this time adding 40 mL of water. With the third cups, add 80 mL of water.

6. **Compare** Observe and compare all six cups.

STEP 2

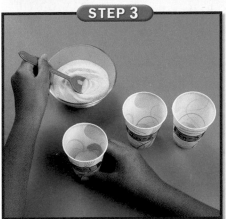

STEP 3

STEP 4

Conclusion

1. **Analyze Data** Which of the IN-cups had the most sugar remaining? Which had the least? How do you explain your observations?

2. **Infer** Why is it important to drink water every day? Use the results of this activity to support your answer. (Hint: Compare the sugar in this activity to body wastes.)

Guided Inquiry

Experiment Repeat this experiment using a double or triple layer of paper towels. How does this **model** the needs of animals with very poor kidneys? In your report, identify variables and draw a conclusion.

Removing Wastes

MAIN IDEA All living things produce wastes. In humans, the excretory system removes wastes and helps maintain water levels.

The Excretory System

Every moment you are alive, a huge number of chemical reactions take place in your body. These reactions break down food into small pieces, bind oxygen in red blood cells, capture the energy from food, and do many more tasks.

As a result of these reactions and other processes, the body produces a lot of waste. A waste is any material that the body cannot use. The job of the **excretory system** is to remove wastes and to maintain water balance.

Unlike other organ systems, the excretory system involves different processes and organs spread throughout the body. The skin, for example, is part of the excretory system because of sweat glands.

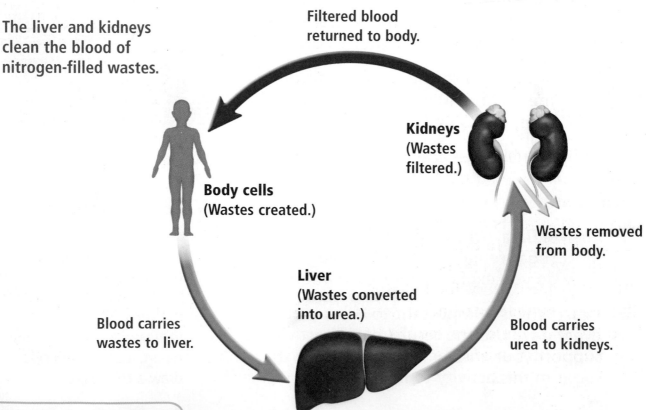

The liver and kidneys clean the blood of nitrogen-filled wastes.

Filtered blood returned to body.

Body cells (Wastes created.)

Kidneys (Wastes filtered.)

Wastes removed from body.

Liver (Wastes converted into urea.)

Blood carries wastes to liver.

Blood carries urea to kidneys.

You already have learned about many wastes. Your lungs remove carbon dioxide, a waste gas that cells release. Other wastes come from the digestive tract. Material that the body does not take in as nutrients is eliminated as solid waste.

Along with carbon dioxide, the blood carries wastes that contain nitrogen. Much of these wastes come from broken-down cells and cell parts. The liver converts nitrogen wastes into a compound called urea.

Filtering urea from the blood is the main job of the kidneys. The **kidneys** are a pair of bean-shaped organs located near the middle of the back. Each is about the size of your fist.

Kidneys filter blood by using a complex system of special cells, pumps, and very small tubes. Curiously, the first step of the filtering process involves the blood dumping out all its liquid parts into a small space in the kidney. Then, nearly all of that liquid returns to the blood. The fraction that stays behind becomes a liquid called urine.

After urine leaves the kidneys, it flows down tubes called ureters. They lead to the bladder. The **bladder** is a muscular bag that holds urine. Sensors detect its size and signal the brain when it needs to be emptied.

Kidneys also help the body maintain the right water balance. If the blood is too watery, the kidneys will form very watery urine. If the blood has too little water, the kidneys keep more water inside the body.

You might guess that kidneys need to be very well protected—and you would be right! Kidneys are surrounded by a layer of fat. They also are kept separate from the body space that holds the intestines and other organs of the digestive system.

CAUSE AND EFFECT How do kidneys change the blood?

Excretory System
The excretory system is responsible for ridding the body of waste. Urine is stored in the bladder, then eliminated.

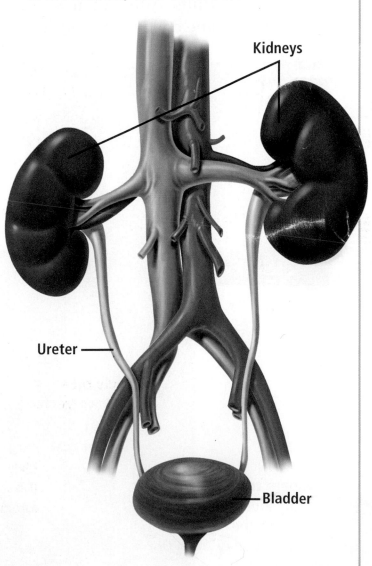

Kidneys

Ureter

Bladder

Excretory System Problems

Picture an aquarium filled with fish. The aquarium needs a filter that traps dirt and other wastes. The water also needs to be changed regularly. Without clean water, the fish will become sick and eventually die.

Something similar will happen if the excretory system works poorly or stops working. Wastes and poisons will gradually build up in the body. If the damage is serious enough, the body cannot survive.

Kidney disease can occur in children and adults. Although it is uncommon, some children are born with missing or damaged kidneys. Kidneys can also become infected, sometimes from infections that travel through the urinary tract. Older adults sometimes suffer from kidney stones, which are masses of salts or minerals. Large kidney stones can block ureters and be very painful.

Kidneys can also be damaged from a physical injury, such as a sharp blow to the lower back or abdomen. A car accident or bad fall could hurt the kidneys this way.

How can you keep your kidneys healthy? Drinking lots of water and eating a healthy diet are two important steps. Following safety rules when you exercise will prevent all sorts of injuries, including those to your kidneys.

◄ Gamma rays were used to take this picture. The kidney at left has normal blood flow, as shown by the red and purple areas. The kidney at right has poor blood flow.

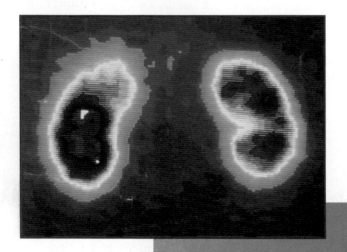

Compare the healthy kidney (left) with the diseased kidney (right). ▶

Dialysis

When kidneys fail, a dialysis machine can replace them. Dialysis has saved many lives.

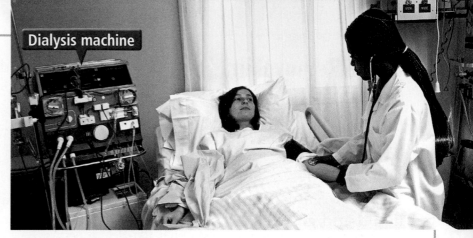

Dialysis machine

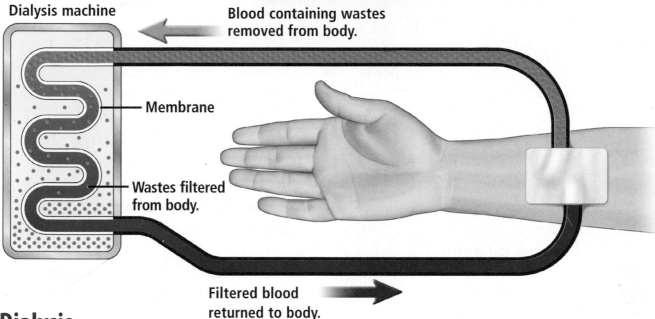

Dialysis machine

Blood containing wastes removed from body.

Membrane

Wastes filtered from body.

Filtered blood returned to body.

Dialysis

Medicines and changes to the diet help some kidney problems. When kidneys stop working completely, however, dialysis is needed. Dialysis is an artificial cleaning of the blood.

In one method, a machine filters waste and extra fluid from the blood. Tubes carry the patient's blood into the machine, then back into the body. In another method, a drug helps turn tissues in the patient's body into a simple blood filter. A machine pumps in the drug, then drains out the wastes.

A long-lasting treatment for faulty kidneys is to transplant a new kidney. In this procedure, a doctor cuts out the damaged kidney and inserts a new, healthy kidney from someone else. If all goes well, the patient can lead a normal life. People need only one working kidney to stay healthy.

Transplants are not always easy or successful, however. Part of the problem is that the body tries to reject organs and tissues that are not its own.

To help the body accept a new kidney, the doctor may prescribe special drugs. It also helps if the kidney comes from a close relative of the patient.

CAUSE AND EFFECT What remedies help a kidney that has stopped working?

Waste Removal in Other Organisms

All organisms produce wastes. They remove wastes in many different ways.

If an organism is small enough, liquid and gas wastes can diffuse directly to the outside. The wet skin of an earthworm, for example, both takes in oxygen and releases waste. This is one reason why earthworms need moist skin to survive.

Snakes and lizards change nitrogen wastes to uric acid, a solid compound. Uric acid can be removed with very little water, which helps snakes and lizards live in dry places. Birds also make uric acid.

Like humans, all mammals make urea, which they flush out with water. The kidneys of some desert animals, however, are able to do this very efficiently. A camel has such powerful kidneys that its urine can be saltier than sea water.

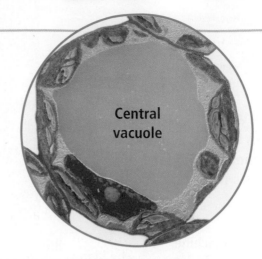

Central vacuole

▲ Plant vacuoles can store cell waste products.

Plants also produce wastes. Plant cells often store wastes in a central vacuole, which is like a large sac in the middle of the cell. Plants may also keep wastes in unwanted parts, such as the leaves a tree drops in autumn.

CAUSE AND EFFECT Why do organisms use different ways of removing wastes?

A camel's well-developed kidneys remove waste without losing a lot of water. How does this help the camel stay alive? ▼

Express Lab

Activity Card 8
Demonstrate How Filtering Works

Visual Summary

The excretory system removes wastes from the body and maintains the body's water balance. Key organs of this system are the kidneys, which filter wastes from the blood and produce urine.

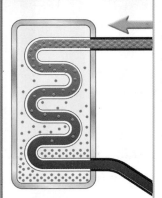

For people with non-working kidneys, dialysis treatment cleans the blood artificially. Transplanting a new kidney is another option.

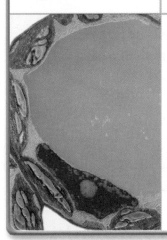

Plants and animals use many different methods of removing wastes. Plants store wastes in a large, central vacuole.

 STANDARD
2.d.

 Technology
Visit **www.eduplace.com/cascp** to find out more about the excretory system.

Reading Review

1 MAIN IDEA What is the role of the excretory system?

2 VOCABULARY How do the *kidneys* connect to the bladder?

3 READING SKILL Describe three examples of the excretory system eliminating waste.

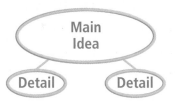

4 CRITICAL THINKING: Evaluate When a patient's blood is channeled into a dialysis machine, the blood may be taken from an arm or a leg. Why can dialysis work on blood far away from the kidneys?

5 INQUIRY SKILL: Analyze Data What can doctors learn by tracking the kidney output of a patient?

 TEST PRACTICE
The kidney filters wastes from the _____.

A. heart

B. lungs

C. large intestine

D. blood

 **STANDARD**
1–5: 2.d., **Test Practice:** 2.d.

Math in Science

The bar graph shows the body length and the length of the digestive tract for four animals. The data apply to typical animals, not all animals of the species.

1. Which is the longest animal of the four listed in the graph? Which animal has the longest digestive tract?

2. For each animal, calculate the ratio of length of digestive tract to body length.

3. How does the information in the bar graph help explain the diets of the four animals?

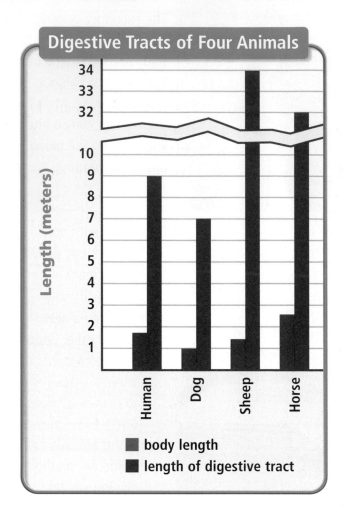

Digestive Tracts of Four Animals

Length (meters)

■ body length
■ length of digestive tract

Writing in Science
Research Report

A huge variety of diseases affect human body systems. Some are quite mild, while others can be very serious. Research a disease that affects one of the body systems you studied. Describe the course of the disease and how it can be treated.

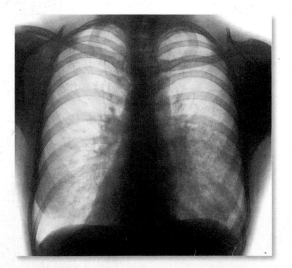

James Colbert

When he was a boy, James Colbert admired the pharmacist who served his family. A pharmacist is an expert on medicine and its effects on the human body. James learned that medicine can make a huge difference in people's lives when it is used properly.

Today, Dr. Colbert is a professor of pharmacy at the University of California at San Diego Medical Center. He has earned many awards for his teaching, research, and work with patients. He also treated wounded soldiers during the Persian Gulf War.

Dr. Colbert encourages students to continue studying throughout their careers. In medicine, as in other fields of science, new ideas and discoveries are always replacing old ones. Patients look to pharmacists for the latest information about their medications.

"I am a living example of how obtaining an education and taking advantage of opportunities can truly elevate your standing in society."
— James Colbert, Pharm. D.

Vocabulary

Complete each sentence with a term from the list.

1. The central organ of the circulatory system is the ___ *heart*

2. Tiny blood vessels that connect arteries to veins are ___ *capillaries*

3. Before passing from the body, urine collects in the ___ *bladder*

4. The ___ *large intestines* churns food, then passes it to the small intestine.

5. Your body uses the ___ *respiratory system* to deliver oxygen and remove carbon dioxide from the body.

6. The ___ brings oxygen and nutrients to all cells of the body, and carries away wastes.

7. The ___ *kidney* removes wastes and maintains healthy water levels in the body.

8. Small food particles travel from the ___ into the blood.

9. Blood vessels called ___ *artery* carry oxygen-rich blood away from the heart.

10. Food travels from the mouth to the stomach through the ___ *esphogasus*   *esophagus*

artery p. 74
bladder p. 91
capillary p. 74
circulatory system p. 74
digestive system p. 82
esophagus p. 85
excretory system p. 90
heart p. 74
kidney p. 91
large intestine p. 86
respiratory system p. 72
small intestine p. 86
stomach p. 85
vein p. 74

Test Practice

Write the letter of the best answer choice.

11. How many chambers are in the human heart?
    A. 2
    B. 3
    C. 4
    D. 5

12. In the lungs, gas exchange occurs in tiny air sacs called ___.
    A. alveoli
    B. trachea
    C. bronchi
    D. villi

13. Saliva works to break down starch into ___.
    A. proteins
    B. vitamins
    C. fats
    D. sugars

14. Where are your kidneys located?
    A. between the heart and lungs
    B. near the middle of the back
    C. behind the stomach
    D. next to the liver

Inquiry Skills

15. Use Numbers If your heart rate is 60 beats per minute, and your classmate's is 80 beats per minute, how many times faster is your classmate's heart rate than your own? Form a hypothesis about why your heart rates are so different.

16. Write a procedure to test which foods earthworms can digest. Identify the independent and dependent variables.

Map the Concept

The chart shows four categories. Place each term or word within a category.

lungs	kidneys
heart	alveoli
trachea	villi
esophagus	bronchi
small intestine	stomach
bladder	capillaries
veins	urine
arteries	sweat

Respiratory System	Circulatory System	Digestive System	Excretory System

Critical Thinking

17. Apply Smoking damages the respiratory system, sometimes by thickening the walls of the alveoli. What health problems would a smoker experience as a result?

18. Synthesize Could the excretory system work without a healthy circulatory system? Explain.

19. Analyze What other body systems does the digestive system affect? Describe the role of the digestive system in the body.

20. Evaluate Why can even the largest fish be healthy with very simple kidneys, much simpler than those of land animals? HINT: Compare the kidneys and environments of a fish and a camel.

Performance Assessment

Draw Your Systems!

Take an outline of a human form provided by your teacher. Use four pieces of tracing paper to draw the respiratory system, circulatory system, digestive system, and excretory system. Draw each system on one piece of tracing paper as it covers the human outline. Label your systems. Next, attach all four pieces of tracing paper onto the outline of the human form. Discuss how each system relates to the others.

Writing Journal

Review your answers to the Lesson Preview questions.

STANDARDS

1–2: 2.b., **3:** 2.d., **4:** 2.c., **5–6:** 2.b., **7:** 2.d., **8:** 2.c., **9:** 2.b., **10:** 2.c., **11:** 2.a., **12:** 2.d., **13:** 2.c., **14:** 2.d., **15:** 2.b., **16:** 2.a., 2.b., **17:** 2.b., **18:** 2.b., 2.d., **19:** 2.c., **20:** 2.d.

Write the letter of the best answer choice.

1. Small openings called _____ allow gases to move through a plant's leaves.
   A. cells
   B. vacuoles
   C. stomata
   D. chloroplasts

2. In which organ does blood receive oxygen?

   A.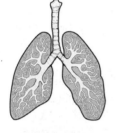

   B.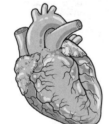

   C.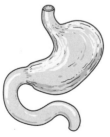

   D.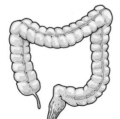

3. The basic unit of all living things is the _____.
   A. cell
   B. organ
   C. tissue
   D. mitochondria

4. Most digestion occurs in the _____.
   A. mouth
   B. lungs
   C. large intestine
   D. small intestine

5. Which part of the plant moves water and nutrients from the roots?

   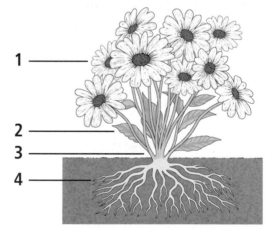

   A. 1 only
   B. 3 only
   C. 2 and 3
   D. 3 and 4

6. Which two structures increase the surface area of their organs?
   A. chloroplasts and stomata
   B. villi and veins
   C. villi and alveoli
   D. alveoli and arteries

7. Which material in a leaf traps energy from sunlight?

    A. carbon dioxide

    B. chlorophyll

    C. oxygen

    D. water

8. The role of the organ system shown here is to remove _____ from the blood.

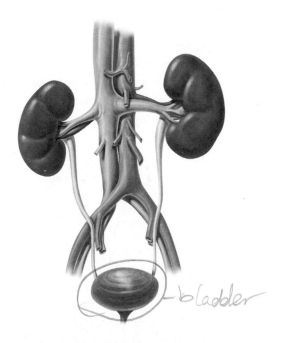

    A. nitrogen-filled wastes

    B. carbon dioxide

    C. oxygen

    D. sugars and other nutrients

Answer the following in complete sentences.

9. Identify the vascular tissues labeled A and B in the drawing. Describe the function of A and B in a vascular plant.

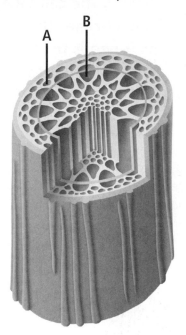

10. Compare the processes of photosynthesis and respiration.

STANDARDS

1: 2.a., **2:** 2.b., **3:** 2.a., **4:** 2.c., **5:** 2.e.,
6: 2.b., **7:** 2.f., **8:** 2.d., **9:** 2.e., **10:** 2.f., 2.g.

You Can...

Discover More

Everything the cell takes in and lets out must pass through the cell membrane. The larger the cell grows, however, the more nutrients it needs to stay healthy. Beyond a certain cell size, the cell membrane cannot take in nutrients quickly enough.

You can compare a cell to a sugar cube. In this cube, the ratio of surface area to volume is 6 to 1.

If the sugar cube doubles in width, the ratio of surface area to volume decreases to 3 to 1. If a cell grew like this, food and oxygen could not diffuse quickly enough for the cell to survive.

Instead of growing larger and larger, cells divide into new cells. To survive, however, each new cell must continue to border a supply of food and oxygen.

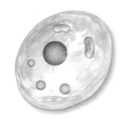
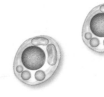

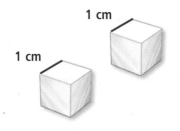

1 cm

Volume: 1 cm³
Surface Area: 6 cm²

2 cm

Volume: 8 cm³
Surface Area: 24 cm²

1 cm
1 cm

Volume: 2 cm³
Surface Area: 12 cm²

In all living things, cell size is limited by the ratio of surface area to volume. Should cell volume increase too much, the demand for food and oxygen would be greater than the amount that diffusion can supply. This explains why each of your cells is about the size of an amoeba. You just have many more of them! Your cells work together to keep you alive.

 Learn more about cell sizes. Go to **www.eduplace.com/cascp** to run a simulation.

EARTH

UNIT B

SCIENCE

Water on Earth

California Connection

Visit www.eduplace.com/cascp/ to learn more about Earth's water.

EARTH SCIENCE
UNIT B

Water on Earth

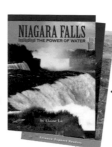

Clouds over the Sierra Nevadas

Water on Earth moves between
the oceans and land through
the processes of evaporation
and condensation.

Chapter 4

Water Resources

Hoover Dam and the Colorado River

LESSON 1

Earth's surface is made up of both land and water. Why is Earth often called the "water planet"?

LESSON 2

Rivers, lakes, and ponds store fresh water. How does water return to lakes and other bodies of fresh water?

LESSON 3

Earth's fresh water isn't always where it is needed. How can water be moved from one place to another?

Writing Journal

In your Writing Journal, write or draw answers to each question.

Vocabulary Preview

Vocabulary

Glossary

Vocabulary Skill

Multiple-Meaning Words
spring

A spring can be a natural flow of water from underground, one of the seasons, or a coiled wire. When you see a word that can have more than one meaning, read the sentence carefully. You must infer the correct meaning.

irrigation
the process of supplying fresh water to farm fields for growing crops

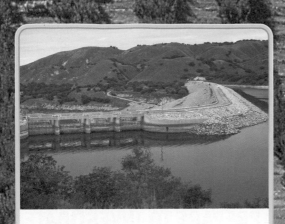

reservoir

a natural or an artificial pond or lake used to collect and store fresh water

spring

a natural flow of water from underground

well

a hole dug or drilled into the ground to provide a supply of water

Start with Your Standards

Standard Set 3. Earth Sciences (Earth's Water)

3.a. *Students know* most of Earth's water is present as salt water in the oceans, which cover most of Earth's surface.

3.d. *Students know* that the amount of fresh water located in rivers, lakes, underground sources, and glaciers is limited and that its availability can be extended by recycling and decreasing the use of water.

3.e. *Students know* the origin of the water used by their local communities.

Standard Set 6: Investigation and Experimentation standards covered in this chapter: 6.g., 6.h.

Where Is Earth's Water?

Building Background

Most of Earth's water is in oceans, and it is much too salty for humans to drink. Only a small fraction of Earth's water is in lakes, rivers, and groundwater. These are sources of fresh water. Humans need fresh water to survive, and its supplies are limited.

 STANDARDS

3.a. *Students know* most of Earth's water is present as salt water in the oceans, which cover most of Earth's surface.
6.g. Record data by using appropriate representations (including charts, graphs, and labeled diagrams) and make inferences based on those data.

PREPARE TO INVESTIGATE

Inquiry Skill

Analyze Data When you analyze data, you look for patterns or other evidence that you can use to make an inference.

Materials

- 6 one-liter plastic bottles
- marker
- masking tape
- graduated cylinder
- blue food coloring
- calculator
- eye dropper

Science and Math Toolbox

For step 3, review **Using a Calculator** on page H4.

Dividing Up Earth's Water

Procedure

Location	Percent	mL to represent the location
Oceans	97.2	
Glaciers	2.1	
Lakes	0.62	
Rivers	0.009	
Underground Water	0.001	

1 **Collaborate** Work with a partner. In your *Science Notebook*, make a chart like the one shown. Label each of the six 1-liter bottles as follows: Earth, Rivers, Lakes, Underground Water, Glaciers, Oceans.

2 **Measure** Pour 1 liter of water into the Earth bottle. Add a few drops of food coloring. This water represents all of Earth's water.

3 **Use Numbers** Recall that 1 liter equals 1000 mL. Calculate how many milliliters equal 1 percent of one liter. Use the data in the chart to calculate the milliliters of water that represent the percent of water in each location. Record each amount in your chart.

4 **Use Models** Measure and pour water from the Earth bottle to fill the other bottles. Save the location of greatest volume for last. Use the graduated cylinder for large amounts and the eyedropper for small amounts. About 20 drops equal 1 milliliter.

Conclusion

1. **Analyze Data** Use the model to compare the amount of salt water on Earth to the amount of fresh water. Oceans hold salt water, the other bodies hold fresh water.

2. **Infer** Where is most of Earth's fresh water? Infer how easy or difficult it would be for your community to get drinking water from that source.

Guided Inquiry

Experiment Make a model that compares the amounts of water in Earth's four major oceans. Describe how the oceans **compare** in volumes of water.

Water on Earth

MAIN IDEA Most of Earth's water is salt water contained in the oceans.

A Watery Planet

Of all the planets in the solar system, Earth is the only one covered mostly by liquid water. Almost all of Earth's water is saltwater in oceans and seas. The oceans surround Earth's continents, which are large masses of land that rise above the ocean surface.

Water is found not only on Earth's surface, but also below and above the surface. Most lands have at least some water in the rocks and soil below them. Water is found in the air in the form of a gas called water vapor. Clouds, which form from water vapor, can produce rain and snow.

The large bodies of water that cover much of the surface help to moderate Earth's climate. These waters also are home to many species of plants and animals, which themselves are made up largely of water.

Did you know that the human body is about 60 to 75 percent water? Each day, a person should take in 8 to 12 cups of water to stay healthy. Without water, no living thing on Earth would survive.

Earth is sometimes called the "Big Blue Marble." Why does Earth look so blue from space?

▲ Oceans cover about 70 percent of Earth's surface. Although oceans support many species, the water is too salty for humans to drink.

Oceans and Seas

About 70 percent of Earth's surface is covered by oceans and seas. Seas are large bodies of water, but are smaller than oceans. Seas are partly or completely surrounded by land.

The most important feature of the water in oceans and seas is its salinity, or its "saltiness." Ocean water is about 3.5 percent salt by weight. That's saltier than anything you could safely drink.

The main source of this salt is **runoff,** rainwater that flows over the land without sinking into the soil. As water moves across the land, it dissolves salts and other minerals in soil and rock. The runoff carries salts and other minerals into streams and rivers.

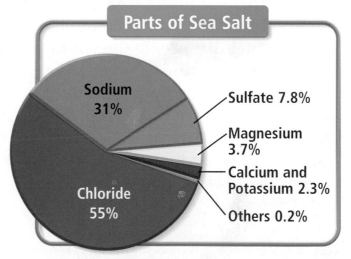

Parts of Sea Salt

Sodium 31%

Sulfate 7.8%

Magnesium 3.7%

Calcium and Potassium 2.3%

Chloride 55%

Others 0.2%

Eventually, the rivers empty into oceans and seas, bringing the salts and other minerals with them. Over time—millions of years—the deposits accumulate, making the water salty.

COMPARE AND CONTRAST What is the most important difference between ocean water and fresh water?

Fresh Water on Earth

Take a drink. Boil a potato. Grow tomatoes in a garden. All of these activities require fresh water. At home or school, fresh water may be as close as a sink or drinking fountain. But large quantities of usable fresh water are not always close at hand.

About 97 percent of Earth's water supply is salt water. Only three percent is fresh water that humans and other living things need to survive. This is why fresh water is an important, valuable resource.

One major problem is that much of Earth's fresh water supply is not available for everyday use. About two-thirds of this water is "locked away" as ice in glaciers and polar ice caps. That leaves less than one percent of Earth's total water supply as fresh water that people can use to drink, cook, and grow food.

There are two main sources of fresh water—surface water and groundwater. Surface water is the water found on Earth's surface. This is the water in lakes, ponds, rivers, and streams.

Lakes are bodies of water surrounded by land. They usually form in low areas where water drains into them faster than it drains out. Ponds are small lakes. A river is a body of water that flows downhill in a channel. A stream is a small river.

By contrast, **groundwater** is water that collects in spaces and cracks in rocks and soil underground. Dig deep enough in just about any spot on land, even a desert, and you'll eventually reach groundwater.

Surface water is the easiest fresh water supply to obtain. However, groundwater makes up about 94 percent of Earth's usable fresh water supply. This water supply is more difficult to reach. In most cases, holes must be dug or drilled down to the groundwater. Then the water must be pumped to the surface.

Fresh water is not distributed evenly over Earth's surface. In some places, rain falls heavily for much of the year. Yet elsewhere, fresh water is scarce. In deserts, rains are often light and brief, and the ground dries up

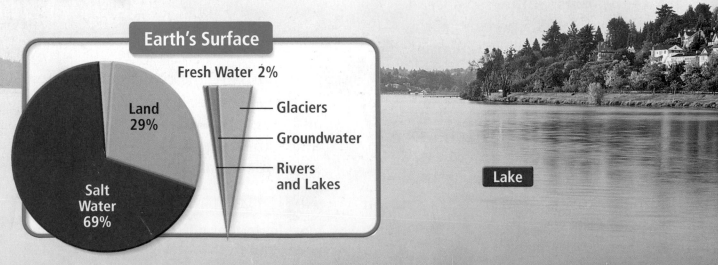

Earth's Surface

Fresh Water 2%

Land 29%

Glaciers

Groundwater

Rivers and Lakes

Salt Water 69%

Lake

quickly. Supplies of fresh water are more difficult to find.

Even in places where fresh water is plentiful, pollution can damage the water supply. Harmful materials may find their way into lakes and rivers, making the water unsafe for drinking.

Groundwater supplies can also be polluted. Chemicals can seep into groundwaters from landfills, factories, farms, and city streets.

Once a freshwater supply is polluted, it can be difficult or impossible to clean up. Fresh water is an important resource that needs to be protected.

COMPARE AND CONTRAST How do the two main sources of fresh water compare?

Ice

River

Lakes, rivers, and ice contain some of Earth's fresh water. Most of Earth's usable fresh water is groundwater, which is water below the surface.

Express Lab

Activity Card 9
Identify Earth's Usable Water

Fresh Water from the Sea

Can ocean water be changed into fresh water? It can happen at a desalination plant. **Desalination** (dee sal uh NAY shuhn) is the removal of salt from salt water to make fresh water. Desalination plants operate all over the world, especially in coastal lands that get little rainfall.

One desalination process is called distillation. First, ocean water is collected and heated. The hot water evaporates and becomes water vapor, leaving the solid salts behind. In a separate chamber, the water vapor is cooled. It condenses back into liquid fresh water.

Another process is reverse osmosis. Salt water is pumped at high pressure through a thin membrane. Holes in the membrane let water molecules pass through, but trap dissolved salts.

Unfortunately, desalination has drawbacks. Plants are expensive to run and they produce brine, an extremely salty waste. Brine can pollute groundwater and make water too salty for living things. For these and other reasons, desalination provides less than one percent of the world's fresh water.

COMPARE AND CONTRAST How are distillation and reverse osmosis alike? How are they different?

Reverse Osmosis

In reverse osmosis, salt is trapped behind a membrane. ▼

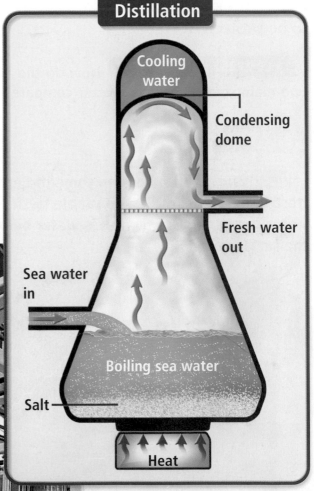

Distillation

Cooling water

Condensing dome

Fresh water out

Sea water in

Boiling sea water

Salt

Heat

▲ **Distillation**
In distillation, sea water is boiled. The water vapor condenses and is collected.

Visual Summary

Most of Earth's water is salt water in the oceans, which cover about 70 percent of Earth's surface. Although oceans are home to many living things, its water is too salty for humans to drink safely.

Earth's fresh water is located in rivers and lakes, underground, and as ice in glaciers. These freshwater supplies are limited and can be difficult to obtain.

At a desalination plant, salt is removed from sea water to make fresh water. Two processes for doing this are reverse osmosis and distillation.

STANDARDS

3.a., 3.d.

Technology
Visit www.eduplace.com/cascp to find out more about the distribution of water on Earth.

Reading Review

1 MAIN IDEA Why is fresh water a valuable resource?

2 VOCABULARY What is *groundwater* and how is it obtained?

3 READING SKILL How does Earth's surface compare to those of other planets in the solar system?

Compare	Contrast

4 READING SKILL: Apply To provide more fresh water for California, would you build a desalination plant by the ocean or a pumping plant on a river? Explain your choice.

5 INQUIRY SKILL Analyze Data Three percent of Earth's water supply is fresh water, and two-thirds of that is frozen in glaciers and ice caps. What can you conclude about the availability of fresh drinking water?

 TEST PRACTICE
What best describes the salinity of Earth's oceans?

A. not salty

B. very salty, but safe to drink

C. too salty for all living things

D. too salty for humans to drink

STANDARDS

1: 3.a., **2:** 3.d., **3:** 3.a., **4:** 3.d., **5:** 6.h., **Test Practice:** 3.a.

117

EXTREME Science

Death by Salt?

What happens when extreme nature meets extreme human actions? Meet Mono Lake.

Water enters Mono by streams and exits by evaporation, leaving minerals behind. As a result the lake was already twice as salty as seawater by 1941. That was the year Los Angeles built an aqueduct to divert water toward the city. The level of the lake began to drop, exposing great calcium formations known as tufas. Salinity went up even more, threatening the brine shrimp and migratory birds. Would Mono Lake die a salty death?

Not yet. After decades of work by conservation groups, Los Angeles reduced its water intake from Mono Lake's streams. The lake has already risen over three meters since 1982, and with continued conservation may recover.

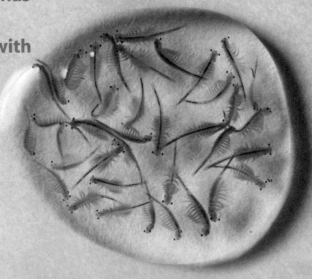

In the summer the Mono ▶ Lake brine shrimp population explodes to 4–7 trillion brine shrimp. A cubic meter of water can have more than 50,000!

Mono Lake Salinity Chart

Date	Water Level (ft above sea level)	Exposed Lake Bed	Salinity (grams of salt per liter of water)
1941 (diversion begins)	1,955 m	0 acres	51.3 g/l
1982 (lowest)	1,942 m	18,500 acres	99.4 g/l
2002	1,945 m	10,000 acres	79.6 g/l
Future stabilization	1,948 m	6,700 acres	69.3 g/l

Tufa formations

Writing Journal

In your journal, write out the pros and cons of diverting water from Mono Lake to the water-thirsty cities of Southern California.

How Do Communities Get Water?

Building Background

Many towns use water towers such as this one in Galt, California. Fresh water is pumped up into the tower from a local source. Inside the tower, the weight of the water generates the pressure needed to keep water flowing through pipes below. In this way the system brings water to homes, schools, and businesses.

PREPARE TO INVESTIGATE

Inquiry Skill

Predict When you predict, you state what you think will happen, based on past observations and experiences.

Materials

- plastic shoebox
- sand
- wax paper
- scissors
- clay
- 2 drinking straws
- small plastic cup

STANDARDS

3.e. *Students know* the origin of the water used by their local communities.
6.g. Record data by using appropriate graphic representations (including charts, graphs, and labeled diagrams) and make inferences based on those data.

Water from the Ground

Procedure

STEP 1

1. **Use Models** Place a 4-cm thick layer of sand in the bottom of a shoebox. Build up one end to form the slope of a flat-topped hill.

2. Cut two sheets of wax paper large enough to cover the slope. Press a thin layer of clay onto one sheet. The clay must extend to the edges of the wax paper.

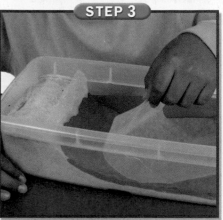
STEP 3

3. Place the clay-covered wax paper on top of the slope. Press the clay against the sides of the shoebox. Cover the clay with the second sheet of wax paper. Press it into place.

4. **Experiment** Use a pencil to poke a hole through the layers of wax paper and clay. Stick a drinking straw through the hole. Press clay around the straw to seal it in place. Add a 2-cm layer of sand over the clay.

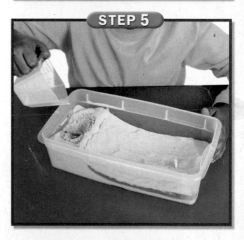
STEP 5

5. **Observe** Make a depression at the top of the sand hill to form a lake, as shown. Then pour water into the lake until the lake is full and no more water sinks into the sand.

Conclusion

1. **Analyze** What happened inside the straw? Explain your observations.

2. **Use Models** What real-world device does the straw represent? What does this device do?

3. **Predict** How deeply must a second straw be sunk to act like the first straw in the model? Predict the answer, then test your prediction.

Guided Inquiry

Ask Questions What is the source of drinking water in your community? How is water brought to homes, schools, and businesses? **Research** the answers. Draw a labeled diagram to show your community's water supply system.

VOCABULARY

aquifer	p. 124
aqueduct	p. 123
irrigation	p. 123
reservoir	p. 123
spring	p. 125
water table	p. 124
watershed	p. 126
well	p. 125

READING SKILL

Main Idea and Details
Use the chart to show the different sources of water for a community.

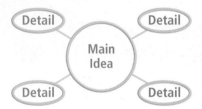

STANDARDS

3.d. *Students know* that the amount of fresh water located in rivers, lakes, underground sources, and glaciers is limited and that its availability can be extended by recycling and decreasing the use of water.
3.e. *Students know* the origin of the water used by their local communities.

Water to Everyone

MAIN IDEA Communities get fresh water from both underground sources and surface sources.

Rivers and Reservoirs

Turn on the tap and fresh, clean water pours out. Where does it come from? Rivers provide much of the drinking water for millions of Californians. For example, the Colorado River, along the state's southeastern border, provides much of the water for communities in southern California. The central part of the state obtains much of its water from the San Joaquin-Sacramento River system.

Yet rivers can be unreliable water sources in their natural state. Only about 35 percent of the rain and snow that falls in California becomes runoff that supplies rivers and lakes. In many hot, dry areas of the state, much precipitation evaporates. Some is lost when it soaks into the ground or is taken up by plant roots.

Reservoirs, wells, and aqueducts all help provide water to Californians. ▼

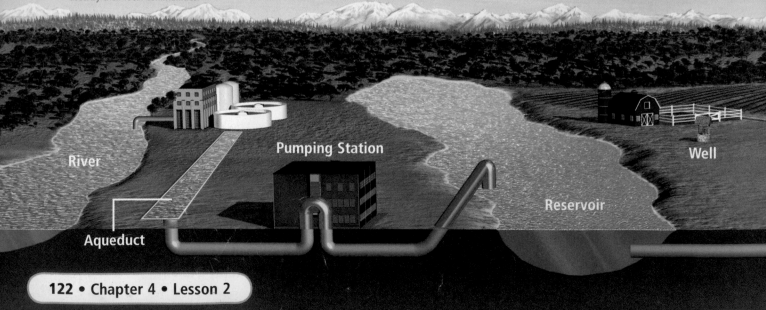

River

Pumping Station

Aqueduct

Well

Reservoir

What's more, most precipitation in California falls between October and April. Most crops need regular watering through spring and summer.

In California, people need ways to make runoff last throughout the year. To this end, the state has built many dams and created reservoirs. A **reservoir** (REZ uh vwahr) is a place that collects and stores water. Some reservoirs are natural ponds or lakes. But many have been made by building dams across rivers.

Sources of fresh water may be far from the people who need it. In such cases, aqueducts are used to transport water. An **aqueduct** (AK wuh dukt) is a system of channels, pipes, and tunnels that carries water a long distance. Some aqueducts are several miles long.

Reservoirs also provide water for **irrigation,** the supplying of fresh water to farm fields. Irrigation systems can be thought of as small-scale aqueducts.

▲ Hoover Dam, on the Colorado River, provides water and electricity for much of southern California.

Dams have other uses, too. Water rushing past them can be used to make electricity. People can boat, swim, or fish on the reservoirs they form.

MAIN IDEA AND DETAILS How do reservoirs help provide fresh water?

Irrigation

Houses

Industry

123

Groundwater

Groundwater supplies drinking water to a little less than half of the people of California. The source of most groundwater is rain and melted snow that sinks into the soil, filling the spaces between soil particles and entering cracks in rock.

Water at the surface seeps downward until it reaches a layer of solid rock or tightly packed clay. Water cannot penetrate this layer, so it fills the spaces in soil and rock above the layer.

An underground layer of rock or soil through which water easily moves is an **aquifer** (AK wih fuhr). Aquifers are usually sand, gravel, sandstone, or rock such as limestone with many cracks. When all the spaces are filled with water, the ground is said to be saturated.

The surface of a layer of saturated ground is the **water table.** Groundwater supplies lie beneath the water table. The water table rises during times of heavy rainfall.

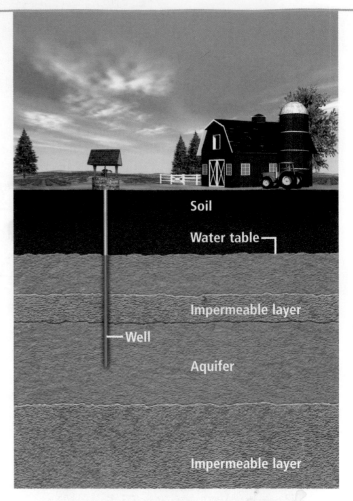

▲ Aquifers may lie deep below the surface. Wells can tap into their water supply.

It sinks during dry periods or when large amounts of water are pumped out of the ground.

In most cases, the water table is hidden underground. But you can sometimes see it. In a low area, the surface of a lake or stream is at the same level as the water table below the surrounding land. A wetland such as a swamp is also at the level of the water table.

◄ Digging a well is a simple way to supply fresh water.

In a desert, a spring may form an oasis. The oasis is home to plants and animals that could not survive without its fresh water. ▶

People often tap supplies of groundwater by drilling down into aquifers or other groundwater supplies. A **well** is a hole dug or drilled into an underground area saturated with water.

Pumps are typically used to raise water from wells to the surface. In *artesian wells*, groundwater flows to the surface without the use of pumps. These wells work where there is enough pressure to force groundwater to the surface.

In many of California's farming areas, such as the San Joaquin Valley, large amounts of groundwater have been pumped to the surface over many years. This has sunk the level of the water table. If the water table drops below the intake pipe of a well, the well runs dry.

Pumping large amounts of groundwater can also sink the land. As water between soil particles is withdrawn, empty space is left. The weight of the land above presses on the soil. In parts of the San Joaquin Valley, the land has sunk more than 6 meters.

In some areas, people also get groundwater from springs. A **spring** is a natural flow of water from underground. Springs form where the water table meets the land's surface. This often occurs on hillsides.

MAIN IDEA AND DETAILS How do people tap fresh water from an aquifer?

Express Lab

Activity Card 10
Build an Aqueduct

125

Water to You

As you have read, much of California's drinking water comes from rivers. A **watershed** is a region of land that drains into a river. Your drinking water may come from a single watershed.

Water from a river, lake, or reservoir is not always clean and safe to drink. So it must first be treated, or cleaned, at a purification plant.

At the plant, the water passes through a screen to remove insects, twigs, and other large objects. Chlorine and other chemicals are added to kill bacteria and other disease-causing organisms.

The next step in the process uses sand and gravel to filter out other unwanted material. Finally, water goes to a storage tank. It is treated with more chlorine to disinfect it. As the diagram shows, the water then flows to homes and businesses in the community.

You use treated water for such things as cooking, bathing, and doing laundry. Then wastewater goes into the sewer system. Pipes carry it to a sewage treatment plant. There it is cleaned and returned to the environment.

MAIN IDEA AND DETAILS What are the main goals of water purification?

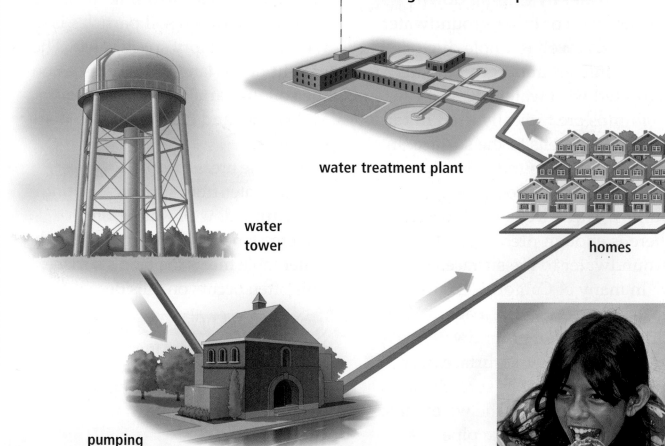

water treatment plant

water tower

homes

pumping station

The next time you take a drink from a fountain, think about how the water came to you.

Visual Summary

The people of California get fresh water from rivers, lakes, and reservoirs. Often this water is transported in long aqueducts to cities and farms.

In some locations, groundwater can be obtained from springs or wells. Groundwater fills about half of California's water needs.

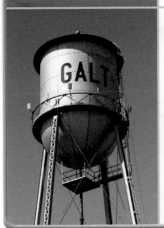

Each community has its own source of fresh water and some means of delivering it to consumers. Waste water is cleaned at a sewage treatment plant.

STANDARDS

3.d., 3.e.

 Technology
Visit **www.eduplace.com/cascp** to find out more about water on Earth.

Reading Review

❶ MAIN IDEA List three sources of fresh water for Californians.

❷ VOCABULARY Explain how the *water table* and a *spring* are related.

❸ READING SKILL Why has the state of California built so many dams and reservoirs? What purposes do they serve?

Main Idea

Detail   Detail

❹ CRITICAL THINKING: Analyze If you saw a sunken area of land in the San Joaquin Valley, what could you infer about its cause?

❺ INQUIRY SKILL: Predict A well is drilled into an aquifer to provide water for a farm. Predict how a long period of wet weather might affect the well. How might a long period of dry weather affect the well?

✔ TEST PRACTICE

For a well to provide water, it must reach _____.

A. above the water table

B. below the water table

C. above an aquifer

D. into a reservoir

STANDARDS

1: 3.d., **2:** 3.d., **3:** 3.e., **4:** 6.h., **5:** 3.e., **Test Practice:** 3.e.

Cleaning Waste Water

On average, each person produces 230 liters (60 gallons) of waste water per day. Even more comes from factories and other industrial uses.

In rural areas, waste water often is treated in septic tanks. These tanks hold chemicals that treat wastes. They are buried close to people's homes or farms.

A town or city, however, relies on a sewer system to collect waste water. The system is a network of pipes that leads to a sewage treatment plant.

What happens at a sewage treatment plant? Study the diagram and read the captions to find out.

1 Screening
Raw sewage contains twigs, stones, and trash. These large objects are screened out, then sent to landfills.

Pumping station

As a city grows, so does its daily volume of waste water. Sewage treatment plants make life in cities possible. ▶

STANDARDS

3.e. *Students know* the origin of the water used by their local communities.
3.d. *Students know* that the amount of fresh water located in rivers, lakes, underground sources, and glaciers is limited and that its availability can be extended by recycling and decreasing the use of water.

READING LINK

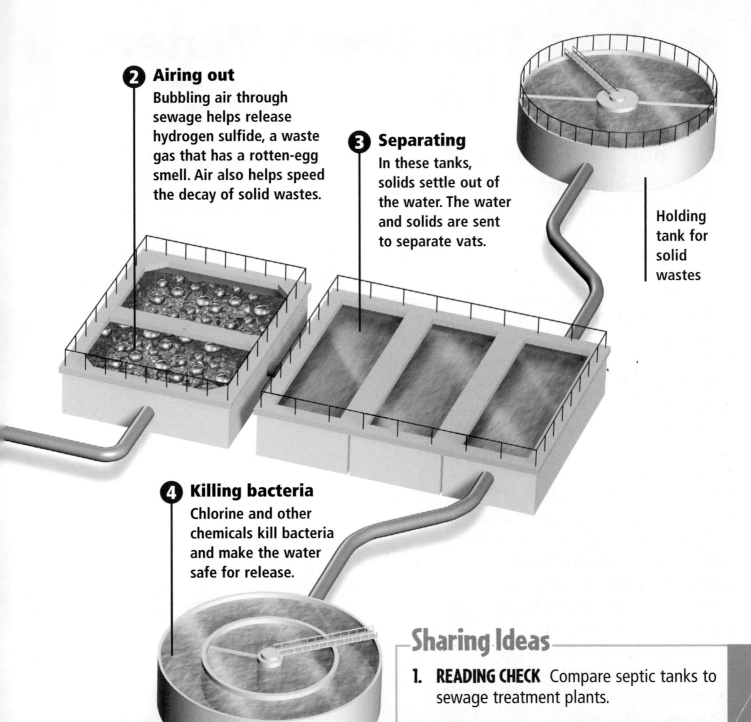

2 Airing out
Bubbling air through sewage helps release hydrogen sulfide, a waste gas that has a rotten-egg smell. Air also helps speed the decay of solid wastes.

3 Separating
In these tanks, solids settle out of the water. The water and solids are sent to separate vats.

Holding tank for solid wastes

4 Killing bacteria
Chlorine and other chemicals kill bacteria and make the water safe for release.

Sharing Ideas

1. **READING CHECK** Compare septic tanks to sewage treatment plants.

2. **WRITE ABOUT IT** What happens at a sewage treatment plant? Briefly describe the steps of the treatment process.

3. **TALK ABOUT IT** Do you know where waste water is treated in your community? Research the answer.

How Can Fresh Water Be Used Wisely?

Building Background

Everyone uses lots of water each day, usually without thinking about it much. But fresh water is an important resource—and a limited one. Using water wisely helps the supply last longer and be available when people need it.

PREPARE TO INVESTIGATE

Inquiry Skill

Use Numbers When you use numbers, you use measurements and other numerical data to describe and interpret organisms, objects, or events.

Materials

- paper
- pencil

 STANDARDS

3.d. *Students know* that the amount of fresh water located in rivers, lakes, underground sources, and glaciers is limited and that its availability can be extended by recycling and decreasing the use of water.
6.g. Record data by using appropriate graphic representations (including charts, graphs, and labeled diagrams) and make inferences based on those data.

Saving Water

Procedure

1. **Collaborate** Work with a partner. Study the table at right, which shows the typical amount of water used during certain common activities.

2. **Record Data** In your *Science Notebook*, list all of the daily activities in which your family uses water. Choose from the activities listed in the table shown in step 1, as well as other activities.

3. **Use Numbers** Estimate the amount of water used to do any activity on your list that is not on the table.

4. **Use Numbers** Calculate the total amount of water used daily by your family.

Conclusion

1. **Analyze Data** Look at the data on your family's daily water use. What surprises you most about how your family uses water?

2. **Research** How could you more accurately estimate the amount of water that your family uses?

3. **Ask Questions** How could your family use less water each day? Propose different ideas. How much of a difference do you think they would make? Test your ideas at home.

STEP 1

Activity	Liters
Bath	100
10-minute shower (typical shower head)	200
10-minute shower (low-flow shower head)	100
Toilet flush	6 to 18
Dishes, in pan without water running	20
Dishwasher, full load	60
Washing machine, full load	120

STEP 4

Guided Inquiry

Ask Questions Has your community ever faced a water shortage? If so, what measures were taken to conserve water? **Research** these questions by asking your teacher, parents, or guardians. You may appoint one class member to interview a local government official about water use.

READING SKILL

Cause and Effect Use the chart to show the effect that water shortages have had on Californians.

Cause ➡ Effect

🐻 **STANDARDS**

3.d. *Students know* that the amount of fresh water located in rivers, lakes, underground sources, and glaciers is limited and that its availability can be extended by recycling and decreasing the use of water.
3.e. *Students know* the origin of the water used by their local communities.

Conserving Fresh Water

MAIN IDEA Water should be conserved in order to make fresh water supplies last longer.

California's Water Needs

California has the largest population of any U.S. state—more than 35.5 million people and growing. California is also the country's leading farming state. Farm fields cover much of the San Joaquin, Imperial, and Coachella Valleys. They provide fruits and vegetables for people throughout the country.

California's growing population and its vast fields of crops require huge amounts of fresh water. But overall, the state's people and farm fields are not close to its major water supplies.

California receives a lot of rainfall every year, but some places are rainier than others. Compare the rainy places to those where water is needed.

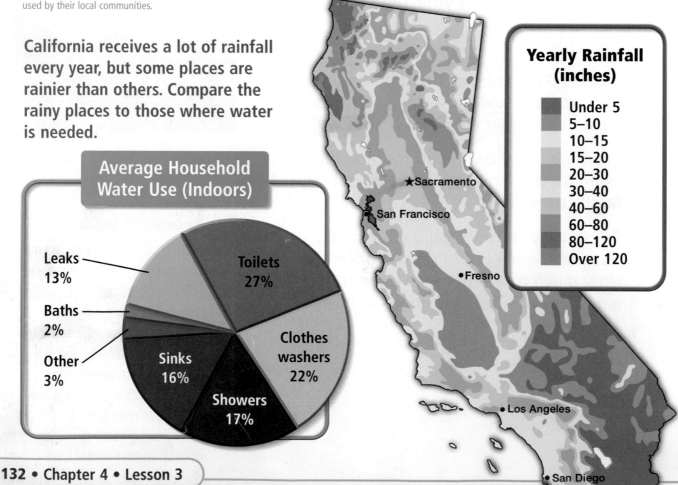

Average Household Water Use (Indoors)

- Leaks 13%
- Baths 2%
- Other 3%
- Sinks 16%
- Showers 17%
- Toilets 27%
- Clothes washers 22%

Yearly Rainfall (inches)

- Under 5
- 5–10
- 10–15
- 15–20
- 20–30
- 30–40
- 40–60
- 60–80
- 80–120
- Over 120

★Sacramento
• San Francisco
• Fresno
• Los Angeles
• San Diego

The average yearly rainfall and snowfall in California is about 58 centimeters (23 inches). Yet about two-thirds of this water falls in the northern part of the state and the Sierra Mountains. Both are thinly populated.

Only about one-third of the rain falls in the central valley and southern California. These places are home to most of the state's people, cities, and farms.

With hundreds of thousands of people moving to California every year, the state faces big challenges in providing water for everyone. Much of the San Joaquin Valley and southern California receive less than 10 inches of rainfall each year. That is not enough to supply water even to the current population.

What is the solution to California's water challenge? For many years now, the answer has been a huge system of canals, pipes, aqueducts, dams, pumps, and reservoirs. This system serves to transfer water from the wet north to the dry south. It allows most Californians to live and farm in areas that would otherwise have too little water to support them.

As you will discover, however, this system works only so well. Californians' water needs have begun to grow greater than their supply. New steps are being taken so that everyone has the water they need.

CAUSE AND EFFECT How has California been supplying water to its major cities and farms?

Most California farms depend on irrigation systems to bring water to crops. Much of the water comes from rain and snow in the northern parts of the state and the Sierra Mountains. ▼

Sharing Water

Californians began to use huge projects to transfer water about 100 years ago. In the early 20th century, the people of Los Angeles worried that their city could not grow without new supplies of fresh water. They built the 238-mile-long Los Angeles Aqueduct to bring water over the mountains from Owens Valley. The aqueduct still supplies about 80 percent of Los Angeles's water.

Today, Californians get most of their water from two main sources—the Sacramento-San Joaquin River system and the Colorado River.

About 1,300 dams and reservoirs, 6 major aqueduct systems, and many other structures shift the water from wetter to drier areas.

The Sacramento-San Joaquin system supplies water to central and southern California. Huge pumps pull fresh water from the Delta, an area where the two rivers meet before flowing toward the Pacific Ocean. Some of this water is sent to thirsty cities and farms in the Central Valley. Farther south, the California State Water Project sends much of this water to people in the southern part of the state, as well as to more than one million acres of farmland.

Southern California gets much of its fresh water from the state's other main surface water source—the Colorado River. The Colorado River Aqueduct carries river water to San Diego, providing about 70 percent of the city's supply. Much of the water also flows by canals to Imperial and Riverside counties. It irrigates some of the state's most productive farmland.

Aqueducts of California

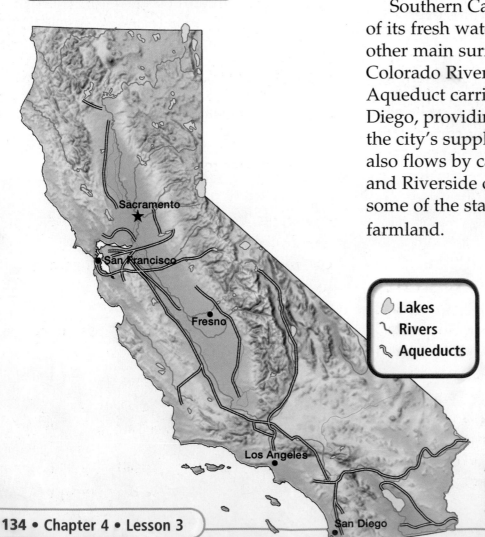

Sacramento

San Francisco

Fresno

Los Angeles

San Diego

Lakes
Rivers
Aqueducts

Aqueducts move water hundreds of miles across California.

Six other states and a part of Mexico share the water of the Colorado River. Each state is entitled to a certain amount of the river's water each year. Yet throughout the 1990s, California had been using much more water than its share. To do this, California had to borrow some of the water allowed to other states.

At first, states such as Arizona and Nevada could allow California to use some of the water they did not need. But as those states and others began to grow, it became clear that the surplus water would not always be available.

With growing populations, other states would soon need the additional water themselves. California could not continue to pull more than its fair share of water from the Colorado River.

In 2000, the Federal government and the states sharing the Colorado's water reached an agreement. Called "The 4.4 Plan," it promotes laws and practices that cut back water use. By the year 2015, California is expected to use no more than the water it is allotted from the Colorado River.

The 4.4 Plan includes many measures to use river water more efficiently. The plan calls for lining canals to stop leaks and for applying water-saving irrigation methods. It also calls on farmers to stop growing crops in parts of the Imperial Valley. Some of the water is to be transferred to San Diego and other growing cities.

As you have read, California and its neighbors get only so much fresh water every year. Desalination plants can supply fresh water from

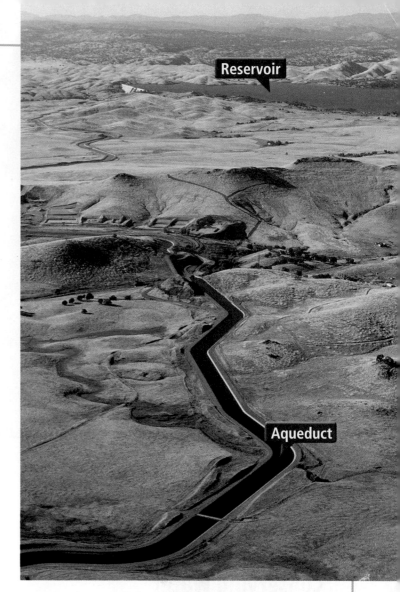

Reservoir

Aqueduct

▲ **This aqueduct snakes through California's Central Valley. It acts like an artificial river, bringing water to people and crops.**

sea water, but they have drawbacks, too. In the years ahead, meeting California's water needs will continue to be an important issue.

 **CAUSE AND EFFECT** How is California's water use changing?

Express Lab

Activity Card 11
See How Quickly a Gallon Empties.

How can water be used wisely in a neighborhood park or community garden?

Tips for Saving Water

- Run only full loads in dish and clothes washers.

- To wash dishes, fill the sink or basin with water. Don't let the faucet run.

- Turn off water while brushing your teeth.

- Take shorter showers. Just one or two minutes less can save up to 3,000 liters a month.

- Install low-flow toilets and shower heads.

- Keep a bottle of cold drinking water in the refrigerator. Don't waste water by running the tap.

Conserving Water

The careful use of a natural resource, such as water, is called **conservation.** Conserving a resource will help it last longer.

Most of California's water is used to irrigate farms, so a lot of water can be saved by irrigating wisely. Irrigation canals flood farm fields with water. Much of this water never reaches crops. It evaporates, runs off the land, or seeps into soil. Newer methods, such as drip irrigation, use much less water and deliver most of it to crops.

The state has also passed laws to encourage water conservation. One law addresses **water reclamation,** the recycling of waste water so it can be used again. Between 50 and 75 percent of waste water from homes and offices can be used to water lawns or plants, or to wash floors and cars.

In the 1990s, new laws encouraged people to replace old toilets with newer models that use less water. This change saves millions of liters of water each year.

You can conserve water, too! Study the tips listed above.

 **CAUSE AND EFFECT** Discuss ways that Californians can conserve water.

Visual Summary

People need fresh water for farms, factories, and personal use. The amount of fresh water in California is limited, especially in the places where it is most needed.

Most of California's rain and snow fall far from its people and farms. A vast water system provides fresh water to the state's communities.

Californians can conserve water by recycling water and by decreasing their use of water. In the years ahead, meeting California's water needs will remain an important issue.

 **STANDARDS**

3.d., 3.e.

 Technology
Visit **www.eduplace.com/cascp** to find out more about the distribution of water on Earth.

Reading Review

1 **MAIN IDEA** List three ways to conserve water.

2 **VOCABULARY** How does *water reclamation* decrease water demand?

3 **READING SKILL:** What has caused the need for water conservation in California?

4 **CRITICAL THINKING:** **Evaluate** Your community has a plan to add reclaimed waste water to its drinking water supply. Is this a good idea? Explain your answer.

5 **INQUIRY SKILL: Use Numbers** Taking a bath uses about 100 liters of water. A ten-minute shower uses about 200 liters. Which would save more water, filling the tub half way or taking a two-minute shower?

 TEST PRACTICE

Which of these bodies of water is the most important source of fresh water for California?

A. Pacific Ocean

B. Mississippi River

C. Colorado River

D. Salton Sea

 STANDARDS

1–3: 3.d., **4:** 3.d., 3.e., **5:** 3.d., **Test Practice:** 3.e.

Math in Science

The Kane family measured their water use over the course of one day. The family uses water in four different rooms of the house, as well as outdoors in the yard and driveway. The table shows the family's results.

1. For each room, calculate the percent of the total water used that day.

2. Which type of graph would best display the percent of water use in each room? Would you choose a line graph, a circle graph, or a bar graph? Explain.

3. If the family repeated their measurements on another day, how do you think the new results would compare to the results shown here?

Room	Water use (liters)
Kitchen	160
Main bathroom	800
Second bathroom	80
Basement	340
Outdoors	620

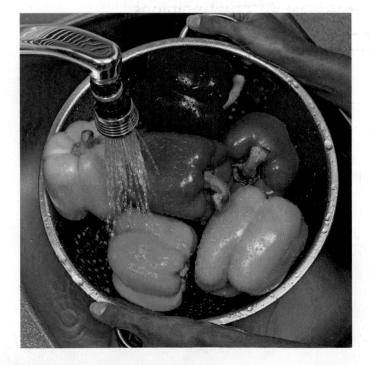

Writing in Science
Persuasive

Do you think people in your community are using water wisely? What do you think Californians should do to help meet the state's water needs? What new laws, if any, should be passed?

Jot down your ideas. Then write a short speech to persuade others that your ideas are worthwhile. Research facts and evidence to support your points.

Spreck Rosekrans

In the late 1800s, the city of San Francisco wanted to build a dam and reservoir in the Hetch Hetchy Valley, part of Yosemite National Park. Many people opposed this plan. But the city needed more fresh water. In 1913, the United States Government finally allowed the dam to be built.

Should that decision be reversed, meaning the dam now be torn down? Spreck Rosekrans says yes, it should. Rosekrans is a water analyst. He works for an organization called Environmental Defense.

"It is important to remember that Hetch Hetchy does not create water," he says. "It is simply one of a number of reservoirs that store the Tuolumne River's supplies." Rosekrans argues that existing reservoirs can take over for Hetch Hetchy. In return, Yosemite would reclaim a beautiful valley.

The state government is listening to Rosekrans, as well as to people who want to keep the dam and reservoir. Californians have different opinions on how best to manage their water, just as they did 100 years ago.

Vocabulary

Complete each sentence with a term from the list.

1. Careful use of a natural resource is called ____.

2. People can tap into groundwater by digging a(n) ____.

3. An underground layer of rock or soil through which water easily moves is a(n) ____.

4. A structure that carries water a long distance is a(n) ____.

5. Water that seeps into the soil may become ____.

6. The ground is dry above the ____.

7. A system of canals and pipes that supply fresh water to farm fields for growing crops is ____.

8. A natural flow of water from underground to the surface is a(n) ____.

9. The recycling of waste water so it can be used again is ____.

10. A place that collects and stores water is a(n) ____.

aquifer p. 124
aqueduct p. 123
conservation p. 136
desalination p. 116
groundwater p. 114
irrigation p. 123
reservoir p. 123
runoff p. 113
spring p. 125
water reclamation p. 136
water table p. 124
watershed p. 126
well p. 125

Test Practice

Write the letter of the best answer choice.

11. The southern part of California contains most of the state's ____.

    A. water
    B. snow-covered mountains
    C. people
    D. natural resources

12. Which of these is NOT a type of surface water?

    A. aquifer
    B. reservoir
    C. stream
    D. ocean

13. Where is most of Earth's water?

    A. glaciers and icecaps
    B. groundwater
    C. lakes and rivers
    D. oceans

14. What is the purpose of a desalination plant?

    A. to purify fresh water
    B. to obtain groundwater
    C. to carry water long distances
    D. to change salt water into fresh water

Inquiry Skills

15. Use Numbers By installing a water-saving device on a showerhead, a family uses 12 liters of water with each use instead of 20 liters. How many times must the family use the showerhead to save 160 liters of water?

16. Isabel waters two identical plants each day for a week with a solution of one cup water and 9 teaspoons of salt. She leaves the plants in the sun. Both plants soon die. What variable should she change to find out the level of salinity that begins to harm plants? Describe an experiment.

Map the Concept

Fill in the concept map to identify major sources of drinking water in California.

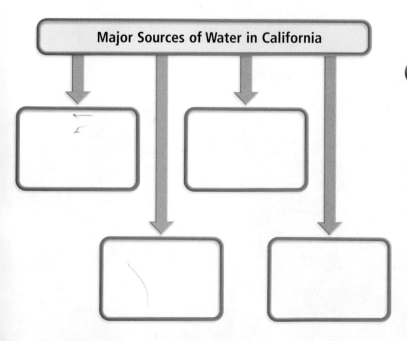

Major Sources of Water in California

STANDARDS

1: 3.d., **2:** 3.d., **3:** 3.d., **4:** 3.e., **5:** 3.e., **6:** 3.a., **7:** 3.e., **8:** 3.d., **9:** 3.e., **10:** 3.e., **11:** 3.e., **12:** 3.d., **13:** 3.a., **14:** 3.e., **15:** 3.e., **16:** 3.a., **17:** 3.e., **18:** 3.a., **19:** 3.e., **20:** 3.e.

Critical Thinking

17. Apply A family digs up its lawn, which required watering each day. The family replaces the lawn with plants that grow naturally in the dry environment of southern California. Does this help conserve water? Explain your answer.

18. Synthesize Although 70 percent of Earth's surface is covered by water, it is still considered to be a limited resource. Explain.

19. Analyze A city gets its drinking water from a nearby river. In drought years, which have become frequent, the river level drops and the water supply runs dangerously low. What might the city do to help ensure a more dependable water supply?

20. Evaluate What watershed district is your community a part of? Does the watershed supply enough fresh water for the community? Explain.

Performance Assessment

Draw a Diagram

Research how your community gets fresh water, then draw a diagram of its water-supply system. Features to include in the diagram include the source of the fresh water, a purification plant, homes and businesses, a sewage treatment plant, and a system to return treated water to the environment. Label your diagram.

Writing Journal

Review your answers to the Lesson Preview questions.

Chapter 5

The Water Cycle

Bridal Veil Falls, Yosemite National Park

LESSON 1

Earth's freshwater supply is limited. Still, each person uses about 350 liters of fresh water each day. Why doesn't Earth's supply run out?

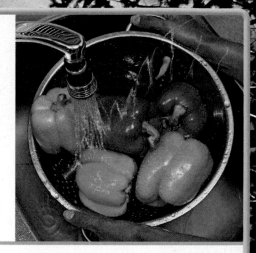

LESSON 2

What are clouds—and what do clouds have to do with your drinking water?

LESSON 3

Even if you never set foot in the ocean, it affects you in many ways. Did you know that the ocean changes the weather of nearby land? How do you think this happens?

Writing Journal

In your Writing Journal, write or draw answers to each question.

Vocabulary Preview

condensation
the change in a substance from gas to liquid

Vocabulary

Glossary

Vocabulary Skill

Root Words
groundwater

A compound word is made from two smaller words joined together. Its meaning often combines the meaning of the two parts. Groundwater is water that collects in the ground.

evaporation

the change in a substance from liquid to gas

precipitation

any form of water that falls to Earth's surface from clouds

transpiration

evaporation through plant leaves

Start with Your Standards

Standard Set 3. Earth Sciences (Earth's Water)

3.a. *Students know* most of Earth's water is present as salt water in the oceans, which cover most of Earth's surface.

3.b. *Students know* when liquid water evaporates, it turns into water vapor in the air and can reappear as a liquid when cooled or as a solid if cooled below the freezing point of water.

3.c. *Students know* water vapor in the air moves from one place to another and can form fog or clouds, which are tiny droplets of water or ice, and can fall to Earth as rain, hail, sleet, or snow.

3.d. *Students know* that the amount of fresh water located in rivers, lakes, underground sources, and glaciers is limited and that its availability can be extended by recycling and decreasing the use of water.

Standard Set 4. Earth Sciences (Weather)

4.a. *Students know* uneven heating of Earth causes air movements (convection currents).

4.b. *Students know* the influence that the ocean has on the weather and the role that the water cycle plays in weather patterns.

Standard Set 6: Investigation and Experimentation standards covered in this chapter: 6.e., 6.g., 6.h.

145

How Does Water Change State?

Building Background

During winter, these mountains are covered in snow. When the weather warms, however, the snow melts to liquid water. Some of the water flows downhill, while some evaporates, meaning it changes to a gas. All of these changes are part of the water cycle—the never-ending movement of water among Earth's land and air.

STANDARDS

3.b. *Students know* when liquid water evaporates, it turns into water vapor in the air and can reappear as a liquid when cooled or as a solid if cooled below the freezing point of water.
6.e. Identify a single independent variable in a scientific investigation and explain how this variable can be used to collect information to answer a question about the results of the experiment.

PREPARE TO INVESTIGATE

Inquiry Skill

Experiment When you experiment, you control variables, changing only one part of your setup at a time.

Materials

- balance
- 2 clear plastic cups
- ice cubes or ice chips
- lamp
- watch or clock with second hand
- ruler

Science and Math Toolbox

For Step 2, review **Using a Balance** on page H9.

Ice Melt

Procedure

1. **Collaborate** Work with a partner. In your *Science Notebook*, make a chart like the one shown.

2. **Measure** Use a balance to find the mass of each of two cups. Half fill each cup with ice, then measure the masses of the half-filled cups. Add ice to one cup so that both cups hold about the same masses of ice.

3. **Experiment** Place one cup directly under a lamp, which will serve as a heat source. Place the second cup in a shaded area. Begin timing the activity.

4. **Observe** Every minute, carefully observe each sample and record what you see. Be sure to note the time when all of the ice has melted in each cup.

5. **Record Data** Continue to observe the cup over the course of the day as the water evaporates. Use the ruler to measure the depth of liquid water in each cup. Fill in the chart with your observations.

Conclusion

1. **Use Variables** Why is it important that the two ice samples have close to the same mass?

2. **Compare** How did the times of melting and evaporation of the two ice samples compare?

3. **Infer** How is energy related to change of state?

STEP 1

Time	Cup (lamp)	Cup (shade)
1 min.		
2 min.		
3 min.		
4 min.		
5 min.		
6 min.		

STEP 2

STEP 3

Guided Inquiry

Experiment Would the results be the same if you changed one independent variable, such as the size of the pieces of ice? Repeat the activity using larger or smaller ice pieces. **Analyze data**, then write a report.

The Water Cycle

▶ VOCABULARY

condensation	p. 149
evaporation	p. 149
precipitation	p. 149
transpiration	p. 149
water vapor	p. 149

◎ READING SKILL

Compare and Contrast
Use the chart to compare
water in its solid, liquid, and
gas states.

Compare	Contrast

STANDARDS

3.b. *Students know* when liquid water evaporates,
it turns into water vapor in the air and can reappear
as a liquid when cooled or as a solid if cooled below
the freezing point of water.
3.c. *Students know* water vapor in the air moves from
one place to another and can form fog or clouds,
which are tiny droplets of water or ice, and can fall to
Earth as rain, hail, sleet or snow.

MAIN IDEA On Earth, water exists in three states: liquid water, solid ice, and a gas called water vapor. Water changes from one state to another in processes that make up the water cycle.

Water in the Environment

Have you ever planned a day outdoors, then have those plans ruined because of rainy weather? You may not always welcome the rain, but it is very important for life on Earth. Rain is part of the water cycle, a natural process that restores and cleans Earth's water supply. In the water cycle, water moves from Earth's surface to the atmosphere and back to the surface again.

As you have read, about 70 percent of Earth's surface is covered with water. Yet most of that water, about 97 percent, is salt water found in Earth's oceans. Less than one percent is the fresh water found in lakes and rivers. The rest of the fresh water is deep underground or is found as ice in glaciers and ice caps.

Condensation
Cooled water vapor condenses into water droplets and forms clouds.

Evaporation
Heat from the Sun causes evaporation of water from oceans, lakes, and rivers. Water vapor rises in the air and cools.

People use fresh water for drinking, cooking, and growing food. But unwanted materials can pollute water on Earth's surface. The water cycle removes many types of pollution. It renews Earth's supply of usable fresh water.

Water exists in three states: solid ice, liquid water, and water vapor. **Water vapor** (VAY pur) is water in the form of a gas. In the water cycle, water changes between states as it is heated or cooled.

To see how the water cycle works, start by looking at how water gets into the air. Energy from the Sun causes liquid water to evaporate from Earth's surface. During **evaporation** (ih VAP uh ray shuhn), liquids change to the gas state.

A great deal of water vapor is also released into the atmosphere by plants. In **transpiration** (tran spuh RAY shuhn), the leaves of plants release water vapor into the air.

Water vapor condenses back into a liquid when it cools. **Condensation** (kahn dehn SAY shuhn) is the change of state from a gas to a liquid. Additional cooling can result in freezing, the change from liquid into solid. At this stage in the water cycle, tiny droplets of water or ice crystals in the atmosphere can form clouds.

When the water droplets or ice crystals become heavy enough, they fall to Earth as precipitation. **Precipitation** (prih sihp uh TAY shuhn) is any form of water that falls to Earth's surface from clouds. It is usually rain, sleet, snow, or hail.

COMPARE AND CONTRAST How does water enter the atmosphere? How does it leave?

Precipitation
Water droplets in the cloud become heavy, and they fall as precipitation.

Express Lab

Activity Card 12
Create Condensation

Runoff

Gulley

▲ Runoff may flow after heavy rains, or from snow melt in the spring. Erosion from runoff may form trenches, called gullies.

Groundwater and Runoff

Most precipitation falls on Earth's oceans. When precipitation falls on land, some of it is absorbed into the ground as groundwater. As you read earlier, groundwater is water that soaks into the ground. It collects in spaces underground between soil and rock.

By contrast, runoff is water that flows downhill across Earth's surface without sinking into the land below. Runoff often comes from rain and the melting of mountain snows. It may flow into streams, rivers, lakes, or the ocean.

Runoff also causes erosion. Erosion is the transport of soil or rocks over Earth's surface. When runoff flows over the land, the water often picks up pieces of land and carries them along. The faster the water is moving, the greater a force of erosion it can be.

Runoff can also pick up harmful chemicals from streets or farm fields, or the chemicals may seep into groundwater. Eventually, the polluted water could taint wells, reservoirs, or other stores of fresh water.

To prevent water pollution, California has enacted laws at the state and local levels to protect water supplies. National laws also require water supplies to be monitored and kept safe.

COMPARE AND CONTRAST Explain the difference between runoff and groundwater.

Lesson Wrap-Up

Visual Summary

Earth's fresh water is an important resource and a limited one. Fortunately, water is cleaned and renewed in the processes that make up the water cycle.

When liquid water evaporates, it changes to water vapor in the air. It can change back to a liquid when cooled, then fall to Earth as rain, hail, sleet, or snow.

Groundwater collects in the soil, while runoff flows over the ground. Runoff can erode the soil and create gullies and other features.

STANDARDS

3.a., 3.b., 3.c.

Technology

Visit **www.eduplace.com/cascp** to find out more about the water cycle.

Reading Review

❶ MAIN IDEA What are the three states of matter in which water can be found?

❷ VOCABULARY What is *transpiration*? What part does it play in the water cycle?

❸ READING SKILL Compare the amount of fresh water readily available on Earth with that of salt water.

Compare	Contrast

❹ CRITICAL THINKING: Apply Are clouds more likely to form during a cold winter night or a warm summer afternoon? Explain.

❺ INQUIRY SKILL: Experiment Which will melt faster on a warm day: a small, frozen puddle or a large, frozen lake? Design an experiment to find out. What variable does the experiment test?

✓ TEST PRACTICE

The unique role played by plants in the water cycle is called _____.

A. precipitation

B. condensation

C. transpiration

D. groundwater

 STANDARDS

1: 3.b., **2:** 3.b., **3:** 3.a., **4:** 3.c., **5:** 6.e., **Test Practice:** 3.b.

Lesson 2

How Does Precipitation Form?

Building Background

When you see rain falling, you're looking at a part of the water cycle. Like all forms of precipitation, rain returns fresh water to Earth's surface to be used again.

 STANDARDS

3.b. *Students know* when liquid water evaporates, it turns into water vapor in the air and can reappear as a liquid when cooled or as a solid if cooled below the freezing point of water.
6.g. Record data by using appropriate graphic representations (including charts, graphs, and labeled diagrams) and make inferences based on those data.

PREPARE TO INVESTIGATE

Inquiry Skill

Use Models When you make a model, you use a representation of a process to better understand or describe how it works.

Materials

- clear plastic container with lid
- water
- small resealable plastic bag
- 4-5 ice cubes
- lamp
- clock or watch
- metric ruler

Science and Math Toolbox

For step 5, review **Measuring Elapsed Time** on page H14.

Water Cycle Model

Procedure

1 **Collaborate** Work with a partner. In your *Science Notebook*, make a chart like the one shown.

2 **Measure** Use a metric ruler to measure 1 cm of water in a plastic container. Place the lid on the container.

3 **Experiment** Place four or five ice cubes in a plastic bag. Seal the bag and place it on the lid of the container.

4 **Use Models** Put the container near a lamp so that the lamp shines on one side of the container. **Safety:** Do not touch the light bulb. It may be very hot. Do not look directly into the light.

5 **Observe** After 15 minutes, carefully observe the container. Look for any changes on the inside and outside of the container. Record your observations in your chart. Make observations every 15 minutes for 1 hour.

Conclusion

1. **Infer** What changes occurred on the inside of the container? Infer what caused the changes.

2. **Use Models** You made a model of Earth's water cycle using a lamp as a source of heat. What source of heat warms the water in lakes, rivers, and oceans on Earth?

STEP 1

Time	Observations	
	Inside of Container	Outside of Container
Start		
15 minutes		
30 minutes		
45 minutes		
1 hour		

STEP 3

STEP 4

Guided Inquiry

Experiment Repeat the experiment, adding food coloring to the water. **Compare** what you see with what you saw in the first experiment. Write a hypothesis to explain the difference.

VOCABULARY

convection current p. 154
dew point p. 158
humidity p. 158

READING SKILL

Sequence Use the chart to show the sequence of events in the formation of rain.

STANDARDS

3.b. *Students know* when liquid water evaporates, it turns into water vapor in the air and can reappear as a liquid when cooled or as a solid if cooled below the freezing point of water.
3.c. *Students know* water vapor in the air moves from one place to another and can form fog or clouds, which are tiny droplets of water or ice, and can fall to Earth as rain, hail, sleet, or snow.

Precipitation

MAIN IDEA Clouds form and release precipitation as rain, snow, sleet, and hail.

Cloud Formation

Why do clouds usually form high in the sky? The answer begins with the Sun. As the Sun warms Earth's surface, the air just above the surface warms, too. Warm air is less dense than cool air, so warm air rises. Temperatures are cooler above Earth's surface, so the air gradually cools as it rises. Cold air is denser than warm air, so the cold air sinks back to the ground.

This process is called convection. A **convection current** is a continuous loop of moving air or liquid that transfers energy.

Another property of air is that warm air can carry more water vapor than cool air. As the warm air rises in a convection current, it carries water vapor with it. When the air cools enough, the water vapor condenses around tiny specks of dust or salt.

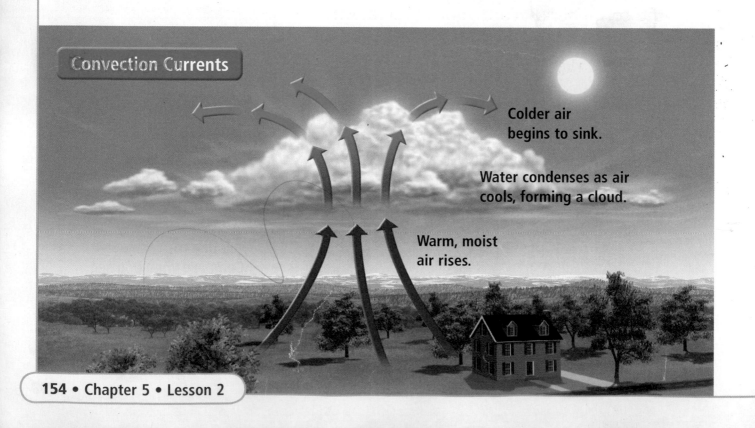

Convection Currents

Colder air begins to sink.

Water condenses as air cools, forming a cloud.

Warm, moist air rises.

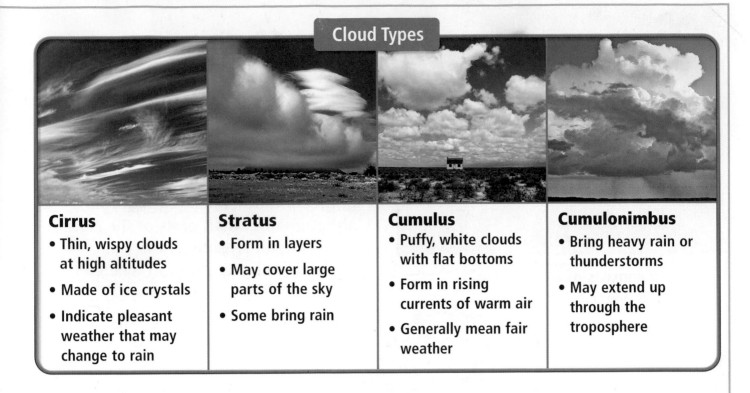

Cloud Types

Cirrus
- Thin, wispy clouds at high altitudes
- Made of ice crystals
- Indicate pleasant weather that may change to rain

Stratus
- Form in layers
- May cover large parts of the sky
- Some bring rain

Cumulus
- Puffy, white clouds with flat bottoms
- Form in rising currents of warm air
- Generally mean fair weather

Cumulonimbus
- Bring heavy rain or thunderstorms
- May extend up through the troposphere

Tiny droplets of liquid water form. The droplets remain suspended in the air, forming clouds.

Sometimes, a cloud can form near the ground. This type of cloud is called fog. Most fogs form when moist air near the ground becomes cool enough for water vapor to condense, forming water droplets.

As you know from observing the sky, clouds can be small or large, thick or thin, and may change shape from moment to moment. They also can be surprisingly heavy. A cloud that is 1 kilometer wide and 100 meters thick has about the same mass as a very large airplane!

So why do clouds stay in the sky? Remember that warm air is rising from the surface. A cloud is less dense than the air below it, so it floats.

Cloud Types

Before the 1800s, scientists thought that clouds were formless objects that could not be classified. They changed their mind because of the work of Luke Howard, an English businessman who studied clouds as a hobby. Howard described four classes of clouds. He chose Latin names because Latin was known to all scientists of the time.

Howard's classification of clouds is still in use today. The photos show Howard's four basic cloud types.

In 1896, a cloud atlas based on Howard's work was published. The ninth cloud in the atlas was an especially puffy, billowy cumulus cloud. Today, people still describe a blissful state as "being on cloud nine."

SEQUENCE What are the steps in the formation of a cloud?

▲ Rain consists of falling drops of liquid water.

▲ Sleet forms when rain freezes as it falls.

▲ Snowflakes can form in many different shapes.

Forms of Precipitation

All precipitation falls from clouds. The type of precipitation depends on both the conditions inside the clouds and conditions of the air between the clouds and the ground.

Each of the four major types of precipitation falls on California, although not on all parts of the state or during all seasons of the year. Which forms are common where you live?

Rain Drops of liquid water are rain, the most common form of precipitation. Rain can form when tiny cloud droplets combine. Cloud droplets can be millions of times smaller than raindrops. So a great number of these droplets must combine to form a raindrop large enough and heavy enough to fall to the ground.

If the droplets fall through air that is warmer than water's freezing point, they reach the ground as rain. Rain can also begin as ice crystals. The crystals melt as they fall through warm air, producing raindrops.

Sleet This form of precipitation begins as small drops of rain. When the raindrops fall through a layer of air that is colder than water's freezing point, they freeze into tiny ice pellets. These pellets reach the ground as sleet.

Snow Small flakes and pellets of ice make up snow. Snowflakes are produced when the temperature in a cloud is cold enough for water vapor to form ice crystals.

▲ Notice the layers of ice inside the hailstone. Hail forms by rising and falling through a tall cloud.

The type of snow that falls depends on the temperature of the clouds. Light, fluffy snowflakes form when the temperature is very low. Warmer temperatures produce heavy, wet flakes.

In California, snow falls during the winter in the Sierra Nevadas and other mountain ranges. In nearby places with lower elevations, snowflakes melt in the air and fall as rain.

Hail Hail is made up of round chunks of ice called hailstones. Hailstones form when drops of rain freeze inside a cloud with strong updraft winds, such as a large cumulonimbus cloud. If the winds are strong enough, they lift the hailstone through the inside of the cloud.

A hailstone may rise and fall many times, each time gaining a new icy coat. Finally, when the hailstone is too heavy for the wind to lift, it falls to the ground.

SEQUENCE Describe the stages in the formation of a hailstone.

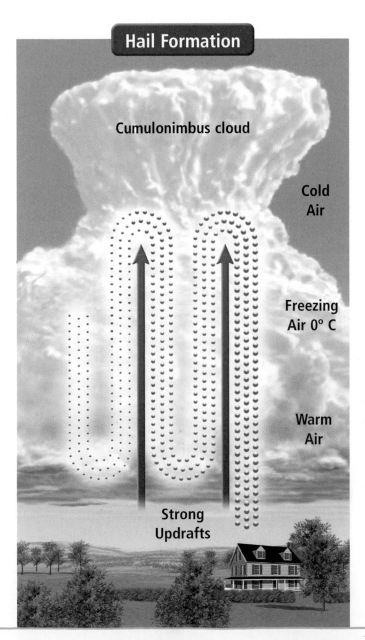

Hail Formation

Cumulonimbus cloud

Cold Air

Freezing Air 0° C

Warm Air

Strong Updrafts

◄ The stronger the updrafts in a cloud, the larger the hailstones that form.

Express Lab

Activity Card 13
Create Humidity

157

Rain forest

Desert

What difference can water make? The air temperature may be the same in a rain forest and desert, but the humidity of the rain forest is much higher.

Humidity

The amount of water vapor in the air can change from day to day, or even from hour to hour. **Humidity** is the amount of water vapor in the air at any given time. The higher the humidity, the stickier the air feels.

One reason that humidity changes is because the temperature changes. As you have read, warm air can hold more water vapor than cold air can.

Relative humidity is the amount of water vapor in the air compared to the greatest amount it can hold at that air temperature. For example, when the relative humidity is 50 percent, air is holding half as much water vapor as it could hold at that temperature.

When air is holding all of the water vapor it can hold, the relative humidity is 100 percent, and the air is said to be saturated. The temperature at which air becomes saturated is its **dew point.** If the air temperature drops below the dew point, water condenses and clouds or fog form.

Recall that water vapor condenses into clouds as humid air rises and cools. This happens because as air cools, its ability to hold water vapor decreases. The rising air becomes saturated. At a certain point, it cools to its dew point. As cooling continues, condensation occurs and clouds form.

SEQUENCE What happens to the relative humidity of warm air as it rises and cools?

Visual Summary

As the Sun heats Earth's surface, warm air rises into the atmosphere, while cold air sinks. The moving air forms a loop called a convection current.

As moist air rises, water vapor condenses and clouds can form. Clouds are made of tiny droplets of liquid water or ice.

Precipitation returns water from the atmosphere to the surface. Forms of precipitation include rain, sleet, snow, and hail.

STANDARDS

3.b., 3.c., 4.a.

Technology

Visit **www.eduplace.com/cascp** to find out more about clouds and precipitation.

Reading Review

❶ MAIN IDEA What must occur before precipitation can fall to Earth's surface?

❷ VOCABULARY Write a sentence to define the term *humidity*.

❸ READING SKILL Describe the steps in the formation of a cloud.

1	
2	
3	
4	

❹ CRITICAL THINKING: Draw Conclusions What does the size of a hailstone show about the cloud where it formed?

❺ INQUIRY SKILL: Use Models How can the formation of water droplets on the outside of a cold glass on a hot day serve as a model for cloud formation?

 TEST PRACTICE

What happens when the temperature of the air falls below its dew point?

A. Hailstones form.

B. Water vapor condenses out of the air.

C. Snowflakes form.

D. The air stops rising.

STANDARDS

1: 3.b., **2:** 3.b., **3:** 3.c., **4:** 3.c., **5:** 3.c., **Test Practice:** 3.b.

Fog in San Francisco

During summer months, the weather for much of California ranges from warm to quite hot. Often the skies are clear, and not much rain falls. Yet San Francisco has cooler weather. And on many mornings, thick fog covers much of the city.

Why is San Francisco so cool and foggy? The answer begins with its neighbor to the west, the Pacific Ocean.

Flowing through all oceans are ribbons of moving water that are called surface currents. The California Current flows by San Francisco. This current begins in the north, so it is especially cold.

When warm, moist air blows in from the south, it is cooled by the cold water of the California below it. As the temperature drops, water vapor in the air condenses into tiny liquid droplets. The droplets make up fog, a low-lying cloud that drifts east over the city.

At any given moment, the weather can be quite different across the San Francisco Bay Area. ▶

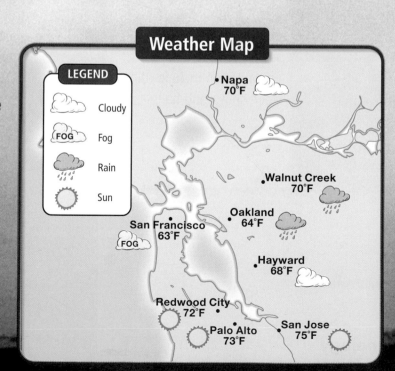

Weather Map

LEGEND

- Cloudy
- FOG — Fog
- Rain
- Sun

- Napa 70°F
- Walnut Creek 70°F
- Oakland 64°F
- San Francisco 63°F — FOG
- Hayward 68°F
- Redwood City 72°F
- Palo Alto 73°F
- San Jose 75°F

STANDARD
3.c. *Students know* water vapor in the air moves from one place to another and can form fog or clouds, which are tiny droplets of water or ice, and can fall to Earth as rain, hail, sleet, or snow.

READING

How Fog Forms in San Francisco

▲ Fog is another name for a cloud that is low to the ground. Cold ocean waters and warm, moist winds combine to bring fog to San Francisco.

Sharing Ideas

1. **READING CHECK** What is the California Current? How does it affect San Francisco?

2. **WRITE ABOUT IT** How does fog typically form over San Francisco?

3. **TALK ABOUT IT** How does weather in San Francisco compare to weather in your community?

How Does the Ocean Affect Weather?

Building Background

All over Earth, places near the ocean have different weather than places farther inland. Oceans add water to the air—water that may form clouds, fog, or precipitation. Oceans also cool the air temperature in summer and warm it in winter. Storms can brew over the ocean, too.

STANDARDS

4.b. *Students know* the influence that the ocean has on the weather and the role that the water cycle plays in weather patterns.
6.g. Record data by using appropriate graphic representations (including charts, graphs, and labeled diagrams) and make inferences based on those data.

PREPARE TO INVESTIGATE

Inquiry Skill

Infer When you infer, you use facts you know and observations you have made to draw a conclusion.

Materials

- 2 large plastic foam cups
- 2 thermometers
- large paper clip
- ruler
- 2 lamps
- water
- sand
- graph paper

Science and Math Toolbox

For step 1, review **Making a Chart to Organize Data** on page H11.

The Ocean and Weather

Procedure

1. **Collaborate** Work with a partner. Fill one plastic foam cup with water and fill the other cup with sand. Make a chart like the one shown.

2. **Experiment** Push one thermometer into the sand 2.5 cm (1 in.) deep. Place a second thermometer 2.5 cm into the water, using tape to attach it to the side of the cup. Record the temperature of the sand and water.

3. **Measure** Place each cup under a hot lamp or in direct sunlight. Measure and record the temperature of each sample every 5 minutes for 30 minutes.

4. **Measure** Move the two cups to a cool, shady place. Measure and record the temperatures every 5 minutes for 30 minutes.

5. **Record Data** Make a line graph to show your data. Note the times when you moved the samples from a warm place to a cooler one.

Conclusion

1. **Analyze Data** What does your data indicate about the heating and cooling of water and sand?

2. **Infer** Based on your observations, how do you think the presence of a large body of water might affect the weather on land nearby?

STEP 1

Time	Sand	Water
5 min.		
10 min.		
15 min.		
20 min.		
25 min.		
30 min.		

STEP 2

STEP 3

Guided Inquiry

Design an Experiment How might you test the inference you made in the Directed Inquiry? What further information is needed? Carry out your experiment. **Communicate** the results to the class.

VOCABULARY

ocean current   p. 165

READING SKILL

Main Idea and Details
Use the chart to show details that support the main idea of this lesson.

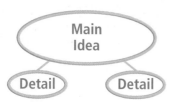

STANDARDS

4.a. *Students know* uneven heating of Earth causes convection currents.
4.b. *Students know* the influence the ocean has on the weather and the role that the water cycle plays in weather patterns.

Water has a relatively high specific heat capacity. It heats up more slowly than land. ▶

Ocean Effects

MAIN IDEA Oceans have a major effect on Earth's weather and climate.

Heating Land and Water

Look at the photograph of the swimming pool. The sun is shining equally on the water in the pool and on the concrete walkway. If you walk across the concrete, you might burn your feet! Yet if you jump into the pool, the water will feel nice and cool. What causes this difference?

The water is much cooler than the concrete because they have different specific heat capacities. This means the two materials heat up and cool down at different rates. As heated air above the warmer surface rises, a convection current is set in motion.

The specific heat capacity of a material is the amount of energy it takes to raise the temperature of 1 gram of the material by 1°C. Water has a much higher specific heat capacity than concrete has. As a result, it takes a lot more energy and time to heat the water in the pool than the concrete around it.

Land and water have different specific heat capacities, too. In general, land heats up faster and reaches higher temperatures than do bodies of water near it. Land areas also lose heat more quickly and drop to lower temperatures.

Cold Water

Hot Cement

Deep Ocean Currents

Ocean currents move hot and cold water around Earth's oceans. This helps moderate temperatures of nearby land. ▶

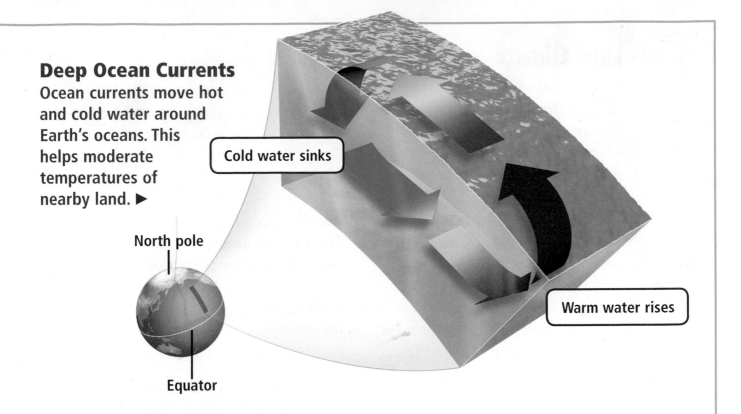

Cold water sinks

Warm water rises

North pole

Equator

Ocean Currents

If you ever swam or waded in the Pacific Ocean you know the waters are quite cold. The coldness is the result of the California Current, a cold ocean current that flows along the coast.

An **ocean current** is a moving stream of water in the ocean. Water that flows within a current has similar temperature and density.

The two types of ocean currents are surface currents and deep currents. The map on the page shows warm and cold surface currents. They move in great circles, driven by surface winds and the effects of Earth's rotation.

Warm currents move warm ocean water from near the equator toward cooler polar regions. Cold currents move in the opposite direction. The currents help balance temperatures at Earth's surface.

Deep ocean currents move vertically within the ocean. These currents form because of differences in temperature and salinity, which is the salt content of the water.

As water becomes saltier, its density increases. So the colder, denser water sinks. It flows back toward the equator along the ocean bottom. Near the equator, the current warms and becomes less salty and less dense. It returns to the surface to complete the cycle.

MAIN IDEA How do ocean currents influence temperatures in coastal areas?

Express Lab

Activity Card 14
Explore Water Density

Oceans and Climate

The oceans play an important role in the water cycle. They also have a great effect on climate—the weather conditions of a place over a long period of time. Ocean currents warm or cool the air above them. That air influences the climate of land nearby.

Oceans also influence climate in other ways. As you have read, water heats up and cools down more slowly than land. That means that oceans hold the summer's heat long into winter. They slowly release that stored energy at a time when the land nearby has already cooled.

During winter, oceans warm nearby lands, which do not get as cold as they would otherwise. During summer, oceans have the opposite effect. Although under the same Sun, ocean waters warm much more slowly than the land. The oceans stay cooler, and they serve to cool nearby lands.

MAIN IDEA How do oceans affect the temperature of land areas near them?

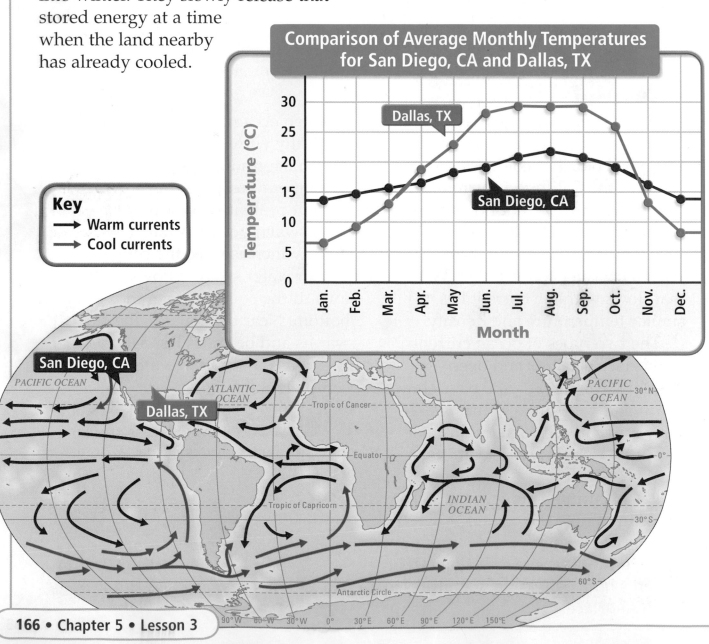

Comparison of Average Monthly Temperatures for San Diego, CA and Dallas, TX

Dallas, TX

San Diego, CA

Key
→ Warm currents
→ Cool currents

San Diego, CA

PACIFIC OCEAN

ATLANTIC OCEAN

Dallas, TX

Tropic of Cancer

Equator

Tropic of Capricorn

INDIAN OCEAN

PACIFIC OCEAN

30° N

0°

30° S

60° S

Antarctic Circle

Visual Summary

Water has a relatively high specific heat capacity. This explains why Earth's oceans warm and cool more slowly than its lands.

Ocean currents are examples of convection currents. They move warm and cold water around the oceans, helping to even out Earth's temperatures.

Oceans help to moderate the climate of places near them, such as California. Winters tend to be warmer and summers tend to be cooler than places further inland.

 **STANDARDS**

4.a., 4.b.

 Technology

Visit **www.eduplace.com/cascp** to find out more about oceans and their effect on weather.

Reading Review

❶ MAIN IDEA How do land and water heat differently?

❷ VOCABULARY What is an *ocean current*?

❸ READING SKILL Why do oceans affect weather and climate?

Main Idea

Detail   Detail

❹ CRITICAL THINKING: Apply
Ocean waters along much of the Atlantic coast of the United States are generally warmer than those along Pacific coast. What is a likely cause for this difference?

❺ INQUIRY SKILL: Infer
If ocean waters were to become much warmer in the polar regions, how might this affect deep-ocean convection currents?

 **TEST PRACTICE**

How does the Pacific Ocean affect weather over land?

A. It makes California winters colder.

B. It causes milder weather over all of the United States.

C. It causes cirrus clouds to form over California.

D. It moderates temperatures of lands near it.

 STANDARDS

1: 3.a., **2:** 4.b., **3:** 4.b., **4:** 4.b., **5:** 4.a., **Test Practice:** 4.b.

167

EXTREME Science

Super Storm!

How powerful is a hurricane? A large hurricane produces as much energy every second as all the electrical power plants on Earth combined!

Where does all this energy come from? The warm waters of the ocean are the hurricane's power source. Think of a hurricane as an extreme example of the water cycle. The violent, swirling winds lift and turn water vapor from the ocean into rain at a tremendous rate— some 20,000 million tons a day in a large storm!

When extreme hurricanes, like Katrina, shown here, come ashore, they can do tremendous damage with wind, rain, high tides, and waves.

Strength	Damage	Winds	Storm Surge
Category 1	Minimal	74–95 mph	4–5 feet
Category 2	Moderate	96–110 mph	6–8 feet
Category 3	Extensive	111–130 mph	9–12 feet
Category 4	Extreme	131–155 mph	13–18 feet
Category 5	Catastrophic	>155 mph	>18 feet

Meteorologists use the Saffir-Simpson scale to divide hurricanes into categories based on wind speed.

Hurricane Katrina was the most destructive hurricane in United States history. Its winds and storm surge caused billions of dollars of damage to Louisiana and Mississippi.

The winds in the strongest hurricanes move three times as fast as cars on a freeway!

Writing Journal

If the force of wind increases with the cube of the wind's velocity, calculate how much more powerful a 140-mph wind is than a 100-mph wind.

Math in Science

1. Choose a city from the chart and find its mean yearly precipitation. Does that value equal the average of the highest and lowest yearly precipitation? Explain why or why not.

2. What is the mean value of yearly precipitation for the 10 cities in the chart? In which city is yearly precipitation closest to the mean?

3. Locate the 10 cities on the map. What conclusions can you draw about precipitation in California?

Yearly Precipitation 1948-2003 (cm)			
City	Lowest	Mean	Highest
Bakersfield	5	15	32
Bishop	5	14	43
Eureka	55	97	170
Fresno	15	27	54
Los Angeles	10	30	74
Sacramento	17	48	87
San Diego	9	25	49
San Jose	15	36	79
Truckee	30	60	138
Victorville	2	11	32

Writing in Science
Narrative

Write a story about a car trip across California. The characters should visit both mountains and oceans, and encounter different kinds of precipitation.

Environmental Science and Protection Technicians

These technicians help monitor pollution. During one week, they might collect samples of air, water, or soil. The next week, they might help analyze those samples in a lab. People in this job often must oversee the proper disposal of hazardous wastes.

What It Takes!

- A high-school diploma
- Courses in applied science or science-related technology
- Strong math, computer, and communication skills

Oceanographer

Oceanographers may study salts in ocean water, rocks from the ocean floor, or the way oceans affect the weather. They also study the ocean's many living things, from tiny algae to huge whales!

Much of the ocean and ocean floor have yet to be visited or studied. What lies in the deep, waiting to be discovered? Most likely, oceanographers will be the ones to find out.

What It Takes!

- Four years of college, plus an advanced degree
- An interest in oceans and science

Vocabulary

Complete each sentence with a term from the list.

1. Water in gas form is called _____.

2. A continuous loop of moving air is called a(n) _____.

3. The amount of water vapor present in the air at a given time and place is called _____.

4. The process by which plant leaves release water vapor into the air is _____.

5. Clouds form from the _____ of water vapor into tiny droplets.

6. Any form of water that falls to Earth's surface from clouds is _____.

7. The temperature at which a parcel of air becomes saturated with water vapor is its _____.

8. The change of state from a gas to a liquid state is called _____.

9. A narrow, fast-moving stream of water moving through the ocean is a(n) _____.

10. Liquids change to the gas state in the process of _____.

condensation p. 149
convection current p. 154
dew point p. 158
evaporation p. 149
humidity p. 158
ocean current p. 165
precipitation p. 149
transpiration p. 149
water vapor p. 149

Test Practice

Write the letter of the best answer choice.

11. The source of drinking water pumped from wells is _____.

    A. ocean currents
    B. groundwater
    C. runoff
    D. transpiration

12. Which of these most influences climate along coastal regions?

    A. transpiration
    B. erosion
    C. ocean currents
    D. runoff

13. Warm air rises and cool air sinks in _____.

    A. a convection current
    B. a surface ocean current
    C. the groundwater supply
    D. the California Current

14. Much of Earth's surface is covered by _____.

    A. groundwater
    B. bodies of fresh water
    C. land areas
    D. bodies of salt water

15. **Draw Conclusions** What can you conclude from the fact that you see a certain type of cloud in the sky whenever it rains? Could you state that this type of cloud is the only one that brings rain? What further evidence would be needed to support or refute that conclusion?

16. You learn that a city on the coast is near a warm ocean current. What can you infer about the climate in that city?

Map the Concept

Copy and fill in the concept map to describe the types of precipitation.

Rain	Snow	Sleet	Hail

17. **Apply** Suppose the temperature of the air high above the ground was warmer than the temperature of the air at the surface below it. How would this affect the operation of the water cycle? Explain.

18. **Synthesize** Why do so few clouds form in the skies above a desert?

19. **Analyze** Are dew point temperatures likely to be higher on a warm, sunny day or on a cool, cloudy day? Explain.

20. **Evaluate** What would you say to someone who claims that land pollution is unimportant, so long as food isn't grown in the affected soil? Give examples of how pollution of soil could affect what people eat or drink.

Performance Assessment

The Water Cycle

Draw a diagram of the water cycle that includes a convection current, evaporation, condensation, cloud formation, precipitation, transpiration, and runoff. Indicate the stage of the cycle where the actions of people are most likely to have an effect.

Writing Journal

Review your answers to the Lesson Preview questions on page 143.

STANDARDS

1: 3.b., **2:** 4.a., **3:** 3.c., **4:** 2.e., **5:** 3.d., **6:** 3.b., **7:** 3.b., **8:** 3.b., **9:** 4.b., **10:** 3.b., **11:** 3.e., **12:** 4.b., **13:** 4.a., **14:** 3.a., **15:** 6.c., **16:** 6.h., **Map the Concept:** 3.c., **17:** 3.b., **18:** 3.b., **19:** 3.b., **20:** 3.d., **Performance Assessment:** 3.b.

Write the letter of the best answer choice.

1. What could this circle graph show?

   A. Earth's surface covered by water and land
   B. Earth's different sources of fresh water
   C. Earth's fresh water and salt water
   D. fresh water resources for California

2. Which is a source of groundwater?
   A. an aquifer
   B. a reservoir
   C. an aqueduct
   D. a canal

3. When will a well no longer provide water?

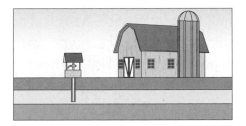

   A. after a week without rain
   B. during most winters
   C. when the water table drops below the top of the well
   D. when the water table drops below the bottom of the well

4. How can Californians conserve fresh water?
   A. Use salt water instead of fresh water.
   B. Use drip irrigation instead of canals and ditches
   C. Get drinking water from aquifers instead of rivers.
   D. Use the dishwasher instead of washing dishes by hand.

5. In which of these directions does an aqueduct move water across California?
   A. from Los Angeles to San Francisco
   B. from San Diego to Los Angeles
   C. from the Sierra Mountains to San Francisco
   D. along the coast of the Pacific Ocean

6. Which of these events leads to the formation of clouds?

   A. Water vapor condenses.
   B. Winds swirl at Earth's surface.
   C. Frost forms.
   D. Droplets of water fall from the atmosphere to the ground.

7. Cumulus clouds often appear in fair weather. Which of these clouds is a cumulus cloud?

   A.

   B.

   C.

   D.

8. What causes convection currents in Earth's atmosphere?

   A. the changing of liquid water into water vapor
   B. uneven heating of Earth's surface
   C. the cooling of air to its dew point
   D. the formation of precipitation

Answer the following in complete sentences.

9. Identify each type of precipitation. Compare and contrast how they form.

   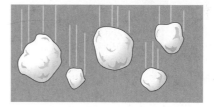

10. Discuss how oceans affect the weather on land. Include at least three examples.

 STANDARDS

1: 3.a., 2: 3.d., 3: 3.e., 4: 3.e., 5: 3.e.,
6: 3.b., 7: 3.c., 8: 4.a., 9: 3.c., 10: 4.b.

You Can...

Discover More

Stalactites are rock formations that form on the ceilings of limestone caves. Droplets of groundwater trickle through tiny cracks in the cave roof. The water dissolves some of the limestone rock. When a water droplet evaporates, it leaves behind a tiny deposit of limestone sediment. Drop by drop, the water adds more limestone sediment to the deposit. Over thousands of years, the deposit grows downward to form a huge stalactite. One stalactite is thought to have taken 4,000 years to grow to a length of 2 m (7 ft).

Stalactites form when drops of water containing minerals drip from the ceiling of a limestone cave.

Stalagmites form when water drops fall to the floor of the cave and evaporate.

Sometimes, stalactites and stalagmites meet. When this happens they form a single column.

Stalactite

Stalagmite

Column

See a cave system grow. Go to **www.eduplace.com/cascp/** to witness a cave's growth over thousands of years.

Weather and the Solar System

Griffith Observatory

The center dome of the Griffith Observatory houses the planetarium, the west dome houses a triple-beam telescope, and the east dome houses a Zeiss Refracting Telescope.

This image of Orion nebulae was taken with the Zeiss Refracting Telescope.

The Foucault Pendulum demonstrates that Earth rotates on its axis.

Weather and the Solar System

A hurricane, viewed from space

Standard Sets 4,5.
Earth Sciences

Energy from the Sun heats Earth unevenly, causing air movements that result in changing weather patterns. The solar system consists of planets and other bodies that orbit the Sun in predictable paths.

Weather

The whirling funnel cloud of a tornado

LESSON 1

Why do your ears pop when you ride on an airplane?

LESSON 2

Look outside—is it windy or calm? What makes the wind blow?

LESSON 3

How do scientists know what the weather will be like tomorrow?

LESSON 4

Some storms are very powerful. What kind of storm caused the damage shown here?

Writing Journal

In your Writing Journal, draw or write answers to each question.

Vocabulary Preview

Vocabulary

Glossary

Vocabulary Skill

Multiple-Meaning Words
front

EVERYDAY LANGUAGE A front often means the part of something that faces forward.

METEOROLOGY In the study of weather, a front is the boundary between two air masses.

weather
the overall condition of the atmosphere at a given time and place

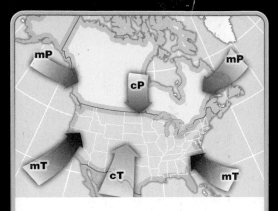

air mass

a body of air that has about the same temperature and moisture throughout

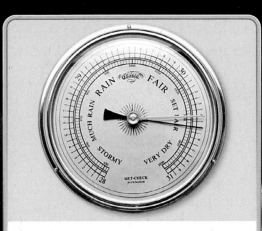

air pressure

the force exerted by air in all directions on an area

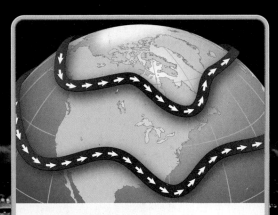

jet stream

narrow belt of high-speed winds in the upper troposphere

Start with Your Standards

Standard Set 4. Earth Sciences (Weather)

4.a. *Students know* uneven heating of Earth causes air movements (convection currents).

4.c. *Students know* the causes and effects of different types of severe weather.

4.d. *Students know* how to use weather maps and data to predict local weather and know that weather forecasts depend on many variables.

4.e. *Students know* that the Earth's atmosphere exerts a pressure that decreases with distance above Earth's surface and that at any point it exerts this pressure equally in all directions.

Standard Set 6: Investigation and Experimentation standards covered in this chapter: 6.f., 6.g., 6.h.

How Does Air Pressure Affect Weather?

Building Background

Imagine what it would be like to float among the clouds. Parachutes allow people to drift with the wind and float down from the sky. Air catches inside the parachute and slows the person's fall. Birds and airplanes both need air to fly.

 STANDARDS

4.e. *Students know* that the Earth's atmosphere exerts a pressure that decreases with distance above Earth's surface and that at any point it exerts this pressure equally in all directions.
6.h. Draw conclusions from scientific evidence and indicate whether further information is needed to support a specific conclusion.

PREPARE TO INVESTIGATE

Inquiry Skill

Collaborate When you collaborate, you work in a team to investigate and experiment.

Materials

- scissors
- 2 round uninflated balloons
- small baby food jar
- 2 thick rubber bands
- toothpick
- transparent tape
- large wide-mouth jar

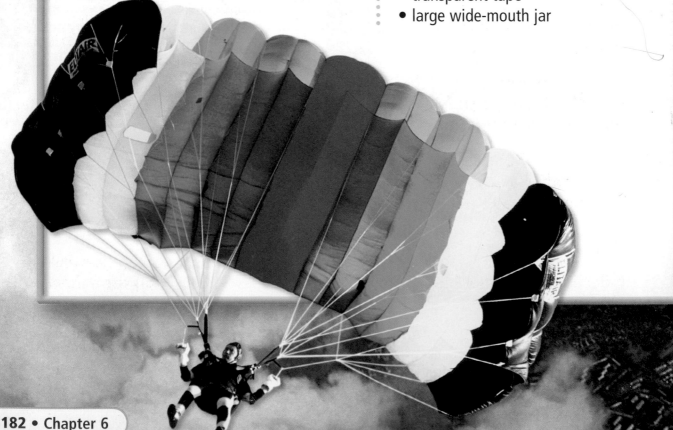

The Pressure's On!

Procedure

Safety: Be careful when using scissors.

STEP 1

1. **Collaborate** Work with a partner. Cut off the tops of two balloons. Then, cut one of the balloons a third of the way down.

2. **Use Models** Stretch the smaller balloon over the mouth of the smaller jar until it is tight. Secure it with a rubber band. Tape a toothpick on the balloon over the center of the mouth of the jar. Leave the toothpick hanging over the lip of the jar.

STEP 3

3. **Use Models** Carefully place the small jar inside the larger jar. Stretch the larger balloon tightly over the mouth of the large jar. Secure it with a rubber band.

4. **Experiment** While one partner holds the large jar, the other partner should push down on the balloon to increase the air pressure inside the jar.

STEP 4

5. **Observe** In your *Science Notebook*, record what happens to the toothpick when the balloon is stretched downward.

6. **Experiment** Repeat step 4, this time pulling up on the balloon. Record what happens to the toothpick.

Conclusion

1. **Infer** How does pulling up on the balloon affect the air pressure inside the jar?

2. **Use Models** What does your model show about how changes in air pressure can be observed?

Guided Inquiry

Experiment How could you modify this experiment to detect actual changes in air pressure? **Compare** your observations with air pressure readings listed in the newspaper.

Earth's Atmosphere

MAIN IDEA Earth's atmosphere is a mixture of gases that surrounds the planet. The atmosphere exerts a pressure that decreases with distance above Earth's surface.

VOCABULARY

air pressure   p. 186
atmosphere   p. 184
weather   p. 184

 READING SKILL

Cause and Effect Select one of the pressure systems described in the lesson. Describe the kind of weather it might produce.

Cause → Effect

STANDARDS

4.e. *Students know* that the Earth's atmosphere exerts a pressure that decreases with distance above Earth's surface and that at any point it exerts this pressure equally in all directions.
4.a. *Students know* uneven heating of Earth causes air movements (convection currents).

Composition of the Atmosphere

When you're going outside, how do you decide what to wear or what you might do? You check on the weather. **Weather** is the overall condition of the atmosphere at a given time and place. Earth's **atmosphere** is a mixture of gases that surrounds the planet. As you know, the condition of the atmosphere—the weather—can change from day to day and even from hour to hour.

Earth's atmosphere is made up mostly of nitrogen and oxygen. As the graph shows, other gases are present in very small amounts.

The amounts of some gases can vary. In desert areas, for example, there is little or no water vapor. However, near oceans or large lakes, water vapor can make up as much as four percent of the air.

Carbon dioxide is another gas that is present in varying amounts. Burning fossil fuels increases the amount of this gas in the atmosphere.

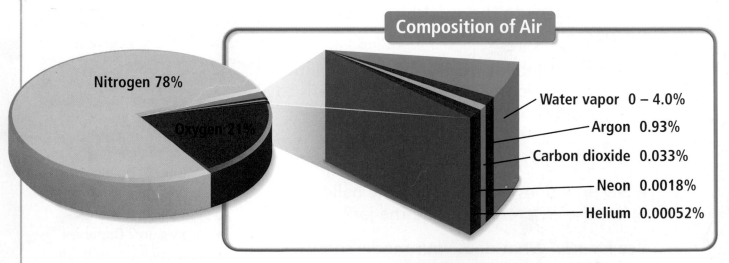

Composition of Air

Nitrogen 78%
Oxygen 21%
Water vapor 0 – 4.0%
Argon 0.93%
Carbon dioxide 0.033%
Neon 0.0018%
Helium 0.00052%

▲ Air is mostly nitrogen and oxygen. Other gases are present in small amounts.

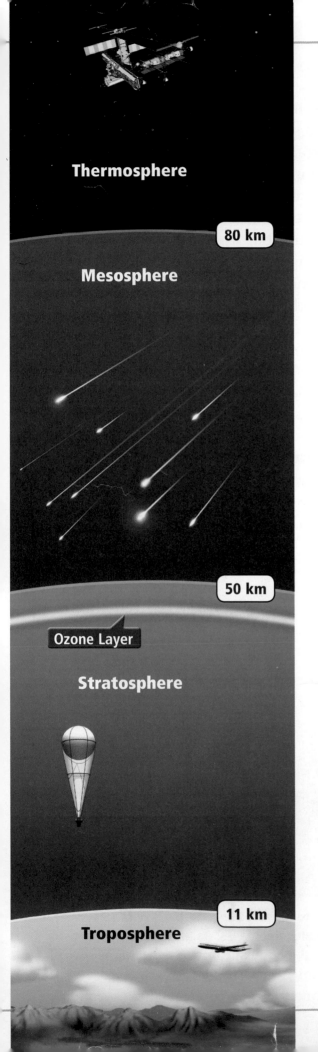

Thermosphere

80 km

Mesosphere

50 km

Ozone Layer

Stratosphere

11 km

Troposphere

Layers of the Atmosphere

Earth's atmosphere can be divided into four main layers. The layer closest to Earth is the troposphere. Here is where almost all weather occurs. Although it is the thinnest layer, the troposphere contains about 75 percent of the air that makes up the atmosphere.

The stratosphere lies above the troposphere. Air in this layer is much colder and drier than air in the troposphere. The stratosphere contains most of our planet's ozone, a form of oxygen. Ozone absorbs certain types of radiation from the Sun that can harm living things.

The mesosphere lies above the stratosphere. The top of the mesosphere is the coldest part of Earth's atmosphere. The very thin air of the next layer, the thermosphere, is the first part of the atmosphere struck by sunlight. Temperatures in the thermosphere can reach 1,700°C.

The living things on the surface are fortunate to have Earth's atmosphere above them. Living things rely on the nitrogen, oxygen, and carbon dioxide that comes from the atmosphere. The atmosphere also keeps surface temperatures from becoming too hot or too cold.

In the illustration, notice the bright streaks drawn in the mesosphere. These are meteors. They are caused by rocks, called meteoroids, that enter the atmosphere from space. Friction with the atmosphere burns up most meteoroids.

CAUSE AND EFFECT Why does most weather occur in the troposphere?

Express Lab

Activity Card 15
Observe Air Pressure

Air Pressure

You can think of the atmosphere as an ocean of air that surrounds Earth. Just like ocean water, air has mass and weight. It exerts a force equally in all directions—sideways, as well as up and down. The force exerted by air on a given area is known as **air pressure.**

As you have learned, most of the air in the atmosphere is found in the troposphere. As you move away from Earth's surface, there are fewer air molecules. The air becomes "thinner," so it exerts less pressure. In other words, air pressure generally decreases with altitude, or distance above Earth's surface.

Measuring Air Pressure Air pressure at Earth's surface is always changing. To keep track of these changes, scientists use an instrument called a barometer to measure air pressure.

There are two types of barometers. A mercury barometer contains a column of mercury in a glass tube. The bottom of the tube is enclosed in a flexible container filled with mercury. Air presses on this container. The column of mercury rises in the tube when air pressure increases and falls when air pressure decreases.

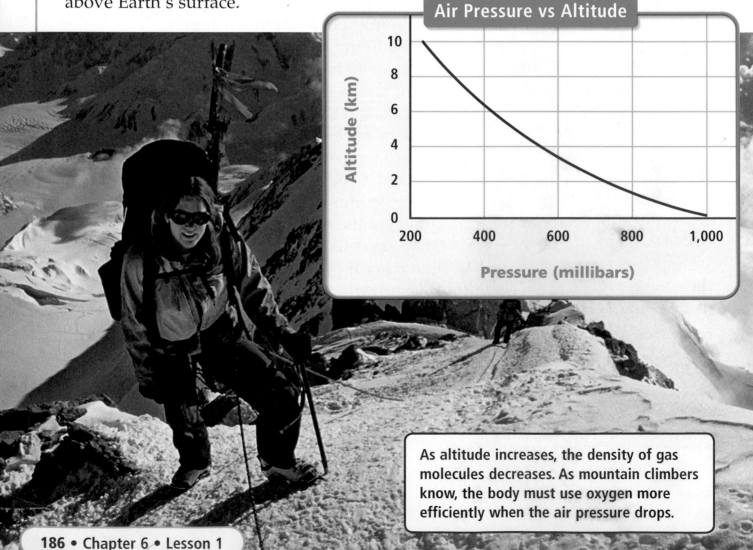

Air Pressure vs Altitude

As altitude increases, the density of gas molecules decreases. As mountain climbers know, the body must use oxygen more efficiently when the air pressure drops.

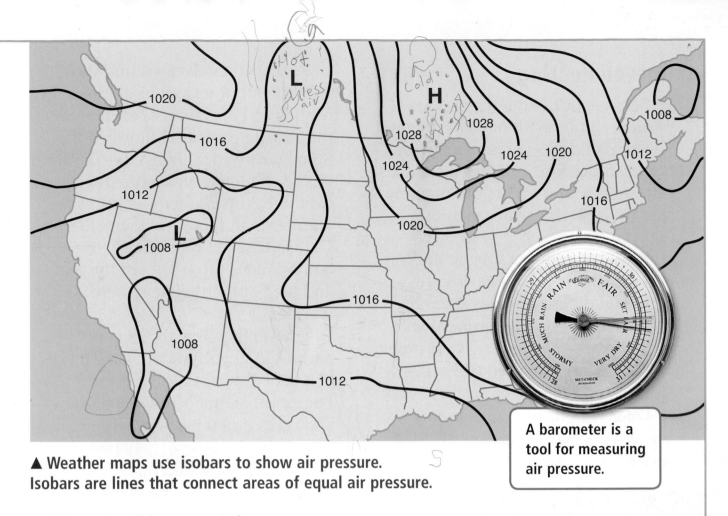

▲ Weather maps use isobars to show air pressure. Isobars are lines that connect areas of equal air pressure.

A barometer is a tool for measuring air pressure.

An aneroid barometer has a dial connected to a small sealed can that contains no air. Air pushes on the sides of the can. When air pressure increases, the sides of the can are pushed in, just as the sides of a rubber ball are pushed in when you squeeze it. When air pressure decreases, the sides move outward.

Any movement of the sides of the can causes the needle of the dial to move. A scale indicates the air pressure.

Pressure Systems Remember that air pressure at Earth's surface is always changing. When air at Earth's surface rises, air pressure decreases. A low-pressure system forms.

In a low-pressure system, air moves in toward the center of the system and then rises. In the Northern Hemisphere, the moving air rotates in a counterclockwise direction. In the Southern Hemisphere, it rotates in a clockwise direction.

When air sinks toward Earth's surface, air pressure increases and a high-pressure system forms. The air moves out from the center of highest pressure. In the Northern Hemisphere, the system rotates in a clockwise direction. In the Southern Hemisphere, the direction is reversed.

High-pressure and low-pressure systems are closely associated with much of the weather you experience. These systems move across Earth's surface, driven by winds that you'll read about later in this chapter.

DRAW CONCLUSIONS What change is indicated by a decrease in the height of the column of mercury in a barometer?

Uneven Heating

Because of Earth's shape, its motions, and the tilt of its axis, the Sun heats Earth's surface unevenly. For example, Earth rotates on its axis, causing day and night. The daytime side of Earth is warmer than the nighttime side.

Because Earth is a sphere, the Sun's rays strike different parts of Earth's surface at different angles. Near the equator, the Sun's rays strike at an angle close to 90 degrees. These direct rays are easily absorbed by Earth's surface and changed to heat.

Polar regions receive the same amount of energy as places near the equator. However, the Sun's rays strike the surface at angles much less than 90 degrees. The energy is spread over a wider area.

Because Earth is a sphere and has a tilted axis, the Sun's energy heats Earth unevenly. ▼

As Earth revolves around the Sun, the tilt of its axis also affects the heating of Earth's surface. Sometimes, the North Pole is tilted toward the Sun. During such times, the Northern Hemisphere receives more direct rays from the Sun, and temperatures are warmer than those in the Southern Hemisphere. At other times, the South Pole is tilted toward the Sun, and the Southern Hemisphere is warmer.

Uneven heating also occurs because different materials heat up and cool down at different rates. For example, the ocean heats up and cools down more slowly than does land. Because of concrete and pavement, cities tend to be warmer than surrounding rural areas.

DRAW CONCLUSIONS How would Earth be affected if its axis were not tilted?

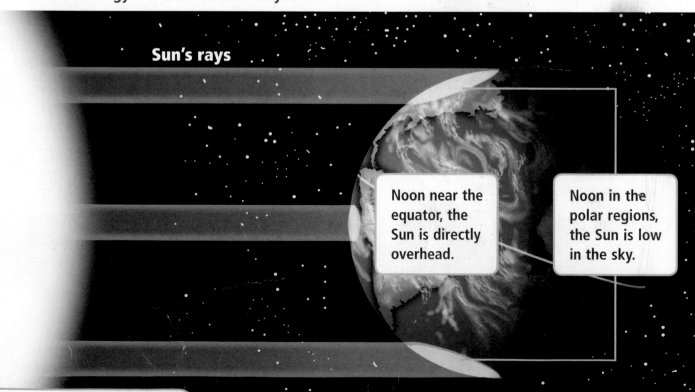

Sun's rays

Noon near the equator, the Sun is directly overhead.

Noon in the polar regions, the Sun is low in the sky.

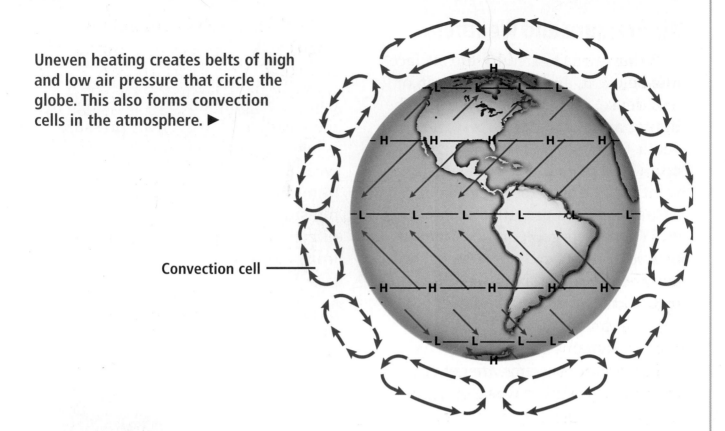

Uneven heating creates belts of high and low air pressure that circle the globe. This also forms convection cells in the atmosphere. ▶

Convection cell

Global Pressure Belts
Uneven heating causes differences in air pressure. Local high-pressure and low-pressure systems affect weather all across the globe.

When air is warmed, it becomes less dense than surrounding air. The warm air is forced upward, and air pressure in the region decreases.

In contrast, when air is cooled, it becomes denser than surrounding air. The dense air sinks, and pressure in the region increases.

The uneven heating also creates global belts of high pressure and low pressure. For example, Earth's surface near the equator is heated intensely by the Sun. The warm air above the surface rises, and its pressure decreases. As the map shows, the rising air forms a low-pressure belt near the equator.

Air near the poles receives the least amount of heat from the Sun. There, air sinks and cools, forming a high-pressure belt.

Four additional pressure belts span the globe. Two belts of high pressure form near 30° north and south latitude. Two belts of low pressure form at the 60° latitudes. These belts change somewhat from season to season.

The belts form loops of rising and falling air. Such a loop is called a convection cell. As you will learn as you read on, winds that blow over the surface are part of convection cells. Both global and local convection cells affect wind patterns and the weather.

 **DRAW CONCLUSIONS** Why does air near the equator rise?

Air Pressure and Weather

When air is heated by the surface just below it, air becomes lighter, or less dense, than surrounding air. The lighter air is forced up. As it rises, it cools. Clouds may form, which can often lead to rainy or even stormy weather. So low-pressure systems are associated with unsettled weather.

When air is cooled, it becomes heavier, or denser, than surrounding air. The dense air sinks, or settles toward the surface. Clouds cannot form under these conditions, so the sky remains clear. That's why high-pressure systems are generally associated with fair weather.

Weather forecasters track pressure systems, knowing that a change is usually accompanied by a change in the weather. However, air pressure is just one of the factors that affects weather. Other factors include humidity, which is the amount of moisture in the air, wind speed and direction, and air temperature. You'll learn more about weather forecasting later in this chapter.

DRAW CONCLUSIONS What type of weather would you expect if air pressure was rising? Explain.

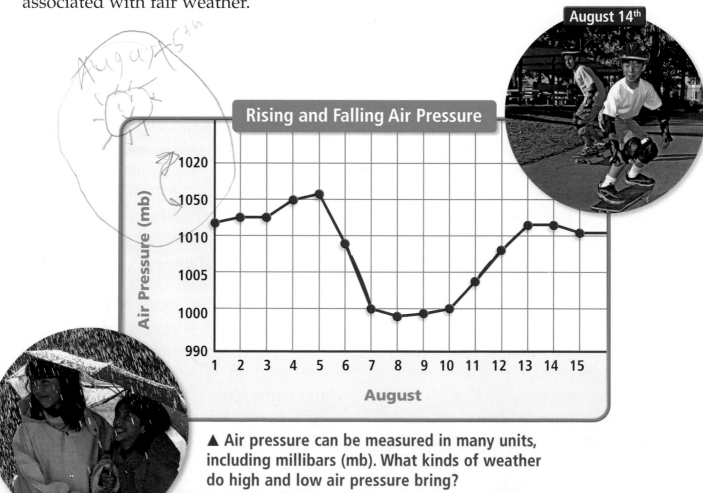

▲ Air pressure can be measured in many units, including millibars (mb). What kinds of weather do high and low air pressure bring?

Visual Summary

Earth's atmosphere is a mixture of gases that surrounds the planet. The atmosphere can be divided into four main layers.

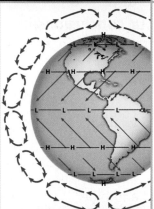

Air pressure is the force exerted by air in all directions. In general, air pressure decreases with altitude. The uneven heating of Earth creates global belts of air pressure.

JRH175MN 018 001
©Michael Newman / Photo Edit
ved by Eva Schorr on 11/14/2005

Air pressure is one of the factors that influences weather. High pressure brings fair weather. Low pressure brings rainy or stormy weather.

 STANDARDS

4.a., 4.e.

Technology
Visit **www.eduplace.com/cascp** to find out more about air pressure.

Reading Review

❶ **MAIN IDEA** Describe how air pressure changes with altitude—the distance from the surface.

❷ **VOCABULARY** Describe Earth's *atmosphere*. What is it made of?

❸ **READING SKILL** Will a parachute slow a sky diver more at a very high altitude or at a lower altitude? Explain.

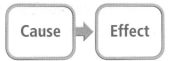

❹ **CRITICAL THINKING: Apply**
A pressure system has remained over an area for several weeks. Plants are wilting from lack of water. What type of pressure system is over the area?

❺ **INQUIRY SKILL: Use Models**
How might sharing air-pressure data gathered in different regions allow scientists to better predict the weather?

 TEST PRACTICE
Rising air usually causes _____.

  A. rising air pressure

  B. rising air temperature

  C. falling air pressure

  D. falling air temperature

 **STANDARDS**

1–2: 4.e., 3: 4.a., 4–5: 4.a., **Test Practice:** 4.e.

Why Does Air Move?

Building Background

Earth is constantly spinning, or rotating. This rotation affects wind direction. Because winds usually blow from west to east across the United States, most weather systems move in this direction, too.

 STANDARDS

4.a. *Students know* uneven heating of Earth causes air movements (convection currents).
6.g. Record data by using appropriate graphic representations (including charts, graphs, and labeled diagrams) and make inferences based on those data.

PREPARE TO INVESTIGATE

Inquiry Skill

Communicate When you report your investigation, include the tests you did, the data you collected, and your conclusions.

Materials

- goggles
- large, clear plastic container
- 2 test tubes
- water
- ice
- food coloring, red and blue

Science and Math Toolbox

For step 1, review **Making a Chart to Organize Data** on page H11.

Circling Around!

Procedure

STEP 1

1 **Collaborate** Work with a partner. Half-fill the large plastic container with water at room temperature. Half-fill one test tube with hot tap water. Add several drops of red food coloring to the hot water.

STEP 2

2 **Experiment** Place your thumb or index finger over the mouth of your test tube and gently lower it to the bottom of the container.

3 **Predict** Predict what will happen to the colored water when you remove your finger from the test tube. Have your partner record your predictions in your *Science Notebook.*

STEP 5

4 **Observe** Remove your finger and observe what happens to the colored water. Record your observations.

5 **Experiment** Switch roles with your partner and repeat the experiment. This time use ice water containing blue coloring and hold the test tube just below the surface of the water in the large container.

Conclusion

1. **Communicate** Draw and label diagrams of any movement you observed of the colored water.

2. **Infer** What caused the movement of the two samples of colored water?

Guided Inquiry

Experiment What changes could you make to your setup to produce a faster-moving current of colored water? Make the changes and **observe** the results.

VOCABULARY

jet stream	p. 198
land breeze	p. 196
mountain breeze	p. 195
planetary winds	p. 198
sea breeze	p. 196
valley breeze	p. 195

READING SKILL

Cause and Effect Copy and complete the graphic organizer to show the factors that cause local winds.

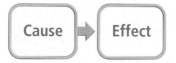

Cause ➡ Effect

STANDARDS

4.a. *Students know* uneven heating of Earth causes air movement (convection currents).
4.e. *Students know* that Earth's atmosphere exerts a pressure that decreases with distance above Earth's surface and that at any point it exerts this pressure equally in all directions.

Moving Air

MAIN IDEA Wind is caused by differences in air pressure. These differences create both local winds and planetary winds.

Winds and Convection Currents

Wind is the movement of air across Earth's surface. What causes air to move? The answer is differences in air pressure. Such differences are caused by the Sun's uneven heating of Earth's surface. Therefore, the Sun is the source of energy that drives winds.

Like air pressure, wind speed and direction often change with altitude. Winds tend to blow faster at higher altitudes than near the surface. That's because winds are slowed by trees, buildings, mountains, and other surface features. For the same reason, winds usually blow faster over smooth oceans than over hilly landscapes.

The wind that fills these sails is created by differences in air pressure. ▶

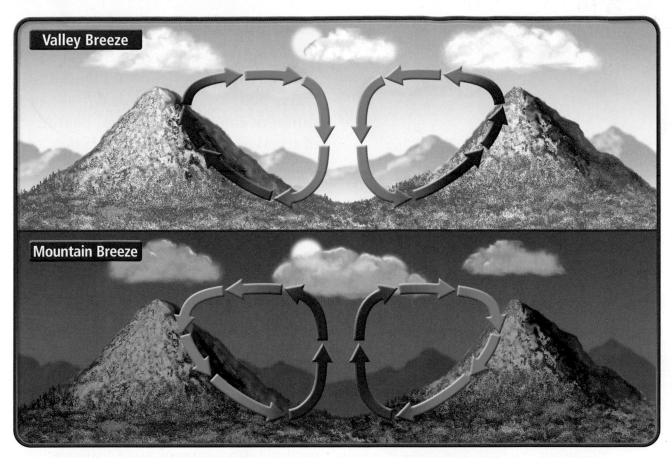

Valley Breeze

Mountain Breeze

▲ Valley breezes flow upslope during the day. Mountain breezes flow downslope during the night. Both breezes are part of convection currents.

Winds are also examples of convection currents. As you learned earlier, a convection current is a loop of moving air or water that transfers energy. Some loops of wind, called local winds, cover relatively small regions of the atmosphere. Global winds cover much larger regions.

Examples of local winds include mountain breezes and valley breezes. During the day, the slopes of the mountain are heated more than the valley floor. As warm air rises from the mountain slopes, cooler air from the valley moves up the slope to replace it, creating a **valley breeze**.

In the Northern Hemisphere, the Sun shines most strongly on slopes that face in a southerly direction, while north-facing slopes receive less sunlight. So valley breezes are particularly strong along south-facing slopes, and may be weak or not present at all on northern slopes.

At night, the direction of the wind reverses. The mountain slopes cool faster than the valley floor. The cooler, denser air above the slopes flows downhill, creating a **mountain breeze**. This cycle of mountain breezes and valley breezes is strongest during the summer, when skies are clear.

 **CAUSE AND EFFECT** What causes wind?

▲ Sea Breeze

A sea breeze flows from the water toward the land.

▲ Land Breeze

A land breeze flows from the land toward the water.

Land and Sea Breezes

If you've ever been to the shore, you may have noticed that land and water heat up and cool down at different rates. The unequal heating of the two different surface types results in local winds known as land breezes and sea breezes.

A **sea breeze** is a local wind that blows from water toward land during the day. During the day, land heats faster than water. As warm air rises over the land, cool air moves in from the water to take its place, creating a sea breeze.

At night, air moves in the opposite way. Land cools faster than water, so the air over the water is warmer. Warm air rises over the water, and cool air moves from land toward water. This movement of air from land toward water is a **land breeze**.

2 Condensation The mountains force the warm, moist air to rise into cooler parts of the atmosphere, causing the water vapor to condense.

1 Evaporation The Sun provides the energy for liquid water to become water vapor, an invisible gas.

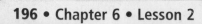

Mountain Effect

Why are some places rainier than others? Coastal mountains can provide part of the answer.

Mountains affect the water cycle—the movement of water between Earth's atmosphere and land. When water evaporates from oceans, it becomes water vapor in the air. The air just above the surface of the water holds a lot of water vapor. A sea breeze will carry that moist air toward the nearby land.

Where coastal mountains are present, the moist air is forced to move up over the mountains. At higher elevations, temperatures are colder, and water vapor condenses to form clouds. Rain or snow may fall along one side of the mountain, called the windward side. Some of the wettest places on Earth are on the windward sides of mountains.

When the air finally crosses to the other side of the mountain, it usually has very little moisture left. Dry winds sweep down this side of the mountain, which is called the leeward side. These dry areas on the leeward slopes are called rain shadows. Desert climates are common in rain shadows.

CAUSE AND EFFECT What effect might a thick cloud cover have on the strength of a sea breeze?

Mountain Effect

3 **Precipitation** As more vapor condenses, precipitation falls on the side of the mountains near the ocean.

4 **Dry Air** By the time the air passes over the mountains, almost all the moisture has fallen out of it.

Express Lab

Activity Card 16
See How Density Affects Buoyancy

197

Global Wind Patterns

Recall that the uneven heating of Earth's surface creates global pressure belts. Differences in air pressure in these belts result in **planetary winds.** Unlike local breezes, planetary winds are long-lasting circulation patterns that affect large areas of Earth.

As the diagram shows, three main wind belts cover each hemisphere. Notice that the winds do not travel in straight lines. They are directed by Earth's rotation and friction with the surface. Planetary winds curve to the right in the Northern Hemisphere and to the left in the Southern Hemisphere.

Another system of global winds occurs in the upper troposphere. These are fast-moving winds called **jet streams.** Winds in these narrow belts can blow as fast as 240 km/hr (149 mph).

Jet streams and planetary winds influence weather systems. For example, jet streams blow from west to east in a wavy pattern. They may shift slightly north or south, or may follow the same path for days on end. Jet streams "steer" weather systems from place to place, affecting both their speed and direction.

Planetary winds also affect the direction in which weather systems move. The prevailing westerlies blow from west to east across the United States. They have a great effect on the weather.

CAUSE AND EFFECT What causes planetary winds to follow curved paths?

Differences in air pressure and Earth's rotation create three major belts of planetary winds. ▶

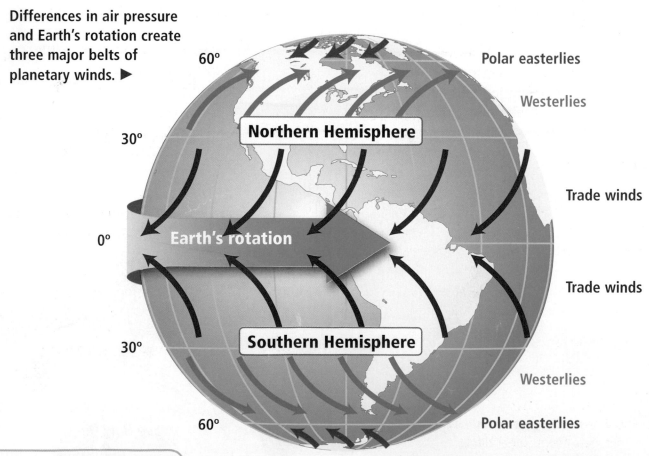

60°
Polar easterlies

Westerlies

Northern Hemisphere

30°

Trade winds

0°   Earth's rotation

Trade winds

30°

Southern Hemisphere

Westerlies

60°
Polar easterlies

Visual Summary

The Sun's uneven heating of Earth's surface causes differences in air pressure. Air moves from areas of high pressure to areas of low pressure.

Local winds include mountain and valley breezes, and land and sea breezes. All winds are parts of convection currents in the atmosphere.

Planetary winds are circulation patterns that affect large areas of Earth. Three belts of winds occur in each hemisphere.

 **STANDARDS**

4.a., 4.e.

 Technology
Visit **www.eduplace.com/cascp** to find out more about global winds.

Reading Review

❶ **MAIN IDEA** Why does air move through the atmosphere?

❷ **VOCABULARY** Write a paragraph describing *mountain breezes* and *valley breezes.*

❸ **READING SKILL** Describe how bodies of water can affect local winds. Use the words *sea breeze* and *land breeze* in your answer.

Cause ➔ Effect

❹ **CRITICAL THINKING: Apply** Airplanes sometimes fly at the same altitude at which jet streams blow. How would a jet stream affect a plane flying from New York to Los Angeles? Explain.

❺ **INQUIRY SKILL: Use Models** Describe the different precipitation patterns found on the windward and leeward side of a coastal mountain range. Include a diagram.

 TEST PRACTICE
What causes convection currents to form in Earth's atmosphere?

A. the jet stream

B. erosion and weathering

C. differences in oxygen levels

D. uneven heating of Earth's surface

 **STANDARDS**

1–3: 4.a., 4.e.; **4:** 4.a.; **5:** 4.a., 4.b.;
Test Practice: 4.a.

Sailing the Global Winds:
The Voyage of Sir Francis Drake

Hundreds of years ago, explorers from Europe sailed the oceans in huge ships. Their goals were fortune, adventure, and a world empire for their king or queen.

How could knowledge of Earth science have helped the explorers? In this play-within-a-play, Sir Francis Drake will learn the answer.

Characters

Narrator

Sir Francis Drake
English explorer

Thomas Doughty
a rival of Drake

Two Sailors

Miwok Indian
a Native American

Critic 1 and Critic 2
audience members

Professor Valero
a meteorologist from the present

STANDARD
4.a. *Students know* uneven heating of Earth causes air movements (convection currents).

READING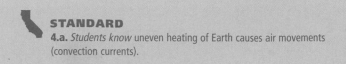

Narrator: Our story begins in December 1577, when Sir Francis Drake set sail from England with five ships. At first, he told the crew they were sailing to Egypt. But soon he revealed the truth.

Drake: Turn the fleet west! We're heading across the Atlantic to the Straits of Magellan. Then into the Pacific Ocean and around the world.

Doughty: Good heavens, how dangerous and unwise! King Philip of Spain claims the Pacific.

Drake: Not another word from you, Mr. Doughty, or I'll try you for treason.

Doughty: Now see here, Drake. When we left—

Drake: That's seven more words than I allowed. Now be quiet!

Critic 1 *(quietly to Critic 2)*: Did Drake really say that?

Critic 2: Maybe not, but these events did happen.

Narrator: Drake and his crew suffered severe storms.

Drake: Roll the sails! Tie the masts! *(aside)* That miserable Doughty, this is all his fault.

Narrator: Near the equator, they suffered hot, humid days with little or no wind.

First Sailor *(mopping his brow)*: The heat, the heat—I can't bear it. Can someone please invent air conditioning?

Second Sailor: Oh, go chew on a lime.

Narrator: They also suffered each other. The crew was ready to mutiny.

Doughty *(to sailors)*: My friends, make me your captain. We'll turn back to England right away.

Drake *(entering)*: What's that you were saying, Mr. Doughty?

Doughty *(slyly)*: Oh, nothing. We were just discussing the weather.

Sailors *(together)*: Oh yes, yes.

Critic 1: Didn't Drake and his crew know about global wind patterns?

Critic 2: Even if they did, I bet an Earth scientist could have helped them a lot.

Professor Valero *(entering)*: I agree!

Drake *(very surprised)*: Goodness gracious! Who are you?

Professor Valero: I am a meteorologist, a scientist who studies the weather. I live in the present day.

Critic 1: Professor, why do winds blow in patterns across the globe?

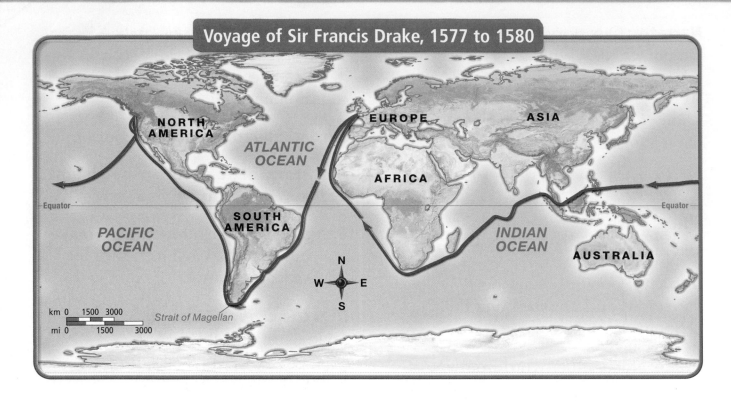

Voyage of Sir Francis Drake, 1577 to 1580

NORTH AMERICA

EUROPE

ASIA

ATLANTIC OCEAN

AFRICA

Equator

Equator

PACIFIC OCEAN

SOUTH AMERICA

INDIAN OCEAN

AUSTRALIA

N
W E
S

km 0   1500 3000
mi 0   1500 3000

Strait of Magellan

Professor Valero: Recall that the Sun heats Earth unevenly. For example, Earth is hottest at the equator and coldest at the poles.

First Sailor: We *know* that!

Professor Valero: There's more. You see, hot air rises and cold air sinks. As a result, Earth's air constantly moves through giant loops above the surface. These loops are called convection cells.

Critic 2: Ah yes, convection. That's the process that spreads heat through a gas or a liquid.

Professor Valero: Correct! The global winds are really part of large convection cells. Look at the diagram on page 189.

Narrator: Thank you, Professor.

(Professor bows, and exits.)

Drake *(confused)*: Page 189?! What does that mean?

Narrator: Eventually, Drake and his crew reached the Pacific Ocean, but with many losses.

First Sailor: One ship sank. Two others turned back to England.

Second Sailor: Some crew members were killed in fights with the Spanish.

First Sailor *(waving treasure)*: But we took their silver and other treasures!

Narrator: In June 1579, Drake and his remaining crew landed somewhere on the Pacific coast of North America.

Drake: I call this land "New Albion."

Miwok Indian (*entering*): Hello, visitors. I bid you welcome.

Drake: Thank you, sir. I don't understand your language, but let us meet together in peace.

Critic 1 (*aside*): New Albion might have been San Francisco, but more likely it was farther north.

Narrator: Drake stayed in New Albion for five weeks, then set sail across the Pacific. He returned to England in 1580, nearly three years after he left.

A recreation of Drake's ship, the *Golden Hinde*

Critic 2: So what do we think of Francis Drake?

Doughty: He was a liar and a pirate! He raided Spanish ships and settlements across South America.

Professor Valero (*entering*): Yet he treated Native Americans kindly and with respect. Most explorers from Europe were quite cruel.

First Sailor: I think Drake was very brave. He circled the globe using only boats, sails, and the global winds.

Second Sailor: Mr. Drake, do you care to have the last word?

All look about the stage for Drake.

Second Sailor: Where did he go?

Narrator: He returned to the history books, I believe. Look there to learn more about him.

Sharing Ideas

1. **READING CHECK** What made Drake's voyage difficult?

2. **WRITE ABOUT IT** What causes global wind patterns?

3. **TALK ABOUT IT** How do you judge Drake's actions?

How Are Weather Forecasts Made?

Building Background

Mt. Washington in New Hampshire is nicknamed "Home of the World's Worst Weather." Scientists here record weather conditions and conduct important research. The research includes testing instruments that can help scientists accurately predict the weather.

PREPARE TO INVESTIGATE

Inquiry Skill

Analyze Data When you analyze data, you look for patterns or other evidence that you can use to make an inference.

Materials

- anemometer
- barometer
- thermometer
- precipitation gauge
- local newspaper weather map and weather forecast

Science and Math Toolbox

For step 5, review **Using a Thermometer** on page H8.

STANDARDS

4.d. *Students know* how to use weather maps and data to predict local weather and know that weather forecasts depend on many variables.
6.f. Select appropriate tools (e.g. thermometers, metersticks, balances, and graduated cylinders) and make quantitative observations.

Local Forecast

Procedure

1. **Collaborate** Work in groups of three or four. In your *Science Notebook*, make a chart like the one shown.

2. **Measure** Set up the weather instruments outside. Select the tool used to measure air pressure and read it immediately. Read it again after one hour. Note whether the air pressure is rising, falling, or unchanged.

3. **Research** Use the Internet or other materials to learn about air-pressure readings. Find out what type of weather is associated with rising or falling air pressure. Predict the next day's weather based on your readings. Record your prediction.

4. **Analyze Data** Study a newspaper weather map and forecast. In your chart, record the newspaper's forecast.

5. **Measure** Using the weather instruments, record the temperature and precipitation amounts throughout the day. Also, observe and record cloud cover and wind conditions.

Conclusion

1. **Compare** How did your weather prediction compare to the newspaper's weather forecast?

2. **Analyze Data** Did the actual weather match the newspaper's forecast? Did it match your prediction? Explain.

STEP 1

	My Weather Prediction	Newspaper Weather Forecast	Actual Weather
Temperature			
Precipitation			
Wind			
Clouds			

STEP 2

STEP 5

Guided Inquiry

Ask questions Collect weather maps for several days. List questions you could answer if you **compare** the maps. Choose one question to investigate and write a report describing your investigation.

Learn by Reading

VOCABULARY

air mass	p. 208
front	p. 209
meteorologist	p. 210

READING SKILL

Main Idea and Details
As you read, write down the main idea and supporting details.

STANDARDS

4.d. *Students know* how to use weather maps and data to predict local weather and know that weather forecasts depend on many variables.
4.a. *Students know* uneven heating of Earth causes air movements (convection currents).

Predicting Weather

MAIN IDEA Scientists gather data about temperature, humidity, wind, and air pressure. They use this information to develop weather forecasts.

Weather Factors

On a fair day, you might describe the weather with just one word, such as *sunny* or *warm*. Scientists describe many different factors when they discuss the weather. Weather involves all of the conditions of the atmosphere at a certain time and place. These variables include temperature, amount of water vapor in the air, wind, and air pressure.

Temperature is a measure of how hot or cold the air is. Humidity refers to the amount of water vapor in air. High humidity can make the air feel damp and sticky. Wind, as you've learned, is the movement of air. Both wind speed and wind direction affect weather. Recall that air pressure is the force exerted by air on a given area.

Clear, sunny weather on Catalina Island

Weather Instruments Each weather factor can be measured using a different instrument. A thermometer measures the temperature of the air in degrees Celsius or Fahrenheit. A rain gauge collects and measures precipitation.

An anemometer (an uh MAHM uht uhr) is used to measure wind speed. A wind vane is used to measure wind direction. Air pressure, as you learned earlier, is measured with an instrument called a barometer.

🎯 **MAIN IDEA AND DETAILS** What variables influence the weather?

Barometer
A barometer measures air pressure in units called millibars.

Thermometer
A thermometer measures air temperature in degrees Celsius or degrees Fahrenheit.

Rain Gauge
A rain gauge measures the amount of precipitation that has fallen in an area.

Anemometer
The cups on an anemometer catch moving air, causing the instrument to spin in the wind. The anemometer records wind speed in kilometers per hour or miles per hour.

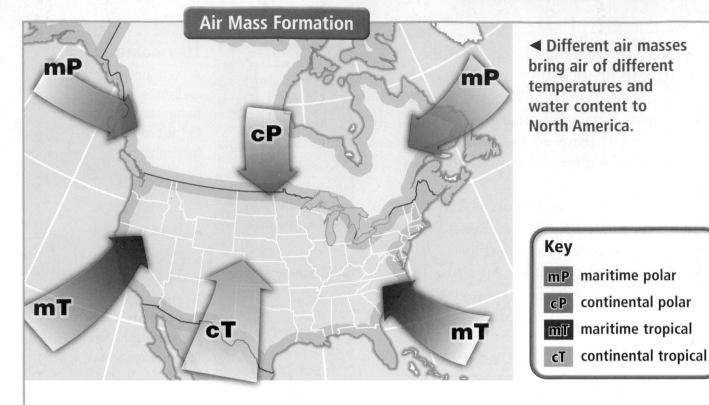

◄ Different air masses bring air of different temperatures and water content to North America.

Key

mP	maritime polar
cP	continental polar
mT	maritime tropical
cT	continental tropical

Air Masses

In the troposphere, where almost all weather occurs, large volumes of air called air masses are always moving. An **air mass** is a body of air that has about the same temperature and moisture throughout.

The temperature and moisture properties of an air mass depend on where it develops. Polar air masses form at middle to high latitudes and are generally cold. Tropical air masses form at low latitudes and tend to be warm. Continental air masses form over land and are generally dry. Maritime air masses form over water and are moist.

The map above shows the types of air masses that affect most of North America. Notice that pairs of letters are used to identify the different air masses. Taken together, each pair identifies the moisture and temperature properties of the air mass.

Lowercase, or small, letters *m* and *c* are used to represent *maritime* (moist) and *continental* (dry). Uppercase, or capital, letters *P* and *T* are used for *polar* (cold) and *tropical* (warm).

Find the mP and mT air masses on the map. These moist air masses are responsible for fog and drizzle in coastal regions. They also bring moisture to the center of the country.

Now locate the cP and cT air masses. These air masses, which form over land, contain little moisture. When such air masses move into an area, they generally bring fair weather.

Now look at the map to find the type of air mass responsible for weather in California. What are its properties? Is it humid or dry? Warm or cold? Does this agree with the type of weather your area experiences?

Fronts

When two air masses meet, a front forms. A weather **front** is the boundary between two air masses with different properties. The approach of a front is usually marked by a change in the weather. Such changes occur because cold air is denser than warm air.

A warm front forms when a warm air mass moves into an area of colder air. The warm air slides up and over the colder air, forming a gently sloping front. A warm front generally brings a large area of clouds and precipitation. On a weather map, a warm front is shown by a red line with red half circles along one side.

A cold front forms when cold air pushes its way into a warmer air mass. The dense cold air forces warmer air to rapidly rise high into the atmosphere. Clouds, heavy rain, and thunderstorms are produced along cold fronts. On a weather map, a cold front is shown by a blue line with blue triangles.

Sometimes when two air masses meet, neither mass moves forward. This type of front is called a stationary front. On a weather map, a stationary front is shown by a line with both red half circles and blue triangles along one side.

 **MAIN IDEA AND DETAILS** How do air masses affect weather?

▲ Warm Front
A warm front forms when warm air moves into an area. Steady light rains are common along warm fronts.

▲ Cold Front
A cold front forms when cold air moves into an area. Heavy rains often form along a cold front.

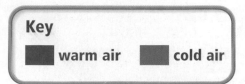

Key
warm air   cold air

Weather Maps

Meteorologists (meet ee uhr AHL uh jists) are scientists who study weather. They make observations and collect data. With the help of computers, they make weather maps like the one shown below. By studying a series of maps, meteorologists are able to forecast future weather conditions.

Like all maps, weather maps use symbols. A key is provided to help understand the map. Study the map and look for the symbols for fronts as described on page 209. Symbols are also used to indicate cloud cover and precipitation.

Notice that colors are used to represent air temperatures. In the United States, temperature is usually reported in degrees Fahrenheit.

Weather maps also identify areas of high and low air pressure. In a high-pressure system, indicated by an H, air sinks to the surface and moves away from the center. These systems usually bring clear weather.

In a low-pressure system, shown by an L, air at the center of the system rises. Air around the system moves in toward the center to take the place of the rising air. These systems often bring cloudy and rainy weather.

Most weather systems move from west to east across the United States. Knowing this, what kind of weather might you expect in Texas in a few days? How do you know?

Data from many sources are combined on weather maps. You can use them to forecast the weather. ▼

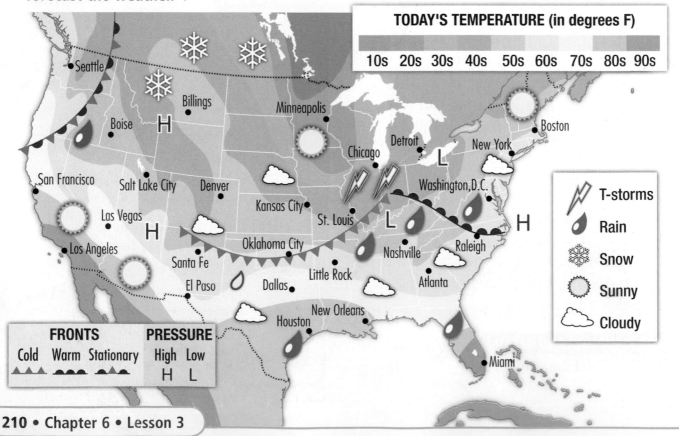

Radar
The colors show thunderstorms moving through Northern California and Nevada. ▼

Reno, NV

San Francisco

▲ Thunderstorm
Dense clouds like these are typical of thunderstorms. Meteorologists can identify such clouds on a radar image.

Weather Radar

Radar is a useful tool for observing and forecasting weather. A weather radar transmitter sends out radio signals. When these signals hit rain, snow, or other forms of precipitation, the signals bounce back to the transmitter and are recorded.

These radar signals can be used to create an image of a storm. You may have seen radar images used in weather reports on television.

The latest radar technology is called Doppler radar. Doppler radar not only picks up images of storms, but also determines the direction they are moving. This helps track and predict weather events, especially thunderstorms and tornadoes.

With this information, forecasters can warn people when severe storms are approaching. In the case of large, destructive storms, early warnings can save lives and property.

The radar image above shows a series of thunderstorms over Northern California and Nevada. A computer added the colors to show the strength of the storms. Yellow and red show the strongest parts. Green and blue show weaker parts.

As time passes, the storms may move through the region, becoming either stronger or weaker. Meteorologists monitor the radar images to predict what will happen.

 **MAIN IDEA AND DETAILS** What weather data can be observed with radar?

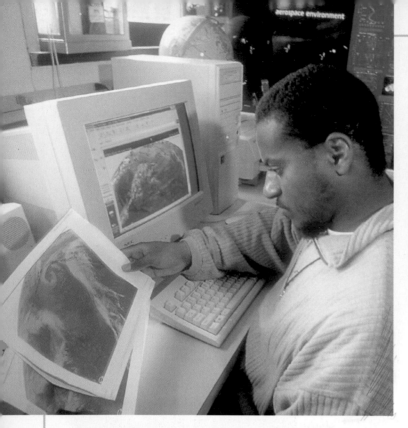

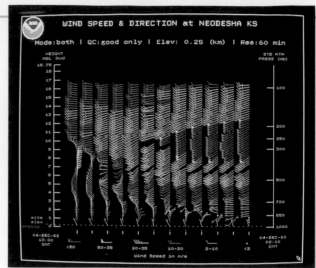

▲ A computer used Doppler radar data to make this graph. It shows wind speeds at different heights during a 12-hour period.

▲ Meteorologists use computers to help analyze complex atmospheric data. This helps them understand how weather forms and what it will do.

More Tools for Meteorologists

Today, a network of Doppler radar stations covers all of the United States and much of the world. Meteorologists even use the Internet to share data from these stations. Studying a radar image of the weather has never been easier!

Of course, meteorologists depend on more than just radar. They collect great amounts of data from weather stations worldwide. They compare these data to radar and satellite images. They also use computers to analyze the data and find trends or patterns.

As you learned earlier, meteorologists use many instruments to gather surface data. Thermometers, barometers, anemometers, wind vanes, and rain gauges all provide important weather information.

Weather conditions in the upper atmosphere are analyzed with the help of weather balloons. They can carry instruments high into the troposphere to collect data.

Weather satellites have become important tools for meteorologists. The earliest weather satellites, launched in the early 1960s, could send back only crude images of clouds. Satellite technology has advanced rapidly, and weather satellites today provide a wide array of data.

Express Lab

Activity Card 17
Forecast Weather

Today, weather satellites can measure cloud temperature, cloud density, water vapor, and land and ocean temperatures. They can also detect the presence and amount of dust and volcanic ash. This information helps meteorologists understand how the weather changes under different conditions.

By using all of these tools, meteorologists are able to track and predict the weather better than ever before. Even so, Earth's atmosphere remains a very complex system. Weather forecasts must take into account changes that are occurring in the upper troposphere, as well as near the surface.

Short-term forecasts predict the weather one or two days in advance. Such forecasts are usually accurate. However, long-term forecasts, which predict the weather more than three

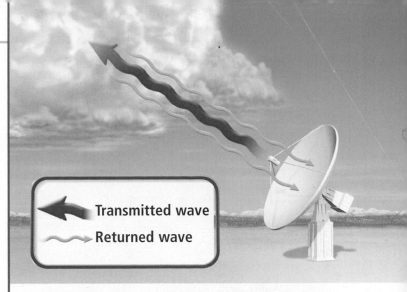

Transmitted wave

Returned wave

Radar works by "bouncing" radio waves off clouds. By comparing the transmitted and returned waves, a computer can plot a cloud's thickness, position, and motion.

days in advance, are not quite as accurate. Too many variables exist to predict long-term weather with certainty.

MAIN IDEA AND DETAILS What types of technology do meteorologists use to predict the weather?

Doppler radar stations, such as this one in Oklahoma, have become important weather forecasting tools.

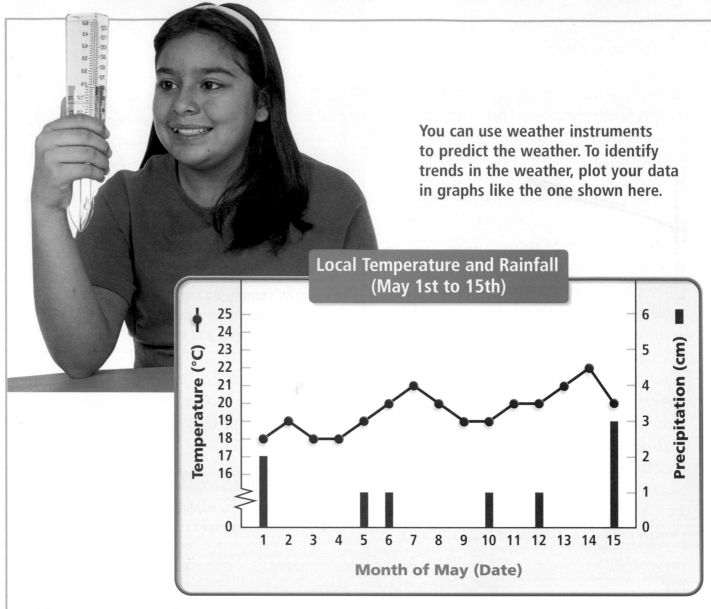

You can use weather instruments to predict the weather. To identify trends in the weather, plot your data in graphs like the one shown here.

Local Temperature and Rainfall (May 1st to 15th)

Month of May (Date)

Be a Weather Expert

Surfing, swimming, skateboarding, and hiking are great ways to spend a summer afternoon. Each of these activities, however, depends on the weather. Wouldn't it be nice to predict the weather so you can plan your day?

You don't have to be a scientist to forecast the weather. All you need are the instruments you read about earlier—a thermometer, a barometer, an anemometer, and a rain gauge. Armed with these tools, you can set up your own weather station at home or at school.

Once you've set up your weather station, use your *Science Notebook* to record weather data. You may find it helpful to graph the data so that you can better recognize patterns and trends.

Compare your results with forecasts in the local newspaper, on a television station, or on the Internet. With practice, you'll find that the accuracy of your forecasts will improve.

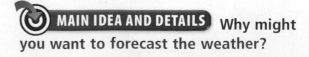 **MAIN IDEA AND DETAILS** Why might you want to forecast the weather?

Lesson Wrap-Up

Visual Summary

Weather involves different variables interacting in the atmosphere. These include temperature, amount of water vapor in the air, wind, and air pressure.

Air masses form in the troposphere. These air masses meet to form fronts, along which weather changes occur.

Different kinds of technology are used to predict the weather, including radar, satellites, and weather balloons.

STANDARDS
4.d., 4.a.

Technology
Visit **www.eduplace.com/cascp** to find out more about weather technology.

Reading Review

1 **MAIN IDEA** Why do scientists gather data about air temperature, humidity, wind speed and direction, and air pressure?

2 **VOCABULARY** What is an *air mass*? What determines its properties?

3 **READING SKILL** How does a warm front form? What kind of weather does it bring?

4 **CRITICAL THINKING: Evaluate** Why are radar images a useful weather tool?

5 **INQUIRY SKILL: Analyze Data** A weather map for your area shows an approaching front represented by a blue line with blue triangles. What kind of front is approaching? What kind of weather do you expect?

 TEST PRACTICE

Weather fronts form when _____.

A. air masses meet

B. air masses form

C. cold air rises

D. warm air sinks

 **STANDARDS**
1: 4.a., 4.d., **2–4:** 4.a., **5:** 4.d., **Test Practice:** 4.d.

215

What Causes Storms?

Building Background

On any given day, most places on Earth experience mild weather. Yet sometimes, the variables that affect weather combine to create storms. A storm is any sudden, extreme weather event.

Storms can bring huge amounts of rain or snow, often with high winds. Being prepared is the key to managing storms and surviving them.

PREPARE TO INVESTIGATE

Inquiry Skill

Record Data You can record and display the data you collect in the form of charts, graphs, maps, and labeled diagrams.

Materials

- outline map of eastern U.S.
- U.S. atlas or Internet access
- ruler

STANDARDS

4.c. *Students know* the causes and effects of different types of severe weather.
6.g. Record data by using appropriate graphic representations (including charts, graphs, and labeled diagrams) and make inferences based on those data.

Storm Reporter

BEFORE

Path of Hurricane Frances, 2004

Date	Storm Center	Top Wind (km/hr)
Sept 2	Bahama Islands	190
Sept 5, early A.M.	Port Salerno, FL	130
Sept 5, late P.M.	Tampa, FL	87
Sept 6	Tallahassee, FL	96
Sept 7	Dothan, AL	83
Sept 8	Rome, GA	46
Sept 9	Pittsburgh, PA	55

Hurricane Frances caused strong winds, heavy rains, and flooding over the southeast United States. Florida alone suffered over $8 billion in damage. A total of 42 storm-related deaths was reported.

DURING

Procedure

1. **Record Data** Use an atlas or the Internet to find the locations of the places listed in the chart. Then plot these places on the outline map. Draw a line to connect them.

2. **Observe** The photos show St. Lucie County, Florida, before, during, and after the hurricane. Record your observations.

AFTER

Conclusion

1. **Analyze** Describe the path of Hurricane Frances. When was it moving most slowly? When was it moving the fastest? Where were its winds the strongest?

2. **Draw Conclusions** What kind of damage can hurricanes cause? Cite evidence to support your answer.

3. **Compare** Compare the property damage from Hurricane Frances to the loss of human life. Were more or fewer people killed than you would have predicted?

Guided Inquiry

Ask Questions The southeast United States has suffered many serious hurricanes, including Hurricane Katrina in 2005. **Research** one of these hurricanes. Report on its strength, path, and the damage it caused.

217

VOCABULARY

blizzard	p. 221
hurricane	p. 222
thunderstorm	p. 218
tornado	p. 219

◎ READING SKILL

Sequence Use the graphic organizer to show the sequence of events that leads to a thunderstorm.

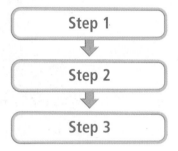

Step 1
↓
Step 2
↓
Step 3

STANDARD

4.c. *Students know* the causes and effects of different types of severe weather.

Severe Weather

MAIN IDEA Severe storms are associated with low-pressure systems. In these systems, warm, moist air rises and cools. Water vapor in the cooling air condenses, forming clouds followed by precipitation.

Thunderstorms

A **thunderstorm** is a storm that delivers lightning, thunder, and heavy rains. It is one of the most common types of severe weather, especially during a warm, humid summer.

Certain conditions must be present for any dangerous storm to form. In the case of a thunderstorm, three things must happen. There must be plenty of moisture in the air. There must be an approaching cold front or extreme heating of the surface to force air to rise rapidly. And the rising air must remain warmer than the surrounding air. When these factors are present, the moisture in the rising air condenses, allowing clouds to form.

How Thunderstorms Form

Warm, moist air rises rapidly upward in the cumulus stage.	Eventually, the cloud builds into a tall cumulonimbus cloud—a thunderhead.	Heavy rains, lightning, and strong winds are associated with the mature stage.

A tornado can develop with a thunderstorm.

Lightning occurs when an opposite charge builds up inside a cloud or between the cloud and the ground.

Thunderstorms often form along cold fronts. At cold fronts, cold air moving at the surface forces warm, moist air to rise rapidly. This action marks the first stage of a thunderstorm, known as the cumulus stage.

In the next stage, called the mature stage, a tall, dark cumulonimbus cloud forms. This type of cloud can extend as high as 15 km (9 mi). Heavy rains and strong winds are part of this stage.

Lightning is also part of the mature stage of a thunderstorm. Lightning occurs when opposite electric charges separate inside a cloud or between the cloud and the ground. The difference in charges builds up until, finally, a powerful electric discharge occurs, releasing a great deal of energy. We see this discharge as a flash of lightning. Lightning heats the air around it, causing a boom of thunder as the air quickly expands and contracts.

In the final stage of a thunderstorm, the air becomes too cool to continue rising. The storm loses energy and eventually dies out.

Thunderstorms are associated with many dangers, including floods, high winds, lightning strikes, and hail. However, the greatest potential danger of a severe thunderstorm is a tornado. A **tornado** is a narrow, spinning column of very fast-moving air. You'll learn more about tornadoes in the Extreme Science feature that follows this lesson.

SEQUENCE Sequence the steps involved in a discharge of lightning.

Floods and Droughts

One of the most common—and costly—dangers associated with severe weather is a flood. A flood forms when a river overflows its banks. It also may follow a short-lasting, but severe thunderstorm. Or it may happen if a front stalls over an area, dropping light but steady rain for several days.

A flood may also follow a sharp warming trend in the spring. Snow on mountains melts quickly. The snowmelt enters streams and rivers, overflowing their banks.

In 1993, the Mississippi River flooded due to a series of severe summer thunderstorms. More than 50 towns along the river were covered by water. More than 45,000 homes were lost, and dozens of people died. The flood caused an estimated $10 billion of damage.

The opposite extreme of a flood is a drought. A drought is a long period of below-normal rainfall. Unlike floods, droughts are associated with high-pressure systems. Recall that air sinks in a high-pressure system. Because the air is sinking, condensation cannot occur and precipitation cannot form.

Droughts can kill crops and drain away water reserves. Communities can manage droughts by conserving water. Often, they will ban lawn sprinklers, car washes, and many activities that use water.

▲ Floods are one of the most common dangers associated with severe weather.

▲ Droughts occur when a high-pressure system stalls over an area for weeks. Ponds and streams may dry up.

SEQUENCE Sequence the events that lead to a drought.

Blizzards

If you live in a cold climate, you know that thunderstorms do not occur very often in winter. There is, however, a type of severe storm that can be just as dangerous.

A **blizzard** is a snowstorm with strong winds and low temperatures. It forms much like a thunderstorm. However, it does not usually bring lightning and thunder.

Like many types of severe storms, blizzards are associated with low-pressure systems. In some regions of the United States, strong, cold winds often blow from north to south during the winter. When these cold winds meet warmer, moist air from the south, the moist air rises. Because temperatures are low, the resulting precipitation falls as snow.

In a blizzard, snowfall is very heavy and winds are very strong. In the "Blizzard of '78," for example, parts of New England received more than 127 cm (50 in.) of snow. The snow formed huge drifts, blown about by winds up to 96 km/hr (60 mph).

In the United States, blizzards are common wherever the winters are cold, such as the Northeast and Great Plains. They also occur in mountainous regions, such as the Sierra Nevada range in California.

The combination of high winds, cold temperatures, and deep snow make blizzards extremely dangerous. People can freeze to death if caught outside during the storm. Moving about is difficult because visibility is

▲ Blizzards bring high winds, heavy snowfall, and low temperatures.

low. Because of deep, drifted snow, it can take a community many days to recover from a blizzard.

To clean snow from roads and highways, many cities and states run a fleet of snowplows, such as the one shown on page 216. Drivers often plow snow all day or all night to keep highways clear.

Many people welcome blizzards, especially in the mountains, because of the snow they bring. Skiing and snowboarding are popular winter sports.

Express Lab

Activity Card 18
Demonstrate Wind Movement

221

Hurricanes

Hurricanes are the most powerful storms on Earth. They form over warm ocean waters in the tropics. These large, rotating storms can grow in size from 160 km (100 mi) in diameter to 1,500 km (930 mi)!

A **hurricane** is a storm with sustained wind speeds near its center of at least 119 km/hr (74 mph). Similar storms are called typhoons in the Pacific Ocean and cyclones in the Indian Ocean.

Water vapor is necessary for hurricanes to form and grow in strength. So it makes sense that a hurricane begins as a low-pressure system over warm, tropical waters. As the system strengthens, thunderstorms begin to rotate around the low-pressure zone. As rotation intensifies, the thunderstorms increase in size.

As warm, moist air continues to rise, pressure in the center of the system falls steadily as the storm strengthens. The warm ocean waters contribute an endless supply of water vapor, and the thunderstorms continue to build. This process intensifies the low pressure at the center of the storm. The hurricane takes the thermal energy from the ocean and turns it into wind.

The hurricane continues to grow in size and intensity while over warm, tropical waters. When the hurricane moves over cooler water, there is less water vapor to fuel the storm, and it begins to weaken. If the storm moves over land, its source of water vapor is cut off, and the storm rapidly loses energy. Friction between the ground and the air mass also slows the storm.

 **SEQUENCE** How does a hurricane begin?

Cross Section of a Hurricane

Air sinks through the eye—the calm, low-pressure center of a hurricane. Air swirls upward just outside the eye, forming extremely strong winds. Thick clouds around the eye bring heavy rains, as do rain bands at the edge of the storm.

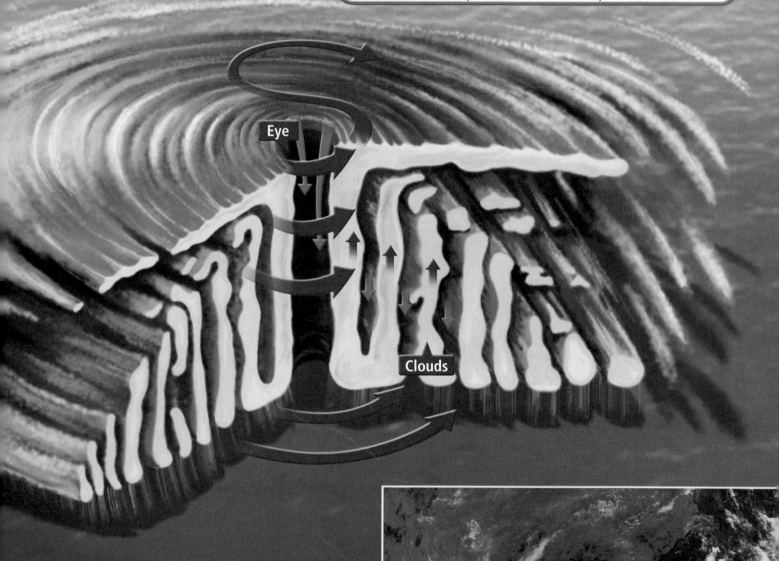

Hurricane Classification

Strength	Damage	Winds
Category 1	Minimal	74–95 mph
Category 2	Moderate	96–110 mph
Category 3	Extensive	111–130 mph
Category 4	Extreme	131–155 mph
Category 5	Catastrophic	> 155 mph

Warm, moist air

Cooler air

Eye

Clouds

This photo from space shows the swirling clouds of a hurricane in the Gulf of Mexico. ▶

Aftermath!

In January 2005, California experienced heavy rains and snowfalls. The steady precipitation saturated the soil on hillsides. Eventually, great quantities of mud slid rapidly down the hills. In La Conchita, California, a mudslide destroyed 15 homes and killed 10 people.

Mudslides are just one of the hazards of severe weather. Hail from thunderstorms can destroy crops and damage property. Lightning can spark forest fires. Strong winds from hurricanes and tornadoes can uproot trees and flatten buildings. Along the shore, huge walls of water, called storm surges, are pushed inland by the wind. They cause severe flooding and extensive damage.

When an area is struck by a severe weather event, the damage to life and

▲ FEMA officials work with communities to help them recover from natural disasters.

property can cost billions of dollars. The Federal Emergency Management Agency (FEMA) was created to help areas deal with natural disasters.

 **SEQUENCE** How can mudslides form?

Heavy rains can cause mudslides such as this one in Laguna Beach, California. ▼

Lesson Wrap-Up

Visual Summary

Thunderstorms bring strong winds, heavy rains, lightning, and thunder. Tornadoes can develop from thunderstorms.

Blizzards are severe snowstorms with heavy snow, high winds, and low temperatures. Blizzards form much like thunderstorms, but in cold weather.

Hurricanes are the most powerful storms on Earth. They form over warm ocean waters in the tropics.

 **STANDARD**

4.c.

Technology
Visit **www.eduplace.com/cascp** to find out more about severe weather.

Reading Review

1 MAIN IDEA What is a common factor associated with most severe storms?

2 VOCABULARY Write a brief paragraph comparing a *hurricane* and a *tornado*.

3 READING SKILL Describe the steps involved in the formation of a thunderstorm.

> Step 1
>
> Step 2
>
> Step 3

4 CRITICAL THINKING: Analyze How are cold fronts related to thunderstorms?

5 INQUIRY SKILL: Record Data What if you were in charge of a network of weather stations in the southeast United States? How would you organize the stations to record data on a hurricane?

✓ **TEST PRACTICE**
Which of the following is associated with a high-pressure system?

A. hurricane

B. thunderstorm

C. tornado

D. drought

 STANDARD

1–5: 4.c., **Test Practice:** 4.c.

225

Twister!

It can rumble like an avalanche. It can roar like a freight train. It can scream like a jet engine. Few things can withstand its fury. It's the mightiest wind on earth— the tornado!

Tornadoes are concentrated, twisting columns of air. They hang from the bottom of special, rotating thunderstorms called supercells. Tornadoes contain the fastest winds on earth. The most powerful reach over 482 km/hr (300 mph)!

In April of 1974, the United States had the biggest tornado outbreak in its history. A total of 148 tornadoes hit 13 states. Called the Super Outbreak, this storm system produced 30 devastating F4 and six incredible F5 tornadoes.

Fujita Scale

F0	40-72 mph	light
F1	73-112 mph	moderate
F2	113-157 mph	considerable
F3	158-206 mph	severe
F4	207-260 mph	devastating
F5	261-318 mph	incredible

The Fujita scale gives scientists a way to classify tornadoes based on wind damage.

Wedge The most powerful tornadoes often have a wedge shape. The largest wedges can span a mile or two across.

Rope Many tornadoes end their lives in what is called the rope stage. Although thin and strung out, the winds of a roped-out tornado can still do great damage.

Writing Journal

The highest wind ever recorded in a tornado was 482 km/hr. In your journal, calculate how many times faster this is than the top highway speed limit of 70 mph in California.

Math in Science

Use a thermometer to track temperature twice each day for one school week. Read and record the temperature just before you leave for school and when you return home. Copy the table to record the temperatures.

When was the highest temperature? When was the lowest temperature? Use the formula below to convert the readings to degrees Celsius.

$$°C = \frac{5}{9}(°F - 32)$$

Day	AM Temp	PM Temp
Monday		
Tuesday		
Wednesday		
Thursday		
Friday		

Writing in Science Narrative

Write a story about a vacation trip in which the weather plays a major role. Explain how weather changes or weather-related events affect travel and vacation activities.

People in Science

California

Harry Yeh

A tsunami is a huge ocean wave caused by an earthquake or volcanic eruption on the ocean floor. In 2003, a strong earthquake struck off the coast of Japan. Yet it caused only a mild tsunami, with waves only about four meters high.

How can tsunamis be predicted accurately? Professor Harry Yeh is trying to find out. After earning his doctorate from the University of California at Berkeley, Yeh has become one of the world's experts in tsunamis and their effects.

Yeh points out that many factors affect tsunamis. Among them are the source of the earthquake and the shape of the ocean floor.

Yeh's advice for surviving tsunamis is very simple. If a tsunami warning is issued for your area, move quickly to high ground!

To study tsunamis, Professor Yeh builds models like this one. A tsunami is a huge wave set in motion by an earthquake. ▼

Review and Test Practice

Vocabulary

Complete each sentence with a term from the list.

1. A scientist who studies weather is a(n) _____.

2. The boundary between two air masses of different properties is a(n) _____.

3. A snowstorm with strong winds and low temperatures is a(n) _____.

4. The force exerted by air in all directions is _____.

5. At night, air moves from the land toward the ocean, forming a(n) _____.

6. The overall condition of the atmosphere at a given time and place is called _____.

7. The mixture of gases that surrounds Earth is the _____.

8. The most powerful type of storm is a(n) _____.

9. A body of air that has the same temperature and moisture conditions throughout is called a(n) _____.

10. During the day, air moving up a mountain slope is a(n) _____.

air mass p. 208
air pressure p. 186
atmosphere p. 184
blizzard p. 221
front p. 209
hurricane p. 222
jet stream p. 198
land breeze p. 196
meteorologist p. 210
mountain breeze p. 195
planetary winds p. 198
sea breeze p. 196
thunderstorm p. 218
tornado p. 219
valley breeze p. 195
weather p. 184

Test Practice

Write the letter of the best answer choice.

11. A _____ is a narrow, spinning column of fast-moving air.

  A. hurricane
  B. thunderstorm
  C. tornado
  D. drought

12. Which of the following is NOT a local wind?

  A. trade wind
  B. sea breeze
  C. land breeze
  D. mountain breeze

13. High-altitude winds, called _____, move weather systems across the United States.

  A. trade winds
  B. polar easterlies
  C. hurricanes
  D. jet streams

14. A sea breeze occurs when air moves _____.

  A. out to sea
  B. toward land
  C. up mountain slopes
  D. downslope

15. **Analyze Data** Suppose you lived in Tampa, Florida, and were planning a picnic. The morning weather report includes the radar image below. How could the weather affect your plans?

16. Which tools would you use to measure the following weather conditions: temperature, air pressure, wind speed, and rainfall amount?

Map the Concept

The chart shows three pairs of terms. Complete the chart to compare and contrast the terms.

Land Breeze	Sea Breeze	Warm Front	Cold Front	Valley Breeze	Mountain Breeze

17. **Synthesize** The amounts of certain gases in the atmosphere can change from time to time. Why do you think this is so?

18. **Evaluate** Which is more reliable—a short-term weather forecast or a long-term weather forecast for your area? Explain.

19. **Analyze** What changes in the atmosphere lead to the formation of thunderstorms?

20. **Synthesize** How do computers help meteorologists to analyze weather data?

Performance Assessment

Use Weather Maps

Predict tomorrow's weather for a specific place on today's weather map. Compare your prediction to the actual weather that place experiences.

Writing Journal

Review and revise your answers to the questions at the beginning of this chapter.

 STANDARDS

1: 4.d., **2:** 4.d., **3:** 4.d., **4:** 4.e., **5:** 4.a., **6:** 4.b., **7:** 4.e., **8:** 4.c.,
9: 4.a., **10:** 4.a., **11:** 4.c., **12:** 4.a., **13:** 4.a., **14:** 4.a., **15:** 4.c.,
16: 6.f., **Map the Concept:** 4.a., **17:** 4.b., **18:** 4.d., **19:** 4.c.,
20: 4.d., **Performance Assessment:** 6.g.

Chapter 7

The Solar System

Earth, viewed from the Moon

LESSON 1

What forms from a spinning cloud of gas and dust, like the Orion Nebula shown here?

LESSON 2

In 1969, astronauts first stepped foot on the Moon. What did they find there?

LESSON 3

Earth has only one moon, a small number compared to other planets. Which planet has more than 60 moons?

LESSON 4

This photo was taken in the space shuttle as it orbited Earth. Why can astronauts "float" in outer space?

Writing Journal

In your Writing Journal, write or draw answers to each question.

Vocabulary Preview

Vocabulary

Glossary

Vocabulary Skill

Sentence Context

sunspot

When you see a word that you do not understand, read the sentence that contains the word, as well as the sentences before and after the word. You can often figure out the meaning of new words by looking for clues in the text.

comet
a small, orbiting body made of dust, ice, and frozen gases

planet
a large body that revolves around the Sun or another star

sunspot
a dark area on the Sun's surface

meteor

a chunk of matter that enters Earth's atmosphere and is heated by friction with the air

Start with Your Standards

Standard Set 5. Earth Sciences (The Solar System)

5.a. *Students know* the Sun, an average star, is the central and largest body in the solar system and is composed primarily of hydrogen and helium.

5.b. *Students know* the solar system includes the planet Earth, the Moon, the Sun, eight other planets and their satellites, and smaller objects, such as asteroids and comets.

5.c. *Students know* the path of a planet around the Sun is due to the gravitational attraction between the Sun and the planet.

The following Set 6: Investigation and Experimentation standards are covered in this chapter: 6.b., 6.g., 6.h.

What Is Earth's Sun Like?

Building Background

The Sun is the closest star to Earth. Other stars are bigger and brighter, or younger or older. But no star is more important to life on Earth. Almost all of Earth's energy comes from the Sun.

 STANDARDS

5.a. *Students know* the Sun, an average star, is the central and largest body in the solar system and is composed primarily of hydrogen and helium.
6.g. Record data by using appropriate graphic representations (including charts, graphs, and labeled diagrams) and make inferences based on those data.

PREPARE TO INVESTIGATE

Inquiry Skill

Compare When you compare, you determine how two or more events are similar and how they are different.

Materials

- 4 sheets of construction paper
- tape
- flashlight
- pencil or pen

Science and Math Toolbox

For steps 1 and 3, review **Measurements** on page H16.

Sun Test

Procedure

STEP 2

1. **Use Models** Tape four sheets of construction paper together to form one very large sheet. The large sheet represents space. The flashlight represents the Sun.

2. **Measure** Hold the flashlight 1 cm directly over the center of the sheet. While one partner holds the flashlight, the other traces the circle of light that the flashlight forms on the paper. Draw a dot on this circle and label it "Mercury."

STEP 3

3. **Measure** Raise the flashlight until the circle is about two and a half times wider than the first circle. Trace this circle. Draw a dot on the circle and label it "Earth."

4. Raise the flashlight again until the circle of light reaches the edges of the paper. Trace this circle. Draw a dot on the circle and label it "Jupiter."

STEP 4

5. **Compare** Move the flashlight up and down to fill each of the three circles again. Compare the different amounts of light in each circle. Record your observations in your *Science Notebook.*

Conclusion

1. **Analyze Data** In your model, how does sunlight compare on Mercury, Earth, and Jupiter?

2. **Infer** How would Earth change if its orbit moved closer to the Sun? How would it change if it moved farther away?

Guided Inquiry

Ask Questions What questions do you have about stars and planets? Which of those questions do you think scientists can investigate? **Research** the answers and report back to the class.

VOCABULARY

nuclear fusion   p. 240

sunspot   p. 239

🎯 READING SKILL

Cause and Effect As you read, use a diagram to list how the Sun's energy affects Earth.

STANDARDS

5.a. *Students know* the Sun, an average star, is the central and largest body in the solar system and is composed primarily of hydrogen and helium.
2.f. *Students know* plants use carbon dioxide (CO_2) and energy from sunlight to build molecules of sugar and release oxygen.

The Sun is a constant source of both light and heat. ▼

The Sun

MAIN IDEA The Sun is the largest and most massive body in the solar system. It provides nearly all the energy needed to sustain life on Earth.

An Average Star

Think about all the stars you can see on a clear night. In addition to these stars, there are billions more you can't see—even with a telescope! There also is one star you see during the day.

The Sun, the closest star to Earth, is a yellow star. It is neither the hottest nor the coolest star. Compared to other stars, the Sun is medium-sized. Study the diagram on the next page to see the range of star colors and temperatures.

The Sun is a giant sphere of hot, glowing gas, called plasma. Its average distance from Earth is 150 million km (93 million mi). The Sun is about 4.6 billion years old. It is so large that more than 1 million Earths could fit inside it!

The Sun is the central body of the solar system. Its gravitational pull is strong enough to keep Earth and the other objects in the solar system in orbit around it. The Sun is the main source of energy for Earth and is essential to life on this planet.

Sun Statistics

Diameter	1,390,000 km
Mass	2×10^{27} metric tons
Surface Temperature	5,500°C
Core Temperature	15,000,000°C
Composition	74% hydrogen, 24% helium, 2% other elements
Age	4.6 billion years

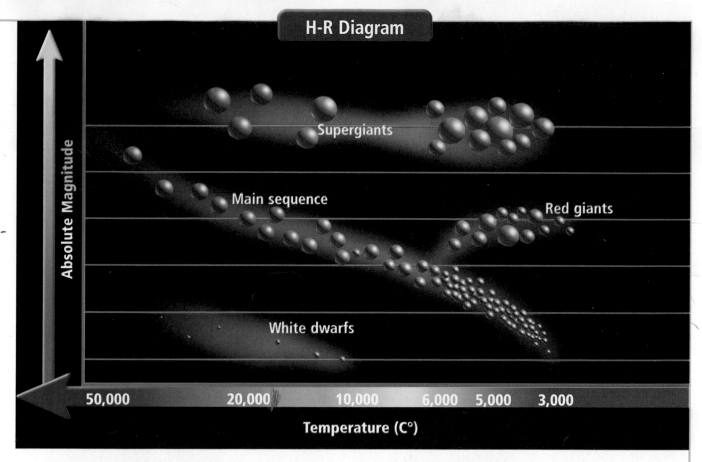

H-R Diagram

Absolute Magnitude

Supergiants

Main sequence

Red giants

White dwarfs

Temperature (C°)

50,000 20,000 10,000 6,000 5,000 3,000

▲ Astronomers Hertzsprung and Russell made this graph of the stars. It shows how a star's temperature relates to its brightness (magnitude).

Sunspots are dark areas on the Sun's surface. They appear dark because they are cooler than surrounding areas. Sunspots often occur in cycles that reach a peak roughly every 11 years. Some scientists suggest that sunspot activity influences climate changes on Earth. Periods of low and high sunspot activity correspond to temperature changes on Earth.

Solar flares are powerful eruptions of particles that shoot into space. The erupting particles strengthen the solar wind, which is made up of fast-moving gases that travel through space. The solar wind can disrupt radio waves. It also causes auroras. Auroras are colorful lights that appear in the sky near Earth's polar regions.

A solar prominence is a huge arc of gas that extends high into the Sun's atmosphere. This feature may hang like a bright curtain for days. Both solar flares and prominences are common during high sunspot activity. Thus, their appearance also varies on an 11-year cycle.

 **CAUSE AND EFFECT** Why do the planets orbit the Sun?

Express Lab

Activity Card 19
See Light Intensity

239

Energy from the Sun

Like other stars, the Sun is made mostly of hydrogen and helium. These are the two lightest elements. Although the Sun is by far the most massive body in the solar system, it is only one-fourth as dense as Earth. Remember that Earth is a rocky planet.

As you might imagine, the Sun is extremely hot. You probably consider it a "hot" day when the temperature rises to near 38°C (100°F). However, the temperature on the surface of the Sun is 5,500°C. At the Sun's core, or innermost layer, the temperature is about 15,000,000°C. Here, hydrogen is converted into helium through a process called nuclear fusion.

In **nuclear fusion,** the nuclei of atoms fuse together to form a larger nucleus. A huge amount of energy is released in the process.

Where does this energy come from? It comes from a small amount of matter in the original nuclei. This "lost" mass is converted into energy!

Physicist Albert Einstein discovered an equation that calculates this energy. The equation is $E = mc^2$, in which E is energy, m is the lost mass, and c is the speed of light.

All stars produce energy by nuclear fusion. As you'll learn later, the types of elements used in nuclear fusion change as a star ages.

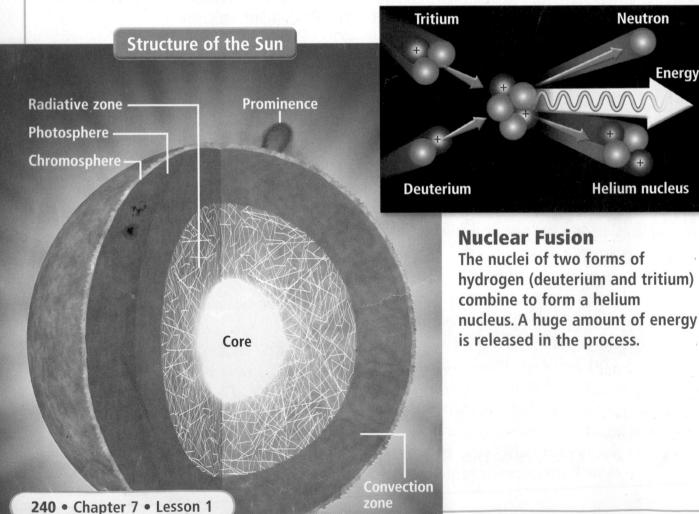

Structure of the Sun

Radiative zone
Photosphere
Chromosphere
Prominence
Core
Convection zone

Tritium
Neutron
Energy
Deuterium
Helium nucleus

Nuclear Fusion
The nuclei of two forms of hydrogen (deuterium and tritium) combine to form a helium nucleus. A huge amount of energy is released in the process.

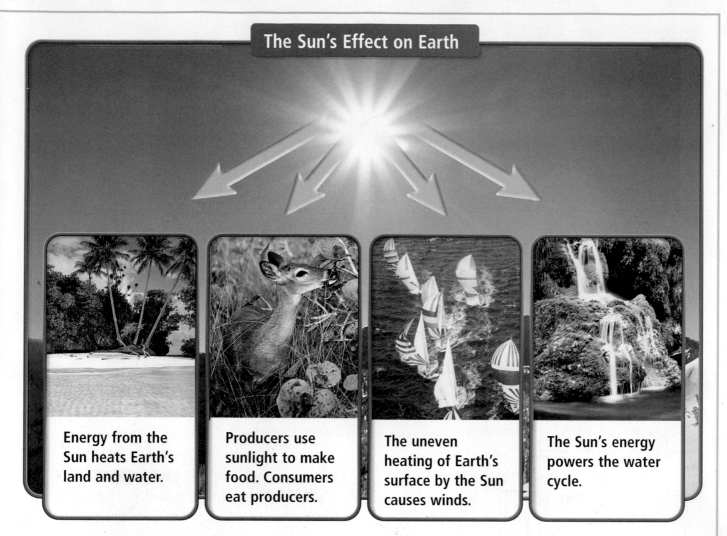

Energy from the Sun heats Earth's land and water.

Producers use sunlight to make food. Consumers eat producers.

The uneven heating of Earth's surface by the Sun causes winds.

The Sun's energy powers the water cycle.

The Sun is the main source of energy on Earth. Solar radiation provides the heat that keeps Earth warm and livable. In fact, temperatures on Earth would be much hotter were it not for the oceans and the atmosphere. These features absorb solar energy and help to moderate temperatures.

What processes does the Sun power? One is photosynthesis. During photosynthesis, green plants and algae use sunlight to produce food. They store some of the energy. When a consumer, such as a deer, eats plants, some of the stored energy is transferred to the deer. When another animal eats the deer, some of the stored energy is transferred again.

In this way, the Sun is the energy source for nearly all living things.

The Sun also drives the water cycle. It causes water on Earth's surface to evaporate, forming water vapor. The water vapor rises into the air, where it condenses into clouds. Eventually, it falls to Earth as precipitation.

Winds also form because of the Sun. Winds blow from regions of high air pressure to low air pressure. Air pressure differences form because of the Sun's uneven heating of Earth's surface.

CAUSE AND EFFECT How is energy produced during nuclear fusion?

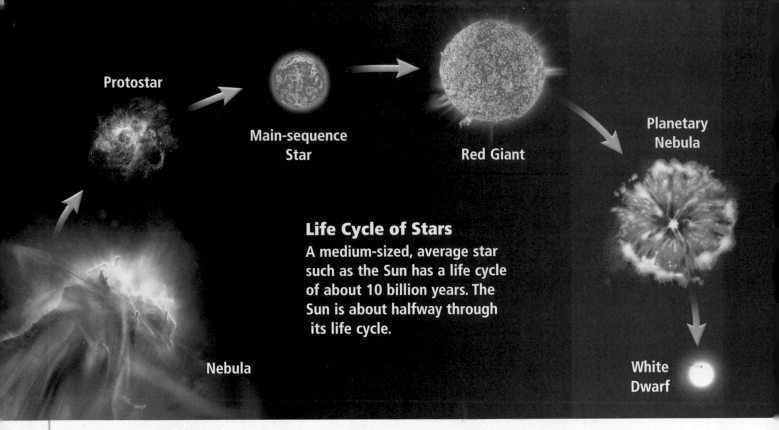

Protostar

Main-sequence
Star

Red Giant

Planetary
Nebula

Life Cycle of Stars
A medium-sized, average star
such as the Sun has a life cycle
of about 10 billion years. The
Sun is about halfway through
its life cycle.

Nebula

White
Dwarf

Life Cycle of Stars

Although stars are not living things, scientists use the idea of life cycles to describe them. A star's life cycle includes a beginning, a middle, and an end. The stages depend on the star's initial mass.

All stars form from enormous rotating clouds of dust and gases—mostly hydrogen. This type of cloud is called a *nebula* (NEB yuh luh).

Over time, gravity and other forces cause the nebula to collapse into a very dense mass. When temperatures rise to a certain point, parts of the cloud begin to glow. This soon-to-be star is called a *protostar*. When temperatures reach at least 10 million°C, nuclear fusion begins. A star is born.

When a newly formed star has stabilized, it becomes a *main-sequence*

star—a stage that can last for billions of years. The Sun is a main-sequence star.

As a star like the Sun approaches the end of the main-sequence stage, its outer part expands while the core contracts. The star becomes a *red giant*—a very bright but cool star. Its diameter is from 10 to over 100 times that of the Sun.

Eventually, the outer layers of the star are released to form a *planetary nebula*. Over a very long period of time, the remaining star shrinks to form a *white dwarf*. In this stage, the star has no nuclear fuel left in its core. The remaining heat radiates into space until the white dwarf fades to a *black dwarf*.

 **CAUSE AND EFFECT** What causes a nebula to collapse into a dense mass?

Visual Summary

The Sun is a medium-sized yellow star. It is the central body of the solar system. It supplies energy to Earth. Plants use this energy to make food.

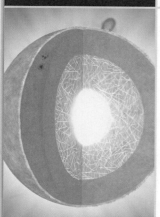

The Sun is made mostly of hydrogen and helium. The Sun's surface has features such as sunspots, solar flares, and prominences. The Sun produces energy by nuclear fusion.

The Sun is a main-sequence star. It will eventually pass through the following stages: red giant, planetary nebula, white dwarf, and finally, black dwarf.

STANDARDS
5.a., 2.f.

 Technology
Visit **www.eduplace.com/cascp** to find out more about the Sun.

Reading Review

1 **MAIN IDEA** Describe how the Sun's energy affects Earth.

2 **VOCABULARY** What is nuclear fusion? Why is it an important process?

3 **READING SKILL** Describe the nuclear fusion reaction that takes place in the Sun. How does this reaction affect Earth?

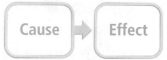

Cause → Effect

4 **CRITICAL THINKING:** **Synthesize** The Sun is often described as an "average star." In what ways is the Sun average?

5 **INQUIRY SKILL: Compare** You are using a golf ball to model Earth. Compare these choices to model the Sun: a beach ball, a flashlight, and a heat lamp. When would you use each choice?

 TEST PRACTICE

The Sun is made up mostly of hydrogen and ____.

A. oxygen

B. carbon dioxide

C. helium

D. water vapor

 STANDARDS
1: 2.f., 4.a., **2:** 5.a., **3:** 5.a., **4:** 5.a., **5:** 5.b.,
Test Practice: 5.a.

243

Lesson 2

What Orbits the Sun?

Building Background

Earth is only one small part of the solar system. The Sun, eight other planets, and thousands of smaller bodies belong to this system, too. Yet only Earth is able to support life—at least as far as scientists can tell. Understanding Earth's position in the solar system is one key to understanding why it supports life.

PREPARE TO INVESTIGATE

Inquiry Skill

Research When you research, you use library reference materials, search the Internet, and talk to experts to learn science information.

Materials

- large index card
- metric ruler
- 2 gummed reinforced rings
- 2 brass fasteners
- string (30 cm long)

Science and Math Toolbox

For steps 1 and 2, review **Measurements** on pages H16–H17.

 STANDARDS

5.b. *Students know* the solar system includes the planet Earth, the Moon, the Sun, eight other planets and their satellites, and smaller objects, such as asteroids and comets.
6.h. Draw conclusions from scientific evidence and indicate whether further information is needed to support a specific conclusion.

A Very Long Trip!

Procedure

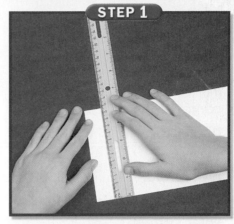
STEP 1

1. **Measure** Use a ruler to mark the midpoints of the two short sides of a large index card. Draw a straight line across the center of the card by connecting the dots.

2. **Measure** Mark two points, each 2 cm in from the edge of the card. Then measure 2 cm in from one of the points and draw a small circle. Label the circle "Sun."

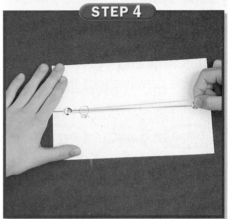
STEP 4

3. **Use Models** Attach reinforced rings over the two marked points on the card. Carefully push the brass fasteners through the rings and the card. Spread the prongs of each fastener.

4. **Use Models** Tie the ends of the string to form a circle with a circumference of about 25 cm. Loop the string around the brass fasteners.

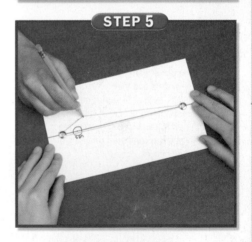
STEP 5

5. **Collaborate** Have a partner hold the edges of the card while you insert the tip of a pencil inside the string loop. Keeping the string tight, draw an ellipse by moving the pencil around the inside of the string. An *ellipse* is shaped like a slightly flattened circle. The ellipse models the orbit of a comet.

Conclusion

1. **Compare** How does the orbit of a comet compare with the orbits of the planets?

2. **Predict** What do you think happens to a comet when it reaches the point in its orbit closest to the Sun?

Guided Inquiry

Ask Questions Find out more about comets. **Research** information at the library or on the Internet. Use your findings to make a poster.

Planets, Moons, and Other Bodies

READING SKILL

Main Idea and Details
Outline details about the solar system.

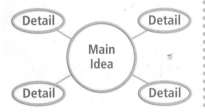

STANDARDS

5.b. *Students know* the solar system includes the planet Earth, the Moon, the Sun, eight other planets and their satellites, and smaller objects, such as asteroids and comets.
5.a. *Students know* the Sun, an average star, is the central and largest body in the solar system and is composed primarily of hydrogen and helium.

MAIN IDEA The Sun and the bodies that revolve around it make up the solar system. The solar system is a small part of a much larger system called the Milky Way galaxy.

The Sun and Its Neighbors

In your neighborhood, your neighbors are the people who live near you. Earth's neighborhood is the solar system. The **solar system** is the Sun and all the bodies that travel, or revolve, around it. Earth is one of many **planets,** large bodies that revolve around the Sun or another star. The planets shine by reflecting the light of a star, such as the Sun.

The Sun is by far the largest and most massive part of the solar system. Its gravity holds the other parts in their positions. Many planets, including Earth, have one or more moons. Smaller members of the solar system include asteroids, comets, and meteoroids.

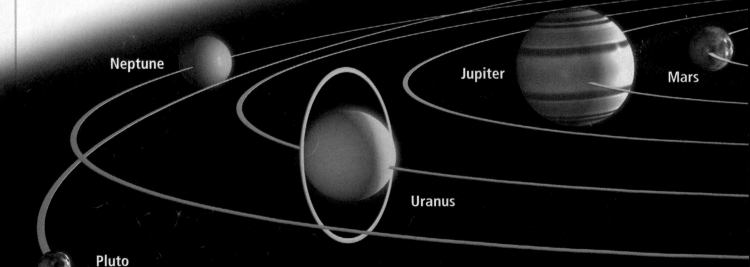

Neptune

Jupiter

Mars

Uranus

Pluto

The solar system is a very small part of a much larger system called the Milky Way galaxy. A **galaxy** (GAL uhk see) is a huge system of gas, dust, and stars.

Scientists believe that the solar system is about 4.6 billion years old. It formed from a hot, spinning cloud of gases and dust. Over time, gravity pulled the gas and dust toward the center of the cloud, causing the cloud to collapse. As it continued to spin, the cloud flattened, and its temperature rose. Eventually, great heat and pressure built up near the center of the cloud. Nuclear reactions produced a star now called the Sun.

Away from the center of the spinning cloud, temperatures were cooler. Matter in this cooler part of the cloud began to come together to form the planets and their moons.

Planets closest to the Sun formed from heavy, rocky material. Farther from the Sun, planets were able to hold onto lighter gases and became much larger. Moons eventually formed around all but two of the planets.

Along with the planets and their moons, other small bodies formed in the solar system. These include asteroids, comets, and meteoroids.

The paths, or orbits, of these bodies range in shape from almost a circle to long, flat ovals. These shapes are called ellipses. The strong gravitational force of the Sun holds all the objects in the solar system in their orbits.

 **MAIN IDEA AND DETAILS** What is the solar system?

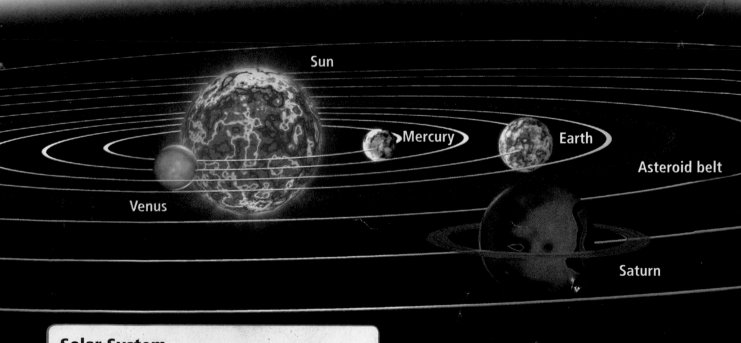

Solar System
The Sun, nine planets and their moons, and many smaller bodies make up the solar system.

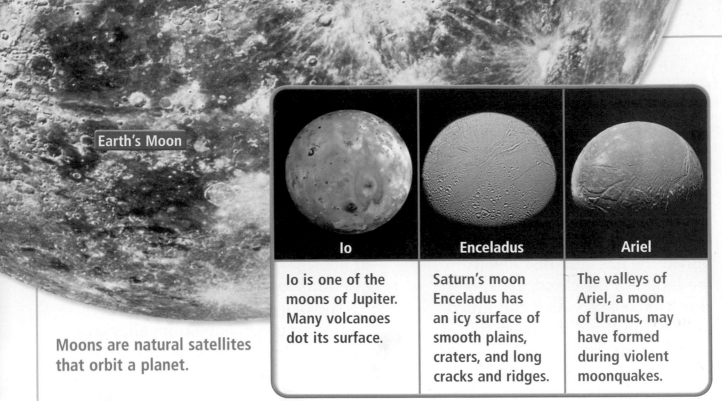

Earth's Moon

Io

Io is one of the moons of Jupiter. Many volcanoes dot its surface.

Enceladus

Saturn's moon Enceladus has an icy surface of smooth plains, craters, and long cracks and ridges.

Ariel

The valleys of Ariel, a moon of Uranus, may have formed during violent moonquakes.

Moons are natural satellites that orbit a planet.

Moons

A moon is a natural satellite. Natural satellites orbit around another body in space.

Earth's moon is the satellite that is often called simply *the* Moon. The Moon has a diameter of 3,476 km—nearly four times smaller than that of Earth. It has motions similar to those of Earth. The Moon rotates on its axis and revolves around Earth. It takes about one month for the Moon to complete one rotation and one orbit.

During its revolution, the Moon goes through phases during which its shape appears to change. The phases of the Moon are caused by the positions of the Moon, the Sun, and Earth in space.

Much of what we know about the Moon comes from space missions. The Apollo missions landed 12 astronauts on the Moon between 1969 and 1972. These astronauts gathered moon rocks and studied the surface of the Moon.

Later missions sent spacecraft only to orbit the Moon and map its surface. Their data indicate that the Moon may have ice at its poles.

Astronaut Dave Scott planted the U.S. flag during the *Apollo 15* mission. ▼

As you have read, other planets have moons, too. In fact, astronomers have discovered about 140 other moons in the solar system. All these moons are held in their orbits by the gravitational attraction of their planets.

Unlike Earth's Moon, two moons have atmospheres surrounding them. They are Saturn's largest moon, Titan, and one of Neptune's moons, Triton. Triton also has geysers. Io, a moon of Jupiter, has active volcanoes.

Still other moons show evidence that water or ice may lie deep beneath their surfaces. Jupiter's Europa, for example, may have vast liquid oceans under its icy surface. In addition, carbon compounds exist on this moon. Both ingredients are necessary for the formation of life as we know it. Scientists are particularly interested in learning more about Europa.

Asteroids

An **asteroid** is a relatively small, rocky object that orbits the Sun. Scientists estimate that millions of these chunks of rock and metal exist in the solar system. Most of them orbit in a band called the asteroid belt, located between the orbits of Mars and Jupiter.

Asteroids range in size from hundreds of kilometers in diameter to only about 1 km. Many asteroids have very peculiar shapes. Some even look like baked potatoes!

One theory about the origin of the asteroids is that Jupiter's strong pull of gravity prevented them from coming together to form a planet. Another, less likely idea is that the asteroids are remnants of several planets that collided and broke apart.

MAIN IDEA AND DETAILS What motions do Earth and the Moon have in common?

Asteroids are small, rocky bodies that orbit the Sun, many in a belt between Mars and Jupiter. ▼

Express Lab

Activity Card 20
Model Orbits

Comet Orbit

A comet's tail always points away from the Sun, regardless of the direction the comet is moving.

Comet Hyakutake

Named for its discoverer, Yuji Hyakutake, this comet was one of the brightest to approach the Sun in the 20th century. ▶

Comets and Meteors

A **comet** is a small, orbiting body made of dust, ice, and frozen gases. The solid center of a comet is its nucleus. Like all objects in the solar system, comets orbit the Sun. However, most comets travel in very long, elliptical paths like the one shown on this page.

When a comet approaches the Sun, frozen solids in its nucleus vaporize. Gases and dust are released, producing a glowing region called a coma. Energy from the Sun causes the coma to grow. Charged particles streaming from the Sun push particles out of the coma, producing a glowing tail that can reach millions of kilometers into space.

The orbits of some comets extend to just beyond the planet Neptune. These comets make one complete trip around the Sun in fewer than 200 years. They are called short-period comets.

The orbits of other comets extend beyond Pluto. These comets can take up to 30 million years to orbit the Sun! They are called long-period comets.

A **meteor** is a chunk of matter that enters Earth's atmosphere and is heated by friction with the air. For a few moments, these chunks burn as they fall, appearing as streaks of light against the night sky.

A few meteors are the size of asteroids. But most are much smaller, even smaller than a grain of sand. Meteors begin as **meteoroids,** which are bits of rock or metal that orbit the Sun. You'll learn more about meteoroids in the feature on page 253.

 **MAIN IDEA AND DETAILS** What causes the tail of a comet to form?

Lesson Wrap-Up

Visual Summary

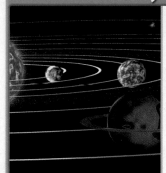

The solar system consists of the Sun, nine planets, their moons, and many other smaller bodies that orbit the Sun.

All but two planets in the solar system have at least one moon. Moons and asteroids are among the smaller bodies in the solar system.

Comets may have short-period or long-period orbits around the Sun. Meteors are bits of matter that burn up when they enter Earth's atmosphere.

STANDARDS

5.b., 5.a.

Technology
Visit www.eduplace.com/cascp to find out more about the solar system.

Reading Review

1 MAIN IDEA What different bodies make up the solar system?

2 VOCABULARY Compare an *asteroid* and a *comet*.

3 READING SKILL Name five groups of objects that make up the solar system. Describe each briefly.

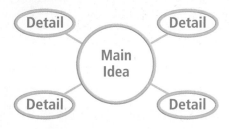

4 CRITICAL THINKING: Apply The Moon's surface has many craters, caused by meteors and other objects in space that strike its surface. Why does Earth's surface have fewer craters than the Moon's surface does?

5 INQUIRY SKILL: Research Find out more about one of the comets that have recently approached Earth or that will approach soon. Research comets at the library or on the Internet.

 TEST PRACTICE
What rocky objects orbit the Sun between Mars and Jupiter?

A. satellites

B. meteoroids

C. comets

D. asteroids

 STANDARDS

1–2: 5.b., 3: 5.a., 5.b., 4: 5.b., Test Practice: 5.b.

Lisa Westberg Peters studied science carefully for her book of poems about Earth. Compare her poem about meteors to the work of a non-fiction writer.

Earth Charged in Meteor's Fiery Death

by Lisa Westberg Peters

The earth was charged Wednesday
in connection with the fiery death
of a large meteor.

"It was a combination of gravity
and thick air," police said.
"That meteor didn't have a chance."

The meteor fell out of orbit
early Tuesday and was vaporized
as it plunged toward the earth.

"It was a fireball!"
said Jose Martinez of Sacramento.
"It lit up my whole backyard."

A hearing will be held next week.

STANDARD
5.b. *Students know* the solar system includes the planet Earth, the Moon, the Sun, eight other planets and their satellites, and smaller objects, such as asteroids and comets.

READING **LINK**

Meteors

Excerpt from *Comets, Meteors, and Asteroids*, by Seymour Simon

Meteors flash in the sky every night. They happen every day, too, but we usually can't see them in the Sun's glare.

Meteor flashes are also called falling or shooting stars. But meteors are not stars. Stars are suns far beyond our Solar System. Meteors begin as meteoroids, bits of rock or metal that orbit around the Sun. We can't see them in space because they are too small and too dark.

But sometimes meteoroids plunge into Earth's atmosphere at speeds faster than a bullet. The friction produced by rubbing against air particles makes them glow red-hot, and they are then called meteors. We see the bright flash for only a few seconds.

Meteors come much closer to the Earth than comets. Some are brighter than the brightest star and are called fireballs.

Several times each year you can see more than a dozen meteors in an hour in the same part of the night sky. This is called a meteor shower. It occurs when Earth passes through an old comet orbit and collides with some of the particles remaining from the comet's nucleus. Each year, Earth passes through the old comet path at about the same date. The Leonids, for example, are meteors from rocks left behind in the orbit of Comet Temple-Tuttle. When the Leonids appear in mid-November, they seem to come from the direction of the constellation (a group of stars) named Leo.

Sharing Ideas

1. **READING CHECK** Why do meteors burn as they enter Earth's atmosphere?

2. **WRITE ABOUT IT** Why do meteor showers appear at certain times every year?

3. **TALK ABOUT IT** Is it reasonable to suggest that Earth causes the death of meteors, as the poem suggests?

Lesson 3

What Are the Planets Like?

Building Background

Do you ever wonder if life exists on other planets? Can studying other planets help us understand life on Earth? Scientists have discovered water in various forms on other bodies in space. On closer inspection, who knows what else could be found there?

PREPARE TO INVESTIGATE

Inquiry Skill

Use Models When you make a model, you are using a representation of an object to better understand how it works.

Materials

- scissors
- pencil
- compass
- construction paper
- calculator
- tape
- metric tape measure

 STANDARDS

5.b. *Students know* the solar system includes the planet Earth, the Moon, the Sun, eight other planets and their satellites, and smaller objects, such as asteroids and comets.
6.g. Record data by using appropriate graphic representations (including charts, graphs, and labeled diagrams) and make inferences based on those data.

Model the Solar System

Procedure

Safety: Exercise caution when using scissors.

1 **Record Data** In your *Science Notebook,* make a chart like the one shown. Use it to make paper scale models of the planets.

2 **Use Numbers** The astronomical unit (AU) is used to measure distances in space. Use the AU value for each planet to convert these values into distances you can measure.

3 **Use Numbers** Convert the radius of each planet and the Sun into a size you can model.

4 **Measure** Use the compass to draw each planet and the Sun on construction paper. Label each and cut them out. If necessary, tape several pieces of paper together to make your models.

5 **Use Numbers** Lay the Sun cutout at one end of the hallway. Use the tape measure to plot the positions of the planets, using the values you calculated in step 3.

6 **Use Models** Place each planet cutout at its proper distance from the Sun. You now have a model of the solar system.

Conclusion

1. **Observe** Look at the positions and sizes of the planets and the Sun. What patterns, if any, do you observe?

2. **Infer** Based on your answer to question 1, do you think Pluto is a true planet?

STEP 1

Planet	Radius in km	Distance from Sun in AU
Mercury	2,439	0.4
Venus	6,052	0.7
Earth	6,378	1
Mars	3,397	1.5
Jupiter	71,490	5.2
Saturn	60,268	9.5
Uranus	25,559	19.2
Neptune	25,269	30.1
Pluto	1,160	39.5

STEP 4

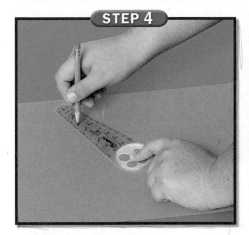

STEP 5

Guided Inquiry

Ask Questions Use the Internet to research the planet-like body, Sedna. **Use Numbers** to modify your scale to include Sedna.

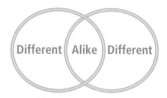

Learn by Reading

VOCABULARY

inner planet   p. 258
outer planet   p. 260

 READING SKILL

Compare and Contrast Use a diagram like the one below to compare and contrast the inner and outer planets.

Different | Alike | Different

STANDARD

5.b. *Students know* the solar system includes the planet Earth, the Moon, the Sun, eight other planets and their satellites, and smaller objects, such as asteroids and comets.

The Planets

MAIN IDEA The four planets closest to the Sun are called the inner planets. The remaining five planets are the outer planets.

Discovering the Solar System

Today, scientists know that the planets and smaller bodies in the solar system orbit the Sun. Long ago, however, people had different ideas about the solar system.

The early Greeks knew of seven bodies in the sky that appeared to circle around Earth. In contrast to the stars, which remained in place in the night sky, these seven bodies moved against the background of stars. The Greeks called these bodies *planetai*, which means "wanderers" in ancient Greek.

The Greeks developed the geocentric model of the solar system. In this model, Earth is at the center of the solar system. The Sun, the Moon, and the planets revolve around Earth. The geocentric model was accepted as correct for nearly 2,000 years.

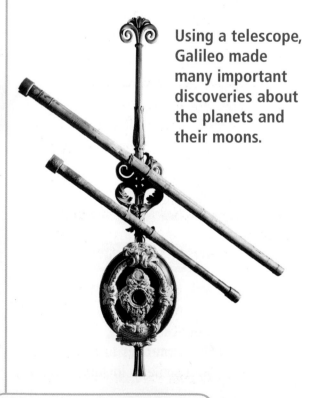

Using a telescope, Galileo made many important discoveries about the planets and their moons.

In 1543, Polish astronomer Nicolaus Copernicus reasoned that the Sun was at the center of the solar system. Earth, he stated, was a planet, not a motionless sphere. It rotated on an axis and revolved around the Sun, just as the other planets did.

Copernicus developed the heliocentric model of the solar system. This states that the Sun is at the center of the solar system and the planets revolve around it. Later, Johannes Kepler figured out that the planets orbit in ellipses.

In 1610, Italian astronomer Galileo Galilei became the first person to study the night sky, using a telescope he built himself. Galileo's observations supported Copernicus's heliocentric model. Galileo also found that Jupiter had four moons that orbited the planet. This proved that not all bodies in space orbit around Earth. Also, Galileo observed

▲ The Chandra x-ray telescope orbits Earth at a distance of more than one-third of the way to the Moon. What advantages do you think this distance provides?

that Venus goes through phases, just as the Moon does. This proved that Venus must orbit around the Sun.

Today, telescopes are still used to explore the solar system and beyond. New types of telescopes gather invisible radiation, such as radio or x-ray waves, to form images.

Clouds and gases in the air may prevent telescopes from picturing objects clearly in space. Thus, many telescopes are set up on mountain peaks. Others are launched into space and orbit Earth. Cameras aboard space telescopes took many of the photographs of planets on the following pages.

Telescopes allow people on Earth to explore the solar system. ▼

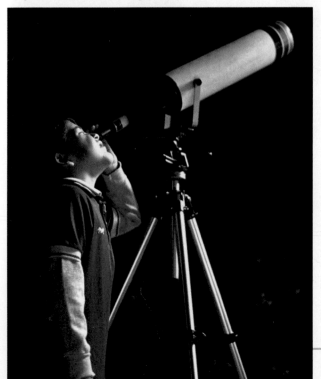

COMPARE AND CONTRAST How does the geocentric model of the solar system differ from the heliocentric model?

Express Lab

Activity Card 21
Model the Distance to the Sun

The Inner Planets

The first four planets from the Sun are Mercury, Venus, Earth, and Mars. These planets are called the **inner planets** because they are closer to the Sun than the other planets are.

The inner planets have certain characteristics in common. They are rocky and much smaller than most of the other planets. Yet if you could travel to the four inner planets, you would find them very different from one another.

Mercury is the smallest of the inner planets and the one closest to the Sun. Mercury's surface temperature varies widely between its day and its night. During the planet's slow rotation, the side facing the Sun becomes extremely hot. Daytime temperatures can rise to a scorching 427°C. Meanwhile, the side facing away from the Sun is experiencing nighttime, when temperatures can plummet to an icy −173°C.

Mercury also has a heavily cratered surface, caused by collisions with asteroids and other objects in space. Its atmosphere is very thin.

Mercury
Mercury's surface has many craters. Some of these may contain frozen water. ▼

Sun

Venus ▲
Venus has a few craters on its surface. A thick, poisonous atmosphere surrounds this planet.

The surface of Venus, the second planet from the Sun, is hidden below a thick layer of clouds made up mostly of sulfuric acid. The atmosphere itself is 96 percent carbon dioxide, creating tremendous pressure and a strong greenhouse effect.

Temperatures at the surface are hot enough to melt lead. The pressure exerted by the atmosphere is bone-crushing—about the same as that found 1 kilometer beneath the ocean's surface on Earth.

You are familiar with conditions on Earth, the third planet from the Sun. It is the only planet known to have liquid water. Earth's atmosphere and oceans help keep its surface temperature within a range that supports life.

Mars, the red planet, is smaller than Earth but has about the same amount of land area. Compared to other planets, Mars has been extensively observed and explored. The Mars Expedition rovers, named Spirit and Opportunity, have visited the surface and sent information back to Earth.

Mars ▲
Like Earth, Mars has ice caps at both poles.

The surface of Mars shows signs of water erosion, indicating that it may once have been more like Earth. While much of its surface is flat and rocky, Mars has deep canyons and the highest volcanic mountain known in the solar system. Olympus Mons stands 24 km (almost 80,000 ft) above the Martian surface.

COMPARE AND CONTRAST What are some similarities among the inner planets?

Earth ▲
Earth's temperature and its atmosphere make it the only planet in the solar system known to support life.

Inner Planets		
Planet	**Diameter (km)**	**Distance from Sun (million km)**
Mercury	4,880	57.9
Venus	12,100	108.2
Earth	12,756	149.6
Mars	6,800	227.9

The Outer Planets

The **outer planets** are Jupiter, Saturn, Uranus, Neptune, and Pluto. Except for Pluto, these planets are larger than the inner planets and consist mostly of gases.

Jupiter, the fifth planet from the Sun, is one of the brightest objects in the night sky. Jupiter takes only about 10 hours to rotate once on its axis. Winds reaching speeds of 670 km/hr (400 mph) form clearly visible bands.

Jupiter is famous for its Great Red Spot. This gigantic storm system has been visible from Earth for more than 300 years.

In addition to its many moons, Jupiter also has rings. The rings are made up of small particles that may have been produced by meteor collisions with Jupiter's moons.

The planet best known for its rings is Saturn, the sixth planet from the Sun. Saturn's band of rings is 250,000 km wide, but only 1 km thick. The rings consist mostly of ice particles.

Saturn is the least dense of any planet. If you could put Saturn in water, it would float! Yet it is massive enough to hold more than 30 moons in their orbits.

Jupiter ▼
Jupiter is a giant—it is the biggest, most massive planet in the solar system. It has more than 60 moons!

Outer Planets		
Planet	Diameter (km)	Distance from Sun (million km)
Jupiter	142,800	778
Saturn	120,000	1,427
Uranus	50,800	2,870
Neptune	48,600	4,500
Pluto	2,300	5,900

Saturn ▲
Thousands of particles make up the rings that surround Saturn.

Uranus, the seventh planet from the Sun, was once called "Herschel" after the astronomer who discovered it. Like other planets, the axis of Uranus is tilted. Yet its axis is tilted so much that it is nearly parallel to the plane of its orbit. Compared to other planets, Uranus is "lying" on its side.

Like Jupiter and Saturn, Uranus consists mostly of gases with a core of rock and ice. Uranus has at least 27 moons and a system of 11 rings.

Neptune, the eighth planet in the solar system, is similar in color and composition to Uranus. Scientists predicted its existence based on observations of the motion of Uranus, but it was not discovered until 1846.

Like all gas giants, Neptune is a windy planet, but its winds are the fastest currently observed in the solar system. They reach velocities of 2,700 km/hr (1,500 mph).

Pluto ▶
Pluto has ice caps at its poles and large dark spots near its equator.

Neptune has at least 11 moons and a system of rings. One of Neptune's rings appears braided, and scientists are trying to understand this unusual observation.

Pluto is usually the farthest planet from the Sun. However, its orbit sometimes brings it closer to the Sun than Neptune. Unlike the other outer planets, Pluto is small, icy, and rocky. Not surprisingly, it is very cold.

In recent years, scientists have discovered moons around Pluto and objects beyond Pluto. They also are debating whether Pluto should be classified as a planet.

COMPARE AND CONTRAST **What do most of the outer planets have in common?**

Neptune ▼
Neptune and its largest moon, Triton, are getting closer to each other. The two probably will collide within the next 100 million years.

Uranus ▲
High concentrations of methane give Uranus a greenish color.

▲ The European Space Agency launched the Mars Express space probe in 2003.

Exploring Space

Today, astronomers still use telescopes to study space. Astronomers also rely on spacecraft to learn even more about the universe.

The space shuttle is a vehicle that takes equipment and people into space. While the shuttle orbits Earth, experiments can be carried out. After a certain time, the shuttle returns to Earth. One major advantage of the space shuttle is that it can be reused again and again.

Another type of spacecraft, a space station, stays in space for long periods of time. It has areas in which astronauts and scientists live, sleep, and conduct experiments. The International Space Station is a joint project involving 16 countries, including the United States.

A space probe is a spacecraft that carries special instruments into space. Some probes are launched into Earth's upper atmosphere. Other probes go much farther, exploring planets and moons that are too distant for humans to visit.

Probes sometimes carry robots that can be lowered to a planet's surface to collect and analyze materials. Twin robots called Spirit and Opportunity have explored Mars.

COMPARE AND CONTRAST How does the space shuttle differ from a space probe?

The space shuttle takes off attached to a rocket. To return to Earth, it lands like an airplane. ▼

Visual Summary

Mercury, Venus, Earth, and Mars are the inner planets. They are small and rocky and have few or no moons.

Jupiter, Saturn, Uranus, Neptune, and Pluto are the outer planets. With the exception of Pluto, the outer planets are large and gaseous, and have many moons.

Space probes can be used to explore regions of space that are too dangerous or difficult for humans to explore directly.

 STANDARD

5.b.

Technology
Visit www.eduplace.com/cascp to find out more about the planets.

Reading Review

❶ **MAIN IDEA** How are the planets of the solar system often grouped?

❷ **VOCABULARY** What is a space station? How does it differ from a space probe?

❸ **READING SKILL** Compare and contrast the characteristics of Earth with those of its two nearest neighbors.

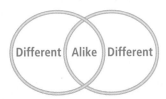

Different | Alike | Different

❹ **CRITICAL THINKING: Synthesize** Why do you think the outer planets have so many moons? Do you think an inner planet could hold so many moons? Explain.

❺ **INQUIRY SKILL: Use Models** Why are models useful to study the solar system? Can a useful model be accurate to both the size of planets and the distances between them?

 TEST PRACTICE

The inner and outer planets are separated by _____.

A. the asteroid belt

B. Jupiter's great storm

C. Earth and its Moon

D. Saturn and its rings

 STANDARDS

1-5: 5.b., **Test Practice:** 5.b.

263

Lesson 4

What Keeps Planets in Their Orbits?

Building Background

When you jump in the air, you fall back to the ground. Why don't you keep rising upwards? You fall because a force pulls you downward.

In fact, this same force pulls on all objects in the universe. The force is gravity. Gravity keeps you bound to Earth, and it keeps the planets in orbit around the Sun.

STANDARDS

5.c. *Students know* the path of a planet around the Sun is due to the gravitational attraction between the Sun and planet.
6.h. Draw conclusions from scientific evidence and indicate whether further information is needed to support a specific conclusion.

PREPARE TO INVESTIGATE

Inquiry Skill

Infer When you infer, you apply logical reasoning to interpret your data.

Materials

- a large plastic bowl with lid
- two marbles of different sizes
- yellow paper
- scissors

Planets in a Bowl

Procedure

1. **Collaborate** Work with a partner. Cut out a small paper circle, and label it "Sun." Tape the circle to the inside bottom of the bowl.

2. **Use Models** The marbles represent planets. Drop one marble along the side of the bowl. Record the results in your *Science Notebook.*

3. Seal the bowl tightly with the lid. Then move the bowl over and over in a circular path, keeping it flat against the table. Observe the motion of the marble inside. Record the results.

4. **Use Variables** Change the way you move the bowl, always keeping it flat against the table. Try moving it slower or faster, or in a wider or narrower circle. Observe the marble's motion.

5. **Compare** Open the bowl and add the second marble. Repeat step 3, making sure the lid is sealed tightly. Compare the motions of the two marbles. Observe what happens when the marbles hit each other.

STEP 1

STEP 2

STEP 3

Conclusion

1. **Use Models** Compare the moving bowl and marbles to the planets of the solar system.

2. **Analyze Data** What would happen if two planets hit each other, or if an asteroid struck a planet? Does evidence from the activity support your answer?

3. **Infer** Why do you think that planets do not crash into the Sun?

Guided Inquiry

Ask Questions If you throw a baseball into the air, it will fall to the ground. How fast would you have to throw a baseball for it to escape Earth's gravity and fly into space? **Research** the answer. Report it to the class.

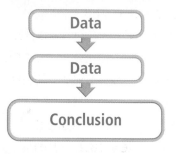

Learn by Reading

READING SKILL

Draw Conclusions As you read, draw conclusions about how the distance between two objects and their masses affects the force of gravity.

Data
↓
Data
↓
Conclusion

STANDARD

5.c. *Students know* the path of a planet around the Sun is due to the gravitational attraction between the Sun and planet.

Gravity

MAIN IDEA The path of a planet around the Sun is caused by the gravitational attraction between the Sun and the planet.

Gravitation

What happens when you throw a ball into the air, drop a dish from a table, or let your bike roll on a steep hill? As you know, the ball and the dish will fall to the ground and the bike will roll downhill.

The force that causes objects to fall back to Earth is called gravitation. Gravitation is an attractive force between objects that have mass. Every object in the Universe attracts every other object.

The gravitational attraction between Earth and objects at or near its surface is usually called **gravity.** The term *gravity* also applies to other massive bodies in space.

The Force of Gravitation

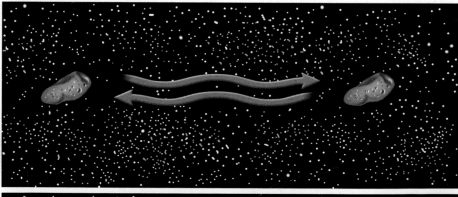

◄ Left alone in space, two large rocks would gravitate toward each other.

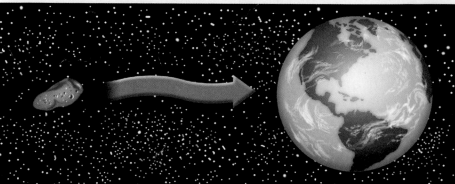

◄ Near Earth, however, objects with small mass fall toward Earth without Earth moving toward them.

◄ When you drop two objects, they accelerate to the ground and not toward each other.

Gravitation is an example of a non-contact force. It acts on objects at a distance, without touching them. Gravitation keeps Earth and the other planets in their orbits around the Sun. It keeps the Moon in its orbit around Earth.

In 1684, Sir Isaac Newton stated that the strength of the gravitational force between two objects depends both on the masses of the objects and on the distance between them. The force is directly proportional to the product of the masses. This means that the greater the masses of the objects, the stronger is the gravitational force between them. If one of the masses were to double, the force would double, too.

The gravitational force between two objects also depends on the distance between them. The smaller the distance between the two objects, the stronger is the gravitational force. The greater the distance between the objects, the weaker is the gravitational force.

Gravitation is a weak force unless the masses involved are very large. To show this, hold two pencils in front of you. Both pencils have mass, so the force of gravitation causes them to attract each other. You cannot feel this attraction, but it's there.

When you release the pencils, will they drift toward each other? No, both pencils are pulled toward Earth. Earth's huge mass attracts each pencil with a much greater force than either pencil attracts the other.

Gravity causes objects to speed up, or accelerate, as they fall. Think about riding a skateboard down a very steep ramp. If you don't apply brakes, you move faster and faster down the ramp.

The acceleration due to gravity at Earth's surface is about 9.8 meters per second per second. This means that objects near Earth's surface accelerate at this rate as they begin to fall. Air resistance, or drag, slows falling objects, however.

DRAW CONCLUSIONS What factors influence the force of gravity between two objects?

Express Lab

Activity Card 22
Show Air Resistance

Formation of the Solar System

Gravity played a large role in the formation of the solar system. Around 4.6 billion years ago, the solar system was born from a cloud of gas and dust called a nebula. The force of gravity collapsed the cloud into a star, planets, and other bodies.

The inner planets formed close to the Sun, where temperatures were very hot. Lighter elements such as hydrogen and helium were vaporized by the intense heat. This is why the inner planets are composed mainly of heavy elements.

In contrast, the outer planets formed farther from the Sun, where temperatures were cooler. The gas giants—Jupiter, Saturn, Uranus, and Neptune—formed from ice, as well as gas and dust. They grew in mass until even light elements such as hydrogen, helium, and methane could not escape their great gravitational pull. This is why the gas giants are composed mainly of light elements.

As you have read, Pluto orbits the Sun beyond the gas giants, yet it is small and rocky. Scientists are not sure how it formed. To help find out, NASA is sending a space probe to explore Pluto. Called *New Horizons*, the space probe was launched in 2006.

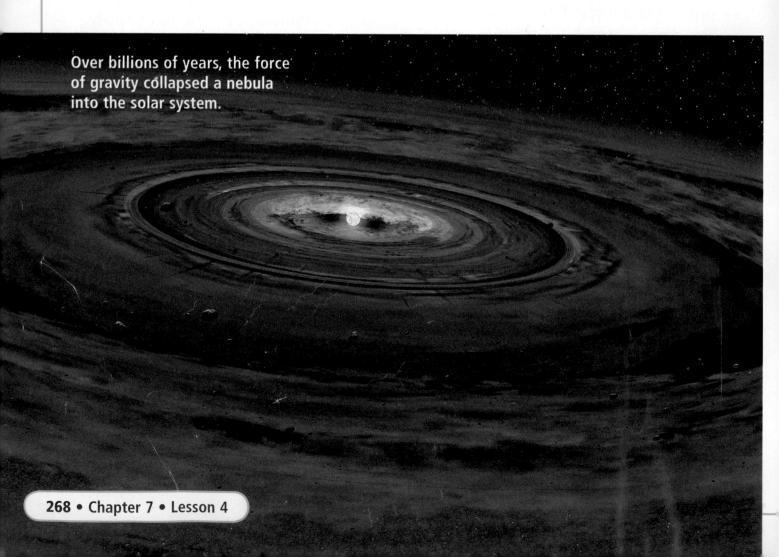

Over billions of years, the force of gravity collapsed a nebula into the solar system.

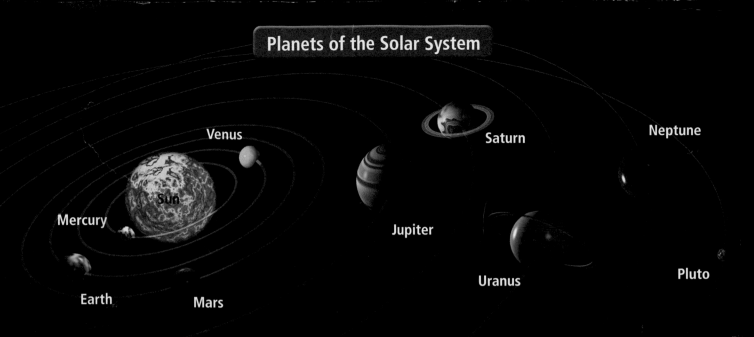

Planets of the Solar System

Venus

Saturn

Neptune

Sun

Mercury

Jupiter

Uranus

Pluto

Earth

Mars

Facts on Four Planets	Mercury	Earth	Jupiter	Pluto
Relative mass (Earth = 1)	0.06	0.06	317.87	0.002
Average distance to Sun (millions of km)	58	58	778	5900
Average orbital speed (km/s)	47.5	29.8	13.1	4.7
Orbital period	88 Days	365 Days	12 Years	248 Years

Planet Orbitals

As Johannes Kepler discovered, the planets travel around the Sun in elliptical orbits rather than circular ones. Kepler also discovered that a planet speeds up as it nears the Sun and slows down when it is farther away.

In addition, Kepler learned that the inner planets travel faster in their orbits than do the outer planets. Because they are much farther from the Sun, the outer planets must cover a greater distance to complete one orbit. The combination of slower orbital speed and longer orbital path means that the outer planets take much longer to complete one orbit than Earth does.

Why do planets remain in orbit around the Sun? Recall that Newton found that the mass of two objects and the distance between them affect the strength of their gravitational attraction. The object with greater mass exerts a greater pull. The Sun is the most massive object in the solar system. It pulls on the planets, keeping them in orbit around itself.

DRAW CONCLUSIONS Why aren't the inner planets made of light elements?

Weightlessness

Your weight is a measure of the force of gravity pulling on your body. If you are falling, and your surroundings are falling at the same rate, you can experience what people call weightlessness.

Have you ever traveled down from a high floor in a really fast elevator? As the floor of the elevator seems to move away from your feet, your body actually feels lighter.

This same sensation occurs in a spacecraft orbiting Earth, but the effect is many times greater. In fact, the craft and the astronauts are in a state called free-fall. They are all falling at the same rate. As the astronauts and their ship fall together toward Earth, they appear to float as though gravity were not affecting them.

Why doesn't the spacecraft fall toward Earth? It has forward motion. Earth's gravity keeps the spacecraft from sailing off into outer space. But the forward motion of the craft balances the Earth's pull of gravity on it. Instead of falling to Earth, the craft follows a curved path around Earth.

In the same way, Earth's gravity draws the Moon toward Earth while the Moon is moving forward. The combined effect of the force of gravity and forward motion keeps the Moon in a curved path around Earth.

The same is true for the planets. The planets would fall toward the Sun if the force of gravity were not balanced by their forward motion.

DRAW CONCLUSIONS How would Earth be affected if there were no gravitational attraction between it and the Sun?

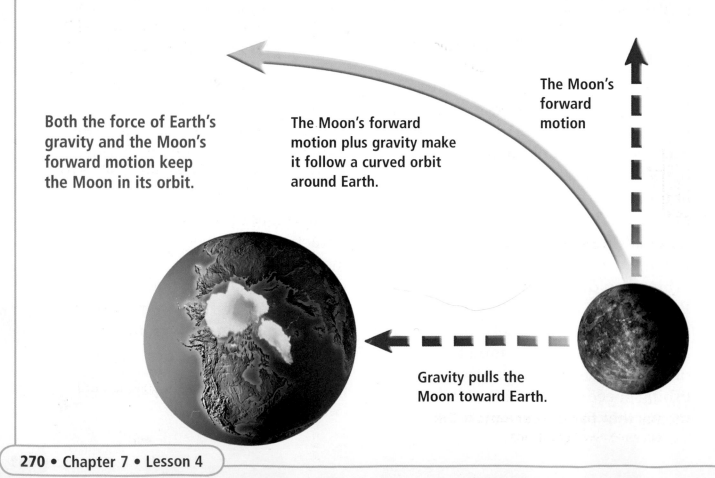

The Moon's forward motion

Both the force of Earth's gravity and the Moon's forward motion keep the Moon in its orbit.

The Moon's forward motion plus gravity make it follow a curved orbit around Earth.

Gravity pulls the Moon toward Earth.

Lesson Wrap-Up

Visual Summary

Gravity causes small objects to fall toward Earth. The strength of the gravitational force depends on the mass of the objects and the distance between them.

The solar system formed from a cloud of dust and gas called a nebula. The gravitational attraction between the Sun and the planets keeps the planets in orbit.

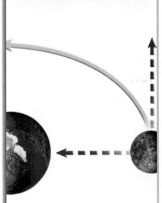

Planets and moons orbit in curved paths. The forward motion of the planet or moon is offset by the inward pull of gravity.

 STANDARD

5.c.

 Technology
Visit **www.eduplace.com/cascp** to find out more about gravitation.

Reading Review

❶ **MAIN IDEA** What keeps the planets in orbit around the Sun?

❷ **VOCABULARY** What is *gravity*? What two factors affect gravity?

❸ **READING SKILL** The first stage of the solar system was a nebula. Why did the nebula contract?

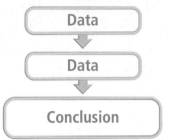

❹ **CRITICAL THINKING: Apply**
The acceleration due to gravity at Earth's surface is about 9.8 m/s². If you dropped a feather from a rooftop to the ground, would it fall that fast? Why or why not?

❺ **INQUIRY SKILL: Infer**
When astronauts orbit Earth in the space shuttle, they can "float" from one room to another! Does gravity not affect them? Explain.

 TEST PRACTICE
The force of gravity affects _____.

A. all objects in the Universe

B. only large objects, such as planets

C. only very small objects

D. only objects close to Earth

 STANDARDS

1–5: 5.c., **Test Practice:** 5.c.

271

STANDARDS 5.c. *Students know* the path of a planet around the Sun is due to the gravitational attraction between the Sun and the planet.

Tides of Io

When you think of tides, you probably think of ocean tides. But did you know that the ground beneath your feet also rises and falls in tides? Like ocean tides, these land tides occur because the Moon's gravitational force pulls hardest on the side of Earth that is closest.

Earth' land tides are too small for you to notice – about 10 cm high. That's nothing compared to the amazing ground tides on Jupiter's moon, Io.

On Io, the enormous gravity of Jupiter pushes and pulls the ground like taffy. The solid surface of Io moves up and down more than 90 meters!

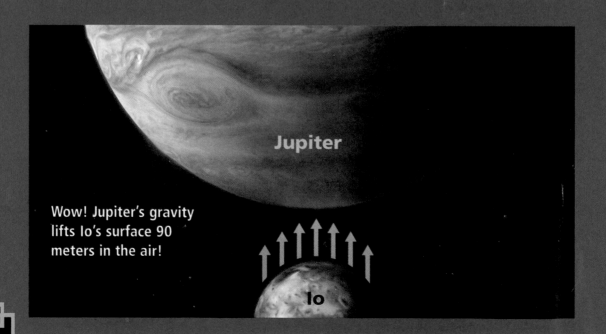

Jupiter

Wow! Jupiter's gravity lifts Io's surface 90 meters in the air!

Io

Sulfur and other minerals give Io its colorful appearance. Some people think Io looks like a giant pizza. What do you think?

Io has more active volcanoes than any planet in our Solar System. This volcanic plume has soared an amazing 300 km above Io's surface.

Writing Journal

In your journal, draw conclusions about the relationship between the extreme tides of Io and the high number of volcanoes there.

273

Math in Science

How much would you weigh on a planet other than Earth? Copy the table. Then fill in the third column by multiplying your weight by each conversion factor.

On which planet or moon would your weight be greatest? On which planet or moon would your weight be least? Where would you be weightless?

Weight on the Nine Planets		
Location	**Conversion Factor**	**Your Weight**
Earth	1	
Outer Space	0	
Earth's Moon	0.17	
Venus	0.90	
Mars	0.38	
Mercury	0.38	
Jupiter	2.36	
Saturn	0.92	
Uranus	0.89	
Neptune	1.13	
Pluto	0.07	

Writing in Science
Research Report

Should Pluto be classified as a planet? Research the debate about this question, then write a report to show what you learned. Discuss people's different opinions and include your own opinion.

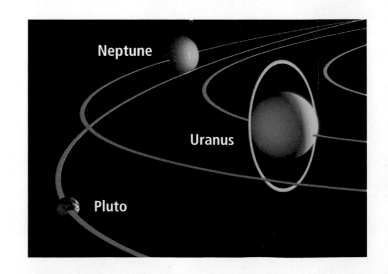

Computer Systems Technician

Who can you call to install a computer or a new computer program? This is a job for a computer systems technician. They often maintain networks of computers, sometimes covering many locations around the world! NASA uses such a system, as do many other government agencies and companies.

What It Takes!

- Training at a technical institute or on the job
- Logical thinking and problem-solving skills
- Ability to work with people and machines

Astronaut

Astronauts work for NASA, the government agency that explores space. They pilot spacecraft, conduct scientific experiments, conduct needed repairs, and perform other tasks in space. Much of their work is done under conditions of very small gravity, which NASA calls microgravity.

What It Takes!

- A degree in engineering or other scientific field
- Rigorous training in simulated spaceflight
- The ability to work in enclosed spaces
- Excellent physical condition

Vocabulary

Complete each sentence with a term from the list.

1. Stars produce energy by _____.

2. Mercury, Venus, Earth, and Mars are classified as _____.

3. Dark, relatively cool areas on the surface of the Sun are called _____.

4. A non-contact force that exists between all objects that have mass is _____.

5. The Sun and all the bodies that orbit around it form the _____.

6. A small, orbiting body made of dust, ice, and frozen gases is a(n) _____.

7. Jupiter, Saturn, Uranus, Neptune, and Pluto are classified as _____.

8. A relatively small, rocky object that orbits the Sun is a(n) _____.

9. A chunk of matter that enters Earth's atmosphere is a(n) _____.

10. The large bodies that revolve around the Sun are called _____.

asteroid p. 249
comet p. 250
galaxy p. 247
gravity p. 266
inner planets p. 258
meteor p. 250
meteoroid p. 250
nuclear fusion p. 240
outer planets p. 260
planets p. 246
solar system p. 246
sunspots p. 239

Test Practice

Write the letter of the best answer choice.

11. Objects in the solar system are held in their orbits by the gravitational pull of _____.

    A. the Sun
    B. the outer planets
    C. Jupiter
    D. the Milky Way

12. All objects in the solar system travel around the Sun in _____.

    A. about 24 hours
    B. about one Earth year
    C. elliptical orbits
    D. circular orbits

13. The Sun is a _____.

    A. main-sequence star
    B. red giant
    C. white dwarf
    D. black dwarf

14. Which of the following is NOT a small, rocky planet?

    A. Earth
    B. Jupiter
    C. Mars
    D. Mercury

Inquiry Skills

15. Use Numbers What units would you use to express distances within the solar system?

16. Dena is looking at the night sky through a telescope. She notices a bright object about the size of a star, and it has a pulsing outer edge. Dena suspects that she has found a comet. Does she have enough evidence to draw a conclusion? Explain.

Map the Concept

Make a flow chart to illustrate the Sun's life cycle. Include the following terms in proper order: main-sequence star, white dwarf, nebula, red giant, protostar, and planetary nebula.

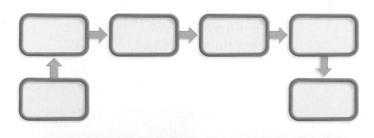

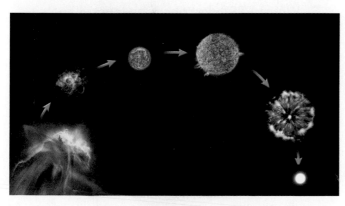

Critical Thinking

17. Analyze What is another way you might divide the planets into two groups other than the inner planets and outer planets?

18. Evaluate What are some advantages of conducting experiments from a space station rather than a space shuttle?

19. Analyze Why do you think so many people accepted the geocentric model of the solar system for so long?

20. Apply You want to view a clear image of the night sky through your telescope. Someone suggests that you take your telescope to a mountaintop. Why would this help?

Performance Assessment

Gravity Demonstration

Develop a demonstration that will illustrate the effects of gravity. When you perform your demonstration, be prepared to define important terms, to describe how your demonstration models gravity, and to explain why understanding gravity is crucial to understanding the solar system.

Writing Journal

Review your answers to the questions on page 233 at the beginning of this chapter. Change your answers, as needed, based on what you have learned.

STANDARDS

1: 5.a., 2: 5.b., 3: 5.a., 4: 5.c., 5–10: 5.b., 11–12: 5.c., 13: 5.a., 14: 5.b., 15: 5.b., 16: 6.h., **Map the Concept**: 5.a., 17–18: 5.b., 19: 5.c., 20: 5.b., **Performance Assessment**: 5.c.

Write the letter of the best answer choice.

1. Which is NOT found within the solar system?
   A. asteroid
   B. comet
   C. nebula
   D. satellite

2. Almost all weather occurs in the ____.
   A. mesosphere
   B. stratosphere
   C. thermosphere
   D. troposphere

3. Which weather-map symbol is shown below?

   A. cold front
   B. warm front
   C. stationary front
   D. stalled front

4. Which statement BEST describes the diagram below?

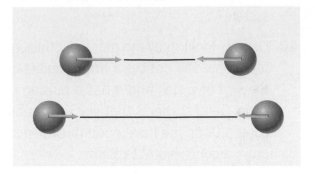

   A. As the distance between two objects increases, the gravitational force between them increases.
   B. As the distance between two objects increases, the gravitational force between them decreases.
   C. As the total mass of two objects decreases, the gravitational force between them increases.
   D. The distance between objects and their total mass does not affect the gravitational force between them.

5. Which BEST describes the inner planets?
   A. They are very cold.
   B. They are gas giants.
   C. They have dozens of moons.
   D. They are small and rocky.

6. A continental polar air mass is ____.
   A. dry and cold
   B. dry and warm
   C. wet and cold
   D. wet and warm

7. What do the lines on the weather map below represent?

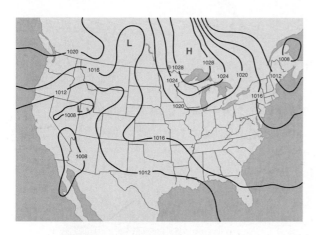

   A. areas of equal air pressure
   B. planetary winds
   C. jet streams
   D. areas of equal elevation

8. The diagram below shows the first four planets in proper order from the Sun. What is the fourth planet?

Mercury → Venus → Earth → ☐

   A. Pluto
   B. Uranus
   C. Mars
   D. Jupiter

Answer the following in complete sentences.

   9. Which of the outer planets is most like the four inner planets? Explain your answer.

10. Describe the importance of the Sun to life on Earth.

STANDARDS

1: 5.b., **2:** 4.e., **3:** 4.a., **4:** 5.c., **5:** 5.b.,
6: 4.a., **7:** 4.d., **8–9:** 5.b., **10:** 5.a.

You Can...

Discover More

Because stars are many light-years away from Earth, they appear as points of light in the sky. What happens to that light when it finally passes through Earth's atmosphere? The answer explains why stars appear to twinkle, or scintillate.

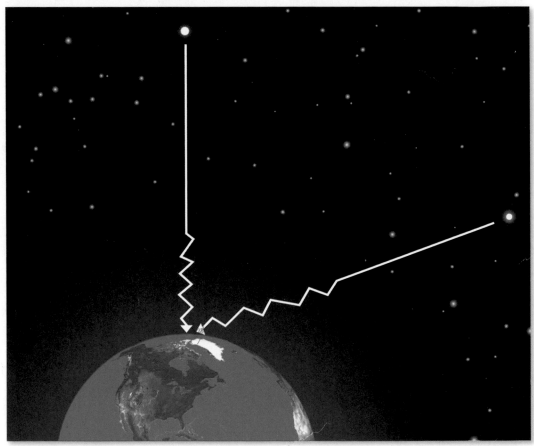

Starlight bends as it passes through Earth's atmosphere. Since the atmosphere is constantly moving and changing, starlight can bend many times! Stars closer to the horizon twinkle more because the starlight passing through the horizon to reach your line of sight travels through more of the atmosphere than starlight passing from directly above. The more atmosphere the starlight passes through, the more it is bent and the more the star appears to twinkle.

 See a star twinkling. Go to www.eduplace.com/cascp to view a Flash ™ movie and to learn more about stars.

PHYSICAL SCIENCE

UNIT D

Elements and Their Combinations

California Connection

Visit www.eduplace.com/cascp/
to learn more about the
structure of matter.

Elements and Their Combinations

Walt Disney Concert Hall, Los Angeles, California

California **Big Idea!**

Standard Set 1.
Physical Sciences

Elements and their combinations
account for all the varied types of
matter in the world.

Chapter 8

Atoms and Elements

The colors of fireworks depend on elements inside them.

LESSON 1

Everything you've ever touched is made of atoms. What are atoms, and what are their parts?

LESSON 2

Some art made of metal has lasted thousands of years. What are metals, and how are they different from other substances?

LESSON 3

This jewelry contains silver, a rare element in Earth's crust. Which elements are common, and which are rare?

Writing Journal

In your Writing Journal, draw or write answers to each question.

Vocabulary Preview

Vocabulary

Glossary

Vocabulary Skill

Synonyms
element

SCIENCE In science, an element is a substance that cannot be broken down into simpler substances. Elements join together to form more complex kinds of matter.

COMMON USE In everyday language, synonyms of the word element include *component*, *constituent*, and *ingredient*.

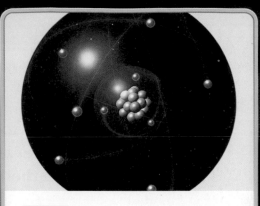

atom

smallest particle of an element that still has the properties of that element

metal

shiny substance that can be bent or stretched, and can conduct electricity

8	9	10
O	**F**	**Ne**
Oxygen	Fluorine	Neon
16	17	18
S	**Cl**	**Ar**
Sulfur	Chlorine	Argon
34	35	36
Se	**Br**	**Kr**
Selenium	Bromine	Krypton

periodic table

a logical arrangement of all known elements

compound

a pure substance made of two or more elements that are chemically combined

Start with Your Standards

Standard Set 1. Physical Sciences

1.b. *Students know* all matter is made of atoms, which may combine to form molecules.

1.c. *Students know* metals have properties in common, such as high electrical and thermal conductivity. Some metals, such as aluminum (Al), iron (Fe), nickel (Ni), copper (Cu), silver (Ag), and gold (Au), are pure elements; others, such as steel and brass, are composed of a combination of elemental metals.

1.d. *Students know* that each element is made of one kind of atom and that the elements are organized in the periodic table by their chemical properties.

1.e. *Students know* scientists have developed instruments that can create discrete images of atoms and molecules that show that the atoms and molecules often occur in well-ordered arrays.

1.h. *Students know* living organisms and most materials are composed of just a few elements.

Standard Set 6: Investigation and Experimentation standards covered in this chapter: 6.a., 6.g., 6.h.

What Are Atoms and Elements?

Building Background

All matter is made up of elements. The smallest piece of an element that still has the properties of that element is called an atom.

For years, scientists could only infer what atoms were like. Today, they use very powerful microscopes that form images of atoms. The photo shows seven uranium atoms, as pictured by a transmission electron microscope.

PREPARE TO INVESTIGATE

Inquiry Skill

Use Numbers When you use numbers, you use measurements and other numerical data to describe and interpret organisms, objects, or events.

Materials

- tape measure
- sharpened pencil
- string
- sticky note
- metric ruler

Science and Math Toolbox

For step 1, review **Measurements** on page H16.

STANDARDS

1.d. *Students know* that each element is made of one kind of atom and that the elements are organized in the periodic table by their chemical properties.
6.g. Record data by using appropriate graphic representations (including charts, graphs, and labeled diagrams) and make inferences based on those data.

A Giant Atom

Procedure

1 **Collaborate** Work in small groups. Use the tape measure to measure a 3.2-m length of string. Tie the ends together to make a loop. Lay the loop of string on the floor to create a circle. Place a sticky note in the middle of the circle.

2 **Use Models** Use a very sharp pencil to make a tiny hole in the center of the sticky note. The string circle represents an atom. The pencil hole in the sticky note represents the nucleus of the atom.

3 **Measure** Use a metric ruler to estimate the diameter of the pencil hole in millimeters. Use the tape measure to estimate the diameter of the atom in millimeters. Record both measurements in your *Science Notebook.*

4 **Use Numbers** Write a ratio in fraction form to compare the diameter of the nucleus to the diameter of the atom in your model.

Conclusion

1. **Analyze Data** The diameter of an actual nucleus is about one ten-thousandth of the diameter of an actual atom. Using the scale of your model, what would the diameter of the pencil hole have to be? (HINT: Divide the diameter of your model atom by 10,000.)

2. **Infer** Almost all of an atom's mass is located in its nucleus. What can you infer about the rest of the atom?

STEP 1

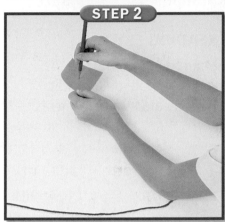
STEP 2

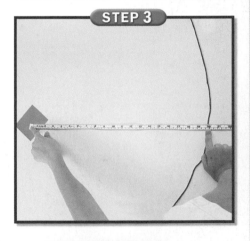
STEP 3

Guided Inquiry

Experiment Pencil "lead" is mostly carbon. Draw a pencil line on a piece of paper. Use a ruler to measure its width. Research the size of a carbon atom. Then **use numbers** to estimate the number of carbon atoms that would fit across your pencil line.

 READING SKILL

Main Idea and Details As you read, note details that describe atoms and elements.

```
        ┌──────────┐
        │   Main   │
        │   Idea   │
        └──────────┘
        ╱            ╲
   ┌────────┐    ┌────────┐
   │ Detail │    │ Detail │
   └────────┘    └────────┘
```

STANDARDS

1.b. *Students know* all matter is made of atoms, which may combine to form molecules.
1.e. *Students know* scientists have developed instruments that can create discrete images of atoms and molecules that show that the atoms and molecules often occur in well-ordered arrays.

Atoms and Elements

MAIN IDEA All matter is made up of particles called atoms, the smallest units of elements. As new tools can picture, atoms often form well-ordered patterns, or arrays.

Matter

Anything that takes up space and has mass is an example of matter—the "stuff" that makes up the universe. In this unit, you will be studying matter and its properties.

All matter is made of elements. An **element** is a substance that cannot be broken apart chemically into other substances. Elements are made up of only one kind of atom. An **atom** is the smallest particle of an element that still has the properties of that element.

You can think of atoms as the tiny building blocks of matter. Although atoms are very small in size, they are made up of even tinier particles.

Atoms consist of a nucleus surrounded by moving electrons. The **nucleus** is the structure in the center of an atom. The nucleus contains two kinds of particles: protons and neutrons. A **proton** is a small, positively charged particle. A **neutron** is a particle that lacks charge. Neutrons and protons have about equal mass.

The nucleus contains almost the entire mass of the atom, although it fills only about 1/10,000 of its space. What fills the rest of the atom? Moving in the space around the nucleus are **electrons,** which are negatively charged particles. The mass of an electron is very small: only about 1/2,000 the mass of a proton or neutron.

◄ **Democritus, a philosopher in ancient Greece, argued that matter was made of atoms. He also believed that things such as taste, feelings, and colors had atoms.**

In every atom, the number of protons equals the number of electrons. A carbon atom, for example, always has 6 protons and 6 electrons. Different carbon atoms may have different numbers of neutrons. While most carbon atoms have 6 neutrons, some have 7 or 8 neutrons.

To understand the electric properties of atoms, scientists assign a charge of $^+1$ to each proton, a charge of $^-1$ to each electron, and 0 charge to each neutron. Because an atom has equal numbers of protons and electrons, the total charge of the atom is 0.

In later lessons, you'll learn how atoms combine to form different substances. One way they do this is by losing or gaining electrons. When this happens, an atom becomes an ion. By gaining electrons, an atom becomes a negatively charged ion. By losing them, it becomes a positively charged ion.

What if an atom's nucleus were enlarged to the size of a quarter? If so, an atom centered on the pitcher's mound would reach to the warning track! ▼

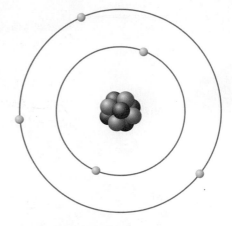

🔴 **Proton** ⚪ **Neutron** ⚬ **Electron**

An atom has a nucleus of protons and neutrons. Electrons reside in orbitals around the nucleus.

Think about something around you: a book, a wall, even specks of chalk dust. All such things are composed of atoms of different elements. Inside those atoms are protons, neutrons, and electrons, each identical from one atom to the next. Keep these facts in mind as you read on! They are the key to the study of matter.

MAIN IDEA AND DETAILS **Where in the atom are protons, neutrons, and electrons?**

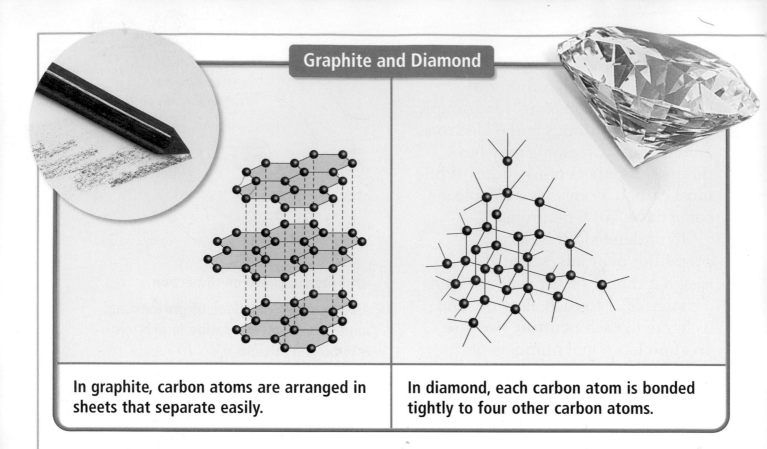

Graphite and Diamond

In graphite, carbon atoms are arranged in sheets that separate easily.

In diamond, each carbon atom is bonded tightly to four other carbon atoms.

Organization of Atoms

Scientists have identified more than 100 different elements, although only about 50 are especially common. Yet the world around you is made of a huge variety of matter. How can matter be so diverse? The answer lies in the way atoms join together.

For example, consider carbon, one of the most common elements on Earth. Even in its element form, carbon atoms can group together in many different ways.

One such grouping is found in coal—a hard, black substance made mostly of carbon and hydrogen. Coal is a very important fossil fuel that forms from dead plants underground.

Another grouping of carbon atoms is found in a substance called graphite. Graphite is gray or black and has a slippery feel. The "lead" in most pencils is actually graphite mixed with clay.

Diamond is another form of pure carbon. Diamonds are formed at high temperature and pressure deep in Earth's crust. They are beautiful, valuable, and the hardest natural substance found on Earth. Low-quality diamonds are put in tools used for cutting and grinding.

How can all these forms of the same element be so different? As shown in the diagrams above, carbon atoms can arrange in different ways. Each arrangement provides different properties.

Express Lab

Activity Card 23
Model an Atom's Diameter

Elements Alone and Joined

As you learned about carbon, an element's properties stem from the atoms that make it up and the way those atoms join together. Examples of properties are color, hardness, and density. Look at the photos on this page. All of these elements are useful for different purposes. What are some of the properties of the elements shown?

A few elements, such as helium, are found in nature only by themselves, never joined with other elements. But most elements typically form compounds. A **compound** is a pure substance that is made of two or more elements that are chemically combined.

Chemical compounds are everywhere! The paper and inks in this book are made of a number of different compounds. The salt and sugar on your dinner table are also compounds. Vinegar is a mixture of two compounds: acetic acid and water.

Many compounds are made of molecules. A molecule is a group of atoms that acts as a single unit. You will learn much more about elements, compounds, and molecules as you read on.

Helium
The helium in these balloons is less dense than air, so they float.

Aluminum
Aluminum is a metallic element that is strong but lightweight.

Copper
Copper can be stretched into wires. It also conducts electricity well.

MAIN IDEA AND DETAILS How can a small number of elements form a huge variety of matter?

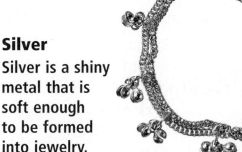

Silver
Silver is a shiny metal that is soft enough to be formed into jewelry.

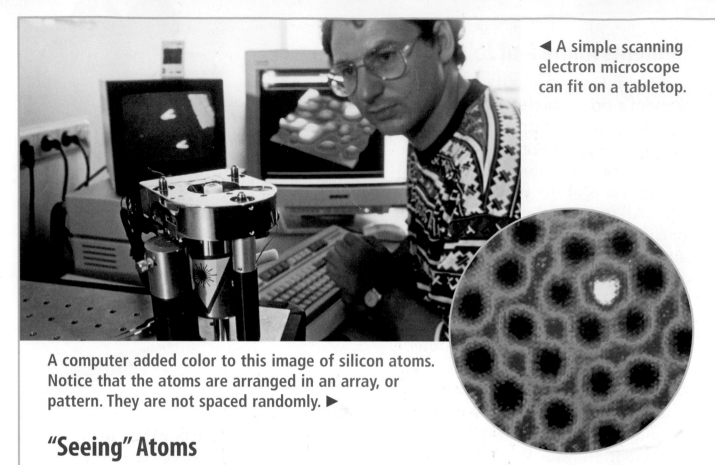

◀ A simple scanning electron microscope can fit on a tabletop.

A computer added color to this image of silicon atoms. Notice that the atoms are arranged in an array, or pattern. They are not spaced randomly. ▶

"Seeing" Atoms

Most microscopes, including those in your school, use lenses and light to magnify images. They work well for studying the tissues that make up living things. Other microscopes study cells not with light but with electrons. Electron microscopes can produce very detailed pictures of cells and cell parts.

While these tools are useful, they are not powerful enough to study atoms. For years, scientists could only infer the structure of atoms. That changed in 1981, when Gerd Binnig and Heinrich Rohrer invented the scanning tunneling microscope (STM).

An STM is a special type of electron microscope. It uses a probe to slowly scan across a solid surface. The probe scans extremely closely— so closely that electrons "tunnel"

between the probe and the atoms of the surface beneath it.

Using STMs, scientists have been able to take pictures of individual atoms and groups of atoms, such as the picture shown above. These pictures show how atoms and molecules often group together in well-ordered patterns, or arrays. Scientists also use STMs to measure the bumps and dips along a surface, such as the circuits of a computer chip.

Although scientists have been studying atoms for hundreds of years, they still have much to learn. What questions about atoms do you have? Do you think new technology could help you find the answers?

 **MAIN IDEA AND DETAILS** What is a scanning tunneling microscope?

Visual Summary

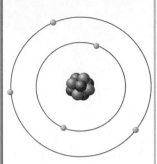

All matter is made of atoms or parts of atoms. Electrons travel in the space around the nucleus, which lies at the center of an atom.

An element is made of only one kind of atom. Atoms of elements can join or group together in different ways. This determines the element's properties.

A few elements, such as helium, are found in pure form. Most elements tend to join into compounds with other elements. Modern tools show that atoms tend to form well-ordered patterns, or arrays.

STANDARDS
1.b., 1.d., 1.e.

Technology
Visit **www.eduplace.com/cascp** to find out more about elements and their combinations.

Reading Review

❶ MAIN IDEA What are atoms? Where can you find atoms?

❷ VOCABULARY Name the three types of particles that make up an *atom*. Describe where they are located in the atom.

❸ READING SKILL What has the scanning tunneling microscope shown about atoms?

Main Idea

Detail   Detail

❹ CRITICAL THINKING: Apply Why is there a greater variety of compounds than of elements and atoms? Give an example to support your answer.

❺ INQUIRY SKILL: Use Numbers A zinc atom loses 3 electrons to become a zinc ion. Do you have enough information to find out the total charge of the ion? If yes, what is that charge?

 TEST PRACTICE
How many elements typically join together to form compounds?

A. all elements

B. most elements

C. only a few elements

D. no elements

 STANDARDS
1–2: 1.b., **3:** 1.e., **4:** 1.b., **5:** 1.d., **Test Practice:** 1.b.

STANDARDS 1.e. *Students know* scientists have developed instruments that can create discrete images of atoms and molecules that show that the atoms and molecules often occur in well-ordered arrays.

ATOMIC CORRAL

Just how small is an atom? If you lined up a million carbon atoms in a row, they would barely be as wide as the period at the end of this sentence. That's small!

Imagine trying to build with something that small. Impossible? That's exactly what scientists are doing in the new field called nanotechnology. (Nano- means "extremely small" or "one-billionth.") Using a device called the scanning tunneling microscope, scientists can not only see but actually move individual atoms with incredible accuracy.

Scientists have used this device to build well-ordered arrays, like this corral, out of just dozen atoms. In time, scientists hope to build complex, molecule-sized machines.

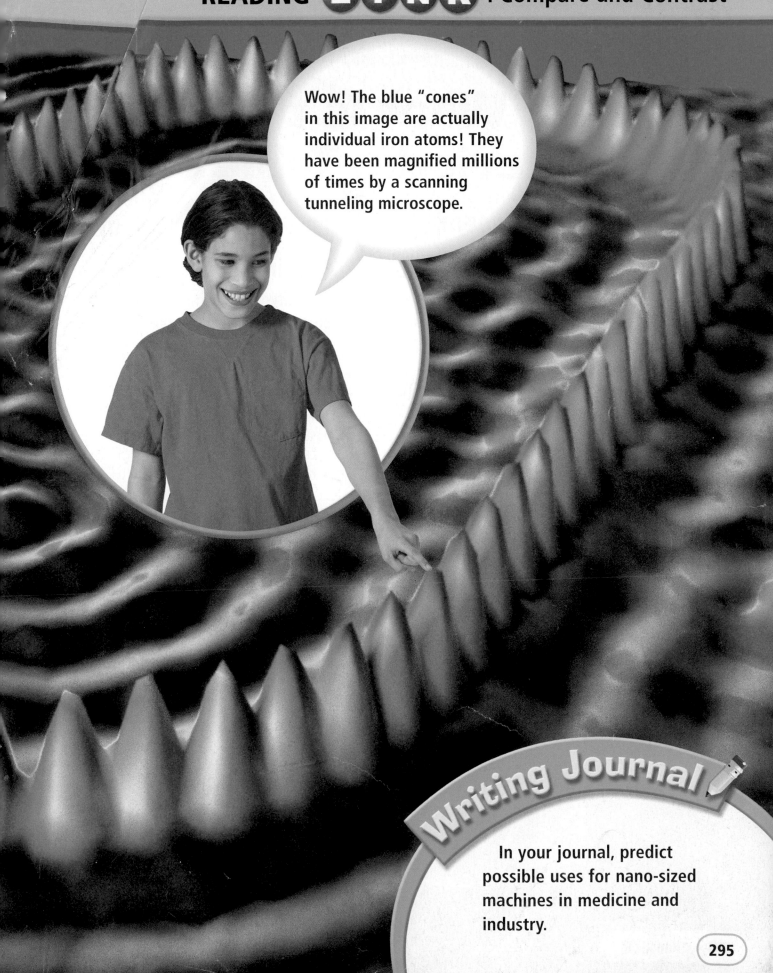

Wow! The blue "cones" in this image are actually individual iron atoms! They have been magnified millions of times by a scanning tunneling microscope.

Writing Journal

In your journal, predict possible uses for nano-sized machines in medicine and industry.

What Is the Periodic Table?

Building Background

Many signs contain neon, argon, or similar gases. The gases glow when an electric current passes through them.

Neon and argon are among the more than 100 known elements. Scientists have grouped all the elements into a table based on their properties.

STANDARDS

1.c. *Students know* metals have properties in common, such as high electrical and thermal conductivity. Some metals, such as aluminum (Al), iron (Fe), nickel (Ni), copper (Cu), silver (Ag), and gold (Au), are pure elements; others, such as steel and brass, are composed of a combination of elemental metals.

6.a. Students will classify objects (e.g. rocks, plants, leaves) in accordance with appropriate criteria.

PREPARE TO INVESTIGATE

Inquiry Skill

Classify When you classify, you sort objects according to their properties.

Materials

- safety goggles
- samples of copper, aluminum, carbon, and sulfur
- hand lens

Science and Math Toolbox

For step 1, review **Making a Chart to Organize Data** on page H11.

Compare Elements

Procedure

Safety: Wear goggles for this investigation.

1 **Collaborate** Work with a partner. Gather the materials listed. In your *Science Notebook,* make a chart like the one shown.

2 **Observe** Look at the samples of copper, aluminum, carbon, and sulfur. Test each sample to find some of its properties. You may observe it closely, feel it, and rub it lightly on a piece of paper. Try to find properties that two or more of the samples have in common.

3 **Record Data** As you examine each element, record the properties you observe in your chart. For example, is the element hard or soft? Stiff or bendable? Dull or shiny?

4 **Classify** How would you classify the elements into two groups? Below your chart, list and describe the two groups.

Conclusion

1. **Analyze Data** Compare your observation of the elements. How are copper and aluminum similar? How are carbon and sulfur similar?

2. **Infer** Based on your observations, what do you think might be some properties of metals and some properties of nonmetals?

STEP 1

Element	Properties
Copper	
Aluminum	
Carbon	
Sulfur	

STEP 2

STEP 2

Guided Inquiry

Experiment How would you **compare** the ability of each element to conduct electricity? Plan a test, then conduct it with your teacher's permission. Write a report that includes a graph, diagram, or chart to display your results.

The Periodic Table

MAIN IDEA Scientists have identified more than 100 elements, including metals, semimetals, and nonmetals. The elements are organized in the periodic table.

Organizing the Elements

Around 450 B.C., the Greek philosopher Empedocles (ehm PEHD uh kleez) suggested that all matter is made up of four elements—earth, air, fire, and water. By the Middle Ages, people began to realize that more than just those four elements must exist.

In the 1600s, English chemist Robert Boyle argued that earth, air, fire, and water could not be real elements. In the 1700s, French chemist Antoine-Laurent Lavoisier made one of the first modern lists of chemical elements.

By the 1800s, scientists had begun to identify many new elements. Scientists were also learning that some elements had similar properties. They began to organize elements into families, or groups, with similar properties. However, they lacked a standardized way of classifying the elements.

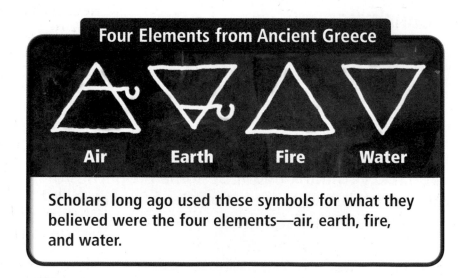

Four Elements from Ancient Greece

Air   Earth   Fire   Water

Scholars long ago used these symbols for what they believed were the four elements—air, earth, fire, and water.

ПЕРИОДИЧЕСКАЯ СИСТЕМА ЭЛЕМЕНТОВ

группы элементов

		I	II	III	IV	V	VI	VII	VIII			0
1	I	H 1 1.008										He 2 4.003
2	II	Li 3 6.940	Be 4 9.02	B 5 10.82	C 6 12.010	N 7 14.008	O 8 16.000	F 9 19.00				Ne 10 20.183
3	III	Na 11 22.997	Mg 12 24.32	Al 13 26.97	Si 14 28.06	P 15 30.98	S 16 32.06	Cl 17 35.457				Ar 18 39.944
4	IV	K 19 39.096	Ca 20 40.0	Sc 21 45.10	Ti 22 47.90	V 23 50.95	Cr 24 52.01	Mn 25 54.93	Fe 26 55.85	Co 27 58.94	Ni 28 58.69	
	V	Cu 29 63.57	Zn 30 65.38	Ga 31 69.72	Ge 32 72.60	As 33 74.91	Se 34 78.96	Br 35 79.916				Kr 36 83.7
5	VI	Rb 37 85.48	Sr 38 87.63	Y 39 88.92	Zr 40 91.22	Nb 41 92.91	Mo 42 95.95	Ma 43 —	Ru 44 101.7	Rh 45 102.91	Pd 46 106.7	
	VII	Ag 47 107.88	Cd 48 112.41	In 49 114.76	Sn 50 118.70	Sb 51 121.76	Te 52 127.61	J 53 126.92				Xe 54 131.3
6	VIII	Cs 55 132.91	Ba 56 137.36	La 57 138.92	Hf 72 178.6	Ta 73 180.88	W 74 183.92	Re 75 186.31	Os 76 190.2	Ir 77 193.1	Pt 78 195.23	
	IX	Au 79 197.2	Hg 80 200.61	Tl 81 204.39	Pb 82 207.21	Bi 83 209.00	Po 84 210	85				Rn 86 222
7	X	— 87	Ra 88 226.05	Ac 89 227	Th 90 232.12	Pa 91 231	U 92 238.07					

★ ЛАНТАНИДЫ 58–71

Ce 58 140.13	Pr 59 140.92	Nd 60 144.27	— 61	Sm 62 150.43	Eu 63 152.0	Gd 64 156.9
Tb 65 159.2	Dy 66 162.46	Ho 67 164.94	Er 68 167.2	Tu 69 169.4	Yb 70 173.04	Cp 71 174.99

Dmitri Mendeleyev left blank spaces in his table for elements that he predicted were yet to be discovered. The photo shows one of his revised tables.

Mendeleyev's Table

In 1869, Russian chemist Dmitri Mendeleyev developed a way to arrange and classify the elements. First, he listed the elements in order of increasing mass. By studying the list, he noticed that the properties of the elements in his list showed a repeating pattern.

Next, he rearranged the list so that elements with similar properties would appear in the same columns of his table. When arranging the elements this way, he had to leave some blank spaces in his table.

Mendeleyev predicted that sometime in the future, scientists would discover the elements that fit in the blank spaces. He thought these elements would have properties similar to those elements above and below them in the table. These predictions were correct, and scientists saw the value of the table.

Today scientists use a table of elements very similar to Mendeleyev's table. Like his table, the modern **periodic table** is a table in which the elements are arranged by their properties. The periodic table is standardized. This means that scientists all over the world can use the same one.

Why is it called a periodic table? Recall that Mendeleyev discovered that the properties of elements have a repeating pattern. The word *periodic* means "repeating."

Although Mendeleyev recognized the pattern among the elements, he could not explain why the pattern should exist. Scientists now can explain how elements in the same column of the table form chemical bonds in similar ways.

COMPARE How does today's classification of elements compare to that of the ancient Greeks?

The Periodic Table

In the modern periodic table, elements are arranged in order of increasing *atomic number*. This is the number of protons in their nuclei.

One example of the periodic table is shown below. The box for each element lists the atomic number, chemical symbol, and name. The **chemical symbol** is an abbreviation of the element's name, sometimes from Latin or Greek.

Each column in the periodic table is called a *group*. Elements within a group have similar properties. For example, look at the group that contains copper (Cu), silver (Ag), and gold (Au). These three elements are all soft, shiny metals.

The horizontal rows in the table are called *periods*. Notice that the periods have an increasing number of elements. Do you see the two rows that seem to have been pulled out of the table? This keeps the drawing of the table from being too wide.

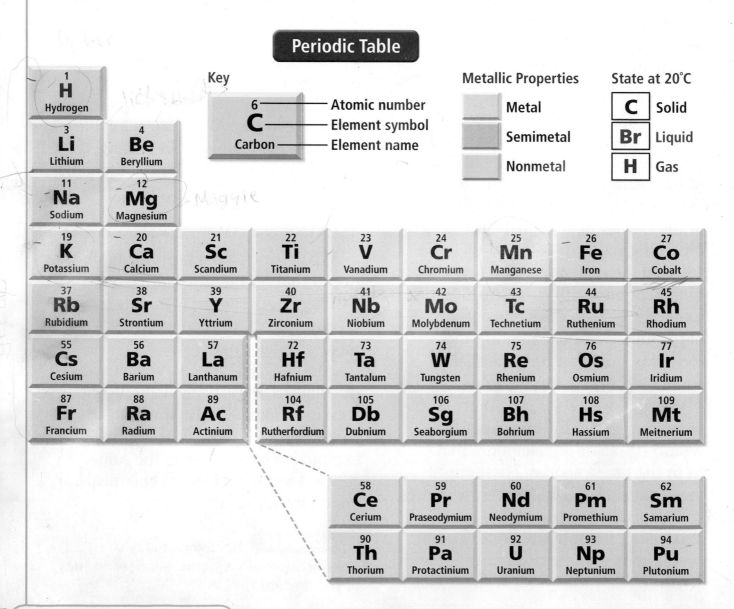

Periodic Table

Elements can be classified in different ways. Below, the colors of the boxes show whether elements are metals, nonmetals, or semimetals.

Metals are usually shiny, can be bent or stretched, and conduct electricity. Most elements are metals.

Many **nonmetals** are gases. Solid nonmetals are usually dull in color, do not conduct electricity, do not bend or stretch very much, and break easily. **Semimetals** are like metals in some ways and like nonmetals in other ways.

Can you find the pattern of metals, nonmetals, and semimetals in the table?

Also notice that the chemical symbols are different colors. The color tells you whether the element is a solid, liquid, or gas at room temperature. Most elements are solids.

In the periodic table below, elements with black symbols are solids. Only two elements, mercury (Hg) and bromine (Br), are liquids at room temperatures. Their symbols are blue. Elements with red symbols are gases.

COMPARE How does Mendeleyev's first periodic table compare to the modern table?

							2 **He** Helium
			5 **B** Boron	6 **C** Carbon	7 **N** Nitrogen	8 **O** Oxygen	9 **F** Fluorine	10 **Ne** Neon
			13 **Al** Aluminum	14 **Si** Silicon	15 **P** Phosphorus	16 **S** Sulfur	17 **Cl** Chlorine	18 **Ar** Argon
28 **Ni** Nickel	29 **Cu** Copper	30 **Zn** Zinc	31 **Ga** Gallium	32 **Ge** Germanium	33 **As** Arsenic	34 **Se** Selenium	35 **Br** Bromine	36 **Kr** Krypton
46 **Pd** Palladium	47 **Ag** Silver	48 **Cd** Cadmium	49 **In** Indium	50 **Sn** Tin	51 **Sb** Antimony	52 **Te** Tellurium	53 **I** Iodine	54 **Xe** Xenon
78 **Pt** Platinum	79 **Au** Gold	80 **Hg** Mercury	81 **Tl** Thallium	82 **Pb** Lead	83 **Bi** Bismuth	84 **Po** Polonium	85 **At** Astatine	86 **Rn** Radon

63 **Eu** Europium	64 **Gd** Gadolinium	65 **Tb** Terbium	66 **Dy** Dysprosium	67 **Ho** Holmium	68 **Er** Erbium	69 **Tm** Thulium	70 **Yb** Ytterbium	71 **Lu** Lutetium
95 **Am** Americium	96 **Cm** Curium	97 **Bk** Berkelium	98 **Cf** Californium	99 **Es** Einsteinium	100 **Fm** Fermium	101 **Md** Mendelevium	102 **No** Nobelium	103 **Lr** Lawrencium

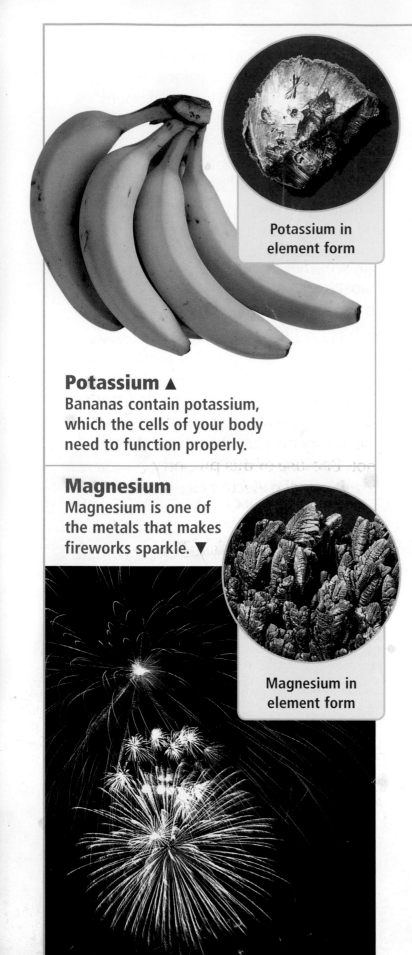

Potassium ▲
Bananas contain potassium,
which the cells of your body
need to function properly.

Magnesium
Magnesium is one of
the metals that makes
fireworks sparkle. ▼

Potassium in
element form

Magnesium in
element form

Metals

In the periodic table on pages
300 and 301, find the red line that
runs through the semimetals. All
the metals fall to the left of this
line. Metals include such familiar
elements as iron, gold, nickel, silver,
and aluminum. Rarer metals include
technetium and francium.

When you think about something
made of metal, you probably think of
a shiny, silver- or gold-colored object.
One of the properties that most metals
have is luster, the ability to reflect light.

Can you think of some other
properties of metals? For example,
how can the shape of metals be
changed? Metal workers can hammer
metals into thin sheets and bend a
metal by using force or by heating it.
The ability to bend is a property of
most metals.

Think of how electricity comes
into your home. Most likely it travels
through copper electrical wires.
Electrical wires make use of two
properties of metals. These properties
are the ability to be stretched or pulled
into thin wires, and the ability to
conduct electricity.

Most metallic objects are made
from more than one metal or from
metals joined with nonmetals. Your
soft-drink can is probably made from
the metals aluminum and manganese.
Your desk might contain steel, which
is made from iron and carbon. Brass
is a mixture of copper and zinc. Even
gold or silver jewelry is made from
metal mixtures, not pure metals.

Calcium ▲
The calcium in milk helps keep your bones strong and healthy.

Calcium in element form

Metals are also found in foods and in your body. However, they usually are combined with other elements in chemical compounds. The calcium in your bones, for example, does not look like the chips of pure calcium shown in the photograph above. Instead, it forms compounds with carbon, oxygen, hydrogen, and other elements.

Silicon ▶
Computer chips are made from silicon.

Semimetals

In the periodic table, semimetals are located between the metals and the nonmetals. These elements have properties of both metals and nonmetals. They are also known as metalloids.

One semimetal is silicon. About 28 percent of Earth's crust is silicon, making it Earth's second most common element. Sand is a compound of silicon and oxygen. Silicon is found in most rocks, in oceans, and even in your body.

Like all semimetals, silicon is a semiconductor. That means that under some circumstances silicon conducts electricity and at other times it does not. Because of this property, silicon is used to make electric circuits found in computer chips.

COMPARE AND CONTRAST What is the difference between a metal and a nonmetal?

Silicon in element form

Nonmetals and Noble Gases

Recall that solid nonmetals are dull in color and do not conduct electricity. They are usually brittle, which means they break easily. One example of a nonmetal is sulfur.

Sulfur is a very important element in the chemical industry. It is used as an ingredient in chemicals such as sulfuric acid, a very strong acid that is found in car batteries. Another nonmetal is phosphorus, which is used to make the striking surfaces of safety matches.

Many nonmetals are gases. Nitrogen makes up about 78 percent of the air you breathe. It is also important in making fertilizers. Oxygen is the most abundant element on Earth. About 21 percent of the air and 47 percent of Earth's crust is oxygen. Oxygen reacts with many metals. Have you ever seen an old, rusty car? Rust is iron oxide—a compound of iron and oxygen.

Compounds of fluorine are added to drinking water to help prevent tooth decay. Chlorine is also often added to drinking water in small amounts to kill bacteria or any other organisms that may be in the water. This has helped stop diseases that once killed huge numbers of people.

The last column, or group, of the periodic table is made of nonmetals only. These are the **noble gases,** the elements that hardly ever combine with other elements to form compounds.

The noble gas helium is used to fill balloons and airships because it is lighter than air. Helium and other noble gases are also used in welding.

Noble gases will glow if an electric current is passed though them. For this reason, they are used to make what are called neon lights, even though neon is not the only gas that is used. Different mixtures of the gases glow in different colors.

COMPARE How do noble gases differ from other elements?

Signs like this one use tubes filled with neon and other noble gases. An electric current makes the gases glow. ▼

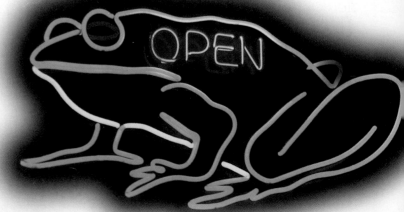

Express Lab

Activity Card 24
Classify Two Elements

Lesson Wrap-Up

Visual Summary

Dmitri Mendeleyev created the first periodic table. He left blank spaces for elements that he believed would be discovered later.

6
C
Carbon

The periodic table presents basic information for each element: name, chemical symbol, and atomic number.

2 He Helium			
7 N Nitrogen	8 O Oxygen	9 F Fluorine	10 Ne Neon
15 P Phosphorus	16 S Sulfur	17 Cl Chlorine	18 Ar Argon
33 As Arsenic	34 Se Selenium	35 Br Bromine	36 Kr Krypton
51 Sb Antimony	52 Te Tellurium	53 I Iodine	54 Xe Xenon
83 Bi Bismuth	84 Po Polonium	85 At Astatine	86 Rn Radon

Elements are classified as metals, semimetals, and nonmetals. Most metals are good conductors of heat and electricity.

 STANDARDS

1.c., 1.d.

Technology
Visit **www.eduplace.com/cascp** to find out more about the periodic table.

Reading Review

❶ **MAIN IDEA** Why is the periodic table a useful tool?

❷ **VOCABULARY** Compare *metals*, *nonmetals*, and *semimetals*.

❸ **READING SKILL** How do the metals in living things compare to the pure form of the metals?

Compare	Contrast

❹ **CRITICAL THINKING: Apply** What can you learn from the periodic table? Give examples of information that the table provides and that it does not provide.

❺ **INQUIRY SKILL: Classify** What if scientists discovered a new element? Where would it fit into the periodic table? Would a new element ever be placed in the first row of the table, next to hydrogen? Explain.

 TEST PRACTICE

What elements are usually shiny, can be bent or stretched, and conduct electricity?

A. nonmetals

B. semimetals

C. noble gases

D. metals

 STANDARDS

1–2: 1.d., **3:** 1.c., **4–5:** 1.d., **Test Practice:** 1.c.

305

People and the Periodic Table

What kinds of scientists work with elements of the periodic table? Read these stories to find out!

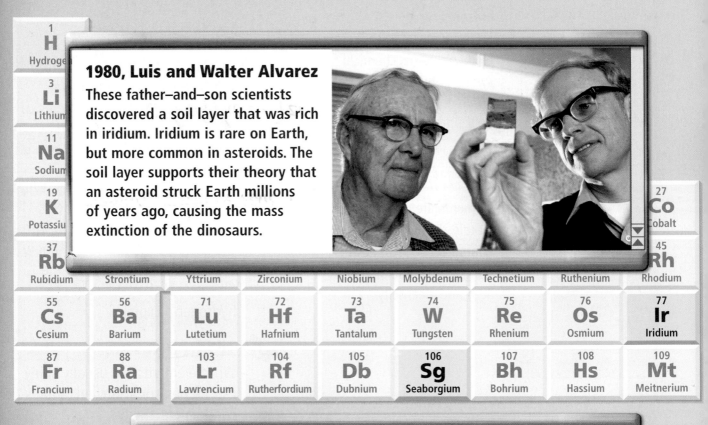

1 **H** Hydrogen								
3 **Li** Lithium								
11 **Na** Sodium								
19 **K** Potassium								27 **Co** Cobalt
37 **Rb** Rubidium	38 Strontium	39 Yttrium	40 Zirconium	41 Niobium	42 Molybdenum	43 Technetium	44 Ruthenium	45 **Rh** Rhodium
55 **Cs** Cesium	56 **Ba** Barium	71 **Lu** Lutetium	72 **Hf** Hafnium	73 **Ta** Tantalum	74 **W** Tungsten	75 **Re** Rhenium	76 **Os** Osmium	77 **Ir** Iridium
87 **Fr** Francium	88 **Ra** Radium	103 **Lr** Lawrencium	104 **Rf** Rutherfordium	105 **Db** Dubnium	106 **Sg** Seaborgium	107 **Bh** Bohrium	108 **Hs** Hassium	109 **Mt** Meitnerium

1980, Luis and Walter Alvarez

These father–and–son scientists discovered a soil layer that was rich in iridium. Iridium is rare on Earth, but more common in asteroids. The soil layer supports their theory that an asteroid struck Earth millions of years ago, causing the mass extinction of the dinosaurs.

62
Sm
Samarium

94
Pu
Plutonium

1974, Glenn Seaborg and the Lawrence Berkeley Laboratories

Glenn Seaborg and other scientists at the Lawrence Berkeley Laboratories in California discovered many of the high-numbered elements. Elements 97, 98, and 106 are named in their honor.

STANDARD

1.d. *Students know* that each element is made of one kind of atom and that the elements are organized in the periodic table by their chemical properties.

SOCIAL STUDIES **LINK**

1880s, Lewis Latimer

The first light bulbs burned out very quickly. Lewis Latimer invented a way to protect the carbon filament, which is the thin, glowing thread in the bulb's center. His work made electric lighting affordable and popular.

2003, Katharina Lodders

Dr. Lodders arranged the elements in a new way. Her periodic table is organized to show how abundant, or common, an element is in the universe. The table helps scientists study how planets form.

5 B Boron	6 C Carbon	
13 Al Aluminum	14 Si Silicon	Pho

28 Ni Nickel	29 Cu Copper	30 Zn Zinc	31 Ga Gallium	32 Ge Germanium	
46 Pd Palladium	47 Ag Silver	48 Cd Cadmium	49 In Indium	50 Sn Tin	
78 Pt Platinum	79 Au Gold	80 Hg Mercury	81 Tl Thallium	82 Pb Lead	
110 Ds Darmstadtium	111 Uuu Unununium*				

63 Eu Europium	64 Gd Gadolinium	65 Tb Terbium	66 Dy Dysprosium	67 Ho Holmium
95 Am Americium	96 Cm Curium	97 Bk Berkelium	98 Cf Californium	99 Es Einsteinium

Sharing Ideas

1. **READING CHECK** How did Luis and Walter Alvarez use iridium in their research?

2. **WRITE ABOUT IT** Choose an element. Research and write about ways it is used.

3. **TALK ABOUT IT** What kinds of scientists work with elements of the periodic table?

Lesson 3

Where Are Elements Found?

Building Background

Elements are everywhere! You can find aluminum in cans, oxygen in the atmosphere, and copper in pipes and wires. Name an example of matter, and you are naming something made of elements.

Different elements have different properties. By combining elements in the right way, scientists have made all sorts of products that you use every day.

STANDARDS

1.h. *Students know living organisms and most materials are composed of just a few elements.*
6.h. Draw conclusions from scientific evidence and indicate whether further information is needed to support a specific conclusion.

PREPARE TO INVESTIGATE

Inquiry Skill

Ask Questions When you ask questions that are based on facts and observations, you should be able to answer them with an experimental test.

Materials

- breakfast cereal with a high-iron content
- clear plastic bowl
- wooden ball or block
- water
- hand lens
- bar magnet

Find the Iron!

Procedure

1 **Record Data** Work with a partner. Study the table of nutrition facts on the package of cereal. Find out how much iron is in the cereal. Record the value in your *Science Notebook.*

STEP 2

2 **Observe** Pour some of the cereal into the bowl, just enough to cover the bottom. Use the hand lens to observe the cereal's color and texture. Record your observations.

3 **Experiment** Add just enough water to cover the cereal. Then use the ball or block to crush the wet cereal into a smooth mash. Continue crushing until the mash is as smooth and even as possible.

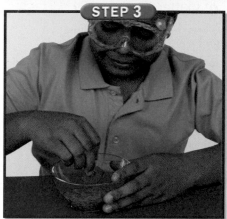
STEP 3

4 **Observe** Lift the bowl and hold the magnet flat against the bottom. Move the magnet slowly in a circle, always keeping it against the bowl. Observe any materials that the magnet attracts.

STEP 4

Conclusion

1. **Compare** How did your observations of the cereal change from the beginning to the end of the investigation?

2. **Classify** In step 4, what property of matter was used to separate the mixture of cereal and water?

3. **Hypothesize** In step 4, do you think you observed iron from the cereal? Describe an experiment or test that could confirm your answer. Tell whether further information is needed to support your conclusion.

Guided Inquiry

Ask Questions Why is iron an important part of your diet? **Research** the answer. Find out the minimum daily recommended dose of iron, foods that provide iron, and the role of iron in the circulatory system.

Elements Everywhere

VOCABULARY

molecule   p. 311

READING SKILL

Cause and Effect Use the graphic organizer to show how a few elements can make a wide variety of matter.

Cause → Effect

STANDARDS

1.b. *Students know* that all matter is made of atoms, which may combine to form molecules.
1.h. *Students know* living organisms and most materials are composed of just a few elements.

MAIN IDEA Most things on Earth are made of only a few elements—far fewer than the more than 100 elements that scientists have discovered.

Rare and Common Elements

Look again at the elements of the periodic table on pages 300 and 301. Most of these elements are quite rare, at least here on Earth. For example, all of the gold that has ever been mined could fill a cube only 19 meters per side. That's not much compared to the volume of Earth's crust!

Other elements are rarer still. Look at the elements after uranium in the periodic table. The nuclei of their atoms readily break apart into smaller nuclei. Many of these elements existed only in laboratories, and only for a few fractions of a second.

In fact, nearly 99 percent of Earth's crust is made of only 8 elements: oxygen, silicon, aluminum, iron, calcium, sodium, potassium, and magnesium. Almost all of Earth's atmosphere is made of two elements: oxygen and nitrogen.

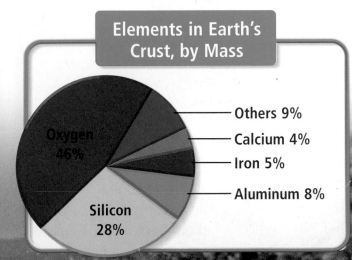

Elements in Earth's Crust, by Mass

Oxygen 46%
Silicon 28%
Aluminum 8%
Iron 5%
Calcium 4%
Others 9%

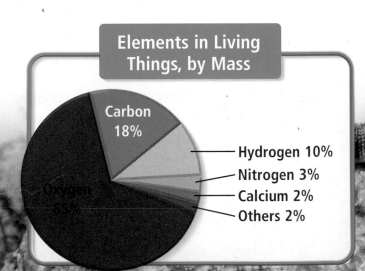

Elements in Living Things, by Mass

Oxygen 65%
Carbon 18%
Hydrogen 10%
Nitrogen 3%
Calcium 2%
Others 2%

Molecules

As you have read, elements can and do combine to form a huge number of compounds. Many of these compounds are made of molecules. A **molecule** is a group of two or more atoms that are chemically joined and that act as a single unit.

Some molecules are quite small. A molecule of water, for example, is made of 2 hydrogen atoms joined to 1 oxygen atom. Most of the gases in the atmosphere—including oxygen, nitrogen, and carbon dioxide—are made of molecules of only two or three atoms.

Other molecules are quite large. Some molecules in your body are made of thousands, millions, or even billions of atoms. Your body makes, uses, and breaks apart such molecules every second of every day. So do the bodies of all other living things on Earth!

As the circle graph shows, living things are made mostly of oxygen, carbon, and hydrogen. Compare the elements in living things to those in Earth's crust.

Acetone (C_3H_6O) molecule

A molecule of acetone is made of 10 atoms. Acetone is used in nail-polish remover. ▶

You can think of atoms as letters, and molecules as words made of letters. Just as many words can be made from only a few letters, so can many molecules be made from only a few kinds of atoms.

For example, consider carbon, oxygen, and hydrogen. Atoms of these elements can combine to form molecules of acetone (found in nail-polish remover), acetic acid (found in vinegar), sucrose (table sugar), and too many other compounds to list!

CAUSE AND EFFECT There are only a few elements. Why is there a huge number of molecules?

Fructose
$C_6H_{12}O_6$

Sugars are an important group of carbon compounds. The sugar in fruits is called fructose, $C_6H_{12}O_6$.

Hydrocarbons
example: C_8H_{18}

Many fuels are mixtures of hydrocarbons. When fuels burn, energy is released.

Protein
—$CH_2(COOH)NH_2$—

Living things contain a variety of carbon compounds. Long chains of amino acids are called proteins.

Carbon Compounds

Carbon forms more compounds than all but one other element, hydrogen. There are nearly 10 million known carbon compounds.

One important group of carbon compounds is the *hydrocarbons*. As the name suggests, these compounds are made of carbon and hydrogen. Hydrocarbons are important fuels. Methane, propane, and the compounds that make up gasoline are all examples of hydrocarbons.

Plastics are also made of hydrocarbons. In plastics, the molecules are linked together into long chains. Such chains are called polymers. Polymers provide strength and flexibility to plastics.

Carbon compounds are also the main parts of all living things. These carbon compounds fall into four main groups.

Carbohydrates provide the body with energy. Most plant tissue is made of carbohydrates. You take in lots of carbohydrates when you eat bread, pasta, and cereal.

Proteins help build muscle and other body tissues. Meats, fish, soybeans, eggs, and dairy products are all rich in protein. Proteins also help the body control chemical changes.

Lipids make up fat tissue. They help the body store energy. Butter, oils, cheese, and nuts are good sources of lipids.

Nucleic acids form very long polymers that help living things grow and develop. DNA is one example of a polymer of nucleic acid. In every living thing, DNA determines every trait in the body.

COMPARE AND CONTRAST Compare the four types of carbon compounds found in living things.

Lesson Wrap-Up

Visual Summary

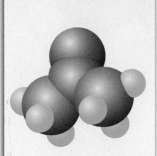

Elements are everywhere! Although there are over 100 elements, nearly 99 percent of Earth's crust is made of only eight elements.

A molecule is made of two or more atoms that are joined together and act as a single unit. Molecules are the "building blocks" for many compounds.

Living things use and make many types of carbon compounds. Four classes of important carbon compounds are carbohydrates, proteins, lipids, and nucleic acids.

 **STANDARDS**

1.b., 1.h.

 Technology

Visit **www.eduplace.com/cascp** to find out more about where elements are found.

Reading Review

❶ **MAIN IDEA** Are most of the elements commonly or rarely found in Earth's crust? Give examples to support your answer.

❷ **VOCABULARY** What is a *molecule*? List at least three examples of molecules.

❸ **READING SKILL** Why do you think living things are not made of uranium, plutonium, or other high-numbered elements?

❹ **CRITICAL THINKING: Analyze** A student is studying a compound. She finds that it is made of only three elements: carbon, hydrogen, and oxygen. Is this enough information to identify the compound? Explain.

❺ **INQUIRY SKILL: Ask Questions** Humans need metals such as zinc, copper, and manganese. Ask questions about how the human body uses these metals, then research the answers.

 TEST PRACTICE

Which is a carbon compound?

A. lipid

B. helium

C. water

D. salt

 STANDARDS

1: 1.h., **2:** 1.b., **3:** 1.h., **4:** 1.b., **5:** 1.h., **Test Practice:** 1.b.

313

Math in Science

The picture models a molecule of acetone. The 3 black spheres represent carbon, the 6 blue spheres represent hydrogen, and the red sphere represents oxygen.

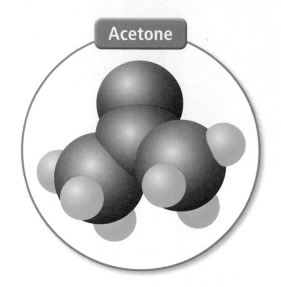

Acetone

1. Of the total number of atoms in an acetone molecule, what percent are carbon atoms? What percents are hydrogen atoms and oxygen atoms?

2. A certain acetone sample contains 3.5 million acetone molecules. What are the percents of carbon, hydrogen, and oxygen atoms in this sample?

3. How could you estimate the volume of the model of acetone? To report the volume, would you use units of cm, cm^2, or cm^3?

Writing in Science
Research Report

Scanning tunneling microscopes (STMs) allow scientists to picture three-dimensional images of atoms and molecules. Research the history of microscopes, from the work of Anton Van Leeuwenhoek to the powerful microscopes of today.

Forensic Chemist

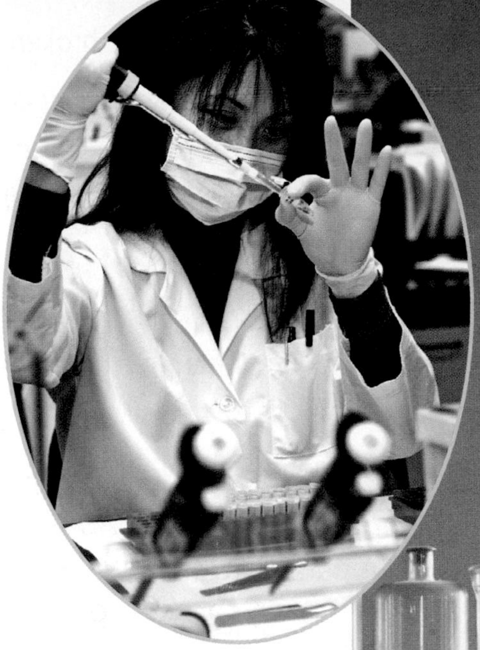

Hundreds of crimes every year are solved with the help of forensic chemists. These scientists carefully examine crime scenes and conduct laboratory tests on evidence.

Forensic chemists might analyze DNA, identify chemicals, or examine such evidence as broken glass, carpet fibers, and strands of hair. They often must report their findings to lawyers and judges.

What It Takes!

- A degree in chemistry, biology, or genetics
- Good analytical and laboratory skills

Food Science Technician

Food science technicians test food for quality and safety. They also test nutrition labels. They check the taste and smell of food, and use microscopes to check food for organisms that could cause disease.

Food science technicians need good listening and speaking skills. Many of these technicians work as assistants to food scientists.

What It Takes!

- A high-school diploma
- Additional job-related courses

Vocabulary

Complete each sentence with a term from the list.

1. A(n) _____ cannot be broken apart into other substances.

2. Elements that hardly ever combine with other elements to form molecules are _____.

3. The center of an atom is called the _____.

4. A(n) _____ is made of two or more atoms joined together and that act as a single unit.

5. An abbreviation of the element's name, sometimes from Latin or Greek, is called a(n) _____.

6. Elements called _____ are like metals in some ways and like nonmetals in others.

7. A particle with a positive charge is a(n) _____.

8. A pure substance made up of two or more elements that are chemically combined is a(n) _____.

9. Elements called _____ are usually shiny, can be bent or stretched, and conduct electricity.

10. The smallest particle of an element that still has the properties of that element is a(n) _____.

atom p. 288
chemical symbol p. 299
compound p. 291
electron p. 288
element p. 288
metal p. 301
molecule p. 311
neutron p. 288
noble gas p. 304
nonmetal p. 301
nucleus p. 288
periodic table p. 299
proton p. 288
semimetal p. 301

Test Practice

Write the letter of the best answer choice.

11. Which of the following is negatively charged?

    A. proton
    B. electron
    C. neutron
    D. compound

12. What kind of element is usually dull in color, does not conduct electricity, does not bend or stretch very much, and breaks easily?

    A. chemical   C. nonmetal
    B. semimetal   D. metal

13. In the periodic table, elements are arranged according to _____.

    A. atomic number
    B. the first letter of their name
    C. the number of neutrons and protons in the nucleus
    D. size and shape

14. An uncharged particle is called a(n) _____.

    A. metal   C. proton
    B. electron   D. neutron

Inquiry Skills

15. **Compare** How is the periodic table different from an alphabetical list of elements?

16. What information about an element can be inferred from its location in the periodic table?

							2 **He** Helium
			5 **B** Boron	6 **C** Carbon	7 **N** Nitrogen	8 **O** Oxygen	9 **F** Fluorine	10 **Ne** Neon

			13 **Al** Aluminum	14 **Si** Silicon	15 **P** Phosphorus	16 **S** Sulfur	17 **Cl** Chlorine	18 **Ar** Argon
28 **Ni** Nickel	29 **Cu** Copper	30 **Zn** Zinc	31 **Ga** Gallium	32 **Ge** Germanium	33 **As** Arsenic	34 **Se** Selenium	35 **Br** Bromine	36 **Kr** Krypton
46 **Pd** Palladium	47 **Ag** Silver	48 **Cd** Cadmium	49 **In** Indium	50 **Sn** Tin	51 **Sb** Antimony	52 **Te** Tellurium	53 **I** Iodine	54 **Xe** Xenon
78 **Pt** Platinum	79 **Au** Gold	80 **Hg** Mercury	81 **Tl** Thallium	82 **Pb** Lead	83 **Bi** Bismuth	84 **Po** Polonium	85 **At** Astatine	86 **Rn** Radon

63 **Eu** Europium	64 **Gd** Gadolinium	65 **Tb** Terbium	66 **Dy** Dysprosium	67 **Ho** Holmium	68 **Er** Erbium	69 **Tm** Thulium	70 **Yb** Ytterbium	71 **Lu** Lutetium
95 **Am** Americium	96 **Cm** Curium	97 **Bk** Berkelium	98 **Cf** Californium	99 **Es** Einsteinium	100 **Fm** Fermium	101 **Md** Mendelevium	102 **No** Nobelium	103 **Lr** Lawrencium

Map the Concept

Fill in the flow chart with the following words. Begin with the smaller structures and work toward the larger. One word is used twice.

atom   electron   molecule
neutron   proton

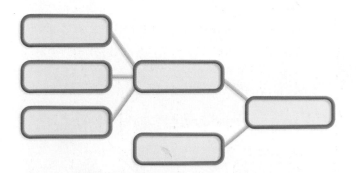

Critical Thinking

17. **Apply** Silicates are minerals that are composed mostly of the elements silicon and oxygen. Some silicates occur in sheet-like form and can be scratched with a fingernail. Others are bulky and so hard that they can scratch glass. How could you explain the differences in these minerals?

18. **Analyze** Two elements in the periodic table exist as liquids at room temperature. What are these elements? If they did occur as solids, would their placement in the periodic table be different? Explain.

19. **Infer** Groundwater can become polluted with heavy metals, such as lead and mercury, and with many toxic compounds. Do you think that water molecules are polluted permanently? If not, how might the water become cleaner? Explain.

20. **Evaluate** Are all elements equally common on Earth? Are they equally common in living things? Give examples to support your answer.

Performance Assessment

Draw an Atom

Oxygen has an atomic number of 8. A typical oxygen atom has 8 neutrons. Draw a model of this atom. Show where the protons, electrons, and neutrons are found. Refer to the atomic model.

Writing Journal

Review your journal writing answers at the beginning of this chapter. Revise and change them if necessary.

STANDARDS

1–2: 1.d., **3–4:** 1.b., **5:** 1.d., **6:** 1.c., 1.d., **7–8:** 1.b., **9:** 1.c., **10:** 1.b., **11:** 1.b., **12:** 1.c., **13:** 1.d., **14:** 1.b., **15:** 1.d., **16:** 1.d., 6.h., **Map the Concept:** 1.b., **17:** 1.b., 1.f., **18:** 1.d., **19:** 1.c., 1.f., **20:** 1.h., **Performance Assessment:** 1.b.

Chemical Compounds

A rusted ship on the California coast

Lesson Preview

LESSON 1

What forms when a greenish gas combines with a metal? The answer may surprise you!

LESSON 2

A beach ball helps you float in water. Why won't steel marbles help you float?

LESSON 3

The color of hydrangea flowers depends on the pH of the soil. What is pH?

Writing Journal

In your Writing Journal, write or draw answers to each question.

Vocabulary Preview

density
the mass per unit volume of an object

Vocabulary

Glossary

Vocabulary Skill

Multiple-Meaning Words
Base

EVERYDAY USE A base can be a home or a center. Baseball players run around bases, and soldiers work at a military base.

SCIENCE In science, a base is a class of compounds that is related to acids. When you read the word *base*, use context clues to determine which meaning is correct.

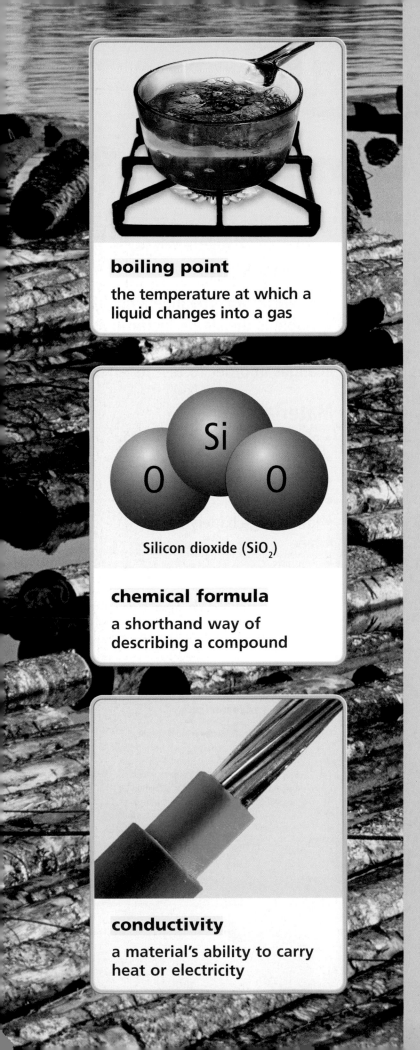

boiling point

the temperature at which a liquid changes into a gas

Silicon dioxide (SiO_2)

chemical formula

a shorthand way of describing a compound

conductivity

a material's ability to carry heat or electricity

Start with Your Standards

Standard Set 1. Physical Sciences

1.a. *Students know* that during chemical reactions the atoms in the reactants rearrange to form products with different properties.

1.f. *Students know* differences in chemical and physical properties of substances are used to separate mixtures and identify compounds.

1.i. *Students know* the common properties of salts, such as sodium chloride (NaCl).

Standard Set 6: Investigation and Experimentation standards covered in this chapter: 6.a., 6.e., 6.f.

What Are Compounds?

Building Background

Have you ever played with "slime" from a toy store? It is gooey and soft, but when you try to pull it apart, it holds together.

What gives the slime these properties? Like most substances, the slime has properties that depend on the chemical bonds that form between its atoms.

PREPARE TO INVESTIGATE

Inquiry Skill

Use Variables The independent variable is the single factor in an experiment that the investigator changes in order to test its effect.

Materials

- plastic cup
- water
- spoon
- baking soda
- low-voltage battery
- tape
- 2 wires

Science and Math Toolbox

Review **Use Variables** on page H5.

STANDARDS

1.a. *Students know* that during chemical reactions the atoms in the reactants rearrange to form products with different properties.
6.e. Identify a single independent variable in a scientific investigation and explain how this variable can be used to collect information to answer a question about the results of the experiment.

Splitting Water

Procedure

1 Collaborate Work with a partner. Fill the cup at least halfway with water. Stir in a spoonful of baking soda. **Safety:** Wear goggles. Use a low-voltage battery only. Never place wires from an electrical outlet into water.

2 Experiment Tape one end of each piece of wire to the battery terminals. Make sure the bare metal ends touch the terminals.

3 Experiment Place the other ends of the two wires in the water. Tape the wires to the sides of the cup so that they do not touch each other.

4 Observe Observe the ends of the two wires in the water. Record your observations in your *Science Notebook*. Note any differences you see at the end of each wire.

5 Predict Predict what would happen if you removed one of the wires from the water. Record your prediction, then test it.

Conclusion

1. **Hypothesize** Water is made up of the elements hydrogen and oxygen, which are gases at room temperature. What do you think the electric current does to the water? How do you know?

2. **Infer** Each molecule of water has two hydrogen atoms and one oxygen atom. Infer how this explains any differences that you observed. Do you have enough information to be sure?

STEP 1

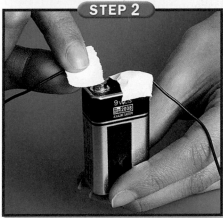
STEP 2

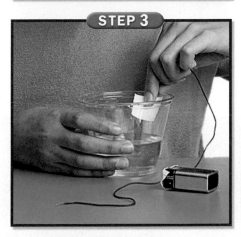
STEP 3

Guided Inquiry

Experiment Repeat the procedure without baking soda. Then replace it with sugar or salt and repeat the procedure again. The substance mixed into the water is the independent variable. **Use variables** to observe its effect.

READING SKILL

Main Idea and Details
Use a graphic organizer to track compounds and their properties.

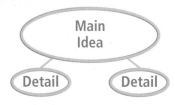

STANDARD

1.f. *Students know* differences in chemical and physical properties of substances are used to separate mixtures and identify compounds.

Compounds

MAIN IDEA Two or more elements can combine to form a compound. Compounds have different properties from the elements that make them up.

Combining Elements

At one time, water was thought to be an element. Recall that an element cannot be broken down into other substances. How did scientists discover that water is not an element? They broke it down into other substances by passing an electric current through it.

Water is a compound. As you have read, a compound is a pure substance made up of two or more elements that are chemically combined. Water is an example of a molecular compound, meaning it is made of molecules. Each water molecule is made of two hydrogen atoms and one oxygen atom.

Compounds have properties that are very different from the elements that make them up. Water, for example, is a liquid at room temperature. Oxygen and hydrogen, however, are invisible gases.

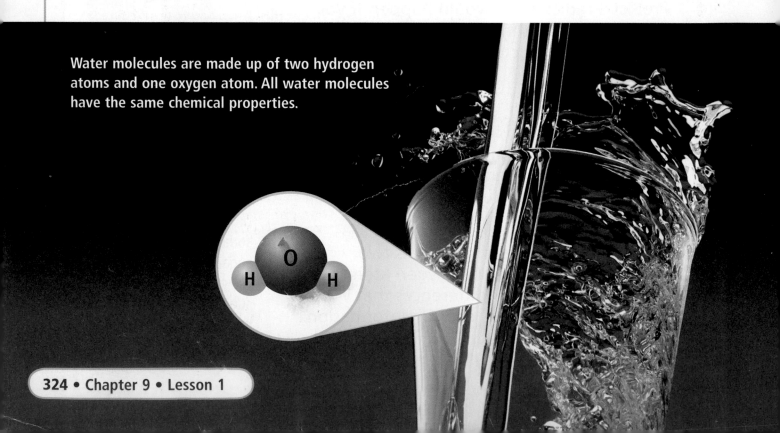

Water molecules are made up of two hydrogen atoms and one oxygen atom. All water molecules have the same chemical properties.

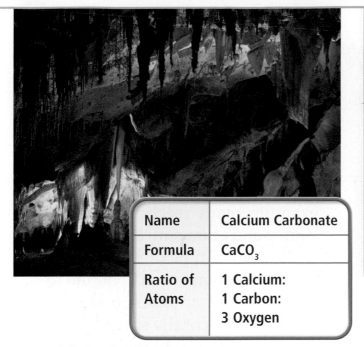

Name	Calcium Carbonate
Formula	$CaCO_3$
Ratio of Atoms	1 Calcium: 1 Carbon: 3 Oxygen

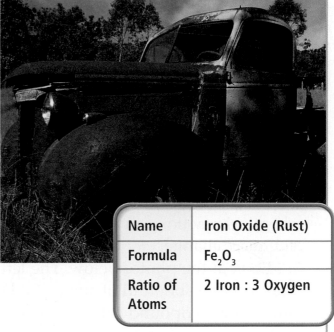

Name	Iron Oxide (Rust)
Formula	Fe_2O_3
Ratio of Atoms	2 Iron : 3 Oxygen

▲ Water evaporates, leaving calcium carbonate behind. This produces formations called stalagmites and stalactites.

▲ Some of the iron in this truck has rusted. Rust is a compound called iron oxide. Rust forms when iron combines with oxygen gas.

Many Compounds

Countless compounds are found in nature. Many more have been created in the laboratory.

Some compounds, like water, are made of just two elements. Each time you exhale, your breath contains the compound carbon dioxide. Molecules of carbon dioxide are made up of one carbon atom and two oxygen atoms.

Other compounds are more complex. Look at the unusual limestone formations in the photo of the cave. Limestone rock is mostly a compound called calcium carbonate. This compound also forms the hard parts of clams, corals, and many other animals.

Calcium carbonate is not made of molecules. Instead, the atoms are arranged in a rigid pattern called

a crystal. Many compounds form crystals in the solid state.

Compounds made of molecules may form crystals, too. A snowflake, for example, is made of crystals of water.

Another familiar compound is iron oxide, also known as rust. Steel is a mixture of iron, carbon, and other elements. When steel is exposed to air and rain, the iron will gradually change into rust. Both salt and water will speed up the rusting process.

COMPARE AND CONTRAST What forms when atoms of two or more elements combine chemically?

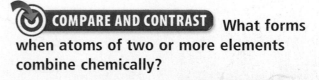

Express Lab

Activity Card 26
Make a Model Water Molecule

Making and Breaking Compounds

To form a compound, the atoms of the elements involved must take part in a chemical reaction. A **chemical reaction** is a process in which one or more substances are changed into one or more different substances. A chemical reaction can also be called a chemical change.

Look at the photos below. The left one shows a spoonful of sugar. Table sugar is a compound called sucrose. It is made up of carbon, hydrogen, and oxygen. One molecule of sucrose contains 45 atoms.

If you heat the sugar over a flame, the sugar will change. First, it will melt. Although the sugar has changed from solid to liquid, it is still sugar. The molecules have not changed. For this reason, melting is an example of a physical change. You will learn about this kind of change as you read on.

If you continue heating the sugar, a chemical reaction will take place. The liquid sugar will change to release gas to the air and leave a black substance behind. This substance is carbon. As with this example, many reactions break down compounds into simpler substances.

In another type of reaction, simple substances can combine to form a more complex substance. In the engines of the space shuttle, for example, liquid hydrogen and liquid oxygen combine to form water. Energy is released in the process. The exhaust from the main engines is steam, tiny droplets of water.

In all chemical reactions, energy is an important factor. Energy is required to break apart water or sugar into elements. Energy is released when elements combine to form water or sugar, and when fuel is burned.

Chemical Reaction

1. Sucrose ($C_{12}H_{22}O_{11}$) is a sugar, a compound of carbon, hydrogen, and oxygen.

2. When heated, the sucrose molecules break down, leaving the element carbon and releasing water molecules.

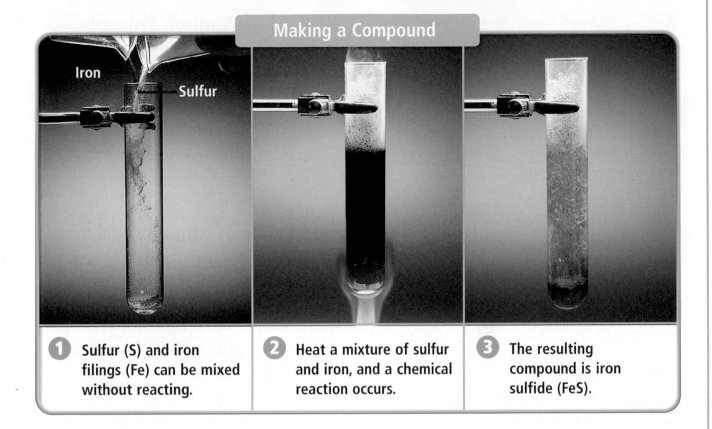

Making a Compound

1 Sulfur (S) and iron filings (Fe) can be mixed without reacting.

2 Heat a mixture of sulfur and iron, and a chemical reaction occurs.

3 The resulting compound is iron sulfide (FeS).

Iron

Sulfur

Compounds and Formulas

The photos show another example of a chemical reaction. When you mix black iron filings and yellow sulfur, they don't react. They are still iron and sulfur. You can use a magnet to separate the iron from the sulfur. However, if you heat the iron-and-sulfur mixture, the iron and sulfur atoms combine to form the compound iron sulfide.

Iron sulfide looks different from the iron and the sulfur from which it is made. It also has different properties. For example, no part of the compound is attracted to a magnet. The iron in iron sulfide has lost its magnetic property.

Scientists use chemical formulas to identify chemical compounds. A **chemical formula** is a shorthand way to describe a compound. Chemical formulas use chemical symbols and numbers to show the makeup of a compound.

For example, the chemical symbol for iron is Fe. The chemical symbol for sulfur is S. The chemical formula for iron sulfide, FeS, tells you that iron sulfide has one iron atom for every sulfur atom.

Often, the elements in a compound do not form a one-to-one ratio. In such cases, the ratio is indicated by small numbers to the lower right of the symbols. Such a number is called a subscript. For example, the chemical formula for water is H_2O. Any sample of water has two hydrogen atoms for every one oxygen atom.

MAIN IDEA AND DETAILS What does a subscript in a chemical formula represent?

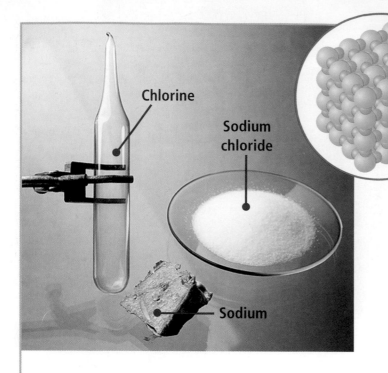

Chlorine

Sodium chloride

Sodium

◀ Sodium Chloride

Sodium (Na) and chlorine (Cl) are the elements that make up the compound sodium chloride (NaCl), or table salt.

Everyday Compounds

Compounds, like elements, are pure substances. Only a chemical reaction will break down a compound into its component elements.

The pictures on these pages show several compounds you probably encounter every day. These compounds, like all compounds, have their own distinctive chemical properties.

For example, common table salt is used in cooking and baking to add flavor to food. Salt is a compound called sodium chloride, or NaCl. As you know, sodium chloride forms hard, whitish crystals. The properties of sodium chloride are very different from those of sodium and chlorine.

In its element form, sodium is a very soft, shiny metal. It is so soft it can be cut with a butter knife. Sodium easily reacts with many substances and must be stored in oil.

When exposed to air, it reacts quickly with oxygen. In water, it violently reacts to form sodium hydroxide and hydrogen gas.

The element chlorine is a greenish, poisonous gas. It is used to kill bacteria and other harmful organisms in drinking water and swimming pools. Chlorine has a strong smell. If you've been swimming in a pool or used bleach, you know what chlorine smells like.

When sodium and chlorine meet, a chemical reaction between them produces salt, or sodium chloride. Salt is a very stable compound, meaning it does not chemically change very quickly or easily.

On the next page, you will read about three other common compounds. All are very different from the individual elements that make them up.

Chemical Formulas	
Compound	**Chemical Formula**
Sucrose	$C_{12}H_{22}O_{11}$
Calcium carbonate	$CaCO_3$
Iron oxide (rust)	Fe_2O_3

▲ These are the chemical formulas for some of the compounds you've already read about in this lesson.

Carbon Dioxide Carbon dioxide (CO_2) is a gas made up of carbon and oxygen. Every time you exhale, your lungs release carbon dioxide. It is also produced when almost anything containing carbon is burned.

Carbonated drinks get their fizz from CO_2. When placed under pressure, small amounts of carbon dioxide will dissolve in water. Release the pressure, and the CO_2 will bubble out. This is why soda slowly goes "flat" if you leave its container open.

Carbon dioxide gas gives soda its fizz and tart taste.

Glass Sand and glass are made mostly of silicon dioxide (SiO_2), a very common compound. SiO_2 is only one of the compounds in glass. It is mixed with others and heated. Then the glass is shaped as it cools.

Glass is an example of an amorphous solid, meaning a solid without form. Unlike the particles of other solids, the particles of silicon dioxide are arranged in a loose, random pattern.

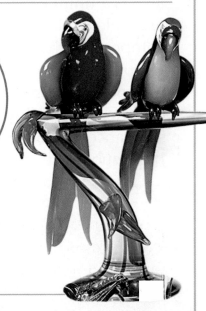

Glass is made of silicon dioxide (SiO_2) and other compounds.

Polymers Some compounds are made up of large molecules called polymers. A polymer is a chain-like molecule made up of repeated units. Many polymers are important to life. For example, many fats, proteins, carbohydrates, and even DNA are polymers. Plastics are polymers that are made from fossil fuels.

MAIN IDEA AND DETAILS Identify three common compounds and their uses.

The nonstick coating of this frying pan is made of a polymer.

Water: Earth's Most Abundant Compound

Water is everywhere on Earth. About three-fourths of Earth's surface is covered with water, and all organisms depend on water to live. Many organisms, such as fish and most single-celled organisms, can live only in water or in moist environments. You need water, too. Your body is about 65 percent water, and staying healthy requires water.

Not only is water abundant, it also is a unique compound. For example, water is one of the few compounds that is a liquid at room temperature.

Another interesting characteristic of water is its ability to dissolve substances. In fact, water dissolves more substances than any other liquid.

One reason for the unique properties of water is its shape. Water molecules have a bent shape. As shown in the diagram, the oxygen end of the molecule has a slight negative charge, and the hydrogen end has a slight positive charge. This uneven distribution of charge gives water its ability to attract and dissolve many compounds.

The charges also cause water molecules to attract one another. The slight positive charge of the hydrogen end of a molecule attracts the slight negative charge of the oxygen end of a second molecule. This is why water is a liquid over a wide range of temperatures.

MAIN IDEA AND DETAILS Name two unique properties of water.

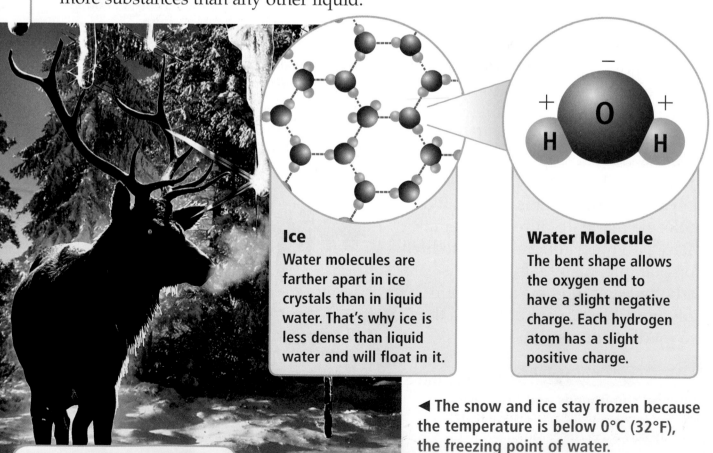

Ice
Water molecules are farther apart in ice crystals than in liquid water. That's why ice is less dense than liquid water and will float in it.

Water Molecule
The bent shape allows the oxygen end to have a slight negative charge. Each hydrogen atom has a slight positive charge.

◄ The snow and ice stay frozen because the temperature is below 0°C (32°F), the freezing point of water.

Visual Summary

The properties of a compound differ from those of the elements that make it up. Sugar is very different from carbon, hydrogen, and oxygen.

A chemical formula describes a compound. The formula for iron sulfide is FeS. The formula for water, H_2O, shows a ratio of 2 hydrogen atoms to 1 oxygen atom.

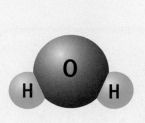

Water is a unique compound that is found almost everywhere on Earth. It is a liquid at room temperature and dissolves many other substances.

STANDARDS

1.f., 1.a.

 Technology
Visit **www.eduplace.com/cascp** to find out more about compounds.

Reading Review

❶ MAIN IDEA Is water an element or a compound? Explain.

❷ VOCABULARY What is a *chemical formula*? Give an example.

❸ READING SKILL Name a chemical reaction that takes place in the world around you. Describe how it changes matter.

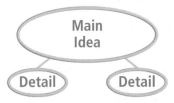

❹ CRITICAL THINKING: Predict Which do you predict is more commonly found in nature—the element sodium or sodium bound into compounds, such as sodium chloride? Explain.

❺ INQUIRY SKILL: Use Variables Will an iron nail rust faster in pure water or salt water? Design an experiment to show how salt affects rusting. Identify the dependent and independent variables.

 TEST PRACTICE
An iron chain will rust the fastest when it is placed _____.

A. on a bedroom table

B. in oil

C. in a plastic container

D. on an ocean beach

 STANDARDS

1: 1.f., **2:** 1.a., **3:** 1.a., 1.f., **4:** 1.a., 1.i., **5:** 1.f., 1.e.,
Test Practice: 1.a.

Glass

What is glass? In the past, scientists had trouble classifying glass. Glass acts like a solid. Yet its atoms are arranged quite randomly, like the particles of a liquid.

Scientists once argued that glass was a slow-moving liquid. Their evidence was 200 year-old window panes that were thicker on the bottom than on top. The scientists thought that the glass had slowly flowed downward. As they researched the windows, however, they discovered the true explanation. The windows had been built with thick bottoms to hold them in their frames.

Today, scientists classify glass as an amorphous solid, meaning a solid without form. Read on to learn how glass is made from sand. Do you agree that "without form" describes glass best?

▲ This glass vessel is over 2,000 years old.

From Sand to Glass

Sand	Glass	Tougher Glass
A sand grain is a crystal of silicon dioxide (SiO_2). Atoms of silicon (Si) and oxygen (O) are arranged tightly in a matrix.	When sand is heated, some of its bonds break apart. They reform when the sand cools. However, if the cooling is fast enough, the bonds reform in a random arrangement. This makes glass!	By mixing sodium carbonate with the sand, sodium ions (Na^+) become part of the glass that results. Sodium makes glass tougher and last longer. You use glass like this in windows, bottles, and other products.

STANDARD
1.g. *Students know* properties of solid, liquid, and gaseous substances, such as sugar ($C_6H_{12}O_6$), water (H_2O), helium (He), oxygen (O_2), nitrogen (N_2), and carbon dioxide (CO_2).

SOCIAL STUDIES LINK

Glass Blowing

In the traditional method, the glass artist blows through a long pipe, called a vessel, to shape the glass as it cools. Chemicals mixed with the melted glass tint it red, blue, purple, and other colors.

Safety Glass

Automobile windshields are stronger and safer than most glass. When they do break, they typically form hundreds of tiny pieces instead of larger, more dangerous shards.

Sharing Ideas

1. **READING CHECK** Describe how sand turns into glass.

2. **WRITE ABOUT IT** What properties of matter describe glass?

3. **TALK ABOUT IT** Compare glass to other materials.

333

What Are Some Properties of Compounds?

Building Background

Different materials each have their own unique physical and chemical properties. Different paints, for example, have different colors. The properties of a material determine ways it can be used. Discovering new properties of a material can lead to new uses and advances in technology.

STANDARDS

1.f. *Students know* differences in chemical and physical properties of substances are used to separate mixtures and identify compounds.
6.f. Select appropriate tools (e.g. thermometers, metersticks, balances, and graduated cylinders) and make quantitative observations.

PREPARE TO INVESTIGATE

Inquiry Skill

Use Numbers When you use numbers, you use numerical data, mathematical skills, and language to describe and compare objects and events.

Materials

- two 250-mL beakers
- vegetable oil
- balance
- water
- cardboard
- plastic wrap
- 2 books
- masking tape
- 2 droppers
- timer or stopwatch

Science and Math Toolbox

For step 1, review **Measuring Volume** on page H7.

Oil and Water

Procedure

1 **Collaborate** Work with a partner. Find the mass of an empty 250 mL beaker. Then add 100 mL of vegetable oil to the beaker. Subtract to find the mass of the oil. Record the results in your *Science Notebook*.

2 **Use Numbers** Repeat step 1 with the other beaker and 100 mL of water. Compare the masses of the two liquids.

3 **Collaborate** Cover the cardboard with plastic wrap. Lean the piece of cardboard against a stack of books to make a ramp. Tape the ramp to the books. Place strips of tape near the top and bottom of the ramp. They are the "start" and "finish" lines.

4 **Predict** Which liquid—oil or water—will travel faster down the ramp? Record your prediction.

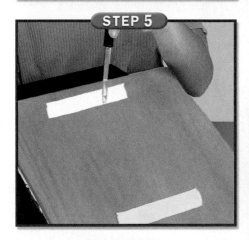

5 **Observe** One partner will start the timer while the other adds five drops of oil to the starting line. Time how long it takes for the oil to travel down the ramp. Repeat with water on the right side of the ramp.

6 **Observe** Pour the water into the oil and stir the mixture. Observe the mixture for about a minute. Record your observations.

Conclusion

1. **Use Numbers** Calculate the density (D) of oil by dividing its mass by its volume ($D = M/V$). Then calculate the density of water.

2. **Analyze Data** How is oil different from water? Cite data from your investigation.

Guided Inquiry

Ask questions about two other materials. What tests could you run to **compare** them and to show their differences? Write a plan. Run the tests with your teacher's permission.

Properties

VOCABULARY

boiling point	p. 339
chemical property	p. 337
conductivity	p. 340
density	p. 338
melting point	p. 339
physical property	p. 337
solubility	p. 340

READING SKILL

Main Idea and Details As you read, write down details that describe different physical properties of matter.

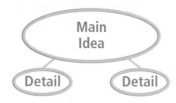

Main Idea

Detail   Detail

STANDARD

1.f. *Students know* differences in chemical and physical properties of substances are used to separate mixtures and identify compounds.

MAIN IDEA Physical and chemical properties are characteristics used to describe, identify, and classify matter.

Using Your Senses

Every object or material you can think of is some form of matter. And every sample of matter has properties that can be used to describe it. You can use your senses to observe certain properties. For example, you might describe an ice cube as cold, colorless, odorless, and cube-shaped. A puff of smoke from a wood fire might be gray and shapeless, with a distinct odor.

Properties can also be used to help identify pure substances—elements and compounds—and to tell one kind of matter from another. The chart on the next page compares some properties of water and glass.

You study, compare, and apply the properties of matter all the time! When you want to write a letter, you choose a sheet of paper. Paper's properties are ideal for writing. When you want to play baseball, you choose a bat made of wood or metal, not paper. What other choices of matter do you make?

Water Bottle
The plastic is dark, lightweight, and flexible. Unlike glass, it won't break when you drop it. ▶

Shoes
Tough, sturdy spikes dig into the ground. The shoe is softer inside, where the foot fits. ▼

Some Properties of Materials		
Property	**Water**	**Glass**
Color	colorless and clear	colorless and clear
State	liquid at room temperature	solid at room temperature
Melting point	0°C	may be greater than 1,000°C
Conductivity	conducts electricity	does not conduct electricity
Reactivity with sodium hydroxide	dissolves sodium hydroxide to form ions	reacts with sodium hydroxide, which etches the glass

Two kinds of properties can be used to describe and classify matter—physical properties and chemical properties. Think about a sheet of paper and a sheet of aluminum foil. Both are thin, flat, and flexible, which are physical properties. Also, note that paper will burn and aluminum will not. These are chemical properties.

A **physical property** can be measured or detected by the senses. Some physical properties include state, size, color, and odor. Many physical properties, such as length, volume, and mass, can be measured. In fact, matter is often defined as anything that has mass and volume.

Glove and Baseball
A glove is shaped like the hand that fits inside it. It is ideal for catching the hard, tough baseball. ▼

A **chemical property** is the ability or tendency of a material to change its chemical makeup. Materials are made of smaller particles—atoms and molecules. When the arrangement of atoms or molecules changes, a new material is formed. The new material has a different identity and different properties from the original material.

You can discover a material's chemical properties by observing how it changes under different conditions. For example, when a piece of paper is held in a flame, the paper will burn. Burning is a chemical change. It produces new matter that is very different from the paper.

MAIN IDEA AND DETAILS Choose two objects. Describe and compare their properties.

Express Lab

Activity Card 27
Compare Densities

Mass, Volume, and Density

Mass is a measure of the amount of matter in an object or a material. It can be measured in grams (g) or kilograms (kg). A large object contains more matter than a smaller object made of the same material. So the larger object has a greater mass.

Volume is the amount of space a sample of matter takes up. The volume of a solid can be measured in cubic centimeters (cm³). Liquid volumes are measured in liters (L) or milliliters (mL). One cubic centimeter is equal to one milliliter.

You can find the volume of a rectangular solid by multiplying its length, width, and height. To find the volume of an odd-shaped solid, sink it in water in a graduated cylinder. The object's volume equals the increase in the water level.

The **density** of a material is its mass per unit volume. To find the density of a sample, measure its mass and its volume, then divide. For example, a 10-mL sample with a mass of 13 g has a density of 1.3 grams per milliliter (g/mL).

All samples of a pure substance kept under the same conditions have the same density. A drop of pure water and a tub of pure water both have densities of 1 g/mL. This is the density of pure water in the liquid state. Liquids with other densities are not pure water.

Remember that density is not the same as mass. For example, lead is much denser than aluminum. If a block of lead and a block of aluminum each have a mass of 10 g, what can you conclude about the volumes of the two blocks?

Some Physical Properties

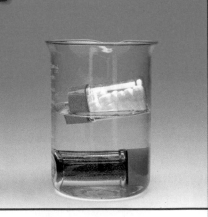

Volume
To find the volume of a solid that does not float in water, measure the volume of water that it displaces. The volume of the orange is the difference of the two water levels.

Mass
The mass of an object can be measured with a balance. Here, the mass of the can equals the sum of the two masses in the right pan.

Density
A bottle filled with plastic foam will float because foam is less dense than water. A bottle filled with sand will sink because sand is denser than water.

Boiling Point
The boiling point of water is 100°C.

Melting Point
The melting point of water is 0°C.

Melting and Boiling Points

Another physical property is state of matter. The three familiar states are solid, liquid, and gas.

Solids are rigid. They have a definite shape and volume. Liquids can flow. They take on the shape of their container, but keep the same volume. Gases have no definite shape or volume. They can expand or contract to fill any container. They typically are much less dense than solids and liquids.

When enough energy is added to a solid, it melts to form a liquid. The temperature at which a solid substance changes to a liquid is called its **melting point.** When enough energy is removed from a liquid, it freezes to form a solid. The freezing point and the melting point for a given substance are the same.

Like density, the melting point is the same for all samples of any given substance. So this property can be used to identify different substances. For example, the melting point of water is 0°C (32°F). The melting point of gold is about 1,060°C (1,940°F).

When enough energy is added to a liquid, it changes into a gas. The temperature at which this happens is called the **boiling point.**

Boiling point can also be used to identify a substance. For example, both water and rubbing alcohol are colorless liquids. Yet at sea level, the boiling point of water is 100°C (212°F), while the boiling point of rubbing alcohol is 82°C (180°F).

 **MAIN IDEA AND DETAILS** How does a substance change state?

Solubility and Conductivity

Stir sugar in water and you can observe the sugar dissolve in the water, meaning it mixes evenly with it. The mixture that results is called a solution. You will learn more about solutions later in this unit.

The measure of how much of one substance can dissolve in another is called **solubility.** Solubility is another physical property of matter. Some substances, such as salt and sugar, are very soluble in water. Other substances, such as oil and sand, are not.

Solubility can be useful for separating substances. If you add alcohol to a mixture of salt and sugar, for example, only the sugar will dissolve.

Another physical property of matter is conductivity. The **conductivity** of a material is its ability to carry energy. Electrical conductivity refers to carrying electricity. Thermal conductivity refers to carrying heat.

Most metals are good conductors of both electricity and heat. For example, copper is used both in cookware and in electric wires.

Materials that have a low conductivity, such as rubber and plastic, are used to insulate conductors. In an electrical cord, insulation around a metal wire prevents both electricity and heat from escaping.

You should never use a current-carrying electrical cord that has frayed insulation. You might get an electrical shock, or heat from the cord could start a fire!

MAIN IDEA AND DETAILS Describe the solubility of sugar in water.

Solubility

Oil and sand will not dissolve in water, so they form separate layers when mixed with water.

Powdered drink mix will dissolve in water, so the two form a colored solution when mixed.

Wire

Insulation

◄ Metal wires have a higher electrical conductivity than plastic insulation has.

Lesson Wrap-Up

Visual Summary

A physical property is a characteristic that can be measured or detected by the senses. A chemical property is the ability or tendency to change chemical makeup.

The measure of how much of one substance can dissolve in another is called solubility. Sand is not soluble in water. Salt and sugar are soluble in water.

Copper wire carries electricity well; plastic insulation does not. People use physical properties, including electrical conductivity, to make useful products and to separate mixtures.

STANDARD
1.f.

Technology
Visit **www.eduplace.com/cascp** to find out more about using properties to identify substances.

Reading Review

❶ MAIN IDEA How are physical and chemical properties useful?

❷ VOCABULARY Is *density* a physical property or a chemical property? Explain.

❸ READING SKILL List five examples of physical properties.

❹ CRITICAL THINKING: Infer Don't swim outdoors during a thunderstorm! A lightning strike could send an electric charge through the water to your body. Which physical property of water explains this safety tip?

❺ INQUIRY SKILL: Use Numbers Toy blocks A and B have the same shape, volume, and color. Yet the mass of block A is 1.5 times the mass of block B. Are the two blocks made of the same material? Explain.

TEST PRACTICE

Which of the following is NOT a physical property of matter?

A. conductivity

B. density

C. reactivity

D. solubility

 STANDARDS
1–4: 1.f., **5:** 1.f., 6.h., **Test Practice:** 1.f.

341

EXTREME Science

STANDARDS **1.g.** *Students know* properties of solid, liquid, and gaseous substances, such as sugar (C $6H_{12}O_6$), water (H_2O), helium (He), oxygen (O_2), nitrogen (N_2), nitrogen (N_2), and carbon dioxide (CO_2).

Rocketing Reactions

Fireworks! Everybody's favorite Fourth of July exothermic reaction! Where do those brilliant colors come from? High-energy chemical reactions are the secret to the brilliant reds, yellows, greens, and blues. Fireworks are based on an explosive compound called black powder, made of potassium nitrate, sulfur, and charcoal. The different colors are achieved by adding compounds of the elements sodium, strontium, copper, or barium.

When potassium nitrate burns, it releases large amounts of oxygen. The oxygen rapidly burns the sulfur and charcoal. The extreme heat and oxygen released by the burning black powder cause the mineral compounds to react, releasing brilliant colored light.

Green comes from barium compounds.

Red fireworks contain strontium compounds.

Copper compounds produce blue.

Sodium compounds produce brilliant yellows.

Writing Journal

Imagine you design fireworks. In your journal, draw a model of an aerial firework. List the chemicals you would use to create the colors you want.

343

What Are Acids, Bases, and Salts?

Building Background

Acids and bases can be found almost anywhere. Many substances you use every day are useful because they are either acids or bases.

 STANDARDS

1.i. *Students know* the common properties of salts, such as sodium chloride (NaCl).
6.a. Classify objects (e.g., rocks, plants, leaves) in accordance with appropriate criteria.

PREPARE TO INVESTIGATE

Inquiry Skill

Classify When you classify substances, you use their properties to organize them into groups.

Materials

- goggles
- stirring rod
- plastic cups
- vinegar
- blue and red litmus paper
- solution of baking soda in water
- lemon juice
- apple juice
- ammonia solution

Science and Math Toolbox

For step 1, review **Making a Chart to Organize Data** on page H11.

Acid Test

Procedure

Safety: Do not taste any of the liquids. Wear goggles as you perform the procedure.

1 **Predict** Predict whether each of the following liquids is an acid or a base: vinegar, solution of baking soda, lemon juice, apple juice, and ammonia solution. Record your predictions in your *Science Notebook.*

2 **Observe** Using a stirring rod, place one small drop of vinegar on a piece of blue litmus paper and one small drop on red litmus paper. Observe and record any color changes. Rinse and dry the stirring rod.

3 **Observe** Repeat step 2 for the other liquids. Remember to use fresh pieces of litmus paper for each liquid.

4 **Experiment** Drop a pinch of baking soda into a small sample of vinegar. Observe the results.

Conclusion

1. **Classify** Blue litmus paper turns red in the presence of an acid. Red litmus paper turns blue in the presence of a base. Classify each liquid as an acid or a base.

2. **Infer** Based on your observations, do you think foods that contain acids taste sour or bitter?

3. **Infer** How do acids and bases react with each other? Give an example from your observations.

STEP 1

Sample	Acid	Base
Vinegar		
Baking soda solution		
Lemon Juice		
Apple Juice		
Ammonia solution		

STEP 2

Guided Inquiry

Experiment Repeat step 4 of the procedure, then place the sample in sunlight. Observe what remains after the liquid evaporates. **Ask questions** about this substance. How might you identify it?

Acids, Bases, and Salts

VOCABULARY

acid	p. 347
base	p. 347
indicator	p. 347
pH	p. 347
salt	p. 348

READING SKILL

Compare and Contrast
Use a Venn diagram to show how acids and bases are alike and how they are different.

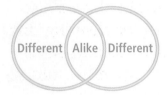

Different | Alike | Different

STANDARDS

1.i. *Students know* the common properties of salts, such as sodium chloride (NaCl).
1.f. *Students know* differences in chemical and physical properties of substances are used to separate mixtures and identify compounds.

MAIN IDEA Acids, bases, and salts are classes of compounds, each with characteristic properties. The strengths of acids and bases are measured with the pH scale.

Acids and Bases

Have you ever tasted lemon juice or vinegar? Both taste sour because each contains an acid. Lemon juice contains a weak acid called citric acid. Vinegar contains another weak acid called acetic acid. Your stomach uses hydrochloric acid to digest food. Hydrochloric acid is an especially strong acid.

If you have accidentally ever tasted soap or shampoo, you know that they taste very bitter. These substances contain bases. Many household cleaners and detergents, including bleach, contain very strong bases.

Acids and bases are important classes of compounds. A definition that applies to most acids

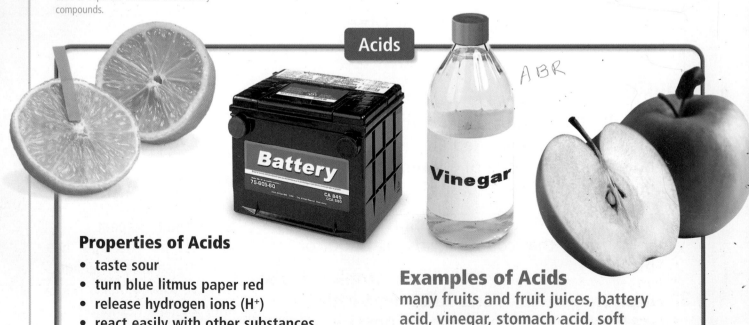

Acids

Properties of Acids
- taste sour
- turn blue litmus paper red
- release hydrogen ions (H⁺)
- react easily with other substances, especially bases

Examples of Acids
many fruits and fruit juices, battery acid, vinegar, stomach acid, soft drinks, sour milk

and bases involves hydrogen ions (H^+). Remember that ions are atoms that have lost or gained an electron. An **acid** typically releases hydrogen ions. A **base** typically receives hydrogen ions.

How can you identify acids and bases? In the laboratory, you should never taste a chemical for any reason! A better way to identify these compounds is to use an acid-base indicator. An **indicator** changes color in the presence of an acid or a base.

One common indicator is litmus paper, which comes in blue and red colors. Acids turn blue litmus paper red. Bases turn red litmus paper blue. Litmus paper stays the same color in the presence of substances that are neither acids nor bases, such as water. Water is an example of a neutral substance.

To measure the strength of acids and bases, scientists use a value called **pH.** The letters stand for potential of hydrogen. The pH scale centers around the number 7, which is the pH of pure water. Acids have pH values less than 7. Bases have pH values greater than 7.

Both acids and bases react easily with other substances and with each other. The stronger the acid or base, the stronger its reaction can be. Sulfuric acid from a car battery will burn your skin. Drain cleaners contain lye, a base that will rapidly dissolve a clogged drain. Bleach also contains strong bases for cleaning dirt from clothes. Strong acids and bases make these products powerful, and also poisonous if swallowed!

COMPARE AND CONTRAST How do acids and bases differ?

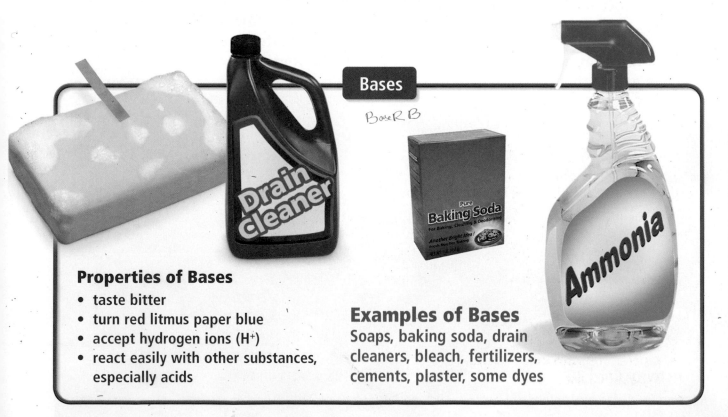

Bases

BaseR B

Properties of Bases
- taste bitter
- turn red litmus paper blue
- accept hydrogen ions (H^+)
- react easily with other substances, especially acids

Examples of Bases
Soaps, baking soda, drain cleaners, bleach, fertilizers, cements, plaster, some dyes

Salts

When a strong acid reacts with a strong base, one of the compounds they form is called a **salt.** Salts are compounds typically made from a metal and a nonmetal. Many salts are hard, brittle, and have high melting points. Most salts, but not all of them, dissolve quickly in water.

You already are familiar with one example of a salt—sodium chloride (NaCl), the salt that you use at the dinner table. In fact, in everyday language, the word salt often refers only to this one compound. However, scientists classify many different compounds as salts.

For example, calcium chloride (CaCl$_2$) is a salt often spread over roads and driveways during a cold winter. Dissolving salt will lower the melting point of water and thus helps melt ice and snow. Calcium chloride does this job better than the more common sodium chloride.

One place to look for salts is the ocean. Ocean water holds a mixture of different salts. Only about 20 percent of that mixture is sodium chloride. In fact, scientists have identified at least 72 different elements in sea salt, although most are present in very small amounts.

Another place to look for salts is in the food you eat. Your body needs sodium, potassium, and other ions found in salts. It also needs iodine, which can be rare. This is why salt from the supermarket is "iodized salt"—sodium chloride with extra iodine added.

◎ COMPARE AND CONTRAST How does sodium chloride compare with other salts?

Calcium chloride (CaCl$_2$) and other salts are often used to help melt ice in the winter. ▼

Sea salt is harvested from the ocean through evaporation, which separates the parts of a solution.

Express Lab

Activity Card 28
Recognize Acids by Taste

Visual Summary

Acids taste sour and turn litmus paper from blue to red. Examples of acids include fruits and fruit juices, battery acid, stomach acid, and sour milk.

Bases taste bitter and turn red litmus paper blue. Examples of bases include soaps, baking soda, and drain cleaners.

A salt is one product of a reaction between a strong acid and a strong base. Most salts are hard, brittle, and have a high melting point. Sodium chloride is table salt. Calcium chloride is used to melt ice.

STANDARDS

1.i., 1.f.

Technology

Visit **www.eduplace.com/cascp** to find out more about acids and bases.

Reading Review

❶ **MAIN IDEA** How could you make a salt from other compounds?

❷ **VOCABULARY** How do acids and bases compare?

❸ **READING SKILL** Is water best classified as an acid, base, salt, or not any of these classes of compounds? Explain.

Different | Alike | Different

❹ **CRITICAL THINKING: Infer** Strong acids and bases can be dangerous and even poisonous. Why do people keep them in their homes? What safety precautions should people take?

❺ **INQUIRY SKILL: Classify** Describe two laboratory tests that would help you classify a compound as an acid, a base, or a salt. What test would you NOT include for safety reasons?

 TEST PRACTICE

What is one product of a reaction between a strong acid and a strong base?

A. salt

B. acid

C. base

D. indicator

STANDARDS

1–2: 1.i., 3–4: 1.f., 5: 1.f., 6.h., **Test Practice:** 1.i.

349

Math in Science

Carbonic acid is a compound found in many products, including your favorite carbonated beverage. The chemical formula for this compound is H_2CO_3.

1. Complete the table by calculating the total number of each type of atom in 2, 4, and 6 molecules of this compound.

2. In any sample of carbonic acid, what is the ratio of hydrogen (H) to carbon (C) to oxygen (O) atoms? Do the results in the table support your answer? Explain.

Number of H_2CO_3 molecules	Number of H atoms	Number of C atoms	Number of O atoms
2	4		
4			
6			18

Writing in Science
Research report

Research a product that contains one or more polymers. Examples of polymers include vinyl, polyester, polyethylene, and Teflon®. Find out how the polymer was developed and how it is used today. Include facts and your opinions in your report.

The nonstick coating of this frying pan is made of a polymer. ▶

California

Mario Molina

In the 1960s and 1970s, people were adding compounds called chlorofluorocarbons (CFCs) to the atmosphere. CFCs were used in refrigerators, spray cans, and other devices. At the time, most scientists thought they were harmless.

Fortunately, California scientist Mario Molina discovered the truth about CFCs. Dr. Molina and his colleague Sherry Rowland showed that CFCs released chlorine atoms in the upper atmosphere. The chlorine was destroying molecules of ozone, a form of oxygen that protects Earth from the Sun's harmful ultraviolet radiation.

Because of these findings, governments across the world banned CFCs. Safer chemicals have now replaced them, and the ozone layer continues to protect Earth.

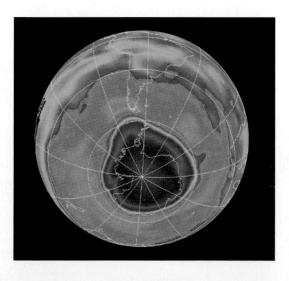

◄ In this satellite map of Earth from 1990, colors are used to show ozone levels. The pink and violet areas show low levels of ozone over Antarctica.

Chapter 9 Review and Test Practice

Vocabulary

Complete each sentence with a term from the list.

1. The temperature at which a solid changes to a liquid is its _____.

2. The ability of a material to carry energy is called _____.

3. The color of a substance is an example of a(n) _____.

4. A shorthand way to describe a compound is a(n) _____.

5. One or more substances are changed into one or more different substances during a(n) _____.

6. A substance that feels slippery, tastes bitter, and turns red litmus paper blue is a(n) _____.

7. The temperature at which a liquid changes to a gas is its _____.

8. The measure of how much of one substance can dissolve in another is _____.

9. A substance that tastes sour or bitter when dissolved in water is a(n) _____.

10. The mass per unit volume of a material is called _____.

acid p. 347
base p. 347
boiling point p. 339
chemical formula p. 327
chemical property p. 337
chemical reaction p. 326
conductivity p. 340
density p. 338
indicator p. 347
melting point p. 339
pH p. 337
physical property p. 337
salt p. 348
solubility p. 340

ABR   B&B.

Test Practice

Write the letter of the best answer choice.

11. What is an example of an acid-base indicator?

A. carbon dioxide
B. water
C. litmus paper
D. calcium chloride

12. What is one product of a reaction between a strong acid and a strong base?

A. acid
B. salt
C. base
D. carbon dioxide

13. What is the ability or tendency of a material to change its chemical makeup?

A. chemical property
B. chemical reaction
C. compound
D. chemical formula

14. A pure substance made up of two or more elements that are chemically combined is a(n) _____.

A. indicator
B. acid
C. compound
D. base

352 • Chapter 9

15. **Compare and Contrast** How are the physical properties of paper and aluminum foil alike and different?

16. You have two liquids, both clear and colorless. Describe a simple test to determine if they are the same or different. To run the test, you may use a balance, hot plate, water bath, barometer, thermometer, calculator, and samples of different salts.

Map the Concept

Fill in the concept map to show how changes and properties of matter can be classified. Use the following terms to complete the concept map: boiling point, chemical change, chemical property, conductivity, density, melting point, physical change, physical property, solubility.

Critical Thinking

17. **Analyze** Lava lamps contain two different liquids. The liquids rise and fall as they heat up and cool. Describe the density changes.

18. **Synthesize** How could you learn whether or not a material conducts electricity? Describe a procedure you could follow.

19. **Apply** Typically, saturated fats are solid at room temperature. Unsaturated fats are liquid (oil). In general, which kind of fat has a higher melting point? Explain.

20. **Evaluate** Sea salt is a product made by evaporating ocean water. How does sea salt compare to sodium chloride?

Performance Assessment

Performance Assessment

You are given a mixture of sugar, sand, and sawdust. Design a method for separating out each part of the mixture.

Writing Journal

Review your answers to the questions on page 319. Revise if necessary.

 STANDARDS

Vocabulary 1: 1.a., **2–4:** 1.f., **5:** 1.a., **6–10:** 1.f., **11:** 1.f., **12:** 1.a., **13:** 1.f., **14:** 1.a., **15:** 1.f., **16:** 1.f., **17–19:** 1.f., **20:** 6.h.

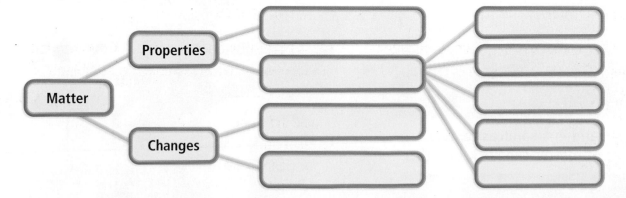

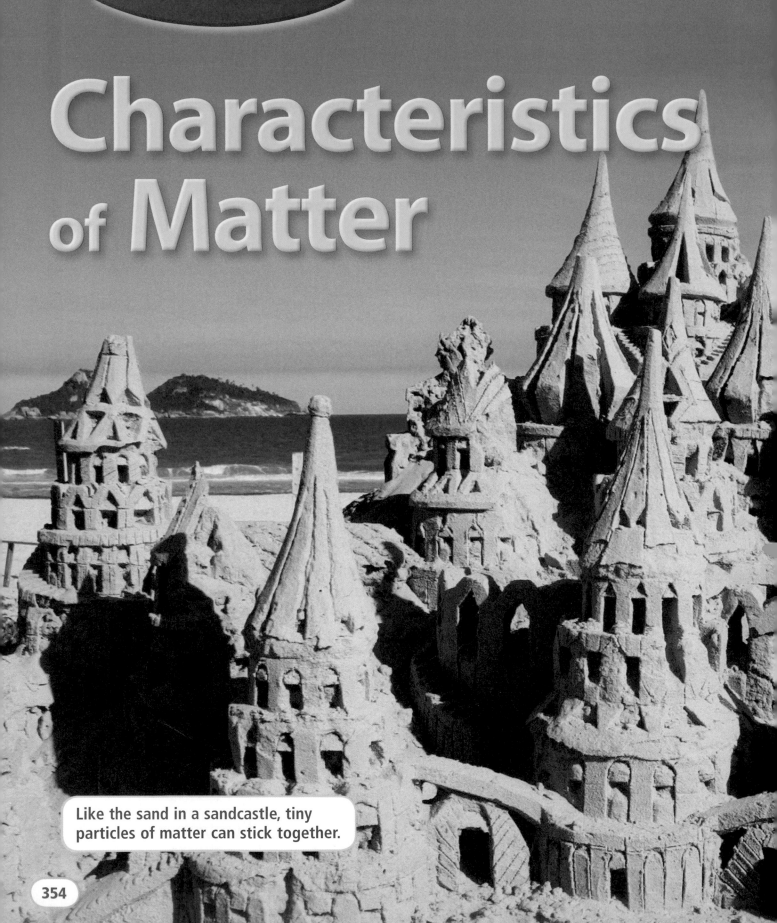

Chapter 10

Characteristics of Matter

Like the sand in a sandcastle, tiny particles of matter can stick together.

Lesson Preview

LESSON 1

In even the largest icebergs, only about 10 percent of the mass lies above the ocean. Why are ice and liquid water so different?

LESSON 2

How can you separate seashells and sand? Put down the tweezers! There's a much easier way.

LESSON 3

Why do ice pops melt when you take them out of the freezer?

LESSON 4

Fireworks are shot into the air, then explode to form colorful trails. How does matter change in fireworks?

Writing Journal

In your Writing Journal, draw or write answers to each question.

mixture
a physical combination of
two or more substances

Vocabulary Preview

Vocabulary

Glossary

Vocabulary Skill

Root Words
mixture

The root word *mix* comes from the
Latin verb *miscere*, which means
"to mix." In everyday language and
in science, a mixture is formed by
combining two or more parts that
each keep their identity.

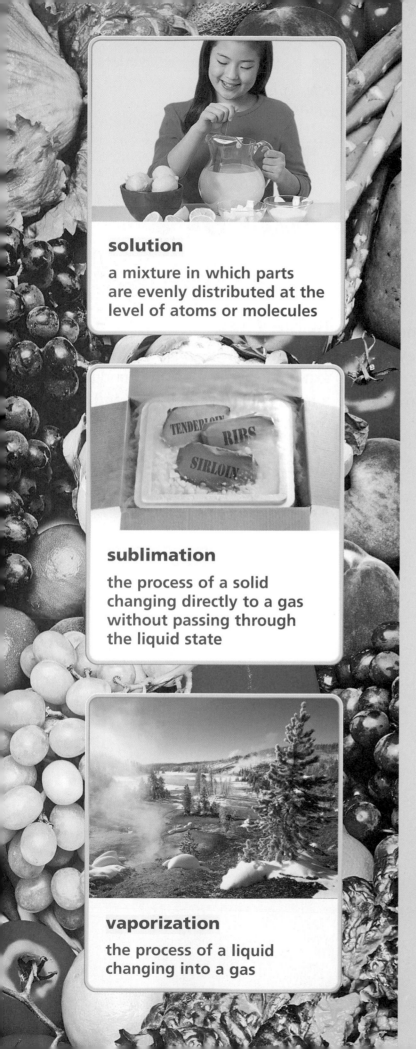

solution

a mixture in which parts are evenly distributed at the level of atoms or molecules

sublimation

the process of a solid changing directly to a gas without passing through the liquid state

vaporization

the process of a liquid changing into a gas

Start with Your Standards

Standard Set 1. Physical Sciences

1.a. *Students know* that during chemical reactions the atoms in the reactants rearrange to form products with different properties.

1.b. *Students know* all matter is made of atoms, which may combine to form molecules.

1.c. *Students know* metals have properties in common, such as high electrical and thermal conductivity. Some metals, such as aluminum (Al), iron (Fe), nickel (Ni), copper (Cu), silver (Ag), and gold (Au), are pure elements; others, such as steel and brass, are composed of a combination of elemental metals.

1.f. *Students know* differences in chemical and physical properties of substances are used to separate mixtures and identify compounds.

1.g. *Students know* properties of solid, liquid, and gaseous substances, such as sugar ($C_6H_{12}O_6$), water (H_2O), helium (He), oxygen (O_2), nitrogen (N_2), and carbon dioxide (CO_2).

Standard Set 6: Investigation and Experimentation standards covered in this chapter: 6.c., 6.f., 6.g., 6.i.

What Are Three States of Matter?

Building Background

Steel is a uniform mixture of solids, mostly iron and carbon. These solids have been heated until they melt. Under the right conditions, most matter can be made to change from one state, or form, to another.

PREPARE TO INVESTIGATE

Inquiry Skill

Experiment When you experiment, you plan and conduct a test in which you identify and use variables to test a prediction.

Materials

- water
- rubbing alcohol
- plastic cup
- paper clips
- eyedropper

Science and Math Toolbox

For step 1, review **Making a Chart to Organize Data** on page H11.

STANDARDS

1.g. *Students know* properties of solid, liquid, and gaseous substances, such as sugar ($C_6H_{12}O_6$), water (H_2O), helium (He), oxygen (O_2), nitrogen (N_2), and carbon dioxide (CO_2).
6.i. Write a report of an investigation that includes conducting tests, collecting data or examining evidence, and drawing conclusions.

Surface Tension

Procedure

Safety: Do not eat or drink in a science laboratory.

1. **Collaborate** Work in small groups. In your *Science Notebook*, prepare a data table like the one shown.

2. Fill a cup with water. Use the eyedropper to raise the level of the water to the rim.

3. How many paper clips do you think the cup can hold, with no water spilled over? Record your prediction.

4. **Record Data** Carefully add paper clips one at a time into the cup of water. Stop when the water overflows. Record the number of paper clips that the cup holds.

5. **Predict** What if you filled the cup with a different liquid, such as rubbing alcohol? Do you think the cup could hold the same number of paper clips? Record your prediction, then test it.

Conclusion

1. **Analyze Data** How did your predictions compare with the results?

2. **Infer** How do you explain the difference between adding paper clips to water and to rubbing alcohol?

3. **Communicate** Write a report about this investigation. Describe the procedure, the results you observed, and your conclusions.

STEP 1

Number of Paper Clips		
	Water	Rubbing Alcohol
Prediction		
Actual results		

STEP 2

STEP 4

Guided Inquiry

Experiment How would temperature, dissolved salt or sugar, or other variables affect the number of paper clips that a cup of water could hold? Form a **hypothesis**, choose tools and materials, then write a procedure.

VOCABULARY

gas   p. 364
liquid   p. 363
solid   p. 362

READING SKILL

Main Idea and Details As you read, pick out the main idea and the details that support it.

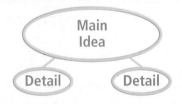

States of Matter

Water can exist as a solid, liquid, or gas. In each state, the particles of matter are arranged in predictable ways. ▶

States of Matter

MAIN IDEA Matter can exist in three familiar states: solids, liquids, and gases. These states are determined by the motion and arrangement of particles.

Solids, Liquids, and Gases

Picture yourself as the captain of a large fishing boat. Your crew has just finished a fishing voyage along the coast of Alaska. As you look at the icy coastline, you realize you are ready to head home to warmer temperatures. Suddenly, you hear a loud cracking and then a huge splash. You watch as a large section of ice from a giant glacier breaks off and falls into the sea.

This scene describes two states of matter interacting on a very large scale. A state of matter is the physical form that matter takes. Three familiar states of matter are solids, liquids, and gases.

Ice is an example of matter in the solid state. Ice is the solid form of water. The ocean water is in the liquid state. The air above the water is a mixture of invisible gases. One of these gases is water vapor. Water vapor is water in the gas state.

Solids

In solids, particles are held together very closely. They vibrate in place.

Particles and State of Matter

You have learned that all matter is made up of atoms and molecules. These particles are always in motion.

The state of any sample of matter depends on the movement and spacing of its particles. In solids, particles vibrate back and forth, but do not move about freely.

For most substances, particles are most closely packed in the solid state. Water is an exception to this rule. Water molecules are slightly farther apart in solid ice than they are in liquid water. However, the molecules in ice still do not move about freely.

In liquids, the particles are also quite close together, but they have a little space in which to move around. Unlike particles in solids, particles in liquids can slip past one another.

Because of this, the arrangement of particles in liquids is disorderly and always changing.

In gases, the particles are spread very far apart compared to liquids and solids. Their arrangement is completely random, and they fill the space of their containers. They are constantly bouncing off one another and the sides of their containers.

Some substances, such as water, can commonly be found in any of the three states. Others, such as iron and helium, are found in only one state in nature. The properties of a substance's particles determine its state.

MAIN IDEA AND DETAILS Describe the arrangement of particles in a solid, a liquid, and a gas.

Liquids

In the liquid state, water particles can slip past one another and move about.

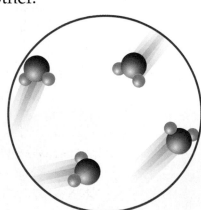

Gases

The particles in gases are spread very far apart. They are constantly moving and bouncing off one another. Water forms an invisible gas called water vapor.

Express Lab

Activity Card 29
See Surface Tension

Solids

A **solid** is a form of matter that has a definite shape and volume. The way that particles in solids are arranged and the way that they vibrate in place give solids certain properties. One property is that solids keep their shape. If you move a solid or place it into a container, its shape will stay the same.

Wood is a solid. A block of wood will keep its shape wherever you put it—on a countertop, in a rectangular cardboard box, or in a circular cake tin. This property is usually described as having definite shape, meaning the shape of a solid doesn't change.

The closeness of the particles in a solid and the small forces of attraction between them keep the particles from moving from place to place. Since the particles stay in position, the shape of a solid doesn't change.

Another property of solids is that they have definite volume. That is, they take up the same amount of space wherever they are. The volume of a solid object stays the same unless you remove a part of the object.

For example, consider a wood block that has a volume of 30 cm³. Wherever you move it, the volume will still be 30 cm³. You can even compress the block, which means to squeeze it. The volume will not change much, if at all.

Many solids might appear to change shape and volume. For example, you can squeeze a foam ball into a smaller volume, and a pillow dents easily when you rest your head on it. In both cases, however, solid matter is surrounded by "pockets" of air. The air changes its shape and volume, not the solid parts.

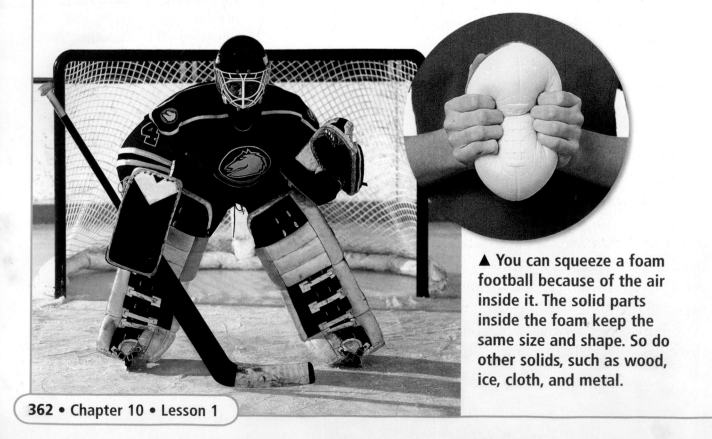

▲ You can squeeze a foam football because of the air inside it. The solid parts inside the foam keep the same size and shape. So do other solids, such as wood, ice, cloth, and metal.

Volume

◀ This liquid was poured into different containers. It changed shape, but kept its volume of 50 mL.

Liquids

What shape is orange juice? You can't answer that question because orange juice is a liquid. A **liquid** is a form of matter that has a definite volume, but no definite shape.

A liquid changes shape to match the shape of its container. Think about what happens when you use a straw to drink apple juice. The juice has one shape in the container and has a different shape when it's in the straw.

Contrast liquid water with ice, which is a solid. When you place an ice cube in a glass, it keeps its cube shape—that is, until it melts into a liquid. Then it takes on the shape of its container.

Liquids have no definite shape because their particles are not rigidly held in place. The particles of a liquid are able to flow past one another to take on the shape of its container. Any substance whose particles can flow freely is called a *fluid*.

Like solids, liquids have a definite volume. To prove this, pour a liquid sample into different containers. Each time, the liquid will take a new shape, but its volume will not change.

Also, like solids, liquids are not very compressible. The particles are close together, so liquids do not easily compress into smaller volumes.

This property makes liquids very useful. For example, a hydraulic device uses a liquid to transfer a force. If you push on one end of the liquid in a sealed tube, the push will be transferred by the liquid to the other end of the tube. The brake system of a car works this way.

Liquids also have a property called surface tension. This is a force of attraction among the particles at the surface of a liquid. Water has a high surface tension, which is one reason why the water stings when you dive into a swimming pool.

 **MAIN IDEA AND DETAILS** What will change the shape of a liquid?

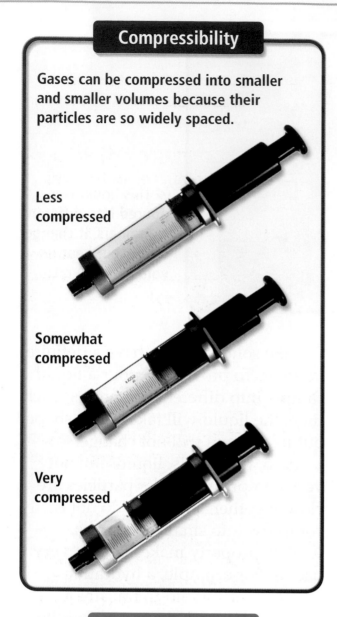

Compressibility

Gases can be compressed into smaller and smaller volumes because their particles are so widely spaced.

Less compressed

Somewhat compressed

Very compressed

States of Matter

Property	Solid	Liquid	Gas
Definite shape	yes	no	no
Definite volume	yes	yes	no
Compressible	no	no	yes
Fluid	no	yes	yes
Particle spacing	close	close	varies

Arrangement   rigid   disorderly   random

The spacing and speed of particles determine state of matter.

Gases

A **gas** is a form of matter that has no definite shape or volume. Common gases include oxygen (O_2), nitrogen (N_2), and carbon dioxide (CO_2).

The particles that make up gases can move about freely. Particles of a gas are constantly moving about and bouncing off one another.

When a sample of gas is placed in a closed container, the particles spread out filling the container and taking its shape. Because the particles are free to move about and flow, all gases are fluids.

Unlike solids and liquids, gases are very compressible. Their particles are so far apart that they can easily be pressed closer together into a smaller volume. For example, helium gas is often compressed and kept in metal tanks. The helium inside the tank has the shape and volume of the tank.

If you were to use the helium in a small tank to fill a large number of balloons for a party, that small volume of helium would take on the different shapes and total volume of all the balloons.

Gases have much lower densities than liquids and solids have. A balloon filled with helium will float in air. This is because the helium-filled balloon is less dense than the air.

MAIN IDEA AND DETAILS How do gases compare with liquids and solids?

Visual Summary

The motion and arrangement of particles in each state of matter give the states their unique properties.

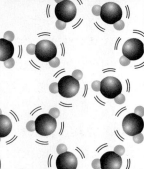

The particles in solids are arranged very close together. They vibrate in place but do not move around.

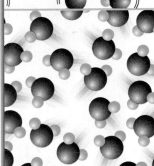

The particles in liquids are close together. They slip past one another as they move about.

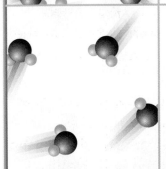

The particles in gases are spread very far apart. They are constantly moving to fill the container that holds them.

 **STANDARDS**

1.g., 1.b.

 Technology
Visit **www.eduplace.com/cascp** to find out more about states of matter.

Reading Review

❶ MAIN IDEA What two factors describe the state of matter of an object or a sample?

❷ VOCABULARY What are three familiar states of matter? Give examples of each.

❸ READING SKILL Using water as an example, explain how particles of matter are organized in a solid, liquid, and gas.

❹ CRITICAL THINKING: Evaluate To keep a gas, why must you use a closed container?

❺ INQUIRY SKILL: Design an Experiment For most substances, particles are spaced farther apart in the liquid state than in the solid state. Design a demonstration to show that this is not true for water.

 TEST PRACTICE
Solids and liquids are similar because both _____.

A. are fluids

B. are compressible

C. have no definite shape

D. have definite volume

 STANDARDS

1–2: 1.g., **3:** 1.b., **4:** 1.g., **5:** 6.c., **Test Practice:** 1.g.

Technology

Plasmas

Solid, liquid, and gas are three common states of matter. Did you know there is a fourth state? It's plasma!

Plasma is an ionized gas, which means that some or all of the electrons are separated from the gas atoms or molecules. Plasmas have special properties. They conduct electricity and can be trapped in a magnetic field.

Any matter will become a plasma if heated to a high enough temperature. In fact, 99 percent of all matter in the universe is in the plasma state! For example, the Sun and other stars are made of plasma. On Earth, plasmas occur naturally in flames, lightning, and auroras. Plasmas are also used in fluorescent lights, neon signs, and plasma-screen televisions.

The photograph shows a donut-shaped device called a tokamak. It uses magnetic fields to hold a hot plasma. Scientists use tokamaks to study nuclear fusion reactions in hot plasmas, which someday could become a new energy resource.

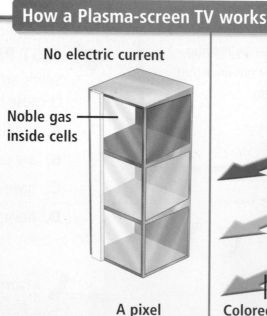

How a Plasma-screen TV works

In a plasma-screen television, each picture element, or pixel, is made of cells filled with noble gases. To form a picture, an electric current ionizes the gases. This turns them into a plasma and causes them to release ultraviolet light. Special coatings on the cells change the light to red, green, or blue.

No electric current

Noble gas inside cells

A pixel

Electric current

Colored light   UV light

STANDARD
1.f. *Students know* differences in chemical and physical properties of substances are used to separate mixtures and identify compounds.

READING **LINK**

▲ The plasma glows pinkish-white. At temperatures of 100 million°C or higher, fusion reactions between hydrogen isotopes can take place.

▲ The large photograph shows the inside of an empty tokamak. The small photograph shows the chamber filled with plasma.

Sharing Ideas

1. **READING CHECK** What is a plasma?

2. **WRITE ABOUT IT** Describe some examples of plasmas, including those used in everyday life.

3. **TALK ABOUT IT** Do you think it is wise to invest money and effort in developing new energy resources? Why or why not?

367

Lesson 2

What Are Mixtures and Solutions?

Building Background

Mixtures are everywhere! Most rocks and the waters of Earth's oceans are mixtures. So are many foods. You can make a useful mixture or separate a mixture if you understand the properties of its parts.

PREPARE TO INVESTIGATE

Inquiry Skill

Predict When you predict, you use observations, patterns, data, or cause-and-effect relationships to anticipate results.

Materials

- goggles
- three 250-mL beakers
- water
- teaspoon
- sand
- salt

Science and Math Toolbox

For step 2, review **Measurements** on page H16.

 STANDARDS

1.f. *Students know* differences in chemical and physical properties of substances are used to separate mixtures and identify compounds.
6.c. Plan and conduct a simple investigation based on a student-developed question and write instructions others can follow to carry out the procedure.

Mixing In

Procedure

Safety: Wear goggles as you perform this procedure.

STEP 1

1. **Collaborate** Work with a partner. Fill two beakers with water.

2. **Observe** Add two teaspoons of sand to one beaker and two teaspoons of salt to the other beaker. Observe what happens in each beaker. Record your observations in your *Science Notebook.*

STEP 2

3. **Compare** Stir the contents of each beaker. Stop stirring, and do not touch or move the beakers for several minutes. Compare the contents of the two beakers. Record your observations.

4. **Predict** What do you think would happen if you added water to a mixture of sand and salt? Record your prediction.

STEP 3

5. **Experiment** Add one teaspoon of sand and one teaspoon of salt to the third beaker, and mix them thoroughly. Fill the beaker with water, and stir. Record your observations.

Conclusion

1. **Analyze Data** What physical property makes sand and salt different, as your results show?

2. **Experiment** Write a procedure for separating a mixture of sand and salt. You may use water and other materials, but the procedure should leave the sand and salt unmixed with other substances.

Guided Inquiry

Experiment Water in ponds and streams may carry dirt, sand, and other large particles. Write a procedure to separate particles from a water sample. **Predict** how well the procedure will work. Try it with your teacher's permission.

► **VOCABULARY**

mixture	p. 370
solution	p. 372

◎ **READING SKILL**

Compare and Contrast Use the information in this lesson to compare solutions with other types of mixtures.

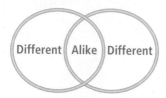

Different | Alike | Different

🏴 **STANDARDS**

1.f. *Students know* differences in chemical and physical properties of substances are used to separate mixtures and identify compounds.

1.c. *Students know* metals have properties in common, such as high electrical and thermal conductivity. Some metals, such as aluminum (Al), iron (Fe), nickel (Ni), copper (Cu), silver (Ag), and gold (Au), are pure elements; others, such as steel and brass, are composed of a combination of elemental metals.

A salad is a mixture. The different parts that make up the mixture have different properties. ▼

Mixtures and Solutions

MAIN IDEA In a mixture, the parts keep their physical properties. These properties can be used to separate the mixture. Mixtures that are evenly mixed at the atomic or molecular level are called solutions.

Types of Mixtures

By eating different parts of a salad, you could taste each vegetable individually. That's because a salad is a mixture.

A **mixture** is a physical combination of two or more substances. The substances in a mixture are not chemically combined as they are in a compound. So a mixture is not a pure substance.

Mixtures may be classified as heterogeneous or homogeneous. In a heterogeneous mixture, like a salad, the materials that make up the mixture are distributed unevenly. Individual pieces are present in some parts and not others.

A homogeneous mixture is uniform throughout. A sample taken from one part of this kind of mixture will be identical to a sample taken from any other part.

Lettuce

+ Tomato

+ Cucumber

+ Pepper

+ Other ingredients

= MIXTURE

To separate a mixture, take advantage of the physical properties of the different parts. What properties of matter are being used to separate mixtures in these two examples?

Sand and pebbles

Corks and marbles

Separating a Mixture

In a mixture, each substance keeps its original properties. If you separated all of the parts of a salad, the tomatoes would still be tomatoes, and the lettuce would still be lettuce.

Mixtures can be separated according to different properties. Think about a mixture of corks and marbles. You could spend hours picking out the cork pieces. However, because cork floats in water, you can separate the mixture by putting it in water and skimming off the floating corks.

Now think about a mixture of sand and pebbles. It would take a long time to pick out the pebbles. Both parts of the mixture sink in water, so adding water does not separate them. But note the different sizes of the pieces. You could use a sieve or a strainer to separate them.

Mixture or Compound?

Mixtures can have variable composition. This means that two mixtures may be made up of the same materials, but in different amounts. Two salads might both be made of lettuce, carrots, olives, and tomatoes. Although they have the same ingredients, one may have more carrots and fewer olives than the other.

Compounds, however, always have the same composition. Every molecule of water has one oxygen atom combined with two hydrogen atoms. The compound's chemical formula describes its composition. Because a mixture does not have a definite composition, it cannot be represented by a simple chemical formula.

 **COMPARE AND CONTRAST** Compare mixtures and compounds.

Solutions

A **solution** is a homogeneous mixture, meaning it is made of two or more substances that are evenly distributed. The parts of a solution mix together at the atomic or molecular level.

You make a solution when you make pink lemonade from a powdered mix. The particles that mix in the water are molecules of sugar, dye, and flavoring.

In any solution, the substance being dissolved is called the solute. The substance that dissolves the solute is called the solvent. In a solution of water and sugar, water is the solvent and sugar is the solute.

Even though you can't see the different parts of a sugar-water solution, it is still a mixture. The properties of the substances that make up the mixture are the same as they were before they were mixed together. The sugar still tastes sweet. The water is still a liquid and still allows light to pass through.

Many solutions, such as lemonade and salt water, have a liquid solvent and a solid solute. However, solutions can have other combinations. Soda water is a solution made of carbon dioxide gas dissolved in water. Air is a solution of several different gases. Brass is a solution of two solids—zinc and copper.

Particles in a solution spread evenly throughout the solution because they mix at the atomic or

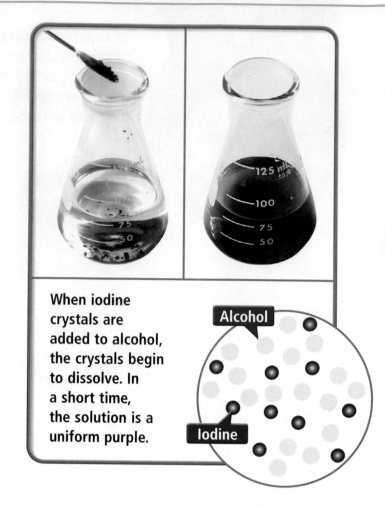

When iodine crystals are added to alcohol, the crystals begin to dissolve. In a short time, the solution is a uniform purple.

molecular level. Think about the solution of iodine and alcohol shown above. Each molecule of iodine has two atoms of the element iodine and is represented by the chemical formula I_2. Each molecule of alcohol has atoms of carbon, hydrogen, and oxygen and is represented by the chemical formula C_3H_8O.

When the two substances are mixed, the iodine dissolves in the alcohol. The particles of iodine spread throughout the mixture. If you could highly magnify a section of the solution, you would see that molecules of the two substances have become evenly mixed.

Sugar from Sugar Cane

First, the cane is prepared for juicing.

Sugar cane juice contains a solution of sugar and water.

Water is removed from the juice, and solid sugar is recovered.

Separating a Solution

To separate a solution, you must make use of the different properties of the mixed materials. You usually cannot use the size of the particles to separate them, because only very special filters are fine enough to trap a molecule.

There are other properties you can use, however. For example, some liquids evaporate at fairly low temperatures. You often can allow a liquid solvent to evaporate, leaving the solute behind.

This happens when a sample of salt water is left in the air over a couple of days. The water slowly evaporates, leaving behind crystals of salt.

A simple way to separate most solutions is to use the different boiling points or melting points of the substances. Sugar is collected in this way. Growers cut down the sugar cane stems and crush them. Then the sugar cane juice is collected and heated. The water boils off at 100°C (212°F), while solid sugar remains behind.

Processes in nature also serve to separate mixtures and solutions. After water falls as rain or snow, it often mixes with dirt, salt, or other materials on the ground. Water may also become polluted with acids or other chemicals.

Yet when even the dirtiest or most polluted water evaporates, only the water molecules rise into the air. The solutes of the solution are left behind on the ground. In this way, nature cleans and recycles water.

COMPARE AND CONTRAST How is allowing a liquid solvent to evaporate different from boiling away the liquid solvent? How are they the same?

Express Lab

Activity Card 30
Compare a Mixture and a Solution

Alloys

A

Mixtures of two or more metals are called alloys. Alloys may also be mixtures of a metal and another solid. Alloys often have combinations of the properties of the materials that form them.

Bronze, for example, is an alloy of copper and tin, and combines the best properties of both. Bronze is malleable, meaning it is easy to hammer into thin sheets. The sheets can then be formed into different shapes. Because of its useful properties, bronze has been used for centuries in tools, weapons, and sculptures.

The amounts of each material in an alloy can affect its properties. Steel is an alloy of iron, carbon, and sometimes other solids. Softer steels, made with less carbon, are used to make nails and chains. Harder steels, made with more carbon, are used to make tools and support beams.

There are many kinds of alloys with different uses. Brass is an alloy of copper and zinc. It is used to make many musical instruments. Sterling silver, an alloy of silver and copper, is used to make jewelry.

COMPARE AND CONTRAST How do the properties of alloys compare to the properties of the materials used to form them?

The body of a typical airplane is an alloy of aluminum, titanium, and other metals. ▶

Copper
+ Zinc
―――――
= Brass

◀ **Brass**
Many musical instruments are made of alloys.

Lesson Wrap-Up

Visual Summary

In many mixtures, the different materials are not uniformly mixed. You often see the individual parts.

Mixtures in which the particles are evenly mixed at the atomic or molecular level are called solutions. You often can see the individual parts.

You can use the physical properties of different parts of a mixture to separate them.

Alloys are solutions of two or more metals or of a metal and another solid.

STANDARDS

1.f., 1.c.

Technology

Visit **www.eduplace.com/cascp** to find out more about solutions.

Reading Review

❶ **MAIN IDEA** How are solutions different from other mixtures?

❷ **VOCABULARY** How are solutes and solvents related to *solutions*?

❸ **READING SKILL** A mixture is made up of evenly spaced atoms of copper and silver. Is the mixture a solution? Explain your answer.

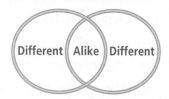

Different | Alike | Different

❹ **CRITICAL THINKING: Apply** Mia makes a delicious soup. How could she separate the solid ingredients from the broth?

❺ **INQUIRY SKILL: Predict** Jars contain different amounts of water. A student adds salt to each jar until no more salt will dissolve. She makes the chart below. Predict how much salt will dissolve in 100 mL of water.

Water	25 mL	50 mL	75 mL	100 mL
Salt	9 g	18 g	27 g	?

 TEST PRACTICE
Which of the following is a type of alloy?

A. salt water

B. gold

C. iodine

D. bronze

 STANDARDS

1–2: 1.f., **3:** 1.f., 1.c., **4:** 1.f., **5:** 6.g., **Test Practice:** 1.f., 1.c.

How Does Matter Change?

Building Background

The teakettle is on the stove. As liquid water in the kettle heats up, changes of state begin to take place. Soon steam comes out of the spout.

Water in the gas state is invisible. But when it hits the cool air, it changes to a cloud of tiny droplets of water you can see. The water has changed from a liquid to a gas and back to a liquid—just like that! Changes of state are part of everyday life.

STANDARDS

1.g. *Students know* properties of solid, liquid, and gaseous substances, such as sugar ($C_6H_{12}O_6$), water (H_2O), helium (He), oxygen (O_2), nitrogen (N_2), and carbon dioxide (CO_2).
6.f. Select appropriate tools (e.g., thermometers, meter sticks, balances, and graduated cylinders) and make quantitative observations.

PREPARE TO INVESTIGATE

Inquiry Skill

Measure When you measure, you select and use appropriate tools and units to make numerical observations.

Materials

- two balloons
- measuring tape
- ice
- warm tap water
- marker
- dishpan
- cool water
- ruler

Science and Math Toolbox

For step 2, review **Measurements** on page H16.

Balloon Bath

Procedure

1. **Collaborate** Work with a partner. Make a chart in your *Science Notebook* like the one shown.

2. **Measure** Draw a circle around the widest part of each balloon. Label one balloon *A* and the other *B*. Measure around each balloon on the lines you made. You can use a string to measure if you need to. Record the measurements.

3. **Experiment** Half fill a dishpan with water and add ice cubes. Place balloon *A* in the ice water. Gently push the balloon into the water with a ruler.

4. **Record Data** Hold the balloon under the ice water for 3 minutes. Then remove it and quickly measure the distance around the balloon as you did in step 2. Record your measurement.

5. **Use Variables** Dump out the ice water and warm the dishpan with warm tap water. Half fill the dishpan with warm tap water.

6. **Compare** Repeat step 4 using warm water and balloon *B*.

Conclusion

1. **Analyze Data** How did the balloon change when it was cold? When it was heated?

2. **Infer** Propose a reason why the balloons changed size.

STEP 1

Balloon	Measurement
A original measurement	
A after cooling	
B original measurement	
B after cooling	

STEP 2

STEP 3

Guided Inquiry

Ask Questions What would happen if you put balloon *A* in a freezer? What would happen if balloon *B* was put in very hot water? With your teacher's permission, ask questions like these and test them. **Analyze data** from your results.

Physical Changes

VOCABULARY

condensation	p. 381
evaporation	p. 381
sublimation	p. 382
vaporization	p. 381

MAIN IDEA A chemical change involves a change in the identity of the matter, whereas a physical change does not.

READING SKILL

Cause and Effect Use a graphic organizer to show examples of physical changes and their causes.

Cause → Effect

STANDARDS

1.f. *Students know* differences in chemical and physical properties of substances are used to separate mixtures and identify compounds.

1.g. *Students know* properties of solid, liquid, and gaseous substances, such as sugar ($C_6H_{12}O_6$), water (H_2O), helium (He), oxygen (O_2), nitrogen (N_2), and carbon dioxide (CO_2).

Changes in Size and Shape

If you have ever sanded a board or sharpened a pencil, you have observed a physical change in matter. The sawdust on the floor and the shavings in the sharpener look different from the board and the pencil. But the chemical makeup of these materials hasn't changed at all.

A physical change is a change in the size, shape, or state of matter with no new matter being formed. In the case of the board and the pencil, only the size of the samples has been changed.

The chemical properties of the sawdust and the shavings are the same as the chemical properties of the objects from which they came.

The students are changing the shape of wood in different ways. Each change is a physical change. ▼

Cutting

Sanding

Drilling

Expansion and Contraction

For most substances, a sample of solid matter will expand, or increase in size, when it is heated. The increase in size of a substance due to a change in temperature is called thermal expansion.

Remember that the particles of solids are constantly vibrating in place. When the temperature of a solid rises, its particles vibrate more rapidly and move farther apart. As a result, the entire sample expands. Compare this to the difference between small and large jumps: When you jump higher, you move through more space.

When a solid sample is cooled, the opposite happens. The particles vibrate more slowly. The sample contracts, or decreases in size. When a solid undergoes thermal contraction due to cooling, it takes up less space.

The molecules of water in ice take up more space than in a liquid. So water expands when it freezes. ▶

Thermal expansion and contraction can strain bridges. Engineers make bridges safer by adding expansion joints. These are spaces between metal parts that allow the bridge to change length without weakening or breaking.

Not all substances get smaller when they get colder. Water expands when it freezes because the molecules in ice crystals are spread farther apart than the molecules in liquid water.

Expansion of water explains why ice floats. Because a given mass of ice has a greater volume than an equal mass of liquid water, the solid ice is less dense than the liquid water.

Although heating or cooling may change the volume of matter, the mass will stay the same. One gram of any substance—solid, liquid, or gas—remains one gram at any temperature.

CAUSE AND EFFECT Why does water expand when it freezes?

◀ Engineers add expansion joints to bridges to ease the strain of expansion and contraction.

Liquid water

Steam

Snow

▲ When spring arrives, the winter's snow melts into liquid water. Steam is made of tiny water droplets. As the droplets rise, they change into water vapor.

Melting and Freezing

In many places, spring brings warmer temperatures. Snow and ice begin changing state from solids to liquids. A change of state is a physical change. The substance involved keeps its identity, and matter is always conserved. A change of state takes place when snow and ice begin melting in the spring.

When energy is added to a solid, its temperature will rise to a certain point. The solid starts melting, or changing from a solid to a liquid, at its melting point.

The process is reversed when energy is removed from a liquid. The temperature drops to the freezing point. The temperature stays the same while the liquid freezes.

For any substance, the melting point and the freezing point are the same temperature. Both the melting point and the freezing point of pure water are 0°C (32°F).

A water solution has a lower melting point than pure water. The more salt or other solute that the water dissolves, the lower the melting point becomes. This is why salt is spread on icy roads, as you read earlier.

Express Lab

Activity Card 31

Observe a Physical Change

Vaporizing and Condensing

Watch a drop of water on a hot frying pan. It sizzles, pops, and disappears. The change of state is caused by a rapid increase in temperature.

Adding energy to a substance makes its particles speed up, raising the temperature. At some point, the particles have so much energy that they break the forces that keep them in the liquid state. The water vaporizes. **Vaporization** is the change of state from a liquid to a gas.

Rapid vaporization is called boiling. The boiling point of a substance is the temperature at which rapid vaporization occurs. Boiling points can be slightly different from place to place because of air pressure. The boiling point for water at sea level is 100°C (212°F).

Slow or gradual vaporization is called evaporation. **Evaporation** takes place at the surface of a liquid. The higher the temperature of the surroundings, the faster evaporation takes place.

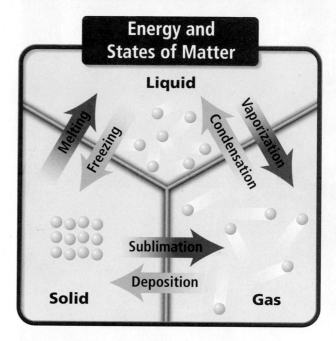

Energy and States of Matter

Liquid · Melting · Freezing · Vaporization · Condensation · Sublimation · Deposition · Solid · Gas

▲ Changes in energy can cause changes in state.

When energy is removed from a gas, it will undergo **condensation,** a change of state from a gas to a liquid. You can observe condensation on a hot day when you make a pitcher of ice-cold lemonade. The pitcher will begin to "sweat," as water droplets form on the outside of the glass. The droplets come from water vapor in the air condensing on the cold glass.

You can also observe condensation on a freezing cold day. The air you breathe out contains water vapor, which condenses when it loses energy to the cold air.

CAUSE AND EFFECT How does energy affect the motion of particles that make up a substance?

◀ The cold bottle removes energy from water vapor in the air that touches it. The water vapor condenses into liquid droplets on the outside of the bottle.

Skipping a Step

Different kinds of matter will change states at different temperatures and at different rates. Each change depends on the particles that make up matter and the forces among the particles.

Sometimes, matter can skip the liquid state! When conditions are right, adding energy to a solid will change it directly to a gas. The process of changing from a solid to a gas is called **sublimation.**

Sublimation explains why dry ice is dry. Dry ice is solid carbon dioxide. It does not melt into a liquid. Instead, it

Sublimation ▶
In sublimation, a solid changes directly to a gas without passing through the liquid state.

◀ Deposition
When energy is removed from water vapor in the air, frost can be deposited on a freezing cold window.

sublimates into carbon dioxide gas. People use dry ice instead of frozen water when they want to keep something cold, but not wet.

The opposite of sublimation is deposition. Deposition is the change of state from gas to solid. When energy is removed from a gas, its particles slow down. Under certain conditions, the gas can change directly into a solid.

Frost is a common example of deposition. Frost forms on grass, cars, and windows when the temperature of these surfaces is below 0°C, the freezing point of water. When water vapor in the air touches these surfaces, it changes directly from a gas to tiny crystals of ice.

CAUSE AND EFFECT What causes frost to form on windows?

Visual Summary

Solids, liquids, and gases are the three common states of matter. Water can be found in nature in all three states.

Removing energy may cause a gas to condense into a liquid, or a liquid to freeze into a solid. Adding energy may cause vaporization or melting.

Frozen carbon dioxide is called dry ice. It changes directly into a gas in a process called sublimation.

Most solids expand when they are heated and contract when they are cooled.

 STANDARDS

1.f., 1.g.

 **Technology**
Visit **www.eduplace.com/cascp** to find out more about changes of state.

Reading Review

1 MAIN IDEA Name three changes of state that can take place when energy is removed from a substance.

2 VOCABULARY Describe the processes of *vaporization* and *condensation*.

3 READING SKILL When will a liquid evaporate, and when will it boil? Explain both changes.

Cause → Effect

4 CRITICAL THINKING: Use Numbers A sample of water vapor is cooled from 134°C to −5°C. Calculate the temperature difference, and describe the changes the sample undergoes.

5 INQUIRY SKILL: Measure To measure the volume of an ice cube, a student first melts the ice, then measures the volume of the liquid with a graduated cylinder. Is this procedure accurate? Explain.

 TEST PRACTICE
During which change of state does a gas change to a solid?

A. deposition

B. sublimation

C. thermal expansion

D. vaporization

 STANDARDS

1–3: 1.g., 4–5: 1.f., **Test Practice:** 1.g.

STANDARDS **1.g.** *Students know* properties of solid, liquid, and gaseous substances, such as sugar (C $6H_{12}O_6$), water (H_2O), helium (He), oxygen (O_2), nitrogen (N_2), nitrogen (N_2), and carbon dioxide (CO_2).

How Cool Is That?

You've heard of "boiling hot." Well, what about "boiling cold?" This rose was "boiled" in one of the coldest liquids known— liquid nitrogen. Liquid nitrogen boils at a temperature so cold it can instantly freeze anything that contains water, such as this rose, or even your skin.

Nitrogen (N_2) is more familiar to us as a gas. It's very familiar, in fact. About 78% of the air we breathe is nitrogen. But when nitrogen is compressed and cooled, it turns to liquid.

How cold is liquid nitrogen? Think how cold an ice cube feels. That's 0° C. Now imagine something 196 degrees colder! Nitrogen liquefies at -196° C. At room temperature, it boils away like water on a hot stove!

A rose, like most living tissue, is largely made of water. That's why it's soft and flexible at room temperature.

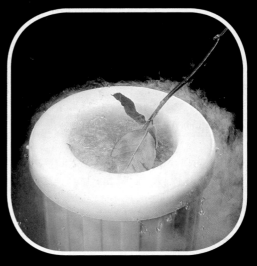

The liquid nitrogen absorbs heat from the rose and boils furiously as it returns to a gas.

After one swift dip in the liquid nitrogen, the rose is frozen solid. It's so brittle, it shatters like glass!

Writing Journal

Helium gas becomes liquid at -270°C. In your journal, infer what would happen if you poured liquid helium into liquid nitrogen. Explain your answer.

385

What Happens in a Chemical Reaction?

Building Background

When you roast marshmallows over a campfire, chemical changes are taking place. The substances in wood combine with oxygen in the air to produce new substances, releasing energy in the process. That energy roasts your tasty treat. But be careful! If you don't watch carefully, the marshmallow will undergo further chemical changes and burn to a crisp.

PREPARE TO INVESTIGATE

Inquiry Skill

Observe When you observe, you use your senses or instruments to identify properties.

Materials

- goggles
- 2 jars
- skim milk
- vinegar

Science and Math Toolbox

For step 2, review **Measuring Volume** on page H7.

 STANDARDS

1.a. *Students know* that during chemical reactions the atoms in the reactants rearrange to form products with different properties.
6.g. Record data by using appropriate graphic representations (including charts, graphs, and labeled diagrams) and make inferences from those data.

Milk and Vinegar

Procedure

① **Collaborate** Work with a partner. In your *Science Notebook,* create a chart like the one shown. Make the chart large enough for you to include written observations.

Safety: Wear goggles during this investigation.

② **Observe** Pour 100 mL of milk into one jar and 100 mL of vinegar into the other jar. Study the properties of each liquid. Record your observations.

③ **Observe** Tightly cover the jar of milk, shake it vigorously, and set it on your work surface. Observe how the milk returns along the sides to the bottom of the jar. Record your observations.

④ **Record Data** Repeat step 3 with the jar of vinegar.

⑤ **Experiment** Uncover the jars and carefully pour a small amount of vinegar into the milk. Observe the interaction of the two liquids. Record your observations.

⑥ **Experiment** Pour the rest of the vinegar into the milk. Stir the mixture and allow it to settle. Record your observations.

Conclusion

1. **Compare** Compare and contrast the properties of milk and vinegar.

2. **Hypothesize** What happened when the milk and vinegar were mixed? Form a hypothesis that answers this question.

STEP 1

	Milk	Vinegar
Properties		
Behavior after shaking		

STEP 2

STEP 3

Guided Inquiry

Experiment Try the experiment with different substances, such as lemon juice, baking soda, water, and salt. **Compare** the result with those obtained when vinegar is mixed with milk.

Chemical Changes

VOCABULARY

product   p. 390
reactant   p. 390

READING SKILL

Main Idea and Details As you read, write down details about chemical changes.

Main Idea

Detail   Detail

STANDARD

1.a. *Students know* that during chemical reactions the atoms in the reactants rearrange to form products with different properties.

MAIN IDEA A chemical change involves making and breaking chemical bonds to form new substances. Chemical changes can either absorb or release energy.

Forming New Substances

When a sample of matter undergoes a physical change, the particles of the substance have the same chemical makeup before and after the change. When a chemical change takes place, however, the result is a new substance with particles that differ in the number or types of atoms or chemical bonds.

In a chemical change, one set of substances changes to form new substances. For example, when a welder lights up a welding torch, the acetylene that fuels the torch (C_2H_2) combines with molecules of oxygen in the air (O_2). The fuel and oxygen undergo a chemical change to produce new substances, which are carbon dioxide gas (CO_2) and water vapor (H_2O). Energy is released in the form of heat and light.

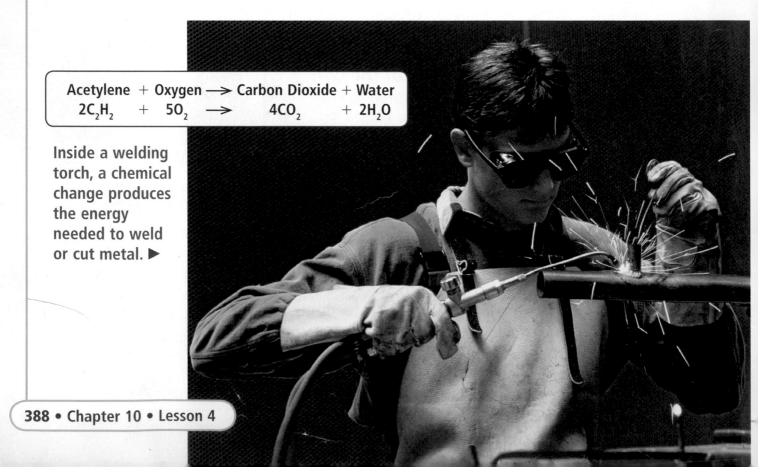

Acetylene + Oxygen $\longrightarrow$ Carbon Dioxide + Water
$2C_2H_2$ + $5O_2$ $\longrightarrow$ $4CO_2$ + $2H_2O$

Inside a welding torch, a chemical change produces the energy needed to weld or cut metal. ▶

Examples of Chemical Changes

Chemical changes take place all around you every day. How do you know that a chemical change is occurring? A change in color often is one sign. For example, when you leave a bicycle chain out in the rain, the iron in the chain undergoes a chemical change, forming brown-red rust. Another chemical change takes place when green bananas turn yellow as they ripen.

Many chemical changes are rapid and give off large amounts of light and heat. Examples include burning, such as burning wood in a campfire, burning natural gas on a stove, or burning wax in a candle. When gasoline in a car engine burns, the chemical change provides energy to make the car run.

Other chemical changes take place more slowly. Think of the changes in your body since you were born, or the changes of other living things in their life cycles. A huge number of chemical changes allow young animals or tiny seeds to grow into adults.

Living things cause chemical changes to their environment, too. The lichens shown at right produce chemicals that slowly break down the rock they grow on. A lichen is a pair of organisms—a fungus and an alga (plural: algae)—living closely together.

MAIN IDEA AND DETAILS List three examples of chemical changes.

$$Iron + Oxygen \longrightarrow Rust$$
$$4Fe + 3O_2 \longrightarrow 2Fe_2O_3$$

▲ When iron (Fe) is exposed to oxygen (O_2) in the air, a chemical change will take place and rust will form. One of the substances in rust is Fe_2O_3.

Lichen

▲ Substances produced by lichens react with substances in the rock in a slow chemical change.

389

▲ When you twist a glow stick, you start a chemical reaction that produces a glowing light.

◄ Burning wood is another example of a chemical reaction.

Chemical Reactions

A chemical change is a change in matter that results in new substances being formed. When a substance enters into and is altered through the course of a chemical change, it is called a **reactant.** A substance that results from a chemical change is called a **product.**

What causes a chemical change? In any sample of matter, forces called chemical bonds hold the atoms or molecules together. Chemical changes involve breaking these bonds and forming new bonds. This creates new substances with new chemical properties.

A chemical reaction is a specific example of one or more chemical changes. Burning wood shows one example. Wood contains cellulose, which is made up of carbon, hydrogen, and oxygen. When wood burns, the atoms of carbon and hydrogen in the wood combine with molecules of oxygen in the air. This chemical reaction releases the products of carbon dioxide gas and water vapor.

Chemical reactions take place all around you every day. How can you recognize them? A change in color sometimes indicates them.

For example, the outer shell of the Statue of Liberty is made of copper, which is a bright, shiny metal. As it was exposed to the weather, chemical changes caused the copper to change color. First, it changed to brown, then to black, and later to the greenish color it is today.

Another sign of a chemical reaction is the release of heat or light. Burning wood and glow sticks are examples.

The forming of gases also may indicate a chemical reaction. Bread rises because of chemical reactions in yeast that release carbon dioxide gas.

Express Lab

Activity Card 32
Observe a Chemical Reaction

Chemical Equations

How do scientists describe the reactants and products of a chemical reaction? They use chemical equations. A chemical equation lists the reactants on the left, then an arrow, then the products. Scientists may use word names for the reactants and products, but typically they use chemical formulas.

In the equations on this page, notice that numbers are written before some of the chemical formulas. These numbers show the ratio of the reactants and products.

For example, in the reaction to the right, 2 water molecules react to produce 2 hydrogen molecules and 1 oxygen molecule. In the reaction below, the ratios include 6 molecules of three compounds.

All chemical reactions include one factor that may not appear in its chemical equation. That factor is energy. Some reactions release energy, while others take it in. Without the energy from light, for example, photosynthesis would not happen.

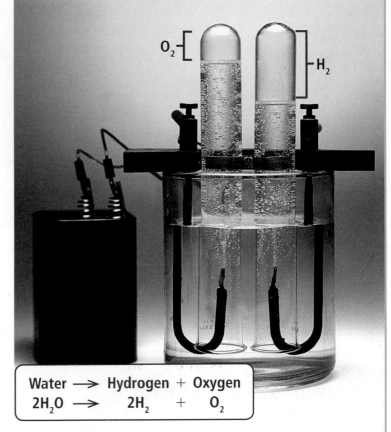

Water $\longrightarrow$ Hydrogen + Oxygen
$2H_2O \longrightarrow 2H_2 + O_2$

▲ In a reaction powered by electricity, water molecules break apart to form hydrogen and oxygen.

MAIN IDEA AND DETAILS What clues show a chemical change is taking place?

Carbon Dioxide + Water $\longrightarrow$ Sugar + Oxygen
$6CO_2 + 6H_2O \longrightarrow C_6H_{12}O_6 + 6O_2$

Plants perform photosynthesis. What are the reactants and products of this reaction? What supplies the energy? ▶

391

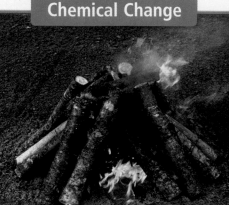

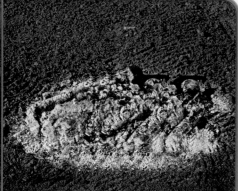

Chemical Change

Original Materials
Wood is mostly a carbon compound called cellulose. When heated, it will react with oxygen in the air.

Chemical Change
Cellulose and oxygen combine to form two gases: carbon dioxide and water vapor. The flames are hot, glowing gases.

New Materials
Most of the wood has been changed into gases. Some carbon remains in ashes.

Conservation of Matter

Regardless of the kind of change taking place in a sample of matter, the amount of matter stays the same. When matter changes, mass is always conserved, meaning that it is neither created nor destroyed.

In a chemical change, this means that the mass of the materials before a chemical change is equal to the mass afterwards. This is true even if you cannot see the materials that form, such as a gas that is produced.

Matter is also conserved in all physical changes. When you place water in the freezer, it undergoes a physical change. The water freezes and becomes ice.

As you may know, the volume of water increases when it freezes. But that does not mean that matter was created. Instead, the arrangement of the water molecules takes up more space in ice than in water.

You can use a scale to prove that mass is conserved when matter changes. For example, fruit changes chemically when it either ripens or decays. Tissues change, new materials form, and gases are released. By covering the fruit and placing it on a scale, you can observe that the mass stays the same even as the fruit changes. Try it!

Sometimes, the conservation of mass is hard to see. For example, when a log burns in a fireplace, only a few ashes remain. The pictures and captions above describe what happens when wood burns.

What if you could measure the masses of the logs, gases, and ashes that take part in this reaction? You would discover that the total mass of the reactants equaled the total mass of the products.

MAIN IDEA AND DETAILS Is matter conserved when wood burns? Explain.

Lesson Wrap-Up

Visual Summary

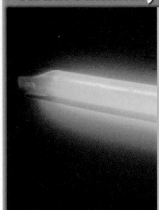

A chemical change involves a change in the identity and properties of matter. The release of heat or light is one sign of a chemical change.

Matter is neither created nor destroyed during chemical and physical changes. When wood burns, its matter changes into gases, smoke, and ashes.

The atoms are rearranged in a chemical reaction, and energy is always involved. Some reactions release energy, others take up energy.

 **STANDARD**

1.a.

 Technology
Visit **www.eduplace.com/cascp** to find out more about changes in matter.

Reading Review

❶ MAIN IDEA What happens to substances during a chemical change?

❷ VOCABULARY What are the *reactants* and *products* of a chemical reaction? Give an example to illustrate your answer.

❸ READING SKILL Write the chemical equation for a reaction. Identify the reactants and products.

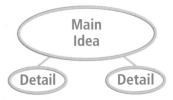

❹ CRITICAL THINKING: Infer When an electric current is passed through a sample of water, bubbles of gas form. Some of this gas will burn when lit. What can you infer about the type of change taking place?

❺ INQUIRY SKILL: Compare Compare the physical and chemical properties of ice and liquid water.

 TEST PRACTICE
In any chemical reaction, the reactants have the same _____ as the products.

A. total mass

B. total volume

C. physical properties

D. colors

 STANDARDS
1–5: 1.a., **Test Practice:** 1.a.

393

Math in Science

When yeast is added to a solution of sugar and water, some of the sugar is changed to ethanol. This process is called fermentation. The chart shows ethanol production from one yeast culture over 6 hours.

Time (hr)	1	2	3	4	5	6
Ethanol produced	1 unit	2 units	3 units	3 units	2 units	1 unit

1. Create a line graph that shows the production rate of ethanol.

2. What if measurements are taken from the culture for 2 additional hours after the sixth hour? What values would you predict for ethanol produced?

Writing in Science
Research Report

Desalination is the process of removing salt from sea water. Research ways this is done. Present your findings in a report that includes text, diagrams, and photos.

Polymer Chemist

What do rubber tires, plastic film, and wool sweaters have in common? They are all made of polymers—large molecules formed by chains of smaller molecules. Polymer chemists are responsible for analyzing and creating polymers. Artificial polymers are used in scientific research, manufacturing, and the newest computer chips.

What It Takes!

- An advanced degree in chemistry or chemical engineering
- Curiosity and imagination

Pyrotechnician

Did you ever wonder who makes the fireworks you see on the Fourth of July? That person is called a pyrotechnician. Pyrotechnicians, literally "crafters of fire," work with flammable and explosive materials. These artists create spectacular and safe visual displays and sound effects.

What It Takes!

- An understanding of basic chemistry
- Artistic creativity
- Following safety rules

Vocabulary

Complete each sentence with a term from the list.

1. A substance with no definite volume or shape is most likely a(n) _gas_.

2. Another name for a homogeneous mixture is a(n) _solution_.

3. The change of state from gas to liquid is called _condensation_.

4. A substance with a definite volume but no definite shape is a(n) _liquid_.

5. The physical combination of two or more substances results in a(n) _mixture_.

6. The change of state from a solid directly to a gas is called _sublimation_.

7. A substance enters into and is altered through the course of a chemical change. It is called a _reactant_.

8. A substance that results from a chemical change is called a(n) _product_.

9. A substance with a definite volume and shape is a(n) _solid_.

10. Boiling and evaporation are types of _vaporization_.

- condensation p. 381
- evaporation p. 381
- gas p. 364
- liquid p. 363
- mixture p. 370
- product p. 390
- reactant p. 390
- solid p. 362
- solution p. 372
- sublimation p. 382
- vaporization p. 381

Test Practice

Write the letter of the best answer choice.

11. A characteristic of a material that can be observed with the senses is ____.

    A. its composition
    B. a reaction time
    C. a physical property
    D. a chemical property

12. Which of the following involves a change in the identity of the matter undergoing change?

    A. melting
    B. boiling
    C. freezing
    D. burning

13. The melting point of a substance is the same as its ____.

    A. boiling point
    B. freezing point
    C. density
    D. chemical formula

14. What best describes an alloy?

    A. a heterogeneous mixture
    B. a solution of a metal and a gas
    C. a metal in its element form
    D. a solution of two metals

Inquiry Skills

15. **Compare and Contrast** How are a solute and solvent different?

16. A scientist places a can containing an unknown liquid in a freezer overnight. The next day, the can does not appear all that different from the day before. What can she conclude about the can and its contents?

Map the Concept

Use a Venn diagram to show examples of physical changes and chemical changes. Fill in the following terms. One example applies to both categories.

Burning wood
Chewing food
Cutting paper
Dissolving sugar in water
Exploding fireworks
Melting ice
Photosynthesis

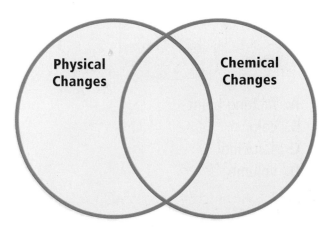

Physical Changes

Chemical Changes

Critical Thinking

17. **Analyze** Iron is attracted to a magnet, but carbon is not. Would you expect steel, an alloy of iron and carbon, to be attracted to a magnet? Explain.

18. **Analyze** Gases can be dissolved in liquids to form solutions. Many carbonated drinks contain dissolved sugar and dissolved carbon dioxide. When a carbonated drink "goes flat" and loses all of its dissolved carbon dioxide, is it no longer a solution?

19. **Apply** A teacher dissolves iodine crystals in alcohol. Which substance is the solute and which substance is the solvent?

20. **Analyze** Could you use a sieve or filter to separate a mixture of sugar and salt?

Performance Assessment

Chemical Equations

Write a chemical equation and explain the reaction that occurs. Label the reactants and products. $2Fe_2O_3$

$$2Fe_2 + O_3 = 2Fe_2O_3$$

Writing Journal

Review your journal writing answers at the beginning of this chapter on page 355. Revise and change them if necessary.

STANDARDS

1: 1.g., **2:** 1.f., **3–4:** 1.g., **5:** 1.f., **6:** 1.g., **7–8:** 1.a., **9–10:** 1.g., **11–12:** 1.a., **13–14:** 1.g., **15:** 1.f., **16:** 6.b., **17:** 1.c., **18–20:** 1.g.

Write the letter of the best answer.

1. Which is NOT an element?
   A. aluminum
   B. carbon
   C. oxygen
   D. water

2. Look at this section of the Periodic Table.

28	29	30
Ni	**Cu**	**Zn**
58.71	63.55	65.8
46	47	48
Pd	**Ag**	**Cd**
106.4	107.8	112.4
78	79	80
Pt	**Au**	**Hg**
195.9	196.9	200.5

   Which element is copper (Cu) MOST likely to resemble?
   A. mercury (Hg)
   B. nickel (Ni)
   C. silver (Ag)
   D. zinc (Zn)

3. Two elements combine chemically to form a new material. This material is called a(n) ____.
   A. atom
   B. compound
   C. conductor
   D. mixture

4. Which pair of properties BEST describes a solid?
   A. compressible, fluid
   B. definite shape, fluid
   C. definite volume, compressible
   D. definite shape, definite volume

5. A solid can change directly to a gas through the process of ____.
   A. condensation
   B. deposition
   C. sublimation
   D. vaporization

6. Which property of sand makes it settle to the bottom of the liquid in the jar?

   A. melting point
   B. color
   C. solubility
   D. volume

7. Which shows a physical change taking place?

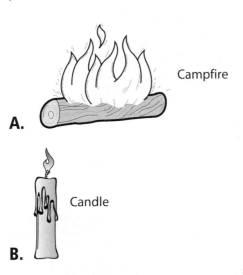

A. Campfire

B. Candle

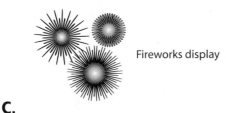

C. Fireworks display

D. Ice cream cone

8. Which property determines how much of a substance can dissolve in another substance?

A. conductivity
B. density
C. mass
D. solubility

Answer the following in complete sentences.

9. Sodium is a soft, silvery metal that burns vigorously when exposed to air. Chlorine is a pale green, poisonous gas. Do these properties tell you anything about the properties of the compound sodium chloride, which is made up of sodium and chlorine? Explain your answer.

10. A bucket of sand also contains a few shells, some strands of seaweed, and a small crab. Is this mixture heterogeneous or homogeneous? Explain your answer.

STANDARDS

1: 1.d., **2:** 1.d., **3:** 1.a., 1.b., **4:** 1.g., **5:** 1.g.,
6: 1.f., **7:** 1.f., **8:** 1.f., **9:** 1.a., **10:** 1.f.

You Can...

Discover More

What do your body, a rocket, and a star have in common? All contain hydrogen: the simplest and most common element in the universe. Although simple in structure, hydrogen is an important building block for all sorts of matter. Read about the different examples below.

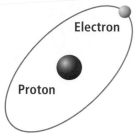

Electron

Proton

Hydrogen atom

Fuels The space shuttle uses liquid hydrogen as a fuel. In the future, hydrogen fuel cells may provide energy for cars.

Stars Inside a star, hydrogen nuclei fuse to form the next simplest element, helium. The process releases huge amounts of energy.

Water Every molecule of water is made of two hydrogen atoms joined to an oxygen atom. Life could not exist without water!

Acids Fruit juice tastes tangy because of acids. Most acids release hydrogen ions when they dissolve in water.

In its element form, hydrogen exists as a molecule of two atoms. However, most of Earth's hydrogen is bound into compounds with other elements, especially carbon, oxygen, and nitrogen. A countless number of hydrogen compounds form and break apart every time you cook a meal, ride in a car, or move a muscle.

Learn about hydrogen fuel cells. Go to www.eduplace.com/cascp to see examples of hydrogen as a fuel.

Science and Math Toolbox

Using a Microscope

A microscope makes it possible to see very small things by magnifying them. Some microscopes have a set of lenses that magnify objects by different amounts.

Examine Some Salt Grains

Handle a microscope carefully; it can break easily. Carry it firmly with both hands and avoid touching the lenses.

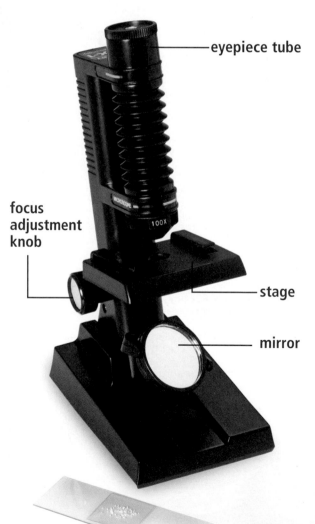

eyepiece tube

focus adjustment knob

stage

mirror

microscope slide

1 Turn the mirror toward a source of light. **NEVER** use the Sun as a light source.

2 Place a few grains of salt on the slide. Put the slide on the stage of the microscope.

3 Bring the salt grains into focus. Turn the adjustment knob on the back of the microscope as you look through the eyepiece.

4 Raise the eyepiece tube to increase the magnification; lower it to decrease magnification.

Making a Bar Graph

A bar graph helps you organize and compare data. For example, you might want to make a bar graph to compare weather data for different places.

Make a Bar Graph of Annual Snowfall

For more than 20 years, the cities listed in the table have been recording their yearly snowfall. The table shows the average number of centimeters of snow that the cities receive each year. Use the data in the table to make a bar graph showing the cities' average annual snowfall.

Snowfall	
City	**Snowfall (cm)**
Atlanta, GA	5
Charleston, SC	1.5
Houston, TX	1
Jackson, MS	3
New Orleans, LA	0.5
Tucson, AZ	3

1. **Title your graph. The title should help a reader understand what your graph describes.**

2. **Choose a scale and mark equal intervals. The vertical scale should include the least value and the greatest value in the set of data.**

3. **Label the vertical axis *Snowfall (cm)* and the horizontal axis *City*. Space the city names equally.**

4. **Carefully graph the data. Depending on the interval you choose, some amounts may be between two numbers.**

5. **Check each step of your work.**

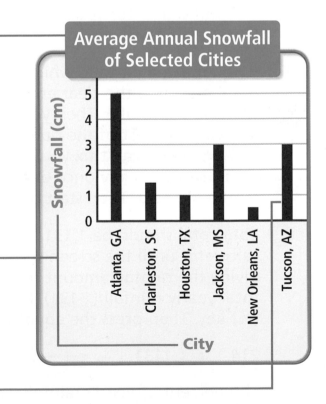

Average Annual Snowfall of Selected Cities

Using a Calculator

After you've made measurements, a calculator can help you analyze your data. Some calculators have a memory key that allows you to save the result of one calculation while you do another.

Add and Divide to Find Percent

The table shows the amount of rain that was collected using a rain gauge in each month of one year. You can use a calculator to help you find the total yearly rainfall. Then you can find the percent of rain that fell during January.

Rainfall	
Month	**Rain (mm)**
Jan.	214
Feb.	138
Mar.	98
Apr.	157
May	84
June	41
July	5
Aug.	23
Sept.	48
Oct.	75
Nov.	140
Dec.	108

1 Add the numbers. When you add a series of numbers, you need not press the equal sign until the last number is entered. Just press the plus sign after you enter each number (except the last).

2 If you make a mistake while you are entering numbers, press the clear entry (CE/C) key to erase your mistake. Then you can continue entering the rest of the numbers you are adding. If you can't fix your mistake, you can press the (CE/C) key once or twice until the screen shows 0. Then start over.

3 Your total should be 1,131. Now clear the calculator until the screen shows 0. Then divide the rainfall amount for January by the total yearly rainfall (1,131). Press the percent (%) key. Then press the equal sign key.

214 ÷ 1131 % =

The percent of yearly rainfall that fell in January is 18.921309, which rounds to 19%.

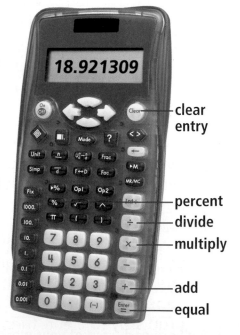

clear entry

percent

divide

multiply

add

equal

Using Variables

Bacteria and other tiny organisms will turn clear soup cloudy. Will adding vinegar or salt to a cup of soup slow the growth of these organisms? With your teacher's help, follow this procedure to find out.

1. Pour equal amounts of clear soup into three plastic cups.

2. Mix a spoonful of vinegar into one cup. Mix a spoonful of salt into the second cup. Add nothing to the third cup, which is the control. Cover the cups with plastic wrap.

3. Compare the soup in each cup after two, three, and four days.

Identifying Variables

- The **independent variable** is the factor that is changed among the test groups. Here it is the added ingredient, either vinegar or salt. One test group is left unchanged and is called the control.

- The **controlled variables** are kept the same among all test groups. They include the amount of soup, the temperature, and the type of cup.

- The **dependent variable** changes because of the independent variable. The clearness of the soup is the dependent variable. If only the salty soup stayed clear, then salt must have been the cause.

STEP 1

STEP 2

Vinegar   Salt   Control

STEP 3

Sample		Observations
Vinegar	2 days	
	3 days	
	4 days	
Salt	2 days	
	3 days	
	4 days	
Control	2 days	
	3 days	
	4 days	

Using a Tape Measure or Ruler

Tape measures, metersticks, and rulers are tools for measuring length. Scientists use units such as kilometers, meters, centimeters, and millimeters when making length measurements.

Use a Meterstick

1 Work with a partner to find the height of your reach. Stand facing a chalkboard. Reach up as high as you can with one hand.

2 Have your partner use chalk to mark the chalkboard at the highest point of your reach.

3 Use a meterstick to measure your reach to the nearest centimeter. Measure from the floor to the chalk mark. Record the height.

Use a Tape Measure

1 Use a tape measure to find the circumference of, or distance around, your partner's head. Wrap the tape around your partner's head.

2 Find the line where the tape begins to wrap over itself.

3 Record the distance around your partner's head to the nearest millimeter.

Measuring Volume

A graduated cylinder, a measuring cup, and a beaker are used to measure volume. Volume is the amount of space something takes up. Most of the containers that scientists use to measure volume have a scale marked in milliliters (mL).

▲ This measuring cup has marks for each 25 mL.

▲ This beaker has marks for each 50 mL.

▲ This graduated cylinder has marks for every 1 mL.

Measure the Volume of a Liquid

1. Measure the volume of some juice. Pour the juice into a measuring container.

2. Move your head so that your eyes are level with the top of the juice. Read the scale line that is closest to the surface of the juice. If the surface of the juice is curved up on the sides, look at the lowest point of the curve.

3. Read the measurement on the scale. You can estimate the value between two lines on the scale to obtain a more accurate measurement.

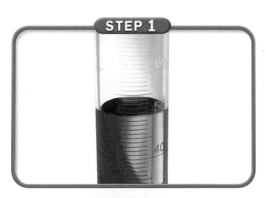

STEP 1

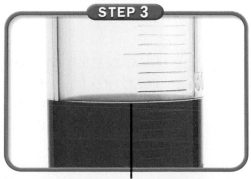

STEP 3

The bottom of the curve is at 35 mL.

Using a Thermometer

A thermometer is used to measure temperature. When the liquid in the tube of a thermometer gets warmer, it expands and moves farther up the tube. Different scales can be used to measure temperature, but scientists usually use the Celsius scale.

Measure the Temperature of a Liquid

1 Half fill a cup with water or another liquid.

2 Hold the thermometer so that the bulb is in the center of the liquid. Be sure that there are no bright lights or direct sunlight shining on the bulb.

3 Wait until you see the liquid in the tube of the thermometer stop moving. Read the scale line that is closest to the top of the liquid in the tube. The thermometer shown reads 22°C (about 71°F).

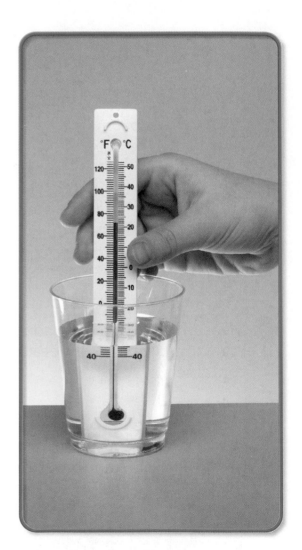

Using a Balance

A balance is used to measure mass. Mass is the amount of matter in an object. To find the mass of an object, place the object in the left pan of the balance. Place standard masses in the right pan.

Measure the Mass of a Ball

1 Check that the empty pans are balanced, or level with each other. When balanced, the pointer on the base should be on the middle mark. If it needs to be adjusted, move the slider on the back of the balance a little to the left or right.

2 Place a ball in the left pan. Then add standard masses, one at a time, to the right pan. When the pointer is at the middle mark again, each pan is holding the same amount of matter, and the same mass.

3 Each standard mass is marked to show its number of grams. Add the number of grams marked on the masses in the pan. The total is the mass of the ball in grams.

Using an Equation or Formula

Equations and formulas can help you to determine measurements that are not easily made.

Use the Diameter of a Circle to Find Its Circumference

1 Find the circumference of a circle that has a diameter of 10 cm. To determine the circumference of a circle, use the formula below.

$C = \pi d$

$C = 3.14 \times 10$ cm

$C = 31.4$ cm

The circumference of this circle is 31.4 cm.

π is the symbol for pi. Always use 3.14 as the value for π, unless another value for pi is given.

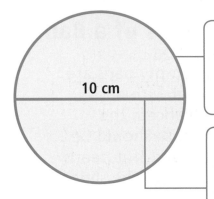

10 cm

The circumference (C) is a measure of the distance around a circle.

The diameter (d) of a circle is a line segment that passes through the center of the circle and connects two points on the circle.

Use Rate and Time to Determine Distance

2 Suppose an aircraft travels at 772 km/h for 2.5 hours. How many kilometers does the aircraft travel during that time? To determine distance traveled, use the distance formula below.

$d = rt$

$d = 772 \times 2.5$ km

$d = 1,930$ km

The aircraft travels 1,930 km in 2.5 hours.

d = distance

r = rate, or the speed at which the aircraft is traveling.

t = the length of time traveled

Making a Chart to Organize Data

A chart can help you record, compare, or classify information.

Organize Properties of Elements

Suppose you collected the data shown at the right. The data presents properties of silver, gold, lead, and iron.

You could organize this information in a chart by classifying the physical properties of each element.

My Data

Silver (Ag) has a density of 10.5 g/cm³. It melts at 961°C and boils at 2,212°C. It is used in dentistry and to make jewelry and electronic conductors.

Gold melts at 1,064°C and boils at 2,966°C. Its chemical symbol is Au. It has a density of 19.3 g/cm³ and is used for jewelry, in coins, and in dentistry.

The melting point of lead (Pb) is 328°C. The boiling point is 1,740°C. It has a density of 11.3 g/cm³. Some uses for lead are in storage batteries, paints, and dyes.

Iron (Fe) has a density of 7.9 g/cm³. It will melt at 1,535°C and boil at 3,000°C. It is used for building materials, in manufacturing, and as a dietary supplement.

Create categories that describe the information you have found.

Give the chart a title that describes what is listed in it.

Make sure the information is listed accurately in each column.

Properties of Some Elements

Element	Symbol	Density g/cm³	Melting Point (°C)	Boiling Point (°C)	Some Uses
Silver	Ag	10.5	961	2,212	jewelry, dentistry, electric conductors
Gold	Au	19.3	1,064	2,966	jewelry, dentistry, coins
Lead	Pb	11.3	328	1,740	storage batteries, paints, dyes
Iron	Fe	7.9	1,535	3,000	building materials, manufacturing, dietary supplement

Reading a Circle Graph

A circle graph shows the whole divided into parts. You can use a circle graph to compare parts to each other or to compare parts to the whole.

Read a Circle Graph of Land Area

The whole circle represents the approximate land area of all of the continents on Earth. The number on each wedge indicates the land area of each continent. From the graph you can determine that the land area of North America is 16% × 148,000,000 km², or about 24 million square kilometers.

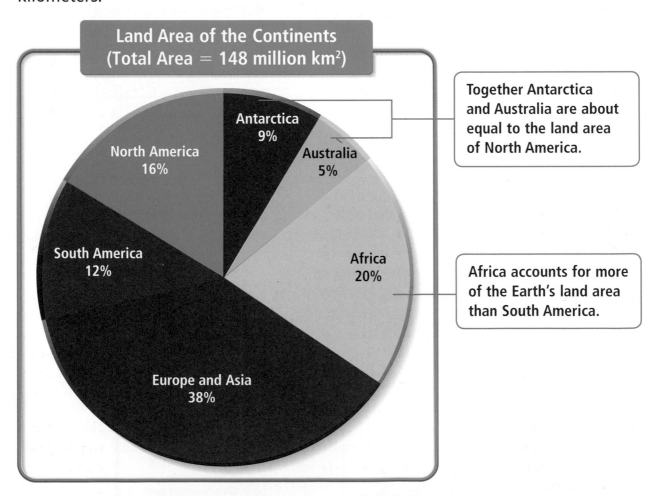

Land Area of the Continents (Total Area = 148 million km²)

Antarctica 9%

Australia 5%

North America 16%

Africa 20%

South America 12%

Europe and Asia 38%

Together Antarctica and Australia are about equal to the land area of North America.

Africa accounts for more of the Earth's land area than South America.

Making a Line Graph

A line graph is a way to show continuous change over time. You can use the information from a table to make a line graph.

Make a Line Graph of Temperatures

The table shows temperature readings over a 12-hour period at the Dallas-Fort Worth Airport in Texas. This data can also be displayed in a line graph that shows temperature change over time.

Dallas-Fort Worth Airport Temperature	
Hour	Temp. (°C)
6 A.M.	22
7 A.M.	24
8 A.M.	25
9 A.M.	26
10 A.M.	27
11 A.M.	29
12 noon	31
1 P.M.	32
2 P.M.	33
3 P.M.	34
4 P.M.	35
5 P.M.	35
6 P.M.	34

1. Choose a title. The title should help a reader understand what your graph describes.

2. Choose a scale and mark equal intervals. The vertical scale should include the least value and the greatest value in the set of data.

3. Label the horizontal axis *Time* and the vertical axis *Temperature* (°C).

4. Write the hours on the horizontal axis. Space the hours equally.

5. Carefully graph the data. Depending on the interval you choose, some temperatures will be between two numbers.

6. Check each step of your work.

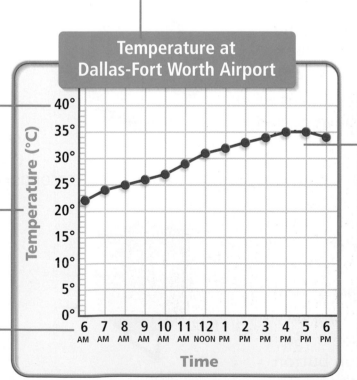

Temperature at Dallas-Fort Worth Airport

Measuring Elapsed Time

Sometimes you may need to find out how much time has passed, or elapsed. A clock is often used to find elapsed time. You can also change units and add or subtract to find out how much time has passed.

Using a Clock to Find Elapsed Minutes

You need to time an experiment for 20 minutes. It is 1:30.

- Start at 1:30.
- Count ahead 20 minutes, by fives to 1:50.
- Stop the experiment at 1:50.

Using a Clock or Stopwatch to Find Elapsed Seconds

You need to time an experiment for 15 seconds. You can use a second hand on a clock.

1. Wait until the second hand is on a number. Then start the experiment.
2. Stop the experiment when 15 seconds have passed.

You can also use a stopwatch to figure out elapsed seconds.

1. Press the reset button on the stopwatch so you see 0:00₀₀.
2. Press the start button to begin.
3. When you see 0:15₀₀, press the stop button on the watch.

Changing Units and Then Adding or Subtracting to Find Elapsed Time

If you know how to change units of time, you can use addition and subtraction to find elapsed time.

1 To change from a larger unit to a smaller unit, multiply.

$2 d = \blacksquare h$

$2 \times 24 = 48$

$2 d = 48 h$

2 To change from a smaller unit to a larger unit, divide.

$78 wk = \blacksquare yr$

$78 \div 52 = 1\frac{1}{2}$

$78 wk = 1\frac{1}{2} yr$

Another Example

Suppose it took juice in an ice-pop mold from 6:40 A.M. until 10:15 A.M. to freeze. How long did it take for the juice to freeze? To find out, subtract.

```
     9 h      75 min
    10 h      15 min      Rename 10 hr 15 min
                          as 9 h 75 min, since
                          1 hr = 60 min.
   – 6 h      40 min
    3 h       35 min
```

You can also add to find elapsed time.

```
    3 h    30 min    14 s
  + 1 h    40 min    45 s
    4 h    70 min    59 s = 5 h 10 min 59 s
```

Units of Time

60 seconds (s) = 1 minute (min)
60 minutes = 1 hour (hr)
24 hours = 1 day (d)
7 days = 1 week (wk)
52 weeks = 1 year (yr)

Measurements

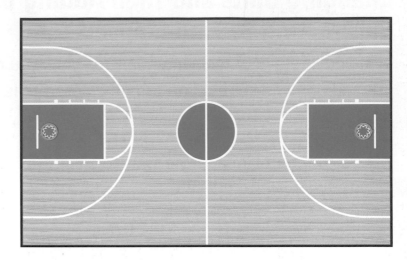

Volume

1 L of sports drink is a little more than 1 qt.

Area

A basketball court covers about 4,700 ft^2. It covers about 435 m^2.

Metric Measures

Temperature

- Ice melts at 0 degrees Celsius (°C)
- Water freezes at 0°C
- Water boils at 100°C

Length and Distance

- 1,000 meters (m) = 1 kilometer (km)
- 100 centimeters (cm) = 1 m
- 10 millimeters (mm) = 1 cm

Force

- 1 newton (N) = 1 kilogram × 1 (meter/second) per second

Volume

- 1 cubic meter (m^3) = 1 m × 1 m × 1 m
- 1 cubic centimeter (cm^3) = 1 cm × 1 cm × 1 cm
- 1 liter (L) = 1,000 milliliters (mL)
- 1 cm^3 = 1 mL

Area

- 1 square kilometer (km^2) = 1 km × 1 km
- 1 hectare = 10,000 m^2

Mass

- 1,000 grams (g) = 1 kilogram (kg)
- 1,000 milligrams (mg) = 1 g

Temperature

The temperature at an indoor basketball game might be 27°C, which is 80°F.

Length/Distance

A basketball rim is about 10 ft high, or a little more than 3 m from the floor.

Customary Measures

Temperature

- Ice melts at 32 degrees Fahrenheit (°F)
- Water freezes at 32°F
- Water boils at 212°F

Length and Distance

- 12 inches (in.) = 1 foot (ft)
- 3 ft = 1 yard (yd)
- 5,280 ft = 1 mile (mi)

Weight

- 16 ounces (oz) = 1 pound (lb)
- 2,000 pounds = 1 ton (T)

Volume of Fluids

- 8 fluid ounces (fl oz) = 1 cup (c)
- 2 c = 1 pint (pt)
- 2 pt = 1 quart (qt)
- 4 qt = 1 gallon (gal)

Metric and Customary Rates

- km/h = kilometers per hour
- m/s = meters per second
- mph = miles per hour

Health and Fitness Handbook

Who is in charge of your health? You! Doctors, nurses, your parents or guardian, and teachers can all help you stay healthy. However, it's up to you to make healthful choices. What are some healthful choices you can make? In this section you'll learn:

- how to keep your body systems strong and healthy
- how to choose healthful foods
- how to exercise your heart and lungs every day
- how to be prepared for emergencies
- the benefits of avoiding alcohol, tobacco, and other drugs

The Muscular System

Your muscular system has three types of muscles.

- *Skeletal muscles* pull on bones to move them. You use them whenever you move your body.

- *Cardiac muscles* make up the walls of your heart and keep it beating.

- *Smooth muscles* line the blood vessels, the stomach, and other organs.

Most skeletal muscles are *voluntary muscles.* You can control them. Cardiac and smooth muscles are *involuntary muscles.* They work without you even having to think about them!

Many skeletal muscles work in pairs. When the biceps muscle in your arm contracts (gets shorter), the triceps muscle relaxes (gets longer). As a result, the elbow bends. How would the muscles work together to straighten the arm?

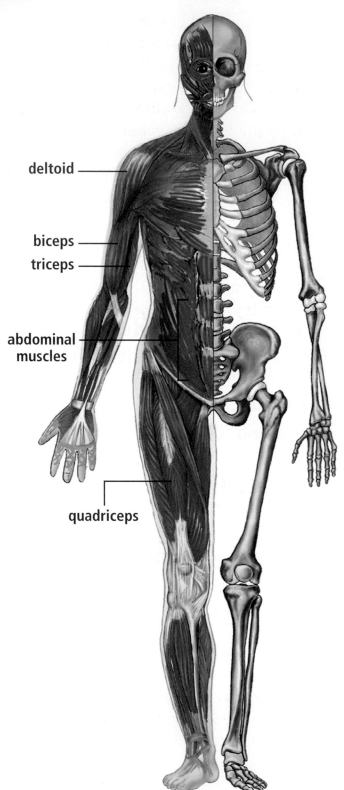

deltoid

biceps

triceps

abdominal muscles

quadriceps

FACTS

- Your muscles receive about 50 messages from your brain every second.

- You have more than 650 muscles.

The Skeletal System

Joints connect bones. If you had no joints, you could not bend or move. Each type of joint allows different kinds of movement. Your elbow has a hinge joint. The arm bends only one way at the elbow. Think about your shoulder. It has a ball-and-socket joint. What movement does it allow?

Your skeletal system gives your body strength and support. It works with your muscular system to move body parts. Your bones also protect your organs.

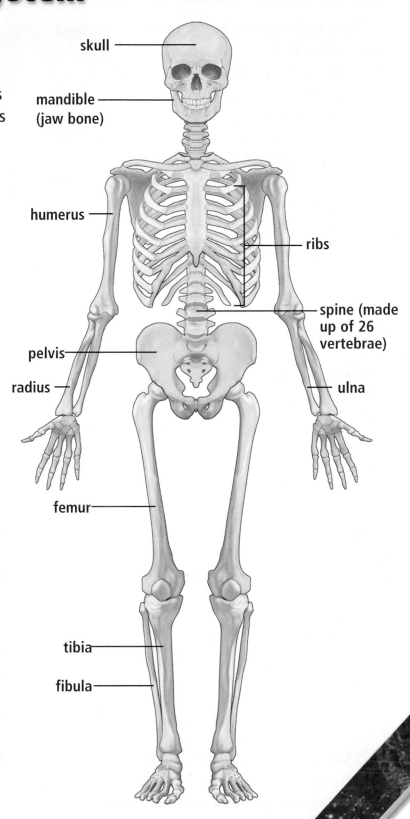

- skull
- mandible (jaw bone)
- humerus
- ribs
- spine (made up of 26 vertebrae)
- pelvis
- radius
- ulna
- femur
- tibia
- fibula

FACTS

- You have 206 bones in your body. More than half of them are found in your hands and feet!

- Your bones come in all shapes and sizes. There's even a bone in your ear shaped like a hammer!

Exercise Your Heart and Lungs

Exercise that makes your heart and lungs work hard is called aerobic exercise. *Aerobic* means "with oxygen." Any kind of steady exercise that raises your heart and breathing rates is aerobic exercise. Jogging, swimming, bicycling, and playing soccer are all good ways to get aerobic exercise.

Five steps toward a great aerobic workout.

1. **Choose your activity.** Pick an activity you enjoy. Do you like exercising with others? Basketball might be a good choice. Do you like exercising to music? Maybe you'd like dancing!

2. **Get the equipment you need.** Make sure you have the right clothes and shoes for your activity. Wear any safety gear you need. Your clothes and safety gear should fit correctly. Ask a parent, guardian, or physical education teacher for help.

3. **Warm up.** Do gentle activity such as walking for five minutes. Then stretch your muscles.

4. **Exercise.** It's best to exercise for at least 20 minutes. Exercise at a level that makes your heart and lungs work. Stop right away if you are injured.

5. **Cool down.** Exercise at a lower level for five to ten minutes to let your heart and breathing rates come back down. Then stretch your muscles again.

Food Labels

The United States Food and Drug Administration (FDA) requires most companies that sell food to label their packages. The facts shown on food labels can help you make smart food choices. Food labels list the ingredients in the food. They are in order by weight. This means that the food contains the most of the first ingredient listed. The label also tells you the name of the company that makes the food and the total weight or volume of the food in the package.

Food labels also include the Nutrition Facts panel. The panel on the right is for a can of chicken soup.

Nutrition Facts	
Serving Size 1 cup (246g)	
Servings Per Container About 2	
Amount Per Serving	
Calories 110	Calories from Fat 20
	% Daily Value*
Total Fat 2.5g	4%
Saturated Fat 0.5g	3%
Cholesterol 25mg	8%
Sodium 960mg	40%
Total Carbohydrate 15g	5%
Dietary Fiber 1g	5%
Sugars 2g	
Protein 9g	
Vitamin A 30%	Vitamin C 0%
Calcium 2%	Iron 4%
*Percent Daily Values are based on a 2,000 calorie diet.	

▲ What nutrients are in the food you eat? Read the Nutrition Facts panel to find out! Calories measure the energy in food.

FACTS

Get Enough Nutrients
- Carbohydrates provide energy. Fiber helps the digestive system.
- Your body uses protein for growth and development.
- Vitamins and minerals are important for many body functions.

FACTS

Limit Some Nutrients
- A healthful diet includes a limited amount of fat. Saturated fats and trans fats can increase the risk of heart disease. Cholesterol is a fat-like substance that can clog arteries.
- Too much sodium can increase the risk of high blood pressure.

Emergency Safety

Earthquakes, hurricanes, and tornadoes are all examples of natural disasters. You can plan ahead so you know what to do when a disaster happens.

Plan Ahead

You might not have fresh running water or electricity during a natural disaster. Here are some items you might want to have on hand.

- flashlights with batteries
- candles or lanterns with matches
- at least two gallons of fresh water
- canned or packaged food that does not need to be cooked
- radio with batteries
- first-aid kit

What To Do

Earthquake Get under something solid like a desk or doorway. Stay away from windows. Also stay away from anything that might fall on you. If you are outdoors, get to a wide open area.

Hurricane If there is some warning that a hurricane is coming, you may be told to evacuate. Tape all windows. Your parents or guardian will probably shut off the gas, water, and electricity.

Tornado If you are inside, go to a storm shelter or basement if you can. If there is no basement, go to an inside room with no windows. If you are outside, lie down in a low area and cover your head.

Tobacco, Alcohol, and Other Drugs

A drug is any substance, other than food, that changes how the body works. Drugs are swallowed, smoked, inhaled, or injected.

Helpful Drugs

Some drugs are helpful. Medicines can treat diseases and relieve pain. Drugs people can buy without a doctor's order are called *over-the-counter medicines.* Medicines that need a doctor's order are called *prescription medicines.*

Medicines can harm you if you use them incorrectly. Only take medicine when your parent, guardian, or doctor tells you to. Follow your doctor's instructions or the instructions printed on the package.

Harmful Drugs

Some drugs can harm your health.

Tobacco is a leaf that is smoked, sniffed, or chewed. Tobacco contains many harmful substances, including nicotine which speeds up the heart. Tobacco is addictive. This means that it is very hard to stop using tobacco once a person starts. Tobacco increases your risk of heart disease and lung disease.

Alcohol is a drug found in drinks such as beer and wine. Alcohol slows brain activity and muscle activity. Heavy drinking can lead to addiction and can damage the liver and other organs. People who drink alcohol are more likely to get into accidents.

Illegal drugs include marijuana, cocaine, ecstasy, LSD, and amphetamines. These drugs can cause serious physical, emotional, and social problems.

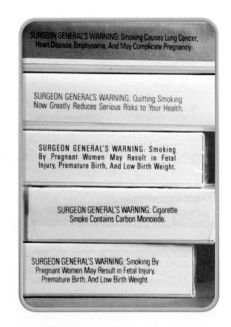

Glossary

English-Spanish Glossary

acid a compound that typically releases hydrogen ions (347)

ácido un compuesto que, por lo general, libera iones de hidrógeno

air mass a body of air that has about the same temperature and moisture throughout (208)

masa de aire cuerpo de aire cuya temperatura y humedad es prácticamente homogénea

air pressure the force exerted by air in all directions on a given area (186)

presión atmosférica fuerza que el aire ejerce en todas direcciones en una zona determinada

aqueduct (AK wuh dukt), a system of channels, pipes, or tunnels that carry water a long distance (123)

acueducto sistema de canales, tuberías o túneles que transportan agua a grandes distancias

aquifer (AK wuh fur) an underground layer of rock or soil through which water easily moves (124)

acuífero capa subterránea de roca o suelo a través de la cual el agua se mueve fácilmente

artery a blood vessel that carries blood away from the heart (74)

arteria vaso sanguíneo que lleva la sangre desde el corazón a otras partes del cuerpo

asteroid (AS tuh royd) a relatively small, rocky object that orbits the Sun (249)

asteroide objeto rocoso relativamente pequeño que orbita alrededor del Sol

atmosphere a mixture of gases that surround a planet (184)

atmósfera capa gaseosa que rodea un planeta

atom the smallest particle of an element that still has the properties of that element (288)

átomo en un elemento, la partícula más pequeña que tiene las propiedades de ese elemento

base a compound that typically receives hydrogen ions (347)

base compuesto que, por lo general, recibe iones de hidrógeno

bladder a muscular bag that holds urine (93)

vejiga bolsa muscular que contiene orina

blizzard a snowstorm with strong winds and low temperatures (221)

ventisca tormenta de nieve con fuertes vientos y bajas temperaturas

boiling point the temperature at which enough energy is added to a liquid to change it into a gas (339)

punto de ebullición temperatura a la que se añade suficiente energía a un líquido para convertirlo en gas

C

capillary a very thin vessel in which gases, nutrients, and wastes pass to and from the body cells (74)

capilar vaso muy fino de las células del cuerpo a través del cual entran y salen gases, nutrientes y desechos

cell the basic unit of all living things (8)

célula la unidad más pequeña de todo ser vivo

cellular respiration the process in which cells break down glucose in plants and animals (19)

respiración celular proceso mediante el cual las células descomponen la glucosa en plantas y animales

chemical formula a shorthand way to describe a compound (327)

fórmula química forma abreviada de describir un compuesto

chemical property the ability or tendency of a material to change its chemical makeup (337)

propiedad química capacidad o tendencia de un material para cambiar su composición química

chemical reaction a process in which one or more substances are changed into one or more different substances (326)

reacción química proceso mediante el cual una o más sustancias se transforman en otra u otras sustancias distintas

chemical symbol an abbreviation of an element's name (300)

símbolo químico abreviatura del nombre de un elemento

chlorophyll (KLAWR uh fihl) the pigment in a chloroplast that absorbs light (43)

clorofila en un cloroplasto, pigmento que absorbe la luz

chloroplast (KLAWR uh PLAST) an organelle in plant cells in which photosynthesis takes place (43)

cloroplasto orgánulo en las células de las plantas en el que tiene lugar la fotosíntesis

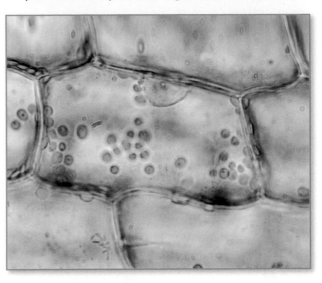

circulatory system a system that works to bring oxygen and nutrients to body cells and takes away carbon dioxide and wastes (74)

sistema circulatorio sistema que sirve para llevar oxígeno y nutrientes a las células del cuerpo y expulsar de ellas dióxido de carbono y desechos

comet a small, orbiting body made of dust, ice, and frozen gases (250)

cometa pequeño cuerpo celeste orbital compuesto de polvo, hielo y gases helados

compound a pure substance made of two or more elements that are chemically combined (291)

compuesto sustancia pura formada por dos o más elementos combinados químicamente

condensation (kahn dehn SAY shuhn), the change of state from a gas to a liquid (149)

condensación cambio de estado de gas a líquido

conductivity a material's ability to carry heat or electricity (340)

conductividad capacidad de un material para transportar calor o electricidad

conservation the careful use of a natural resource, such as water (136)

conservación uso prudente de un recurso natural, como el agua

convection current a continuous loop of moving air or liquid that transfers energy (156)

corriente de convección bucle continuo de aire o líquido en movimiento que transfiere energía

cytoplasm (SY toh plaz uhm) gel-like material located between the nucleus and the cell membrane (10)

citoplasma material gelatinoso localizado entre el núcleo y la membrana celular

density the mass per unit volume of a material (338)

densidad masa por unidad de volumen de un material

desalination (dee sal uh NAY shuhn), the removal of salt from salt water to make fresh water (116)

desalinización eliminación de la sal del agua marina para hacer agua potable

dew point the temperature at which air becomes saturated (158)

punto de condensación temperatura a la cual se satura el aire

diffusion (dih FYOO zhuhn) a process that spreads substances through a gas or liquid (21)

difusión proceso mediante el cual las sustancias se propagan a través de un gas o un líquido

digestive system an organ system that breaks down food to release nutrients (82)

sistema digestivo sistema que separa los alimentos para liberar los nutrientes

electron a negatively charged particle that moves in the space around the nucleus of an atom (288)

electrón partícula con carga negativa que se mueve en el espacio que rodea el núcleo de un átomo

element a substance that cannot be broken apart chemically into other substances (288)

elemento sustancia que no puede dividirse químicamente en otras sustancias

esophagus (uh SAHF uh gihs) a muscular tube that pushes food toward the stomach (85)

esófago tubo muscular que empuja los alimentos hacia el estómago

evaporation (ih VAP uh ray shuhn), the change in state from a liquid to a gas; slow or gradual vaporization (149; 383)

evaporación cambio de estado de líquido a gas; vaporización lenta o gradual

excretory system an organ system that removes wastes and maintains water balance (92)

sistema excretorio sistema de órganos que elimina los desechos y mantiene el equilibrio del agua

front the boundary between two air masses (208)

frente el límite entre dos masas de aire

gas a form of matter that has no definite shape or volume (364)

gas tipo de materia que no tiene forma o volumen definidos

grana stacks of membranes inside a chloroplast that contain chlorophyll (43)

grana conjunto de membranas dentro de un cloroplasto que contienen clorofila

gravity the gravitational attraction by Earth, or any massive body in space, on objects at or near its surface (90)

gravedad atracción gravitacional de la Tiera o cualquier cuerpo gigantesco en el espacio sobre los objetos que están cerca o sobre su superficie

groundwater water that collects in spaces and cracks in rocks and soil underground (114)

agua subterránea agua que se acumula en los espacios y grietas de las rocas y del suelo subterráneo

heart a muscular organ at the center of the circulatory system that pumps blood through a network of blood vessels (76)

corazón órgano muscular en el centro del sistema circulatorio, que bombea sangre a través de una red de vasos sanguíneos

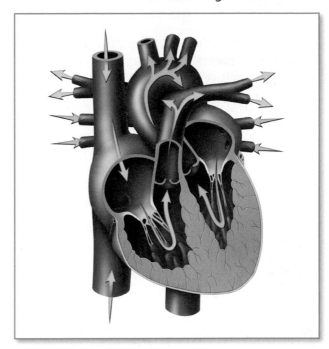

humidity the amount of water vapor in the air at any given time (158)

humedad cantidad de vapor de agua que hay en el aire en un momento determinado

hurricane a tropical storm with sustained wind speeds near its center of at least 119 km/hr (74 mph) (222)

huracán tormenta tropical con vientos cuyas velocidades cerca de su centro son de al menos 119 km/h (74 mph)

indicator a substance used to show the presence of an acid or a base in a substance (347)

indicador sustancia que se usa para identificar la presencia de ácidos o bases

inner planet any of the first four planets (Mercury, Venus, Earth, and Mars) from the Sun (258)

planetas interiores cualquiera de los cuatro planetas más cercanos al Sol (Mercurio, Venus, Tierra y Marte)

irrigation the process of supplying fresh water to farm fields for growing crops (123)

riego proceso mediante el cual se suministra agua dulce a los campos agrícolas para su cultivos

jet stream narrow belt of high-speed winds in the upper troposphere (198)

corriente de aire círculo estrecho de vientos a alta velocidad en la capa superior de la troposfera

kidney a bean-shaped organ that filters wastes from the blood (93)

riñón órgano con forma de frijol que filtra desechos procedentes de la sangre

land breeze a local wind that blows at night from land toward water (196)

viento terral viento local que sopla de noche desde la tierra hasta el agua

large intestine the organ into which food and other substances pass and where water and minerals from food are absorbed (86)

intestino grueso órgano a través del cual pasan alimentos y otras sustancias y donde se absorbe agua y minerales de los alimentos

liquid a form of matter that has a definite volume, but no definite shape (363)

líquido foma de materia que tiene volumen definido, pero no forma definida

melting point the temperature at which a solid substance changes to a liquid (339)

punto de fusión temperatura a la cual un sólido cambia a líquido

metal a shiny substance that can be bent or stretched, and can conduct electricity (301)

metal sustancia brillante que se puede doblar o estirar y que conduce electricidad

meteor a chunk of matter that enters Earth's atmosphere and is heated by friction with the air (250)

meteoro pedazo de materia que entra en la atmósfera terrestre y se calienta por la fricción con el aire

meteoroid a bit of rock or metal that orbits the Sun (250)

meteorito trozo de roca o de metal que gira alrededor del Sol

meteorologist a scientist who studies weather (210)

meteorólogo científico que estudia el tiempo atmosférico

mixture a physical combination of two or more substances (270)

mezcla combinación física de dos o más sustancias

molecule a group of two or more atoms that are chemically joined and that act as a single unit (311)

molécula grupo de dos o más átomos unidos químicamente y que actúan como una sola unidad

mountain breeze a local wind that flows downhill and is produced by cooler, denser air above the mountain slopes (195)

brisa de montaña viento local producido por aire más frío y denso que se desliza por las pendientes de las montañas

neutron an atomic particle that lacks charge (288)

neutrón partícula atómica sin carga

noble gas an element that hardly ever combines with another element to form a compound (304)

gas noble elemento que es difícil combinar con otro elemento para formar un compuesto

nonmetal an element, usually in the form of gas, that cannot conduct electricity, does not stretch or bend very much, and can break easily (301)

no metal un elemento, generalmente en forma de gas, que no conduce la electricidad, no se dobla o estira mucho y que se rompe con facilidad

nonvascular plant a plant that lacks true leaves, stems, and roots (54)

planta no vascular planta que carece de hojas, tallo y raíces

nuclear fusion the process in which the nuclei of atoms fuse together to form a larger nucleus (240)

fusión nuclear proceso mediante el cual los núcleos de los átomos se funden para formar un núcleo mayor

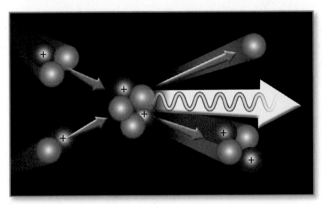

nucleus (NOO klee uhs) the structure in the center of an atom that contains protons and neutrons (288), the cell part that contains DNA and directs cell activities (10)

núcleo estructura en el centro de un átomo que contiene protones y neutrones; la parte de la ciélula que contiene el ADN y que controla la actividad celular

ocean current a moving stream of water in the ocean (165)

corriente oceánica corriente de agua en el océano

organ a group of related tissues that perform a specific function (27)

órgano grupo de tejidos relacionados que realizan una función específica

organelle a structure that performs specific functions in the cell (10)

organelo estructura que realiza funciones específicas en la célula

organ system a group of organs that work together to accomplish a task (28)

sistema de órganos grupo de órganos que trabajan juntos para realizar una tarea

osmosis (ahz MOH sihs), a special form of diffusion that works to keep water inside the cells (21)

ósmosis método especial de difusión que sirve para mantener agua dentro de las células

outer planet any of the five planets farthest from the Sun (Jupiter, Saturn, Uranus, Neptune, and Pluto) (260)

planeta exterior cualquiera de los cinco planetas más alejados del Sol (Júpiter, Saturno, Urano, Neptuno y Plutón)

periodic table the table that logically arranges all known elements (299)

tabla periódica tabla que ordena de forma lógica todos los elementos conocidos

pH (potential of hydrogen) the value of measured strength of acids and bases (347)

pH (potencial de hidrógeno) valor de la fuerza medida en ácidos y bases

phloem (FLOH ehm) a vascular tissue that conducts food that is made in the leaves downward to the rest of the plant (56)

floema tejido vascular que transporta hacia el resto de la planta el alimento producido en las hojas

photosynthesis (foh toh SIHN thih sihs) the process by which plants transform energy from sunlight into chemical energy (42)

fotosíntesis proceso mediante el cual las plantas transfoman energía de la luz solar en energía química

physical property any characteristic of matter that can be measured or detected by the senses (337)

propiedad física cualquier característica de la materia que pueda ser medida o detectada a través de los sentidos

planet a large body that revolves around the Sun (246)

planeta gran cuerpo estelar que gira alrededor del Sol

planetary winds long-lasting wind patterns that cover a large area of Earth (198)

vientos planetarios patrones duraderos de vientos que cubren un área grande de la Tierra

precipitation (prih sihp uh TAY shuhn), any form of water that falls to Earth's surface from clouds (198)

precipitación agua proveniente de las nubes que, en cualquiera de sus formas, cae sobre la superficie de la Tierra

product a substance that results from a chemical change (390)

producto sustancia que resulta de un cambio químico

proton a small, positively-charged atomic particle (288)

protón pequeña partícula atómica de carga positiva

R

reactant a substance that enters into and is altered through the course of a chemical change (390)

reactivo sustancia que entra en un cambio químico y se altera durante el transcurso del mismo

reservoir (REZ uh vwahr), a natural or artificial pond or lake used to collect and store fresh water (123)

embalse lago natural o artificial que se usa para recoger y almacenar agua dulce

respiratory system a system of organs that exchange gases with the environment (72)

sistema respiratorio sistema de órganos que intercambia gases con el ambiente

runoff rainwater that flows over land without sinking into the soil (113)

escurrimiento agua de lluvia que fluye por la tierra sin penetrar en el suelo

S

salt a compound formed when a strong acid reacts with a strong base (348)

sal compuesto que se forma cuando un ácido fuerte reacciona con una base fuerte

sea breeze a local wind that blows from water toward land during the day (196)

brisa marina viento local que sopla desde el mar hacia la tierra durante el día

semimetal an element that is like a metal in some ways and like nonmetal in other ways

semimetal un elemento que tiene características de los metales y de los no metales

small intestine in humans, a long, coiled organ where most digestion takes place (86)

intestino delgado en los humanos, órgano largo y enrollado donde tiene lugar la mayor parte de la digestión

solar system the Sun and all the bodies that travel, or revolve, around it (246)

sistema solar el Sol y todos los cuerpos que se mueven, o giran, a su alrededor

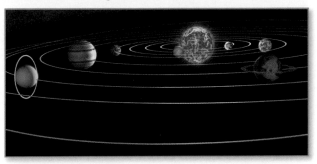

solid a form of matter that has a definite shape and volume (362)

sólido estado de la materia que tiene forma y volumen definidos

solubility the measure of how much of one substance can dissolve in another (340)

solubilidad medida de la cantidad de sustancia que puede disolverse en otra sustancia

solution a mixture in which parts are evenly distributed at the level of atoms or molecules (372)

solución mezcla distribuida en partes iguales a nivel de átomos o moléculas

spring a natural flow of water from underground that forms where the water table meets the land's surface (125)

manantial corriente natural de agua subterránea que aparece donde el nivel hidrostático se une con la superficie de la tierra

stomach a muscular organ that mixes and stores food and passes it to the small intestine (85)

estómago órgano muscular que mezcla y almacena alimento y lo pasa al intestino delgado

stomata (STOH mah tuh) small openings in the bottom of a leaf through which gases move (44)

estomas pequeñas aperturas en la parte inferior de una hoja a través de las cuales fluyen los gases

sublimation the process of a solid changing directly to a gas without passing through the liquid state (384)

sublimación proceso por el cual un sólido pasa directamente a estado gaseoso sin pasar por el estado líquido

sunspot a dark-appearing area on the Sun that is cooler than surrounding areas (239)

mancha solar zona oscura del Sol que es más fría que las zonas que la rodean

thunderstorm a storm that delivers lightning, thunder, and heavy rains (218)

tormenta perturbación atmosférica acompañada de fuertes lluvias, truenos y relámpagos

tissue a group of similar specialized cells that work together (27)

tejido grupo de células con una especialización similar que trabajan juntas

tornado a narrow, spinning column of very fast-moving air (219)

tornado columna estrecha de aire que se mueve muy rápidamente en círculos

transpiration the evaporation of water through a plant's leaves (149)

transpiración evaporación del agua a través de las hojas de una planta

valley breeze a local wind produced by the movement of cooler air from the valley that moves up a mountain slope (195)

brisa del valle viento local producido por el movimiento de aire más frío del valle, que se mueve montaña arriba

vaporization the process of a liquid changing into a gas (383)

vaporización proceso por el cual un líquido cambia a gas

vascular plant a plant that has specialized structures for transporting food, water, and other materials between plant parts (54)

planta vascular planta que tiene estructuras especializadas para transportar alimentos, agua y otros materiales a las diversas partes de la planta

vein a blood vessel that carries blood back to the heart (74)

vena vaso sanguíneo que transporta sangre de vuelta al corazón

water reclamation the recycling of waste water so it can be used again (136)

recuperación del agua reciclaje de agua residual para que pueda usarse de nuevo

water table the surface of a layer of saturated ground (124)

nivel hidrostático superficie de una capa de suelo saturada de agua

water vapor (VAY pur), water in the form of a gas (149)

vapor de agua agua en forma de gas

watershed a region of land that drains into a river (126)

divisoria de aguas zona cuyas aguas desembocan en un mismo río

weather the overall condition of the atmosphere at a given time and place (184)

tiempo condiciones climatológicas de la atmósfera en una hora y lugar determinado

well a hole dug or drilled into the ground to provide a supply of water (125)

pozo hoyo excavado o taladrado en el suelo para proporcionar suministro de agua

xylem (ZY luhm) a vascular tissue that conducts water and minerals through a plant (56)

xilema tejido vascular que conduce agua y minerales a través de la planta

Index

Acknowledgements

Excerpt from *Comets, Meteors, and Asteroids*, by Seymour Simon. Copyright © 1994 by Seymour Simon. Reprinted by permission of William Morrow and Company, an imprint of HarperCollins Publishers.

Earth Charged in Meteor's Fiery Death from *Earth Shake: Poems From the Ground Up*, by Lisa Westberg Peters, illustrated by Cathie Felstead. Text copyright © 2003 by Lisa Westberg Peters. Illustrations copyright © 2003 by Cathie Felstead. Reprinted by permission of HarperCollins Publishers.

Photography

Front cover © Randy Morse/Golden State Images. **Back cover** (Harbor seal) © WorldFoto/ Alamy. (water background) © Randy Morse/ Golden State Images. **Spine** © Steven J. Kazlowski/Alamy. **Title page** © Steven J. Kazlowski/Alamy. **v** © Mark Keller/SuperStock. **vi-vii** © Corbis. **ix** ©Gene Blevins/LA Daily News/Corbis. **S1** © Mark E. Gibson/Corbis. **S3** © David Shale/Nature Picture Library. **S4** © Paul Nicklen/National Geographic Society/ Image Sales. **Nature of Science Opener** © Pete Oxford/Nature Picture Library **S9** © LB Goodman/Omni-Photo Communications. **S10** Courtesy of Dr. Dale Brown Emeagwali. **S10-11** © Microfield Scientific Ltd./Photo Researchers, Inc. **S12-13** (bkgd) © Picmpact/Corbis. **S14** (bkgd) © Marc Muench/Muench Photography, Inc. **S16-S17** (bkgd) © HMCo. **S18** (t) © Mitsuhiko Imamori/Minden Pictures, (b) © Cassandra Wagner. **S19** © Janet Hostetter/ AP/Wide World Photos. **S20-21** (b) © Brand X Pictures/Punch Stock, (bkgd) © PhotoDisc, Inc./Punch Stock. **S22** © Stephen Frink/Corbis. **Unit A Opener** © Wendy Shattil /Bob Rozinski. **1** © Len Kaufman Photography **2-3** (bkgd) © David McCarthy/Science Photo Library/Photo Researchers, Inc. **3** (t) © Leonard Lessin/ Peter Arnold, Inc., (c) © VVG/Science Photo Library/Photo Researchers, Inc., (b) ©Ariel Skelley/Corbis. **4** (t) © Andrew Syred/Science Photo Library/Photo Researchers, Inc., (b) © Innerspace Imaging/Photo Researchers, Inc. **4-5** (bkgd) © Motta/Photo Researchers, Inc. **6-7** © Mitsuaki Iwago/Minden Pictures. **8** (r) © Dennis Kunkel Microscopy, Inc., (l) © Mark Tomalty/Masterfile Stock Photo Library. **9** © David Shale/Nature Picture Library. **12** © Dr. Jeremy Burgess/Science Photo Library/ Photo Researchers, Inc., (c) © Professors P. Motta & T. Naguro/Science Photo Library/ Photo Researchers, Inc., (b) © CNRI/Science Photo Library/Photo Researchers, Inc. **13** (t) © Dennis Kunkel Microscopy, Inc., (b) © Professors P. Motta & T. Naguro/Science Photo Library/Photo Researchers, Inc. **14** (br) © Dr. Jeremy Burgess/Photo Researchers, Inc., (c) © Volker Steger/Peter Arnold, Inc., (bl) © Dave King/Dorling Kindersley Picture Library, (t) © Peter Beck/Corbis. **15** (tl) © Andrew Syred/Science Photo Library/Photo Researchers, Inc., (tr) © A. Smith/Photo Researchers, Inc., (b) © Tom Hollyman/Photo Researchers, Inc., (c) © Science VU/IBMRL/Visuals Unlimited. **16** (b) © Raoul Minsart/Corbis. **16-17** (bkgd) © Chip Henderson/Index Stock Imagery. **18** (bl) © Ant Photo Library/NHPA. **19** © Bob Daemmrich/PhotoEdit, Inc. **20** (t to b) © Dr. Yorgos Nikas/Photo Researchers, Inc., © David McCarthy/Science Photo Library/Photo Researchers, Inc., © Lee Strickland/Getty Images., © Franz Lanting/Miden Pictures. **22** (r) © NHPA/Rod Planck, (c) © Francois Gohier/Ardea London Ltd., (l) © NHPA/Andy Rouse. **23** © Ant Photo Library/NHPA, (b) © Franz Lanting/Miden Pictures. **24-25** © Dr.

David M. Phillips/Visuals Unlimited, Inc. **26** © Innerspace Imaging/Photo Researchers, Inc. **29**© Innerspace Imaging/Photo Researchers, Inc. **30-31** © Steve Gschmeissner/Science Photo Library. **30** (br) Associates of Cape Cod, Inc., E. Falmouth, MA. **32** © HMCo./Allan Landau. **33** (t) © Alamy Images, (b) ©Jim Whitmer Photography, (bkgd) © Roy Lawe/Alamy Images. **36-37** © Steve Hopkin/Getty Images. **37** (t) © Barry Runk/Stan/Grant Heilman Photography, Inc., (b) © Eduardo Garcia/Taxi/ Getty Images. **38-39** © Muench Photography Inc. **39** (t) © Andrew Syred/Science Photo Library/Photo Researchers, Inc., (b) © Edward Parker/Alamy Images. **40-41** © Medford Taylor/National Geographic Society. **42** (r) © Barry Runk/Stan/Grant Heilman Photography, Inc. (l) © PhotoDisc, Inc. **44** (l) © Runk/ Shoenberger/Grant Heilman Photography, Inc., (r) © Runk/Shoenberger/Grant Heilman Photography, Inc. **45** © Andrew Syred/Science Photo Library/Photo Researchers, Inc. **46** © Claus Meyer/Minden Pictures. **47** (t) © PhotoDisc, Inc. **48** © HMCo./Allan Landau. **49** (r) © Inga Spence/Visuals Unlimited, Inc., (l) © Photodisc/Punch Stock. **50** (l to r) © Alex Kerstitch/Visuals Unlimited, Inc., © Norbert Wu/Peter Arnold, Inc., © Ed Reschke/Peter Arnold, Inc. © Inga Spence/Visuals Unlimited, Inc. **51** (b) © The Granger Collection, New York, (t) © Patrick Johns/Corbis, (r) © Mario Tama/Getty Images. **52-53** © Peter Marbach/ Grant Heilman Photography, Inc. **54** (l) © Richard Cummins/Corbis, (c) © Dr. Jeremy Burgess/Photo Researchers, Inc. **56** © Sheila Terry Photo Researchers, Inc., (b) © Alfred Pasieka/Science Photo Library/Photo Researchers, Inc. **58** © Nick Hawkes; Ecoscene/ Corbis. **59** © Richard Cummins/Corbis. **60-61** FogStock LLC/Index Stock Imagery. **62** (t) © David Brooks/Corbis, (b) © Richard Cummins/Corbis, © Philadelphia Museum of Art/Corbis. **63** (bkgd) © Adam Jones/Visuals Unlimited, © Nilsa Bosque-Perez. **65** © Richard Cummins/Corbis. **66-67** © Philippe Montigny/ Vandystadt. **67** (t) © Simon Fraser/Photo Researchers, Inc. (c) © Michael Newman/ PhotoEdit, Inc., (b) © Steve Gschmeissner/ Photo Researchers, Inc. **68-69** (bkgd) © Dr. Kessel & Dr. Kardon/Tissues&Organ/Visuals Unlimited. **70-71** Stephen Frink/Corbis. **72** (c) © Jerry Young/Dorling Kindersley Picture Library, (t) © Ron Boardman/Corbis, (b) © T. C. Nature/ Animals Animals. **74-75** © HMCo./Lawrence Migdale. **78** © David M. Grosman/Photo Take. **79** © Zephyr/Science Photo Library/Photo Researchers, Inc., (t) © Mediscan/Visuals Unlimited, Inc., (l) © Dr P. Marazzi/Science Photo Library/Photo Researchers, Inc., (b) © Science VU/Visuals Unlimited, Inc. **80** (b) © Stone/Getty Images. **80-81** (bkgd) © Photodisc/ Punch Stock. **82** © PhotoDisc/Punch Stock. **83, 84** © HMCo./Ken Karp Photography. **85** © E.R. Degginger/Color Pic, Inc. **88-89** Chris Fallows/apexpredators.com. **89** (tr) © Jeffrey L. Rotman/CORBIS. **90** (b) ©Robert W. Ginn/ PhotoEdit. **90-91** (bkgd) © Tony Freeman/ PhotoEdit, Inc. **94** (b) © Arthur Glaubeman/ Photo Researchers, Inc. **95** (c) © CNRI/Science Photo Library/Photo Researchers, Inc., © BSIP/Phototake © BSIP/Phototake. **96** (t) © Dr. Jeremy Burgess/Science Photo Library/Photo Researchers, Inc., (b) © Hanne Jens Eriksen/ naturerpl.com. **97** © Dr. Jeremy Burgess/ Science Photo Library/Photo Researchers, Inc. **98** © Simon Fraser/Photo Researchers, Inc. **99** (b) © James Colbert, (bkgd) © Michael Donne/ Science Photo Library/Photo Researchers, Inc. **Unit B Opener** © Tim Fitzharris/Minden Pictures, **105** © Nature Picture Library. **106** ©

Wernher Krutein/PhotoVault. **107** (c) © Michio Hoshino/Minden Pictures, (b) © David McNew/ Getty Images. **108-109** (bkgd) © Michael S. Lewis/Corbis. **109** (c) © QT Luong/Terragalleria. com, (b) © David Young Wolff/PhotoEdit, Inc., (t) Scott Clark. **110** © Mark E. Gibson/Corbis. **112** © Science VU/GSFC/Visuals Unlimited, Inc. **113** Georgette Douwma/Photo Researchers, Inc. **114-115** © Greg Probst/Panoramic Images/ National Geographic Society Image Sales. **115** (c) © Thomas Hallstein/Outsight Photography, (t) © Carsten Peter/National Geographic Image Collection. **116** (l) © Roslan Rahman/AFP/Getty Images. **117** (t) © Georgette Douwma/Photo Researchers, Inc., (c) © Greg Probst/Panoramic Images/NGSImages, (b) © Roslan Rahman/ AFP/Getty Images. **118-119** © Jose Fuste Raga/ CORBIS. **118** (bl) Pascal Goetgheluck/Science Photo Library/Photo Researchers, Inc. **120** © Bob West/AG Pix. **123** © Bernhard Edmaier/ Photo Researchers, Inc. **124** (b) © David Young Wolff/PhotoEdit, Inc. **125** © Roger Powell/ Nature Picture Library. **126** © David Young Wolff/PhotoEdit, Inc. **127** (c) © Roger Powell/ Nature Picture Library, (b) © Bob West/AG Pix, (t) ©Bernhard Edmaier/Photo Researchers, Inc. **128** © Lester Lefkowitz/Corbis. **130** © Corbis, (bkgd) © Sunniva Harte/Garden Picture Library. **133** © Kevin Fleming/Corbis. **135** © R.Perron/Visuals Unlimited, Inc. **136** © Rachael Epstein/PhotoEdit, Inc. **137** (b) © Rachael Epstein/PhotoEdit, Inc., (c) © R.Perron/Visuals Unlimited, Inc., (t) © Kevin Fleming/Corbis. **138** © Punch Stock. **139** (bkgd) © Galen Rowell/ Corbis, © Spreck Rosekrans. **142-143** © Paul Nicklen/National Geographic Society/Image Sales. **143** (c) © John Eastcott & Yva Momatiuk/ National Geographic/Getty Images, (b) © Jonathan Nourok/Photo Edit, Inc., ©Photodisc/ Punch Stock. **144** (bkgd) © Kathleen Brown/ Corbis. **145** (t) © Robert Folz/Visuals Unlimited, Inc. (c) © Richard Hamilton Smith/Corbis. **146** © Galen Rowell and Odyssey Productions, Inc. **150** (tr) © Inga Spence/Visuals Unlimited, Inc., (tl) © Science VU/Visuals Unlimited, Inc. **151** © Science VU/Visuals Unlimited, Inc. **152** (b) © White Cross Productions/Getty Images. **152-153** (bkgd) © Anthony Redpath/Corbis. **155** (l to r) © Darryl Torckler/Taxi/Getty Images, © Richard Hamilton Smith/Corbis, © David R. Frazier/Photo Researchers, Inc., © Matthias Clamer/Getty Images. **156** (l) © David Cavagnaro/Visuals Unlimited, Inc., (l inset) © Nigel Cattlin/Photo Researchers, Inc., (l inset) © Marion Owen dba Carotte, Inc./Alaska Stock LLC., (r inset) © E.R. Degginer/Color-Pic, Inc., (r) © Mary Clay/Dembinsky Photo Associates, (l) © Darrell Gulin/DRK photo. **157** (r) © Warren E. Faidley/DRK Photo, (t) © Jeff J. Daly/Visuals Unlimited, Inc. **158** (tl) © Gregory G. Dimijian/ Photo Researchers, Inc., (tr) © Mark Gibson/ VIsuals Unlimited, Inc. **159** (c) © David R. Frazier/Photo Researchers, Inc., (b) © Jeff J. Daly/Visuals Unlimited, Inc. **160** © Jim Sugar/ Corbis. **162** © Mike Dobel/Masterfile Stock Photo Library. **164** (b) © Creatas/Punch Stock, **167** © Creatas/Punch Stock, (b) © Mike Dobel/Masterfile Stock Photo Library. **168-169** © NOAA/CORBIS. **169** (tr) AP Photo/Ric Feld. **171** (c) © Gabe Palmer/Corbis, (t) © Robert Yin/ Corbis, (bkgd) © Corel. **173** © David Cavagnaro/Visuals Unlimited, Inc. **Unit C Opener** Courtesy Goddard Space Flight Center/ NASA. **177** NASA. **178-179** ©Eric Nguyen. **179** (cl) © Jochen Tack/Peter Arnold, Inc., (t) © Firefly Productions/Corbis, (b) © Jim Reed/ Photo Researchers, (cr) © Georgette Douwma/ Getty Images. **180-181** (bkgd) © Rob Matheson/Corbis, © Karl Shone/Dorling Kindersley Picture Library. **182** (b) © Gerard

scar